SEWING for
20th CENTURY DOLLS
Volume II
by Johana Gast Anderton

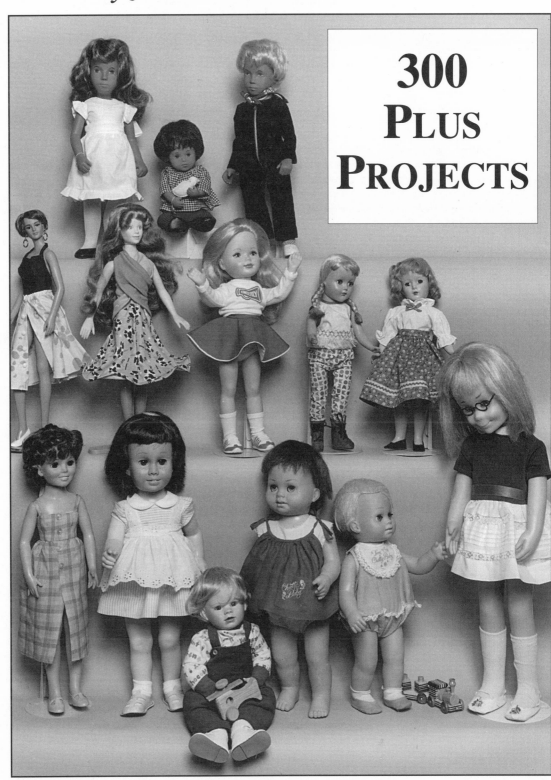

300 PLUS PROJECTS

Published by

Hobby
House
Press™

Hobby House
Press, Inc.
Grantsville, MD
21536

DEDICATION

In memory of my father and mother, Joseph Rudolph Gast, Sr. and Nellie Catherine Margarette Blankenship Gast

ACKNOWLEDGMENTS

As with any such work, there would be no book without the constant cooperation of many people. Editors, layout people, printers, binders, all contribute to the end product.

In the beginning, before the book is a book, however, some extension of belief, of trust in the author's worth, ability to bring a project to fruition, must be forthcoming from those who lend dolls and clothing, from a spouse who complacently lives in utter pandemonium as a way of life, even or perhaps more especially, from a publisher...all of whom I thank most sincerely.

Those who have allowed me to disrobe their dolls and handle the costumes are among the ones most necessary to the project. Alphabetically, they are: Nancy Anderson, Florida; George and Kathleen Bassett, Bassett's Babies, Washington; Madeleine Bennett, Florida; Juanita Bishop, Georgia; Joyce Brooks, Florida; Diana Serra Cary, California; Cathie Clark, Ohio; Elaine Elsberry; Arlene Foster, West Virginia; Carol and Ernie Gardner, Childhood Reflections, Florida; Maria Gates, Florida; Marion Reed Getty; Linda Ghiorse, Florida; Carol Gast Glassmire, CJ Gifts, Florida; Anne Hanna, Arkansas; Margaret Hill, Florida; Jerry Kennedy, Doll Alley, Florida; Ruth A. Lane; Mary Lord, Florida; Shirley Gast Lynn-Smith, Kansas; Barbara A. Meyer, North Carolina; June McNulty, Grandma Goldie's Dolls, Florida; Carmen and Frank Pedota, Anything Goes, Florida; Joyce H. Phelps, Maryland; Nancy Provoncha, Nana's Dolls, Florida; Lanell Rowland, Lanell's Dolls, Florida; Susan Schroeder, Florida; Carmen Smotherman, C & B Antique Doll Hospital, Florida; Betty Snider, Georgia; Carol Stover; Billie Nelson Tyrell, California; and Margaret Ann Watkins, Colorado.

In handling such a large amount of material, mistakes occur. If I have overlooked anyone, I apologize and thank you most sincerely for your contributions.

And, finally, eternal gratitude to most excellent proofreaders Cynthia Anderton and Mary Ruth Bateman.

-JGA

WHAT THE COPYRIGHT MEANS

Back Cover: Top Row, L to R: *Sasha, Sasha Baby, Gregor.* **Middle Row, L to R:** *Lady Luminous, Wild Styles Radonna, Kimberly,* two 1950s Hard Plastic Girls. ***Front Row, L to R:*** *Beautiful Crissy, Chatty Cathy, Peaches, Chatty Baby, Tiny Chatty Baby, Charmin' Chatty.* ***Front Cover: Top Row, L to R:*** First Communion Hard Plastic, Composition *Patricia,* Unmarked Hard Plastic. **Middle Row, L to R:** *Sarah* by Nicholas Bramble, 1930s Ideal Composition. ***Front Row, L to R:*** 21in (53cm) Antique Bisque Kestner marked DEP 7//54, 21in (53cm) Antique Bisque Morimura Bros., Japan.

TABLE OF CONTENTS

INTRODUCTION

During my nearly thirty years as a doll dress designer, the most frequently asked question has been, "Where can I buy well-designed, easy-to-make patterns?" My customers were sewing for antique and collectible dolls (the dolls of the early years of this century on into the 1960s and 1970s). They wanted solid styles typical of the clothes in which the dolls were first sold.

My husband is a well-known doll doctor in Florida and I have dressed many of the dolls he has restored. Johana's first volume of *Sewing for Twentieth Century Dolls* has been invaluable through the years as a source of patterns and research on dolls that were brought to our doll hospital for rejuvenation. The book was sent home many times with my dressmaking friends and helpers, Dottie and Alice. They made frog bodies for Bye-lo babies and dresses for *Schoenhuts, Shirley, Patsy, Buddy Lee, Sweet Sue,* and all the rest with phenomenal success, using Johana's wonderful patterns.

In addition, I recommended the book to many of my customers who were dressing their own dolls. For anyone wishing to dress dolls in authentic styles, that book was the source.

Now comes a new volume of doll clothes treasures. Pictures and accurate drawings of original wardrobe items are invaluable when restoring dolls to an approximation of their original condition. Johana Anderton's newest book makes a further huge contribution in this field.

There are patterns for lady and child dolls of the early decades of this century, *Shirley Temple* dolls of several eras, *Baby Peggy* and *Dolly Rosebud* of the 1920s, the *Dionnes* and other composition dolls of the 1930s, the *Littlechaps* of 1963, the *Crissy* family of the 1970s, and dozens of others.

As an example of the thoroughness of her presentation, all of the best of the early 1960s fashions are represented in the display of gorgeous street dresses, evening attire, and bridal finery for the 1961 *Miss Seventeen* fashion doll from Louis Marx & Co. Inc. The original in-box folder for these fashions is shown as a

further reference to authenticity. The 18in (46cm) patterns Johana has drafted will also fit, and are appropriate for, the later *SuperSize BARBIE®* doll and other slim fashion dolls. Given also are instructions for reducing and enlarging these patterns to fit fashion dolls of other sizes, including the standard-size *BARBIE®* doll.

Patterns for the 12in (31cm) *Shirley Temple* of 1982 have been detailed to perfection. A great quantity of these dolls were sold in the early 1980s. Because they were a nice play size and were fun to dress, they were often played with to the point of complete destruction of their clothing. Many of the little girls of the early 1980s are young mothers today and have decided to re-dress their dolls for their own enjoyment or to hand on to their little girls. Within these pages is all they will need to bring their Shirleys back to life.

Johana finishes off with some marvelous patterns for the artist dolls of the 1980s and 1990s, including wardrobes for original artist dolls and reproduction dolls. She also gives suggestions for adapting patterns to the dressmaker's needs and encourages creativity in combining patterns in new ways, teaching us to develop our skills and to trust our own judgment in such matters.

Altogether, this book represents a treasure trove of information, original patterns, and adaptable material. Johana has written easy-to-follow instructions, drawn detailed construction sketches and well-drafted patterns, and has put it all together for us. No doll collector, professional or just-for-fun doll dressmaker should be without it.

In this book, Johana has answered the question for us all, "Where can I find the patterns?"

Susan Schroeder, Senior Designer
S & S Doll Hospital, Kissimmee, Florida

FOREWORD

The original clothing of old dolls tells a story as compelling as any to be found in fiction. Just as the construction and the materials used in the manufacture of old dolls themselves act as technological indicators, so the various articles of clothing in which the dolls were dressed serve as mute socio-economic testimony of the times in which the dolls were made. In addition, antique and original doll clothes sometimes offer clues to the patterning and construction of obsolete articles of apparel which often are not readily evident to the modern researcher studying contemporary fashion periodicals such as *The Delineator* and *The Godey's Lady's* Book.

It is with these thoughts in mind that many collectors

seek out the antique or collectible dolls that remain in all-original condition; that is, those dolls that retain the clothing in which or with which they were sold, or the wardrobes that were especially created for them by contemporary professional seamstresses.

Original, as the word pertains to doll clothes, may refer to the clothes in which the doll was dressed for sale to the retail public as well as to the additional wardrobe items marketed especially for a particular model, either in separate units or as part of a "set" in a suitcase, trunk, wicker basket, or wardrobe case.

Over the years, there have been thousands of different sets offered by manufacturers. These were made up of a doll or dolls and several items of apparel plus accessories such as soap, towel, even a bathtub, all artfully arranged in a case, or more economically, in a simple cardboard gift box. Fortunate the collector who locates even one such set in good condition. They were made to be played with and were, often to the point of destruction or complete disintegration of the box and clothing.

Other collectors also try to obtain clothing made from authentic patterns professionally created for particular dolls. A number of examples come to mind: the various wardrobe patterns created by pattern companies for the Effanbee *Patsy* Family dolls, for the Ideal *Shirley Temple* dolls, for Vogue's *Ginny* Family dolls, and more recently, for Mattel's *BARBIE*® Doll Family. The patterns often constitute collections in themselves; some doll collectors attempt to acquire complete sets of every commercial pattern ever issued for their dolls.

Many collectors appreciate being able to reproduce authentic clothing for their dolls using both contemporary patterns and books of more recent publication which treat the subject. Those who make it possible for the average collector to produce authentic reproductions of original clothing perform a real service.

Doll collectors who seek to create costumes for their dolls as near to the originals as possible are to be commended. Theirs is not the simple path. It is much easier to follow the expedient route, to create a period costume of readily available polyester or nylon than to spend time and money in search of authentic old fabric or a suitable substitute. It takes far less time to sew a "reasonable facsimile" using known construction techniques than to set aside time to study and understand the construction principals of long-ago fashions.

As we have noted, any doll, regardless of its age, is a product of the era in which it was made. For this reason, a collector interested in presenting a well-rounded picture of the history of dolls will spend time in careful research before attempting to choose a suitable costume for her doll. Each decade seems to bring to mind a special look, a silhouette, a face of fashion that represents that period more completely than mere words describe.

A few examples will serve to illustrate. Try thinking of the word, "Flapper," the name given to the fashionable young woman of the 1920s in America. The very word evokes the fashion picture of a slim, almost boyish figure, of "marcelled" hair and "spit curls," of long-waisted dresses and rolled-down stockings, of cloche hats and rouged cheeks.

When we hear "Gibson Girl," most of us immediately experience a clear vision of a certain hairstyle, a certain lift of chin, a certain outline of costume. All these were elegantly and eloquently pictured for us in the idealized pen and ink illustrations of Charles Dana Gibson and have become for us a symbol of the 1890s.

Each of these decades is reflected in the dolls of the period and in their clothing, which is also true of previous and subsequent decades from which collectible dolls are available.

Doll collectors owe a debt of gratitude to the mothers and aunts and grandmothers who preserved the childhood relics which collectors now treasure so highly. For every bit of lacy underclothes, for every tiny shoe or stocking, for every dress or skirt or coat thus salvaged from destruction, other millions of items were lost, burned or thrown away.

It follows, therefore, that a doll collector must see herself or himself not as owner of the dolls and clothing in his or her collection, but rather as steward of these miniature historical artifacts. Preservation must become a by-word for collectors if the original clothing and accessories we find, as well as the authentic patterns, fashion magazines, and catalogs of former years, pass on to future generations for their study, enrichment, and understanding.

In the past few decades the number of collectors seeking to acquire comprehensive collections has risen like a mighty ground swell. On the other hand, time has taken its toll of the delicate fibres and fugitive colors of antique and collectible doll clothing. Consequently, there are not enough original doll clothes extant to satisfy the demands of the ever-increasing number of doll collectors seeking them.

There is a further problem. In recent years interest in collecting vintage clothing has nearly dried up a major source of old fabrics suitable for making authentic doll clothes. This scarcity has added noticeably to the difficulties of duplicating original clothing. The collecting and preservation of vintage garments is a valid occupation, but it has also created a moral dilemma for the doll couturier who must ask herself if she can conscionably destroy vintage garments of good condition.

It is for all these reasons that I have attempted to present here, as carefully drafted as possible, my own interpretations of the original styles belonging to Twentieth Century Dolls.

-JGA
7 May 1997

This essay, in its original form, appeared in *Dolls — A Complete Bibliography*, edited by Nancy Ann Lutz, Newport Beach, California; The Doll Works, 1981. Reprinted by permission of the author.

MAKING THE PATTERNS IN THIS BOOK WORK FOR YOU

THE MAGNIFICENT COPYING MACHINE AND HOW TO USE IT LEGALLY

When I wrote and illustrated the first volume of *Sewing for Twentieth Century Dolls*, I explained how to trace, enlarge or reduce the patterns given in the book. Using the time-honored grid system, I explained how a seamstress could convert a given pattern to a different size as needed. What I did not say, but what everyone knows is true, is that such techniques are not only time-consuming and aggravating but also tend to be painfully frustrating. (Who has the time for such nonsense?)

In 1972, copy machines were a novelty, having only recently become available to the general public. The one in my office in 1974 took up more floor space than a standard office desk. Today small copiers may be found in drug stores, grocery stores, office supply outlets, post offices, train stations, airports, and many homes. Not all of these readily available copiers, however, have the capacity for enlargement or reduction. Today, newer machines with such capacities may be found in speed print shops and office supply outlets which abound in most towns.

Along with the benefits of this modern miracle of technology have come problems. Copyright infringement is a daily occurrence. Although admittedly often unintended and quite innocently committed, it is infringement nevertheless.

Infringement, simply put, is copying another person's work without permission and/or without paying for the privilege, for the purpose of profiting from that person's work. This is not an acceptable practice, I am sure most of us would agree. Another thing most people will agree on is that there seem to be gray areas in the copyright laws. The laws are convoluted and confusing. Perhaps it is possible to clarify the situation, at least in the matter of the doll clothes patterns in this book.

The purpose of this book is to provide doll collectors and costumers with authentic patterns with which they may dress a doll as near original as possible or at the very least in the style of the doll's period.

For the book to be of any value to anyone, it must therefore follow that certain permissions are automatically granted regarding the use of the work of the author as shown in this book. You *do have permission* to copy these patterns, either by tracing with tissue and pencil, or by modern copy machine. You *do have permission* to make doll clothes from these patterns for yourself or for sale as a business or hobby (the clothes, not the patterns).

You *do not have permission* to copy the patterns and give or sell them to another person or use them in any other way for profit other than as outlined above. I recently found several pages from my first sewing book had been copied and the copies were being offered for sale on a table at a doll show. That is infringement, unconscionable and against the law.

In another case, I discovered that someone had traced several pages from my first sewing book and published it as their own work in a national magazine, without acknowledgment of the source or payment to me. When I brought the matter to the attention of the publisher, I was paid at my usual rate for the pages published plus an equal amount in exemplary damages, with apologies for their mistake. (There is some justice in the universe after all.)

Now that we've said all that, please know that you do have permission to make copies on a copier for your own use. You do have permission to reduce or enlarge the patterns to fit your doll. And be thankful at the same time that in most instances it is no longer necessary to lay out patterns and try to transfer the forms to a graphed sheet of paper in a larger or smaller size. (More about this later).

FIGURING REDUCTIONS

Figuring reductions and enlargements is difficult for some people. In reality, it is only a matter of understanding a few basics of the method and memorizing a wonderful little formula I've devised: Divide what you want (W) by what you have (H) to obtain the percentage of reduction (R) or enlargement (E) you must use to obtain the size you want (W). Thus we have the formula $W \div H = R/E$ (reduction or enlargement). Memorize this formula. Write it on a bit of paper and post it in full view of your work area.

Examples may help to illustrate. If you have a pattern designed for a 20in (51cm) doll, but your doll is a mere 16in (41cm), divide 16 (W) by 20 (H) and you get 80 (R). Your reduction is 80% of the original size. Set the machine accordingly.

If that seems overly simple, let's try another to double-check our method. Your doll is 8-1/2in (22cm) tall (W) but the pattern is for an 11in (28cm) doll (H). Again, divide. *Divide the pattern size you want by the pattern size you have:* 8-1/2in (22cm) divided by 11in (28cm); answer 77%. An 8-1/2in (22cm) pattern is 77% the size of an 11in (cm) pattern, so set the machine at 77%. Get it?

FIGURING ENLARGEMENTS

Enlargement uses the same formula. If you have a 16in (41cm) pattern (H) and your doll measures 20in (51cm) (W), then divide what you want by what you have. You want a 20in (51cm) pattern and you have a 16in (41cm) pattern, so divide 20 by 16 which equals 1.25, or 125%. A 20in (51cm) pattern is 125% the size of the 16in (41cm) pattern. Set the machine at 125% enlargement. Easy!

If a copy machine is not available to you, then the graph system is your only option. Even then, you need the methods outlined above to determine what percentage of enlargement or reduction is required.

Trace the pattern from the book onto white tissue or plain typing paper. Draw lines across the paper at 1in (3cm) intervals, keeping lines parallel. Turn paper and draw lines at 1in (3cm) intervals crossing previous lines. Be careful to maintain the 1in (3cm) measurements. This is your 100% same-size copy.

Now, if you have calculated your enlargement at 125%, for example, you must draw a new graph on blank paper (a larger piece of paper) with the lines 1-1/4in (3cm) apart (125% of 1in [3cm]). Working square by square, transfer the curves and lines of the pattern to the larger sheet with the larger squares and you have completed a 125% enlargement of the original pattern.

If you need to reduce to 75% of the original size, for example, simply draw lines on your copy of the pattern at 1in (3cm) intervals as above, then draw lines on a separate piece of plain paper at 3/4in (2cm) (75%) intervals. Transfer your original pattern, square by square, to this new, smaller size grid and you have the 75% reduction.

For future reference, here is what you write on a small card or piece of paper to keep in your wallet or hang on the wall:

To reduce or enlarge a pattern, divide what you want by what you have (pattern sizes): W ÷ H = E/R.

Or it may be easier for you to remember the formula in algebraic form:

$$\frac{W}{H} = E/R$$

Simple!

LEARNING TO USE FABRICS AND PATTERNS CREATIVELY

Patterns, contrary to popular opinion, lend themselves to adaptation. All that is required is the courage to try something new. By mixing and matching fabrics and pattern parts, the designer in you may be released.

Here are a few ideas of what can be done with a little imagination:

1. Use a slip bodice to make a dress. Find a sleeve pattern that will change the slip into a dress or blouse. Add a Bertha collar or a bit of lace or a ruffle to the neckline, the sleeves, or the hem of the garment.

2. Use florals, plaids, or checks in combination with matching plain fabric. Pick up the pink in a rosebud, the yellow in a daisy, or the soft green of a leaf.

3. Use sheer white or pale pastel organdy or organza over a flower print for a softened effect.

4. Vary the fullness of a gathered or pleated skirt.

5. Add rows of tucks even though the pattern doesn't call for them. Allow for the extra width or length needed as you cut the fabric.

6. Borrow collars, sleeves, cuffs, a jacket or skirt from another pattern.

7. Lengthen a bodice; shorten a skirt, or shorten a bodice and lengthen a skirt.

8. Use the extra fullness intended for gathers to create darts for a fitted look.

9. Reverse a button-down-the back bodice pattern to create a shirtwaist dress.

10. Cut the collar and cuffs wider or narrower.

11. Pleat a skirt that calls for gathers; gather a skirt that calls for pleats.

12. Make jeans, shorts, or slacks by lengthening a panty pattern.

13. Borrow a slacks or dress pattern from another decade and adapt it to the style of the period of your doll.

14. Make an entire dress of lace:
   A) Make a basic dress (use white or pastel organdy, or fabric of your choice) from the desired pattern. Overlay the entire dress with lace. Begin at the bottom of the skirt, sewing row after row of flat lace over the skirt. Continue over the entire dress.
   B) Omit the basic dress and sew lace together, referring to the pattern as you proceed. This is real adventure!
   C) Pin lace fabric and base fabric together, smoothing out all wrinkles. Pin pattern on and cut both fabrics as one. Pin or tack the two layers together as you carefully remove patterns and pins. Sew both layers as one.

15. Seek out unique trims (buttons, braids, bindings, broken jewelry, bits of fabric that could be appliquéd to a garment). Apply these trims in new ways.

16. Combine fabrics in unusual combinations (it's done all the time in the fashion industry).

17. Make a memorable gift for a child. Translate scraps from your family's clothing into corresponding garments for a doll.

And now, congratulations! You have become a fashion designer.

MAKING DOLL BODIES

As with people, dolls come in all shapes and sizes. Unlike real people, they were and are made from a large number of different materials: Kid leather, cloth, celluloid, metal, rubber, hard plastic, and vinyl, among others. Replacement of some of these materials is easier than others. We are concerned here with replacing doll bodies of leather and cloth.

Cloth bodies were used with nearly every type of head. We have all seen China heads with cloth bodies, many of them obviously homemade. As well, we have seen heads of bisque, rubber, composition, celluloid, hard plastic, and vinyl on cloth bodies. Although cloth is effective for adult doll bodies, it is especially appropriate for a baby doll; its softness makes a baby doll seem almost as cuddly as the real thing.

There are many modern fabrics, some especially designed for dollmaking, that may do the job quite satisfactorily. These fabrics are eminently suitable for making modern artist dolls, especially those using needle-molding techniques. The choice when replacing an old body, however, if one is out to return a doll to something of its original state, should be a fabric similar to the original.

Most old cloth doll bodies were made of muslin or a similar material. A few were made of a rubberized fabric and some were of heavy pink cotton sateen. Since low-cost unbleached muslin is economical, most companies opted for this fabric. In my opinion, nothing works as well for replacing old cloth doll bodies as good quality unbleached muslin.

In some instances, especially for larger dolls, double thicknesses of muslin may be used and sewn as one. I have seen a marvelous duplication of a 30in (76cm) antique kid leather body with universal joints, constructed of double thicknesses of muslin. Every detail had been addressed and the stuffing was done with equal care and skill. The results were breathtaking.

Most doll restorers would prefer to use kid leather to construct a replacement kid body and I agree with that choice. My point here is that in a pinch it can be done with fabric.

RECLAIMING AN OLD BODY

Sometimes it is not necessary to replace a cloth doll body. If the fabric is merely soiled but is otherwise in good condition, carefully remove the head, clean it, set it aside, and remove and discard the stuffing from the body and all extremities. If the doll has legs and arms of another material, these must also be separated from the cloth parts.

Inspect the body to be sure all the stuffing has been removed, then tenderly wash the piece with a mild soap or detergent. If the fabric is heavily stained, it may be necessary to resort to a mild bleach. Identify the type of stain (rust, dirt, oil, etc.) before selecting a bleaching agent since all bleaches do not work on all stains. Lipstick and ball-point pen marks are especially difficult, if not impossible, to remove.

Read package instructions carefully and, when finished, rinse thoroughly to remove all soap and bleach. Any residue may come back to haunt you in future years, evidenced by accelerated deterioration of the fabric.

Some old bodies were stamped by the manufacturer with the company's logo, address, a date, or the name of the doll. These marks are vital clues to the origin of the doll and must be treated reverently. Consider carefully before laundering a marked body; it may be possible to clean around the mark. Place the body flat on a terry towel and sponge surrounding areas while protecting the mark from cleaning materials and water. If the body has disintegrated to the point of being unusable, it may be possible to cut around the mark, allowing material for turning under. This piece then becomes a "label" that may be sewn to the new body in the position it appeared on the original.

If a body has a sewn-in tag, care should be taken to preserve it from bleaching or washing away valuable information. If the body is being replaced, sew the tag into the new body as it was in the original, or open it out flat and whipstitch it to the body label-fashion.

DUPLICATING AN OLD BODY

To duplicate the body, remove all stitching and press the pieces flat. Make paper patterns from these parts, mark any darts or tucks, identify the doll from which it was taken and file for future use. Long, business-size envelopes are perfect for storing most patterns. Someday you may find a head needing a body of just this design and you will be ready to produce that body. Remember also that your pattern may be reduced or enlarged to make bodies for smaller or larger heads.

Send your doll into the future with the best possible replacement body; use the best quality fabric possible, do the best job you can in sewing and stuffing the body.

Baste before machine stitching to ensure proper alignment of the parts. Use small stitches (even double-stitching of seams is advisable).

Use heavy thread when attaching heads or limbs by hand or closing neck openings. Avoid wire for use in attaching flange-neck heads and you avoid chances of future rust. Instead use heavy thread such as carpet weight thread.

Duplicate the stuffing style of the original, allowing for what time may have done in compacting the stuffing. Some dolls were hard-stuffed; others were fluffy-stuffed. Polyester fills are the modern stuffing of choice because they are clean, efficient, hypo-allergenic, and washable. Such fillings may be stuffed soft, hard, or fluffy, but care should be taken that the body is never "lumpy."

Polyester fill makes a doll much lighter in weight than some of the old dolls. This problem may be solved by adding pellets of heavier material which are generally available from dollmaking supply sources.

Kid bodies and bodies of some of the early compositions were stuffed with cork, straw, excelsior, sawdust, bran, horse hair, or combinations of these and other materials. If you choose to use such materials, be advised problems may arise in the future. Sawdust is a wood product and contains acids and oils which could bleed through your doll's body cover, causing staining and other damage not only to the body, but also to the costume. Insects are sometimes attracted to wood, bran, and other materials. Horse hair may bring along its own set of problems, including allergic reactions.

CHOOSING THE CORRECT BODY SIZE

I am often asked if a doll's measurements are from shoulder to toe. Of course not. They are taken from top of head to bottom of heel just as the measurement of a man who is six feet tall is taken from the top of his head to the floor.

The confusion may stem from the problem of determining the overall height of a doll when only the head is available. Recognizing the age-type of the head is essential since the proportion of the head to overall height varies with the age of the figure represented. In other words, the proportion of a baby's head to its total length is far different from an adult's head-to-height proportion. Following is a chart of average proportions. Measurements for the head are taken from bottom of chin to top of head.

Babies – 3-1/2 to 4 times head height
Toddlers – 4 to 4-1/2 times head height
Six-year-olds – 5 to 5-1/2 times head height
Eight-year-olds – 6 to 6-1/2 times head height
Ten-year-olds – 6-1/2 to 7 times head height
Twelve-year-olds – 6 to 7 times head height*
Fourteen-year-olds – 7 to 7-1/2 times head height
Sixteen-year-olds – 7 to 7-1/2 times head height
Adult Women – 7 to 7-1/2 times head height
Adult Men – 7-1/2 to 8 times head height
Adult Fashion Figures – 9 times head height

*Bear in mind that as the person matures, the head size changes. You will note, therefore, that proportions change in irregular increments.

MAKING DOLL SHOES

The feet of dolls vary in size and shape to such a degree that it is almost impossible to draft a generic pattern. Shoes for one 18in (46cm) doll, for example, will not fit every 18in (46cm) doll. (Look carefully at the shape of the sole of your doll's foot and compare it to the shapes of various shoe soles given in this book.)

It is therefore extremely important to check the pattern fit before cutting into good leather or other material.

Cut one shoe from heavy muslin or even oilcloth and sew it together, checking the fit on the doll's foot at each stage of the process.

Make any required alterations and construct a second shoe using the altered pattern to confirm your findings. Then, and only then, proceed to the use of the good material.

Cut all pieces and make two piles, separating left and right pieces. Construct both shoes at the same time, step by step, to ensure they will match.

Refer to the first volume of this work for further information on making doll shoes and for additional patterns.

WARDROBE FOR
18in (46cm) ANTIQUE
BISQUE-HEAD
GIRL DOLL
ca. 1905

View 1

View 2

View 3

View 4

View 5

View 6

View 7

WARDROBE FOR 18in (46cm) ANTIQUE BISQUE-HEAD GIRL DOLL
ca. 1905

View 1
DRESS
Pattern Pieces A, B, C

Use any fine silk, organdy, cotton lawn, or other soft, lightweight fabric. Keep lace width in proportion to size of doll. A 2in (5cm)-3in (8cm) wide lace, for example, would not be appropriate for most dolls, yet we often see such widths of trim used on otherwise wonderfully crafted doll outfits.

Remember always to check the pattern against your doll. Old dolls vary in size and shape just as human children do. If you have doubts, cut a checking garment from an old sheet or shirt, sew it up, make any required adjustments, and then cut from good fabric.

Note that these patterns may be enlarged to fit the popular artist dolls of the 1980s and 1990s.

1. For back opening, snip pattern piece A from top to dot on center back line. Cut a self-bias piece 3/4in (2cm) wide to face this opening.

2. Attach lace to neckline with self-bias, sew lace and bias as one, turn bias to inside. Finish with blind stitch. Lace should stand up along neckline.

    A. If using organdy, silk, or other sheer or fine fabrics, the yoke B may be made double. Construct as above, except sew the two pieces together along neckline and down back. Attach skirt to one thickness only of yoke, attach sleeves to same piece. Turn under edges of underneath piece of yoke and blind stitch to wrong side of skirt and sleeves for finished inside.

    B. If constructing a double yoke, attach lace to one yoke B, leave folded down, attach remaining yoke, turn and press so lace stands up.

3. Gather or pleat skirt front and back to yoke B. Lay out flat.

4. Gather sleeve and lace shoulder ruffle as one between dots (see illustration) to fit sleeve opening.

    A. Check length of sleeve on doll and trim any excess length, allowing for narrow hem. Attach lace at lower edge of sleeve and tie off securely. Run double gathering thread along double dash line, pull to a loose fit. Finish by sewing narrow lace over gathers. The location of the gathering line may need to be adjusted, according to length of doll's arm. Note that this pattern also may be made without the lace wrist trim or shoulder ruffle.

5. Pin and baste sleeve/dress side seams, matching underarm seams. Sew seams.

6. Blind-stitch lace edge so raw edges are neatly finished.

7. Hem to suit your doll using careful blind stitches, making no less than a 1in (3cm) hem, or trimming length to accommodate a narrow "handkerchief" hem with tiny hand stitches.

View 2
DRESS
Pattern Pieces D, E

This dress is easy to construct and finish. It would be considered an "everyday" dress and is similar to dresses that many of the moderately priced antique dolls wore when they were new. Most often these dresses were of lightweight white cotton lawn, batiste, organdy, or some other inexpensive fabric.

The neck is finished with slightly wider lace than that used in the View 1 Dress. The same lace is also used at the wrists or mid-forearms, depending on which length sleeve is chosen. A loose belt defines the dropped waistline and effectively gathers the dress to form.

The belt length is determined by measuring around the doll, over the dress and underwear, and adding 2in (5cm). Use this measurement to cut a piece of fabric 3in (8cm) wide for the 18in (46cm) doll. Adjust the width for a smaller or larger doll. Fold the piece along the length, then seam, leaving an opening for turning. Trim the seam and turn. Carefully blind-stitch the opening. Work a buttonhole in one end of the belt; sew a button on the other end.

If desired, crocheted belt loops may be attached to the dress, or the belt may be buttoned to the sides or back with additional buttonholes worked on the belt at appropriate locations.

View 3
JUMPER/APRON
Pattern Pieces F, G

This simple garment was a staple in every little girl's wardrobe during a time when automatic washing machines were as yet unheard of. For protection of a school dress or everyday dress, it was usually made of a serviceable white cotton, often without the bottom ruffle and extra fullness. Fashioned of crisp organdy or other finer material, trimmed with lace, with stiffly starched butterfly ruffles at the armhole openings, the garment became a lovely addition to a Sunday or Holiday outfit.

To point up the versatility of the patterns, look through this book for suitable sleeve patterns with which to create additional dress designs. Do not be afraid to mix and match pattern pieces to achieve different looks, always adjusting for fit.

A reversible garment may be made by cutting from two different fabrics of essentially the same weight. (Example: Blue chambray backed with a cotton print of yellow or pink flowers.) Sew the garments separately along shoulder, back edge, and side seams, turn, press and blind-stitch remaining seams.

A pattern for the bottom ruffle is not given since much depends on your own eye as a seamstress/designer. How deep the ruffle, how full the gathers, and how the bottom edge is finished (wide hem, simple "hanky" hem or narrow lace) is left in the hands of the reader.

View 4
NIGHTGOWN & SLIPPERS
Pattern Pieces A, B, C

Lengthen pattern piece A to nightgown length, allowing for ruffle width and seam. Construct gown as for dress, following illustration for placement of lace. Lightweight flannel or soft cotton prints are excellent choices for this garment.

For slippers, use either the gown fabric or a matching felt. Trim with pompons or ribbon bows. For soles, draw around doll's foot and check against the pattern given. Cut four pieces from this pattern for double thickness soles, making left and right soles. Consult slipper patterns elsewhere in this book for finishing instructions and other ideas.

View 5
SLIP & BLOOMERS
Pattern Pieces H, J

This slip is quite simple but may be adorned with lace and tucks for a more luxurious garment. The sketch shows three tucks across the skirt. Measure your doll from top of shoulders to desired length, then add 1/2in (1cm) for each 1/4in (.65cm) tuck or 1/4in (.65cm) for each 1/8in (.31cm) tuck. Always mark tucks carefully, measuring up from finished hem; baste then press before final stitching.

This pattern may be cut off just below the waist to make a camisole.

The bloomers are of standard construction and are shown made quite plain. If tucks are desired, extend length of leg as above. Mark legs for a casing for elastic, then add tucks below the casing. Finish with plain hem or narrow lace to match the slip.

View 6
DRESS & HAT
Pattern Pieces A, B, C

This view shows an alternate treatment of the pattern pieces used for the View 1 Dress, and again illustrates the versatility of a pattern in the hands of an imaginative dressmaker. Here we see the trim treatment does not employ lace; rather the entire dress is of the same soft fabric with ruffles cut of various widths of dress fabric from narrow at the neck to quite wide for the bottom ruffle.

The hat is a simple concoction of dress fabric and lace as shown, or may be made entirely of dress fabric, to match the dress described above. The lace brim is shown to remind the dressmaker that the bottom ruffles of the dress skirt and sleeves may be made of lace to match the hat illustrated.

For the hat, measure around your doll's head along the line where the hat will sit. Depending on your vision of the fullness of this crown, either increase the measurement by 50% or double it.

Cut a circle of test fabric using this measurement as the diameter. Run double gathering threads around the circumference of the circle and pull to fit doll's head (with wig on, of course).

How do you like the effect? Is it too large, too "poufy"? Or perhaps too small? Make adjustments accordingly, then do another test piece. It will be worth the effort to have it just the way you want it to be.

Now cut good fabric using your final measurement. If the fabric is organdy, cut two, gather both pieces as one and firmly tie off the gathering thread. If the hat is to be made of heavier fabric, the lining should be cut of organdy.

If using dress fabric for the brim, do another test to decide just how full you want the ruffled brim to be. Cut a piece of scrap fabric the width you desire for the brim and 12in (31cm) long. Run a gather stitch alone one long side and pull to the desired fullness; tie off. Measure the gathered side. To determine how long the ruffle piece should be cut for your hat, we'll do a little math.

If your doll's head measures 12in (31cm) around and your ruffled sample measures 4in (10cm), you will need to cut three times as much ruffle material as in your sample (12in [31cm] x 3 = 36in [91cm]). This ratio makes a very full ruffle which will result in a lovely brim for an all-organdy hat. Remember to cut the brim double. In this example, the piece of dress fabric would be 36in (91cm) long by twice the desired finished width of the brim plus seam allowance.

Attach the ruffle to the crown with the seam to the outside of the hat, then cover the seam with ribbon. (Inside of hat will be completely finished.) Add ribbon rose and streamers for a very romantic chappeau.

Nothing gives a doll better "hand," that certain feel when it is handled, than a complete outfit with all the proper underthings, a nice dress and finally a lovely coat. When the fabrics and style are well-chosen and the garments carefully color-coordinated and skillfully sewn, the beauty and personality of the doll are revealed. This coat and bonnet will finish off your doll's couture beautifully.

For a winter coat, use soft wool, wool blends, or soft, wool-like synthetics. Make every effort to find a fabric that looks like wool and not like a modern fabric. Soft, fine corduroy is an acceptable alternative, as are velvet or velveteen. Using fabrics from old garments is sometimes acceptable. (See my essay on the subject elsewhere in the book).

For a spring coat, navy linen or a heavy cotton will do nicely. A double organdy coat over a matching organdy dress makes a nice ensemble. You may wish to experiment with two shades of organdy, using a pastel shade as lining in a white organdy coat. Construct the lining separately, insert into coat, wrong sides together, and blind-stitch in place.

When trimming the coat, the imagination and creativity of the dressmaker again come into play. You may choose to embroider delicate vines, leaves, and roses around the collar and down the front of the coat, making each buttonhole a blossom with the button as its center. Or use matching or contrasting woven braid, remembering it must not be too wide. Always check for proportion. Trim the bonnet to match. Or tack a ribbon bow at the neck opening to match the bonnet illustrated.

Change the look of the coat entirely by squaring or rounding the collar. Add pockets with or without flaps. Use squared flaps with a squared collar, rounded flaps with a rounded collar.

Given are three choices of bonnet styles, all suitable for wear with this coat. One is the soft or "mushroom" style as in View 6. The other two are slightly more tailored. Note that the brim of this latter style may be varied according to the design chosen for the collar-a straight edge or a scalloped edge made by following the dot-dash line on the pattern.

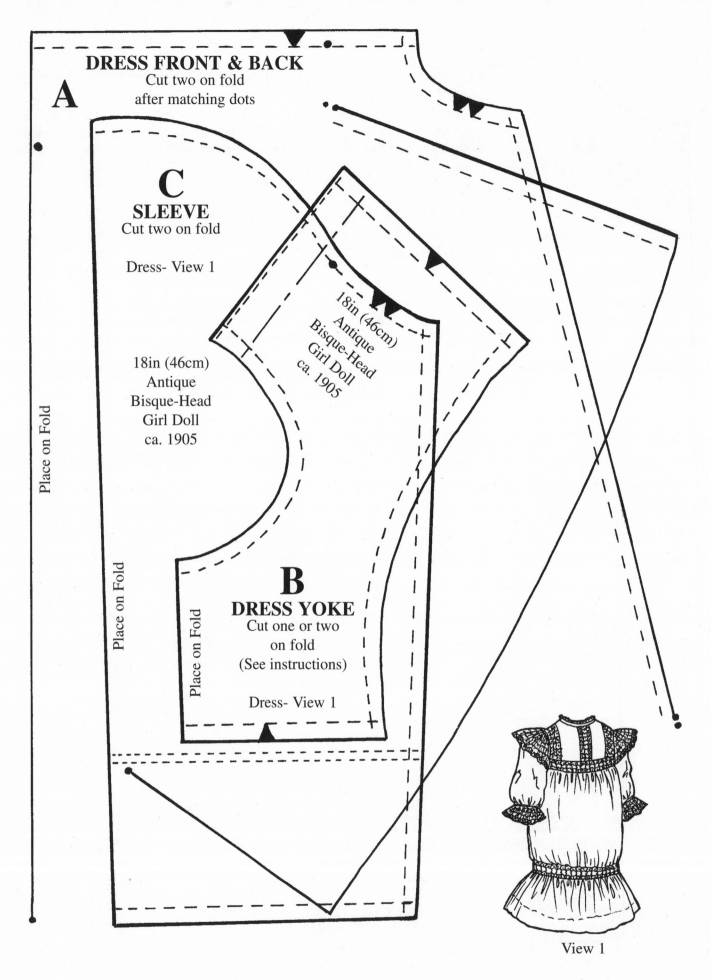

DRESS FRONT & BACK
Cut two on fold
after matching dots

A

Place on Fold

C

SLEEVE
Cut two on fold

Dress- View 1

18in (46cm)
Antique
Bisque-Head
Girl Doll
ca. 1905

18in (46cm)
Antique
Bisque-Head
Girl Doll
ca. 1905

Place on Fold

Place on Fold

B

DRESS YOKE
Cut one or two
on fold
(See instructions)

Dress- View 1

View 1

14

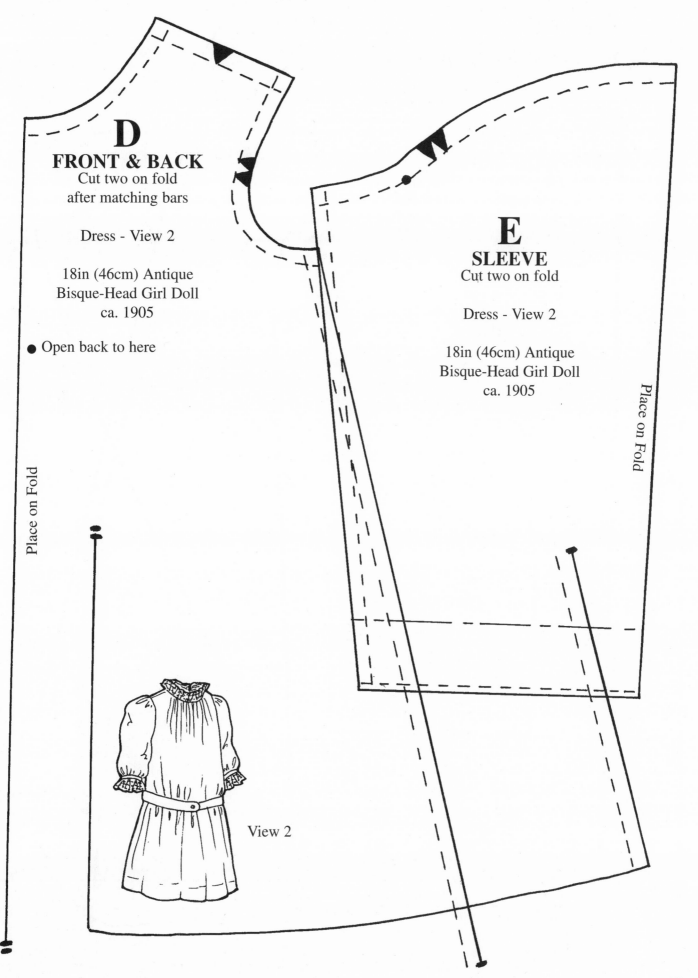

D
FRONT & BACK
Cut two on fold
after matching bars

Dress - View 2

18in (46cm) Antique
Bisque-Head Girl Doll
ca. 1905

● Open back to here

Place on Fold

E
SLEEVE
Cut two on fold

Dress - View 2

18in (46cm) Antique
Bisque-Head Girl Doll
ca. 1905

Place on Fold

View 2

15

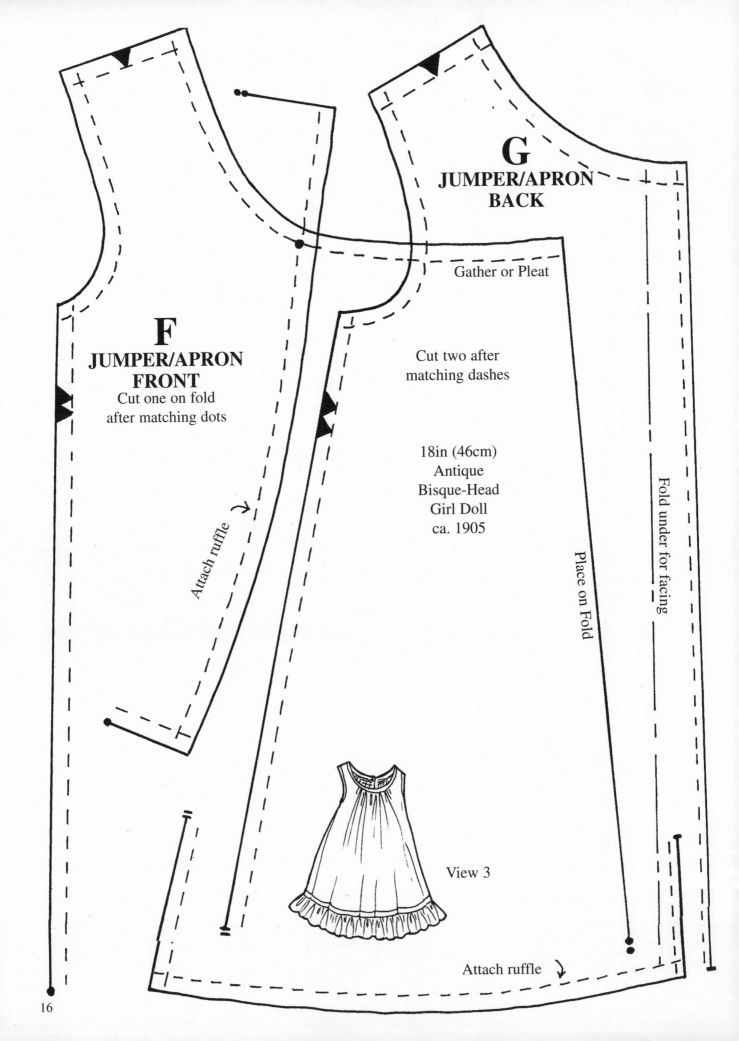

G
JUMPER/APRON BACK

Gather or Pleat

Cut two after matching dashes

18in (46cm) Antique Bisque-Head Girl Doll ca. 1905

Place on Fold

Fold under for facing

F
JUMPER/APRON FRONT
Cut one on fold after matching dots

Attach ruffle

View 3

Attach ruffle

16

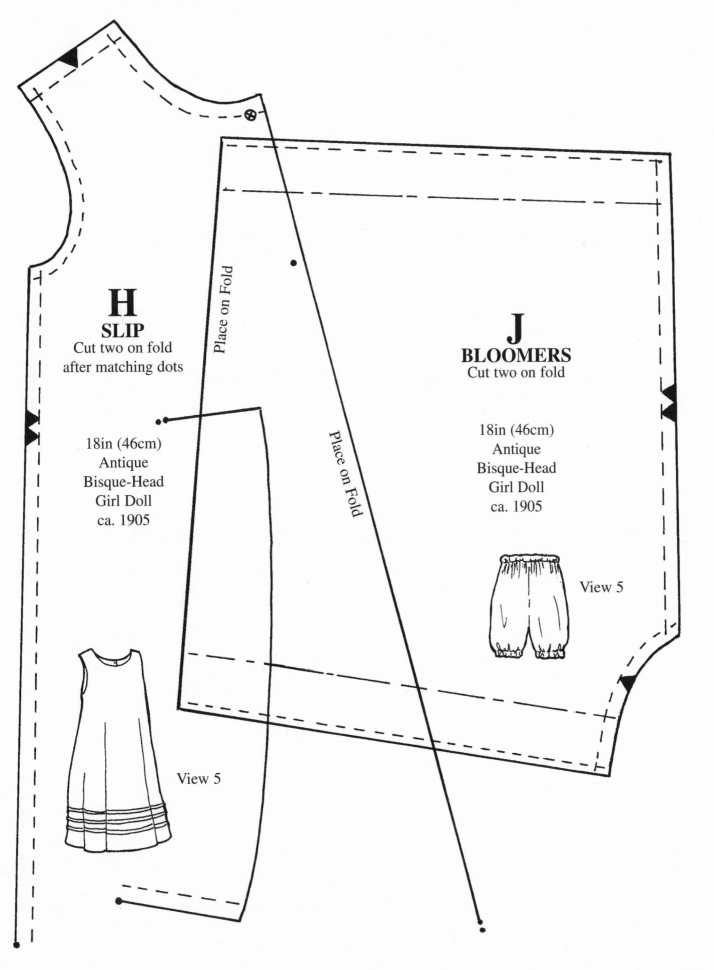

H
SLIP
Cut two on fold
after matching dots

18in (46cm)
Antique
Bisque-Head
Girl Doll
ca. 1905

Place on Fold

Place on Fold

View 5

J
BLOOMERS
Cut two on fold

18in (46cm)
Antique
Bisque-Head
Girl Doll
ca. 1905

View 5

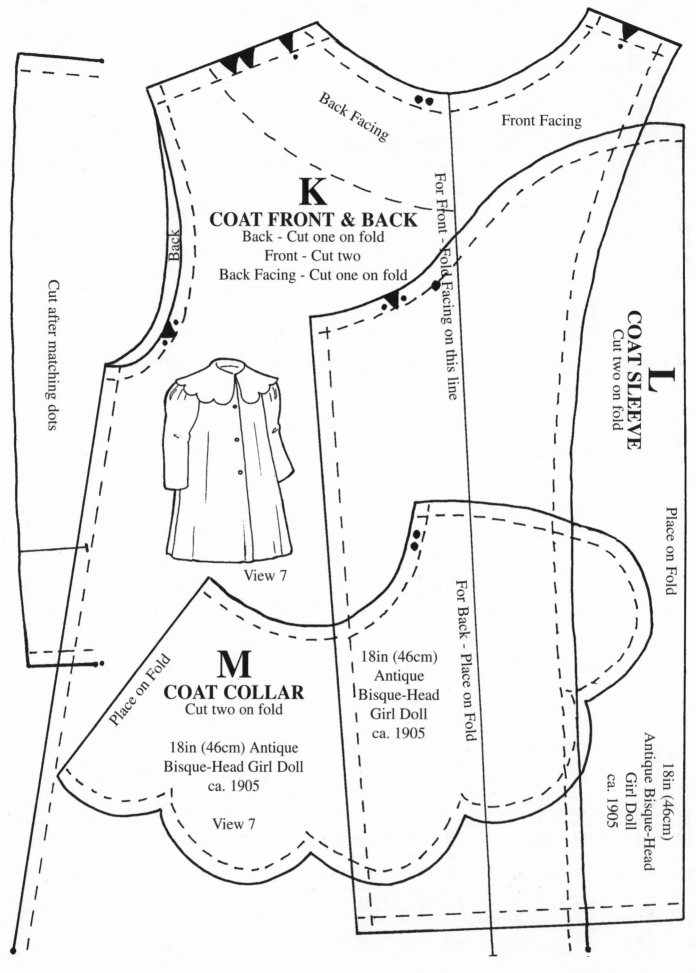

K
COAT FRONT & BACK
Back - Cut one on fold
Front - Cut two
Back Facing - Cut one on fold

Back Facing

Front Facing

For Front - Fold Facing on this line

Back

Cut after matching dots

L
COAT SLEEVE
Cut two on fold

Place on Fold

M
COAT COLLAR
Cut two on fold

18in (46cm) Antique
Bisque-Head Girl Doll
ca. 1905

View 7

Place on Fold

For Back - Place on Fold

18in (46cm)
Antique
Bisque-Head
Girl Doll
ca. 1905

18in (46cm)
Antique Bisque-Head
Girl Doll
ca. 1905

View 7

18

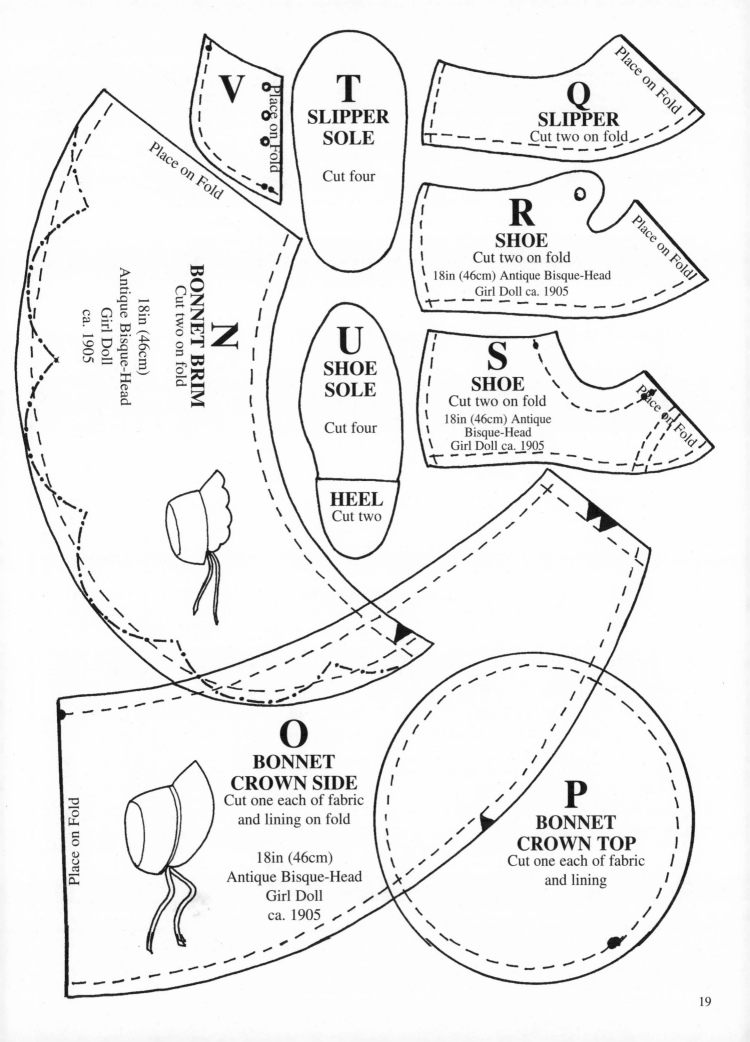

V

Place on Fold

T

SLIPPER SOLE

Cut four

Q

SLIPPER

Cut two on fold

Place on Fold

R

SHOE

Cut two on fold

18in (46cm) Antique Bisque-Head
Girl Doll ca. 1905

Place on Fold

N

BONNET BRIM

Cut two on fold

18in (46cm)
Antique Bisque-Head
Girl Doll
ca. 1905

Place on Fold

U

SHOE SOLE

Cut four

HEEL

Cut two

S

SHOE

Cut two on fold

18in (46cm) Antique
Bisque-Head
Girl Doll ca. 1905

Place on Fold

O

BONNET CROWN SIDE

Cut one each of fabric
and lining on fold

18in (46cm)
Antique Bisque-Head
Girl Doll
ca. 1905

Place on Fold

P

BONNET CROWN TOP

Cut one each of fabric
and lining

View 4

View 1

View 2

View 3

AN EARLY TWENTIETH CENTURY
WARDROBE FOR A 15in (38cm)
LADY DOLL

View 5

View 6

View 7

View 8

All designs are original JGA concepts based on the actual styles of the period - 1890-1919.

AN EARLY TWENTIETH CENTURY WARDROBE FOR A 15in (38cm) LADY DOLL
1890-1919

These original patterns were created for the doll featured in my short story, "The Last Christmas Doll," which was written for the UFDC Region IV 1990 Conference in Lincoln, Nebraska. The story, a pattern for the doll, and a paper doll were featured in the conference souvenir book and were reprinted later that year as part of a pattern booklet. The paper doll and doll-only pattern also appeared in the Winter 1990 issue of *DOLLMAKING* magazine.

General Instructions

The patterns may be used to dress a Kestner *Gibson Girl* or other lady dolls of the period. Since dolls differ in size and shape as much as humans differ, it may be necessary to make adjustments. Always check a pattern on a doll before cutting good fabric.

In the story, the doll and her clothes were created by a non-dollmaker using scrap fabrics. If you wish to achieve the "old" effect, wash and press all the fabric before pinning on the patterns.

Use fine-woven, lightweight fabrics that hang softly. Synthetic fabrics are not appropriate for these fashions. Choose small prints, tiny checks, miniature plaids, and narrow stripes that are in proportion to the size of your dolls. Buttons and other fasteners should always be appropriately proportioned.

Make gathers by sewing two parallel rows of tiny running stitches no more than 1/8in (.31cm) apart. Pull both threads carefully at the same time, creating even gathers. Leave ends of threads loose until seam is complete (to allow for making adjustments), then tie off gathering threads.

Pin paper patterns to fabric and cut out all pieces according to instructions. Stitch all darts, then clip and press. Pin pieces right sides together and stitch. Always press seams open; the garment will look and fit much better. Pin the cut fabric pieces of each garment together if you will not be completing the garment immediately.

Keep the paper pattern pieces in separate envelopes for each garment and paste the sketch of the garment on the outside of the envelope. Be sure to note the size of the doll. If you plan to use the pattern more than once, you may wish to make notations of any changes, alterations, or embellishments you've devised. Refer to the instructions below for lists of pattern pieces for each garment.

Hand-sewing or machine-stitching, that is the question. Some seamstresses believe that sewing the darts by hand using tiny, even stitches is much easier and neater than sewing them by machine. It takes little or no additional time when you consider all that stopping to clip threads, lining up the machine needle in the dart, reversing the machine for knotting the stitches, etc. The choice, however, is yours.

Important: If using a sewing machine, be sure to set the stitch size to a small setting.

You may notice as you create this wardrobe that the outfits seem to represent more than one fashion period. There is a very good reason for this. Victoria, the woman of my story, was a farm woman of moderate means. Clothing was precious and had to last many seasons. Sometimes an outfit was updated by recutting or reseaming or merely adding a "new-style" ornament or trim. Garments were rarely discarded. The "good" fabric of a skirt might be enough to make a child's dress. Buttons and trim were always saved for "later." Thus we have here a mixed bag of styles, making the wardrobe even more charming and interesting.

It may be that you are sewing for a much larger doll. Below is a chart showing enlargement increments for several additional sizes. You need only take your pattern to a photocopy machine with enlargement capabilities and use the enlargement percentages shown to obtain the larger patterns.

Using the pattern given here for a 15in (38cm) doll you may enlarge as follows:

For 18in (46cm) doll — enlarge 120%
For 20in (51cm) doll — enlarge 135%
For 25in (64cm) doll — enlarge 165%

NOTE: These pattern pieces may be combined to construct various dresses of the period. Consult fashion plates of the time and use your imagination to create more outfits.

View 1
HOBBLE SKIRT DRESS
Pattern Pieces T, U, H

Recommended Fabrics - Lightweight wools, cottons

Cut 1 pattern piece T dress front on fold as indicated, extending to desired length plus hem allowance. Cut 2 pattern piece U dress back, extending to desired length plus hem allowance. Cut neck facings using dress back and dress front patterns as guides.

Sew darts as indicated. Sew shoulder seams and press flat. Place assembled facings on dress, right sides together, stitch all around, clip corners and turn. Turn plackets to inside and tack in place.

Sew wide lace trim around neckline as indicated on illustration and pattern, mitering corners neatly. Sew side seams and press open. Attach lace trim to skirt as indicated on pattern and illustration.

Sleeves -Using pattern piece H, cut two. Sew underarm seams, press seam open and turn. Insert sleeve into armhole, easing fullness. Turn up 1/4in (.65cm) hem to outside of sleeve. Cover hem raw edge with lace cuff. See illustration.

Recommended Fabrics-Very fine crepe or some other softly falling fabric such as silk charmuese

Bodice Back - Use pattern piece W bodice back, bottom line A.

Bodice Front - Use pattern piece K. Run gather stitches between black dots. Match neckline to front yoke J, stitch J to back of K, leaving seam in view on front (wrong side of bodice should show a finished seam). On remaining piece of section J, press under 1/8in (.31cm) and tack-stitch this piece over seam on front and along shoulder seam. Turn under all edges of trim M and press carefully. Blind-stitch this piece over the seam as shown in illustration. Assemble back and front bodice at shoulder seams and install soft stand-up collar N. Sew side seams of bodice and press open.

Sleeves - Cut two each of pattern pieces H sleeve and L cuff. Sew underarm seams of sleeves and seams of cuffs. Press seams open. Insert cuff into sleeve, right side of cuff facing wrong side of sleeve and seam. Turn cuff to right side. Turn back 1/8in (.31cm) of cuff and press. Blind-stitch cuff to sleeve.

Skirt - Cut a rectangle 12in (31cm) wide and 10in (25cm) long. Gather along one 12in (31cm) edge to within 1in (3cm) of each end. Sew the two 10in (25cm) edges together to within 2in (5cm) of gathered edge. Attach to bodice, allowing for placket along back opening. Finish back placket, using either tiny buttons or thread knot buttons and worked buttonholes, or very small snaps.

Belt and Rose - Using dress material, cut a strip 4-1/2in (12cm) x 1-1/2in (4cm), fold right sides together, stitch all around, leaving opening at center for turning. Turn, blind-stitch opening. Make rose using either matching color velvet or satin ribbon or dress fabric. See illustrations.

A decorative antique button or cameo earring may be used to simulate a brooch at the neckline.

Afternoon Dress construction

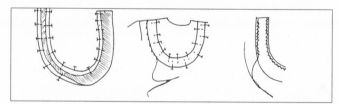

Afternoon Dress Construction.

Coat Body - Measure doll and draw pattern pieces TT and UU to proper length. Sew shoulder darts, clip, and press open. Join pieces at shoulder seams, press seams open.

Cut two pattern piece XX collar, sew right sides together, leaving seam open between dots. Clip seam and collar points, turn and press. Pin, then baste collar to neckline, matching center back at half-notch. Pin, baste, and seam front facing TT to fronts of coat, right sides together. Clip seams and turn. Finish back neck with matching bias or cut a facing using neckline of coat back as pattern. Sew side seams, matching notches. Press open.

Sleeves - Run gather stitches as indicated but do not pull. Stitch underarm seams, press open and turn. Sew cuff pieces along end seams only, matching single and double dots. Clip seam, turn and press. Insert cuff into sleeve as shown in illustration and seam together. Turn cuff to outside, sew button on rounded end at dash mark.

Pull gather threads to fit sleeve into opening and stitch armhole seam, matching notches. Clip seams to ease as required.

Work buttonholes and attach buttons as indicated on pattern. Hem coat.

Pocket - Cut four pattern piece ZZ. Seam two right sides together for each pocket, leaving small opening along bottom for turning. Clip seams and turn. Slipstitch opening. Fold down flap and tack in place. Position on coat and stitch in place.

NOTE: This coat may be lined if desired, using very lightweight silk or wool. Use coat body pattern and construct as for coat. Insert into coat before sewing on coat collar, cuffs and front facings. Sew pockets to coat before inserting lining.

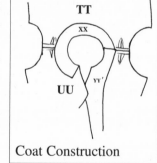

Coat Construction

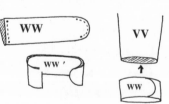

Coat Cuff Construction

WEDDING DRESS
Pattern Pieces
JJ, KK, LL, MM, NN

Recommended Fabrics - Heavy silk, lightweight satin

Victoria, the woman of my story, was married in 1896, two years after the wedding of her sister, Elizabeth. When Elizabeth learned of the impending marriage of her sister, she insisted that Victoria wear her wedding dress. (This began a family tradition that Mary Bethel, her cousins, their daughters and their granddaughters carried on. The 1894 wedding dress is now carefully preserved, awaiting yet another generation's brides.) So it was thAT Victoria created a wedding dress of the 1894 style for Mary Bethel's doll.

Sleeves - Baste lace ruffle along top edge of sleeve. Run gathering stitches through lace and fabric between dots. Do not pull gathers at this time. Sew underarm seams and press open. Turn sleeve facing to right side and tack in place. Cover raw edge of facing and sleeve with lace trim.

Bodice - Cut one bodice front pattern piece NN of dress fabric and one of lace fabric. Pin and baste together. Sew darts, clip and press. Sew shoulder and side seams, press open. Insert sleeves, pulling gathers evenly. Pin, baste, and sew. Gather center of sleeve between X's. Attach bow over stitching.

Skirt - Sew side seams, press open. Run gathering threads between dots on both panels. Sew back seam to double dots, press seam open. Pin skirt and bodice right sides together at waist. Adjust gathers in back and soft pleats in front to fit. Pin, baste, and stitch. With silk thread, topstitch by hand with tiny decorative feather stitching.

Turn under back placket. Pin, baste and sew collar to bodice. Crochet a chain of white thread the length of the back opening. Attach to back edge of left side of bodice, leaving openings to form button loops. Sew on tiny pearl buttons or make thread knot buttons. (These are especially beautiful if silk floss is used).

Sash - Cut four 6in (15cm) lengths of 3in (8cm) wide matching satin ribbon. Following illustration, construct bow. Cut one 20in (51cm) length of same ribbon. Attach bow as shown in illustration. Attach hook and eye to fit. (*Note:* Lengths must be adjusted depending on size of doll. These measurements and others in these instructions are for a 15in [38cm] doll.)

Headdress and Veil - Construct headdress and veil using bits of ribbon, lace, and tulle as in illustration. Add seed pearls, beads, miniature flowers as desired. For the Victorians, more was better, so have fun with this.

DRESSING GOWN & NIGHTDRESS
Pattern Pieces
O, P, Q, R, W

Recommended Fabrics- Very fine wool, wool jersey, or soft cotton flannel

Bodice - Using pattern piece Q, run gathering stitches as indicated on pattern. Attach Q to front yoke P.

Bodice Back - Cut pattern piece W on fold, using facing fold line as center back line and bottom line B. Stitch shoulder seams and install stand-up collar using collar N with front opening.

Sleeve and Cuff - Using pattern pieces O and R, run gathering stitches between dots. Attach cuff to sleeve, wrong sides together, sew underarm seams, turn cuffs and blindstitch to sleeve. Insert sleeve into armhole and seam, arranging even gathers.

Skirt - Cut 14in (36cm) x 10in (25cm) rectangle. Run double gathering stitches along one 14in (36cm) edge to within 1in (3cm) of each end and attach to bodice, keeping gathers even. Turn facings to right side and stitch along bottom, then hem garment. Turn facings, whipstitch edges, and baste down. Press. Work buttonholes and sew on buttons as indicated in illustration.

Sash - Cut one piece 18in (46cm) x 1-1/2in (4cm), turn right sides together and stitch all around, leaving 2in (5cm) opening at center for turning. Turn and blindstitch opening. Crochet tiny chain-stitch belt loops of embroidery floss and attach at either side seam or sew a loop of several threads at each side and work buttonhole stitches on loop.

Embroider a feather stitch chain or other decorative stitch in matching or contrasting colors across yoke, cuffs, collar, and down front, if desired. Keep proportion in mind; make stitches tiny enough not to overwhelm the garment.

NIGHTDRESS
Pattern Pieces
O, P, Q, R, X

Recommended Fabric- Lightweight wool or cotton flannel

Use same pattern pieces as used for Dressing Gown, except: For skirt, extend sides of bodice back and bodice front to length required for a full-length garment. Leave front open to just below fifth button. Use collar X from *Gibson Girl* blouse pattern. Construct as above.

LINGERIE
Pattern Pieces
CC, DD, E, EE, FF, GG

Recommended Fabrics- Lightweight silks, cottons, jerseys

Bloomers - Using pattern piece CC, cut two on fold. Working each piece as a unit, sew leg seams and hem bottom edges with rolled hem using blind stitches. Baste tucks at waist, catching with one or two stitches at top. Sew front seam, matching X's and XX's, continue on with back seam to back opening marked with dot. Finish back opening with rolled hem and blind stitches. With a length of bias tape begin six inches from end of tape and bind waist, leaving another 6in (15cm) length of tape at other end. Stitch open edges closed for ties.

Camisole - Using pattern piece DD, cut two on fold. Sew shoulder and side seams, hem neckline, armholes, and bottom with narrow rolled hem. Trim with tiny line of embroidery stitches over hem lines. Note: Neck and armhole may be faced or bound with bias if desired.

Long Silk Chemise - Using pattern piece EE, cut two on fold, using dot-dash line as guide for back piece, extending length to desired measurement plus hem allowance. Sew side seams, turn top edges to right side of fabric and tack. Cover with lace trim. If using cotton, an eyelet trim is appropriate. Attach ribbon straps at large dots.

Corset - Using pattern piece FF, cut two from silk plus one from unbleached muslin for interlining. Stitch darts in each piece and carefully trim excess from seam; join by tacking together with right sides of silk out (a silk, muslin, silk sandwich). Stitch along lines indicated on pattern to simulate boning or stitch 1/8in (.31cm) matching ribbon along "boning" lines. Bind all around with self bias or ribbon. Work matching pairs of tiny eyelet holes along two back edges. Lace with 1/8in (.31cm) ribbon.

Fanny Pad - Using pattern piece GG, cut two of fine cotton, seam with right sides together, leaving 1in (3cm) opening. Turn and pad lightly with bit of cotton batting. Close opening with blindstitching. Attach ribbon ties at dots.

Bosom Pad - Using pattern piece HH, cut two of fine cotton, seam with right sides together, leaving 1in (3cm) opening. Turn and pad lightly with bit of cotton batting. Close opening with blindstitching. Attach ribbon ties at dots.

Stockings - Using pattern piece E, cut two of fine lisle, cotton underwear knit, or silk jersey. Sew back seam, matching darts. Sew toe seam, matching dots. Finish top of stocking with fine rolled hem or very narrow lace.

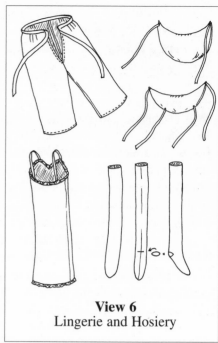

View 6
Lingerie and Hosiery

If you wish to insert a small gusset at the heel, completely finish the stocking and try it on the doll. Mark with a pen where the gusset will go on the heel and remove the stocking. Snip carefully and insert small gusset, making a no-seam joining all around. Remember, you will be cutting the back seam, so be sure to overstitch at both points to strengthen the joining.

View 7
HOUSEDRESS & APRON Pattern Pieces F, G, W

Recommended Fabric-Any soft, fine 100% cotton (men's worn shirts, old blouses, etc.)

Skirt - Cut 10in (25cm) square of dress fabric and assemble as for Afternoon Dress, except insert a 1in (3cm) x 2in (5cm) placket facing, cut from same fabric, at center front of skirt and match to bodice opening. See sketch.

Bodice - Use pattern piece W, bodice back, bottom line B and bodice front pattern piece F. Run gather stitches between dots at neckline and waist of front pieces. Join shoulder seams and side seams of W and F. On sleeve pattern piece G, run gathering stitches between dots, sew underarm seams, fit sleeve into armhole, adjusting gather stitches to fit and matching notches.

Fold front facing back along dotted line. Bind neckline, and bottom of sleeves with contrasting bias tape. Note: Bodice is open to waist. Construct skirt and bodice separately, then assemble, matching front openings. Work buttonholes as marked on pattern. Use tiny buttons or make thread knot buttons. (See illustrations.)

APRON Pattern Piece S

Recommended Fabric-White cotton lawn

Bodice - Cut one pattern piece S on fold and one waistband piece 3/4in (2cm) x 4in (10cm). On bodice, run gathering stitches on dotted lines, turn back and tack at double dots. Pull gathers to fit bodice to waistband. Sew bodice to one piece of waistband, with raw seam at front and finished seam on wrong side. Bind top edge of bodice with self bias.

Skirt - Cut 8in (20cm) x 8in (20cm) square of fabric. Make a narrow rolled hem along two opposite sides of square and press. Run gathers along one remaining edge; make a 3/4in (2cm) hem in the opposite 8in (20cm) edge. Cut a pocket from 2-1/2in (6cm) x 2-1/2in (6cm) square.

Turn back all edges 1/4in (.65cm) and press. Turn one edge down an additional 1/4in (.65cm) press, and blindstitch. Turn one edge down an additional 1/4in (.65cm). Attach to skirt, leaving double-hemmed side open.

Pull gathers and seam skirt to waistband, with finished seam at wrong side and raw seam to front. On remaining piece of waistband turn under 1/8in (.31cm) all around and press. Blind-stitch to front of apron.

By hand, topstitch hem, pocket top, and bias seam with matching embroidered decoration in white if desired.

Apron ties - Cut two 11in (28cm) x 2in (5cm) strips, fold over lengthwise, and seam together leaving 2in (5cm) opening in center for turning. Turn and blind-stitch opening. Attach to apron at double dots.

24

View 8
GIBSON GIRL BLOUSE
Pattern Pieces
V, W, X, Y

Recommended Fabrics-Cotton lawn, eyelet, pique, organdy

Bodice Front - Using pattern piece W, cut two, using bottom line C. Using pattern piece Y, cut one on fold, using bottom line C. With tiny, even stitches, top-stitch along fold to dot. Fold along next line and top-stitch to dot, continuing across bodice (see sketch). Check shoulder edges with those of bodice back as you work; shoulder edges must match in length. Run gathering stitches along waistline as shown, pull to fit doll, and tie off. Join bodice back W and bodice front

Y at shoulder and side seams. Press open.

Fold back facing along dash line, right sides together, seam at bottom edge and turn. Hem bottom edge all around.

Collar - Using pattern piece X, cut four. Seam two pieces right sides together, leaving small opening for turning. Turn, press, and close opening with blind-stitching. Attach collar units, matching dots; cover seam with self-bias facing.

Turn back facing to inside. Finish with worked buttonholes and knotted thread buttons, tiny pearl buttons, or tiny snaps if desired. (Buttons recommended.)

View 8
GIBSON GIRL SKIRT
Pattern Pieces
Z, AA, BB

Recommended Fabrics-Lightweight cotton, wool, or silk faille, serge, or broadcloth

Front - Using pattern piece Z, cut one on fold, extending length as needed, plus adding hem allowance. Using pattern piece BB, cut two, extending length as above, adding hem allowance. Tack pleat as indicated and seam pieces together, matching dart and dots.

Back - Using pattern piece AA, cut two, extending length as needed, adding hem allowance. Sew in darts and

sew back seam to placket opening at dot. Press back seam open.

Waistband - Cut one piece 6-3/4in (17cm) x 1in (3cm). Try on doll to check waist size. Trim off unneeded length. Allow 3/8in (.9cm) for overlap to sew on fastener. Turn right sides together and stitch at both ends.

Assembly - Sew skirt side seams, matching darts. Bind placket with self-bias and press flat. Construct back pleat to cover placket and tack at waistline. Attach waistband and sew hook and eye at waistband closing.

ALL VIEWS SHOES & BOOTS
Pattern Pieces
OO, PP, QQ, RR, SS

Cut 2 pattern pieces QQ or RR of kid leather, depending on which shoe is desired. (Cut one at a time and flip the pattern for the second piece, thus maintaining right and left.)

For soles cut 2 each of pattern piece SS of heavier leather for outer sole and 2 each of pattern piece SS from heavyweight linen-weave stationery for inner lining.

For innersoles, cut 2 each of pattern piece PP of lightweight cardstock such as file folder or index card stock.

Assemble shoes as shown in illustrations.

Tips on Making Shoes

Cut all pieces - side pieces, innersoles, outersoles, and any other sections. Lay out in sets for each shoe. Complete each step on both shoes before proceeding to the next step. In this way, the shoes will be a matching pair, and will also be easier to finish.

Place stockings on doll's feet. Attach inner lining to bottom of doll's stockinged foot with bit of floral clay. Fold seam allowance to bottom, snip to ease all around, dot glue all around innersole and folded-over section, allow glue to set a bit, then put together. Allow to dry, then glue on outersoles. (Additional reinforcement may be made by stitching back and forth across bottom of foot before gluing. See illustrations.)

Glue on heel modeled from a commercial air-drying clay, low-temperature oven-dried clay, or other modeling

material. Heels may also be carved from small blocks of soft wood or cut from sandwiches of light cardboard. Glue several layers of cardboard together until required thickness is achieved. Dry under heavy weight. Cut with sharp craft knife. Paint edges to resemble leather or to match the shoe.

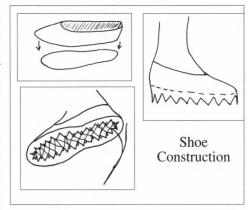

Shoe Construction

View 1
STRAW PICTURE HAT

Using narrow (about 1/8in (.31cm)-1/4in (.65cm) nylon lace (to simulate milliner's horsehair lace), begin at center crown, sewing lace round and round, fitting and shaping crown as you sew. When crown is complete, continue sewing as before, shaping outward for large, flat "picture" brim. Brim should measure from 4in (10cm) to 4-1/2in (12cm) in diameter for a 15in (38cm) doll.

To stiffen further, spray with "hard" hair spray or extra stiff spray starch on inside of crown. Allow to dry well, spray outside. Shape and stuff crown with well-crumpled waxed paper. When dry, spray underside of brim. When dry, place hat on piece of waxed paper and spray outside of crown and topside of brim. Spray shellac may be used instead of starch. Always work in a well-ventilated area when using such chemicals.

SILK HAT

For crown, use drawing compass to make a 4in (10cm) circle pattern. Cut two 4in (10cm) circles of silk and one 4in (10cm) circle of muslin. Lay out flat and stack: One silk circle face down, muslin, remaining silk circle face up. Tack together, taking care to smooth out wrinkles. Run gather stitches around outer edge through all three pieces of fabric. Do not pull gathers at this time.

For brim, using drawing compass, draw a pattern for a 4in (10cm) circle. Without lifting the point of the compass, draw a 2in (5cm) circle in the exact center of the first circle. Carefully cut out and discard the 2in (5cm) circle. The remaining piece is your pattern for the brim.

Cut one brim piece from muslin and two brim pieces from silk. Stack one silk circle face down, then muslin, then remaining silk circle face up. Tack together, then run basting stitch all around inside and outside edges. Bind outer edge with very narrow self-bias. Turn under and blind stitch, keeping a very narrow edge.

Pull gather threads of crown to fit inner edge of brim and pin to brim. Raw edges of seam should be on outside of hat. Cut a piece of self-bias 3/4in (2cm) wide, turn both edges under 1/8in (.31cm), and apply flat over raw seam with blind-stitching. Trim all around over bias with bit of gauzy lace or veiling and finish off with decorative antique button.

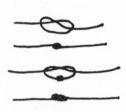

THREAD KNOT BUTTONS

Continue until correct size has been achieved; tie off with a triple knot.

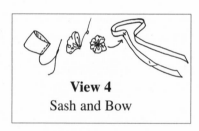

View 4
Sash and Bow

Silk Hat

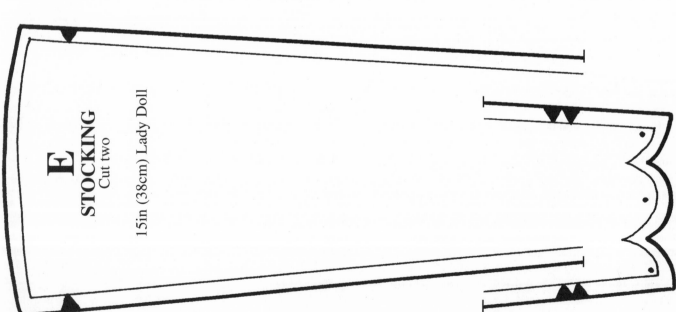

E
STOCKING
Cut two

15in (38cm) Lady Doll

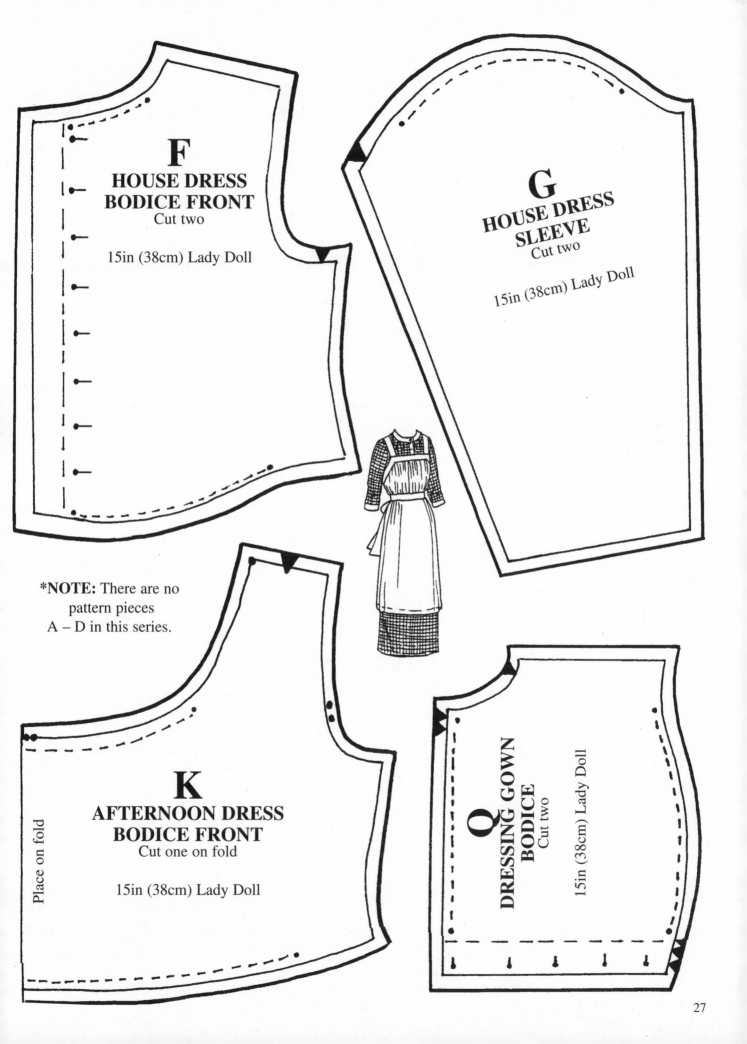

F
HOUSE DRESS
BODICE FRONT
Cut two

15in (38cm) Lady Doll

G
HOUSE DRESS
SLEEVE
Cut two

15in (38cm) Lady Doll

*NOTE: There are no
  pattern pieces
  A – D in this series.

K
AFTERNOON DRESS
BODICE FRONT
Cut one on fold

15in (38cm) Lady Doll

Place on fold

Q
DRESSING GOWN
BODICE
Cut two

15in (38cm) Lady Doll

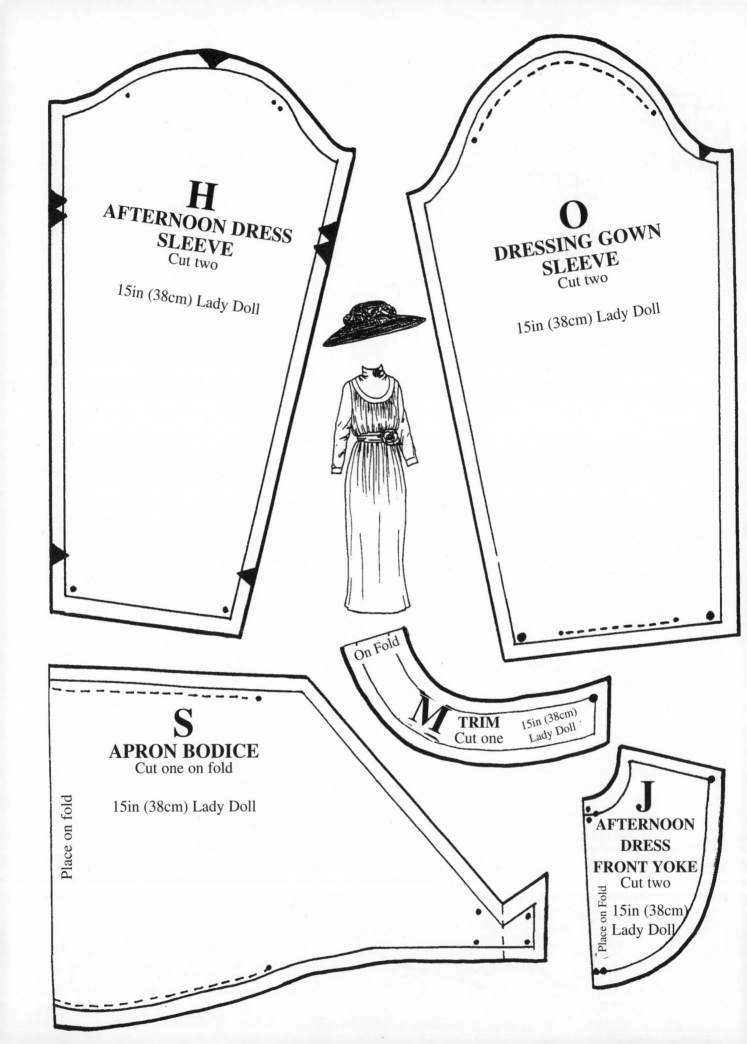

H
AFTERNOON DRESS
SLEEVE
Cut two

15in (38cm) Lady Doll

O
DRESSING GOWN
SLEEVE
Cut two

15in (38cm) Lady Doll

On Fold

M **TRIM**
Cut one   15in (38cm)
            Lady Doll

S
APRON BODICE
Cut one on fold

15in (38cm) Lady Doll

Place on fold

J
AFTERNOON
DRESS
FRONT YOKE
Cut two

15in (38cm)
Lady Doll

Place on Fold

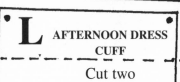

L **AFTERNOON DRESS CUFF**
Cut two

15in (38cm) Lady Doll

Z **AFTERNOON DRESS COLLAR**
Cut two

15in (38cm) Lady Doll

Place on Fold

P **DRESSING GOWN FRONT YOKE**
Cut two

15in (38cm) Lady Doll

DRESSING GOWN CUFF
Cut two

15in (38cm) Lady Doll **R**

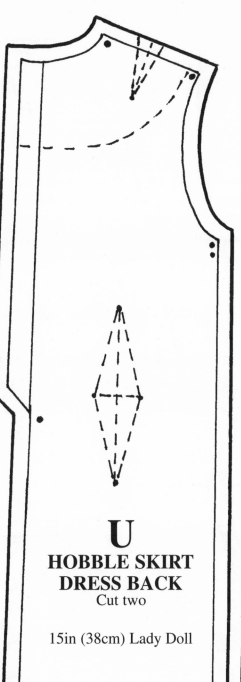

U
HOBBLE SKIRT DRESS BACK
Cut two

15in (38cm) Lady Doll

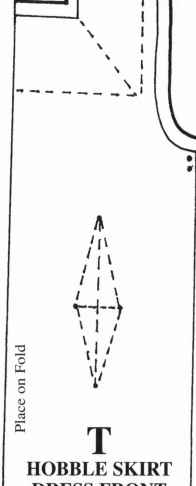

Place on Fold

T
HOBBLE SKIRT DRESS FRONT
Cut two

15in (38cm) Lady Doll

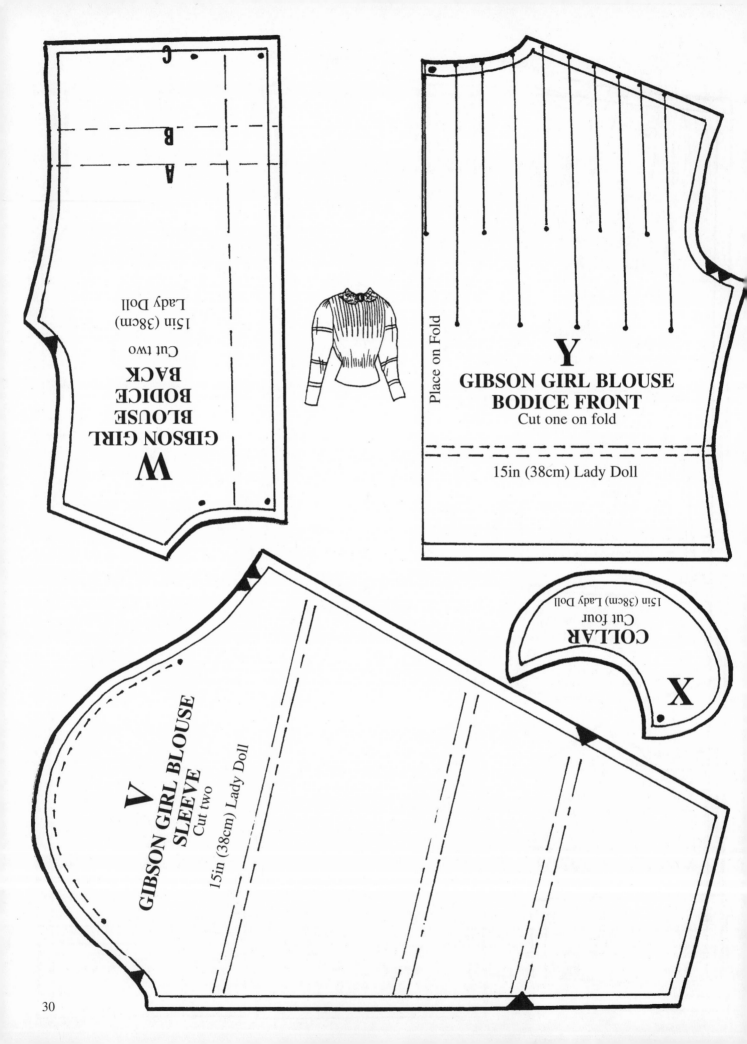

C

B

A

Lady Doll
15in (38cm)

Cut two

**BACK
BODICE
BLOUSE
GIBSON GIRL
W**

Place on Fold

Y

**GIBSON GIRL BLOUSE
BODICE FRONT**

Cut one on fold

15in (38cm) Lady Doll

15in (38cm) Lady Doll

Cut four

COLLAR

X

V

**GIBSON GIRL BLOUSE
SLEEVE**

Cut two

15in (38cm) Lady Doll

30

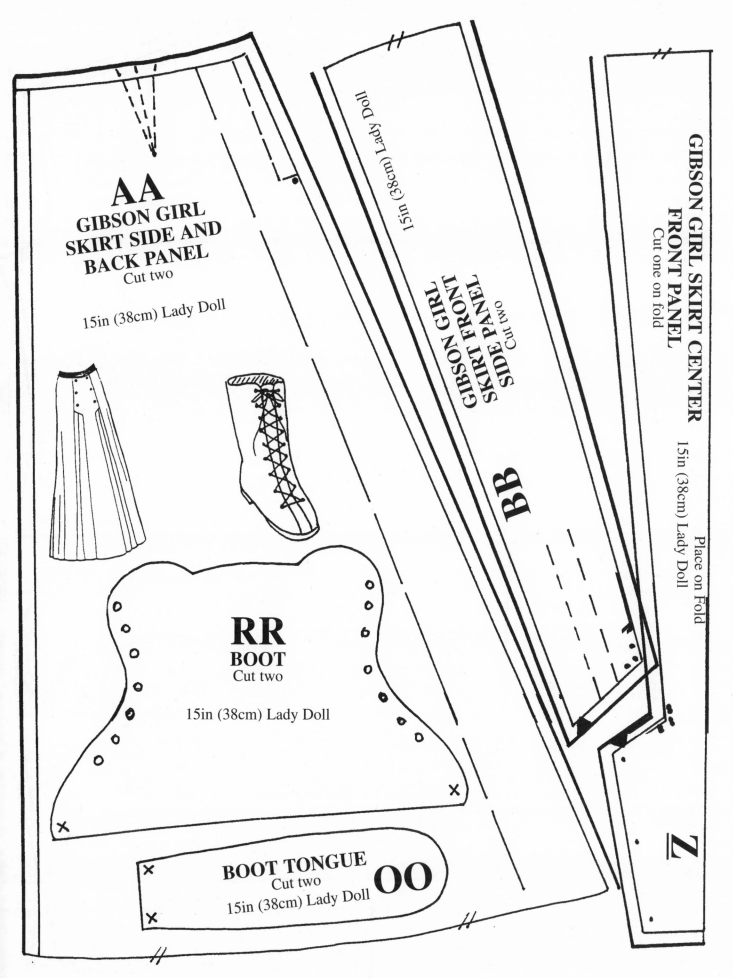

AA
GIBSON GIRL
SKIRT SIDE AND
BACK PANEL
Cut two

15in (38cm) Lady Doll

RR
BOOT
Cut two

15in (38cm) Lady Doll

BOOT TONGUE
Cut two
15in (38cm) Lady Doll
OO

15in (38cm) Lady Doll

GIBSON GIRL
SKIRT FRONT
SIDE PANEL
Cut two

BB

GIBSON GIRL SKIRT CENTER
FRONT PANEL
Cut one on fold

15in (38cm) Lady Doll

Place on Fold

Z

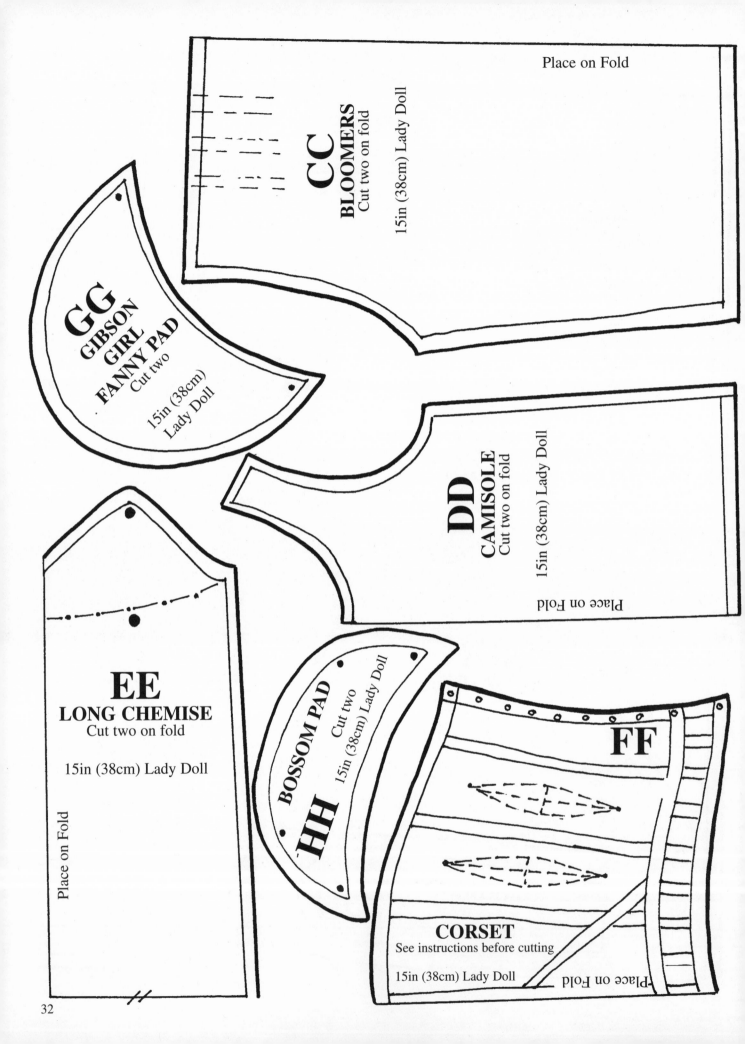

CC
BLOOMERS
Cut two on fold

15in (38cm) Lady Doll

Place on Fold

GG
GIBSON GIRL FANNY PAD
Cut two

15in (38cm) Lady Doll

DD
CAMISOLE
Cut two on fold

15in (38cm) Lady Doll

Place on Fold

EE
LONG CHEMISE
Cut two on fold

15in (38cm) Lady Doll

Place on Fold

BOSSOM PAD
Cut two
15in (38cm) Lady Doll

HH

FF

CORSET
See instructions before cutting

15in (38cm) Lady Doll

Place on Fold

32

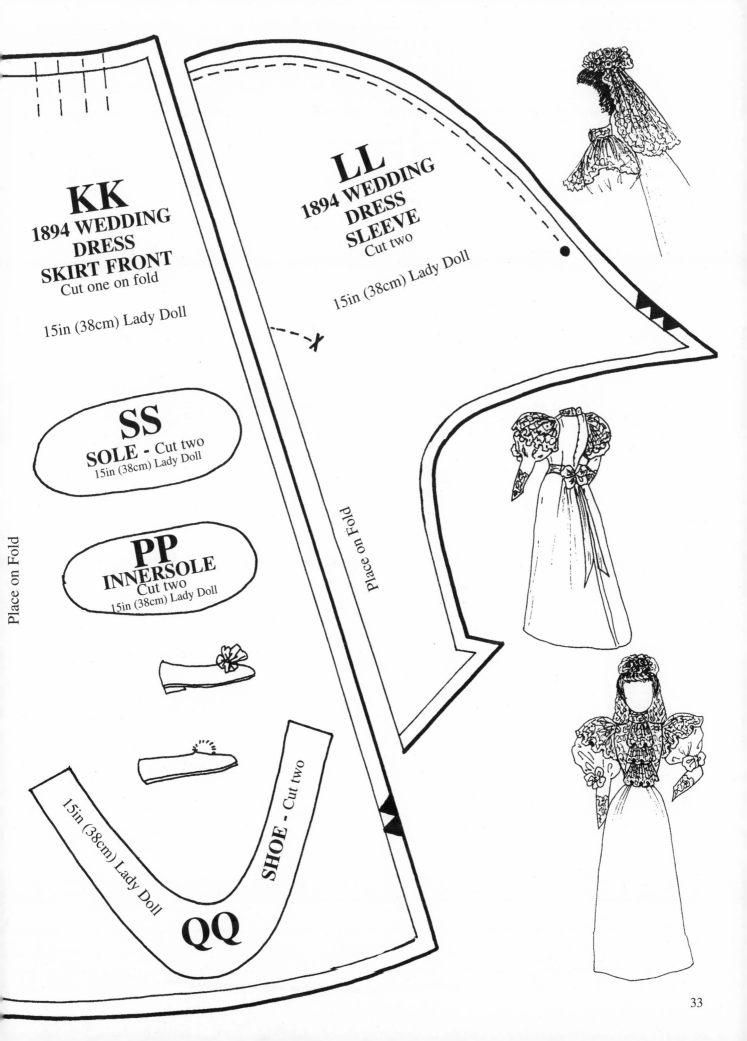

KK
1894 WEDDING DRESS SKIRT FRONT
Cut one on fold

15in (38cm) Lady Doll

Place on Fold

SS
SOLE - Cut two
15in (38cm) Lady Doll

PP
INNERSOLE
Cut two
15in (38cm) Lady Doll

LL
1894 WEDDING DRESS SLEEVE
Cut two

15in (38cm) Lady Doll

Place on Fold

15in (38cm) Lady Doll

SHOE - Cut two

QQ

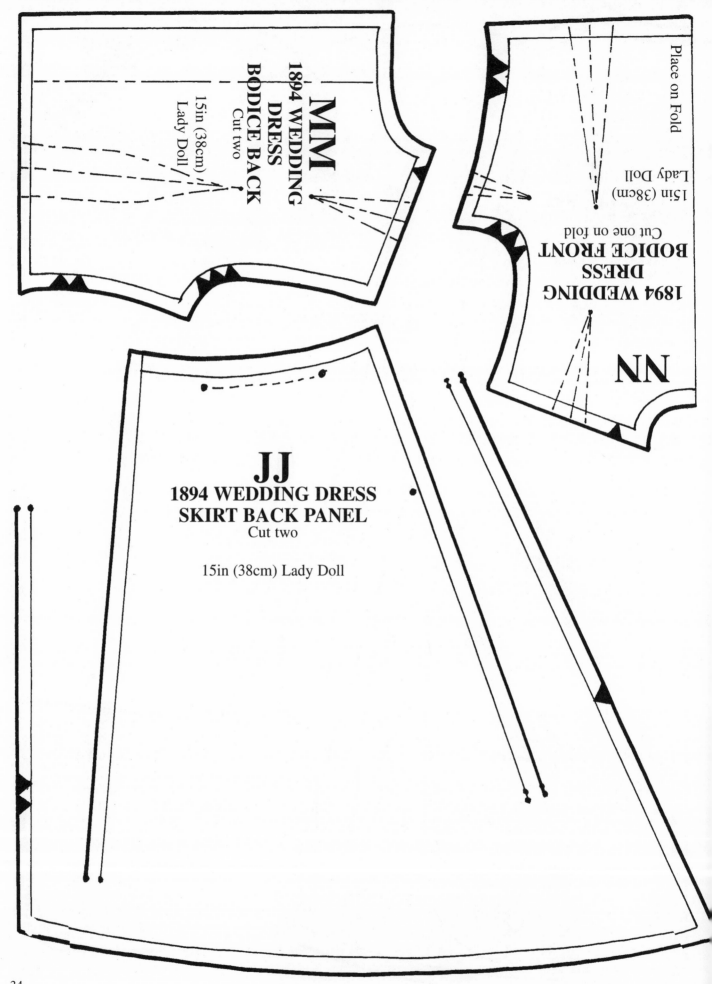

MM
1894 WEDDING
DRESS
BODICE BACK
Cut two

15in (38cm)
Lady Doll

Place on Fold

1894 WEDDING
DRESS
BODICE FRONT
Cut one on fold

15in (38cm)
Lady Doll

NN

JJ
1894 WEDDING DRESS
SKIRT BACK PANEL
Cut two

15in (38cm) Lady Doll

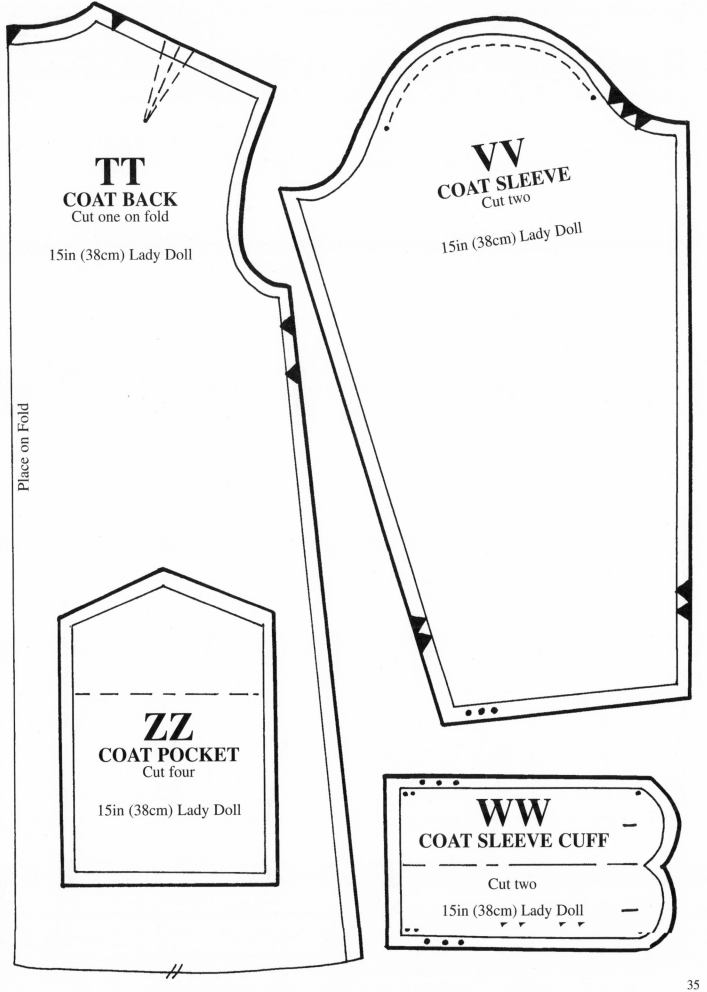

TT
COAT BACK
Cut one on fold

15in (38cm) Lady Doll

Place on Fold

VV
COAT SLEEVE
Cut two

15in (38cm) Lady Doll

ZZ
COAT POCKET
Cut four

15in (38cm) Lady Doll

WW
COAT SLEEVE CUFF

Cut two

15in (38cm) Lady Doll

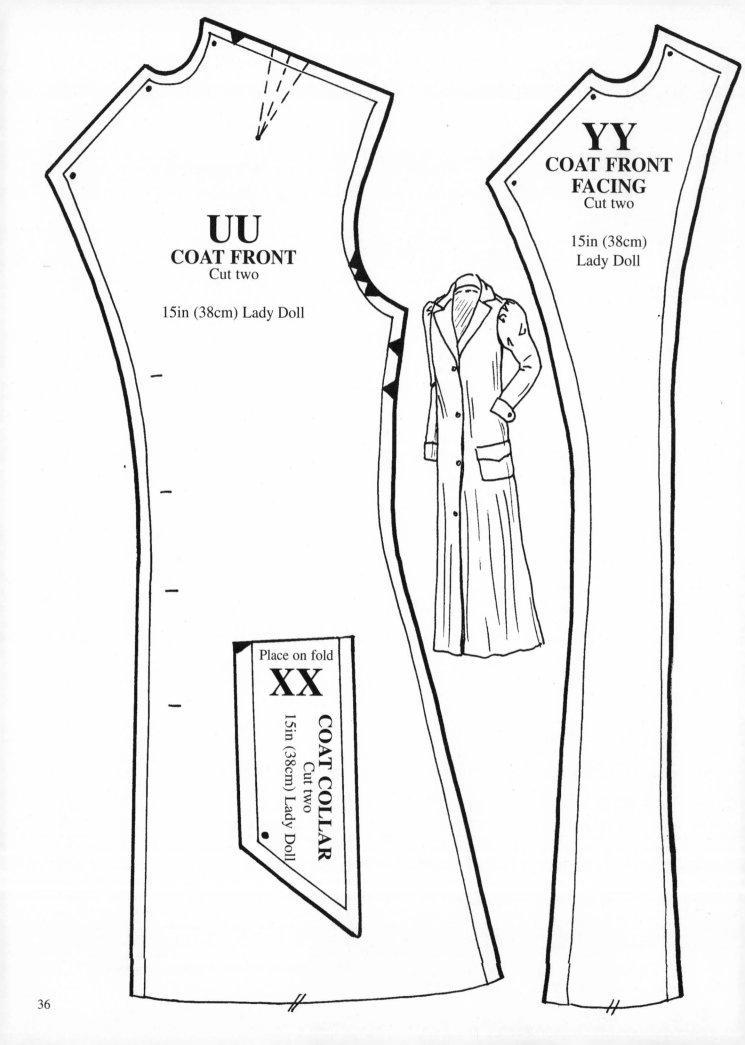

UU
COAT FRONT
Cut two

15in (38cm) Lady Doll

YY
COAT FRONT
FACING
Cut two

15in (38cm)
Lady Doll

Place on fold
XX
COAT COLLAR
Cut two
15in (38cm) Lady Doll

View 1

View A

Wardrobe for
20in (51cm)
DOLLY ROSEBUD
by E. I. Horsman - 1928

View 2

View D

View C

View 5

View 2

View 3

View B

View 4

View 5

WARDROBE FOR 20in (51cm) DOLLY ROSEBUD
by E. I. Horsman, 1928

This wardrobe was gleaned from several sources. The patterns for the clothes in Views 1, 3, 4, and 5 are based on catalog illustrations and dolls I have seen in private collections and at doll shows. Many dealers and collectors allowed me to examine and sketch their dolls' clothes.

The dress in View 2 was found original on a composition doll, without a bonnet. Later, I was able to confirm the identity of the doll (which was marked only "Horsman") as *Dolly Rosebud*. She is shown in the exact dress I had seen, along with the bonnet, on page 229 of *Twentieth Century Dolls* in an illustration from the 1928 Sears Roebuck catalog.

Large collars were much in vogue and those in Views A through D were taken from fashion illustrations of the period. These collars may be used with other dress patterns for a nearly unlimited variety of styles.

The dresses were made of silk organza, satin, organdy, crepe, lawn, or dimity and were trimmed lavishly with lace, eyelet, embroidery, and ribbon rosettes and streamers. The cape may be of cotton flannel or of fine wool, lined with satin, silk, or flannel. Or, as in this case, it may be of unlined felt.

I have seen these large dolls dressed in many different dress designs and combinations of fabrics. For example, a pleated white satin or crepe dress and large collar, trimmed with rose or red satin ribbon rosettes and knotted streamers. Or rows of lace on white organdy, embroidered with tiny rosebuds and leaves. Or a large collar of organdy trimmed with French knots and lazy daisy stitch. Perhaps a peach silk organza lavishly embellished with rows of ecru lace and peach satin ribbons.

It seems to me that dolls manufactured after the Great Stock Market Crash of 1929 were, understandably, somewhat less luxuriously dressed than earlier ones, although those already in stock in October of that year had been dressed for the booming market that many expected to continue forever. Therefore, as curators of our collections, we are correct in dressing our compositions in whatever lovely fabrics we wish to use so long as they are suitable for the period and the type of doll.

The coat, View 5, may be made of rose, blue, ecru, or peach satin trimmed with white rabbit fur. The lining is also satin, but of a lighter weight fabric than the coat. Front fastening is a single large pearl button. The back has a deep pleat that is stitched down about 4in (10cm). Real rabbit fur serves as the collar and trims the cuffs. The bonnet is cut from coat fabric, is lined with the coat lining, and is tied with matching satin ribbons.

Following is a list of pattern pieces required for each View:

1. Lace-trimmed silk organza dress: K and L
2. Cotton organdy dress and bonnet: C, D, E, X, V, W
3. Red Riding Hood cape: F and G
4. Eyelet-trimmed cotton dress: M, N, O, P, Q, R
5. Fur-trimmed coat and bonnet: A, B, H, J

A-D. Only two pattern pieces make all these views and more: S/T and U.

Not illustrated is a combination garment (pattern pieces Y, Z, A2) which was usually made of simple cotton fabric. If desired, a very narrow lace may be used to trim the neck edge and hems. This pattern was drafted from the original garment found on the *Dolly Rosebud*. Notice that in this case the drawers are attached to the petticoat, whereas in some other such garments (*Shirley Temple* for example) the skirt is attached to a full undersuit.

For hood of cape, cut one 12in (31cm) circle from felt cape fabric. From any point on circle measure across for an 8in (20cm) line (see illustration). Cut off this small section of the circle and discard. Seam a casing on inside as shown, using bias tape. Run a gathering cord but do not pull. Attach to completed cape along straight side, adjusting gathers. Tie off gathering cord.

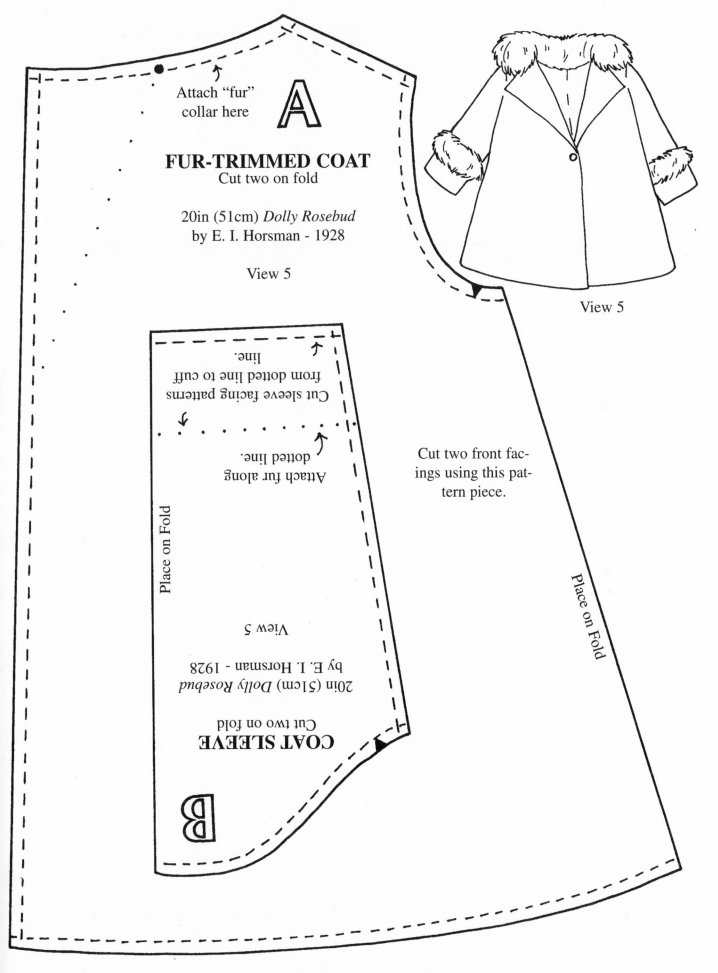

A

Attach "fur" collar here ↑

FUR-TRIMMED COAT
Cut two on fold

20in (51cm) *Dolly Rosebud*
by E. I. Horsman - 1928

View 5

View 5

Cut sleeve facing patterns from dotted line to cuff line. ↑

Attach fur along dotted line. ↑

Cut two front facings using this pattern piece.

Place on Fold

Place on Fold

View 5

20in (51cm) *Dolly Rosebud*
by E. I. Horsman - 1928

COAT SLEEVE
Cut two on fold

B

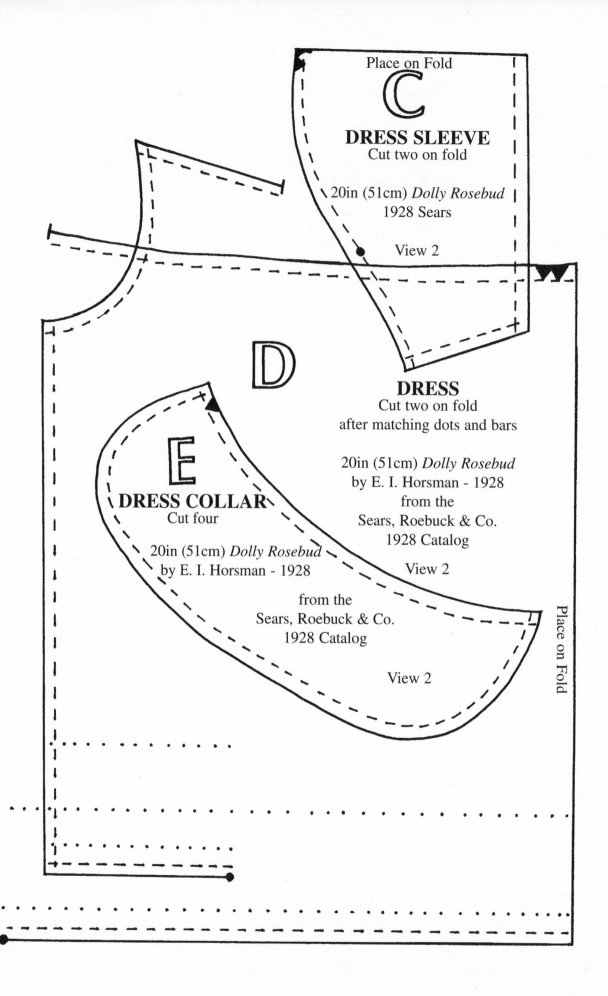

Place on Fold

C

DRESS SLEEVE
Cut two on fold

20in (51cm) Dolly Rosebud
1928 Sears

View 2

D

DRESS
Cut two on fold
after matching dots and bars

20in (51cm) Dolly Rosebud
by E. I. Horsman - 1928
from the
Sears, Roebuck & Co.
1928 Catalog

View 2

E

DRESS COLLAR
Cut four

20in (51cm) Dolly Rosebud
by E. I. Horsman - 1928

from the
Sears, Roebuck & Co.
1928 Catalog

View 2

Place on Fold

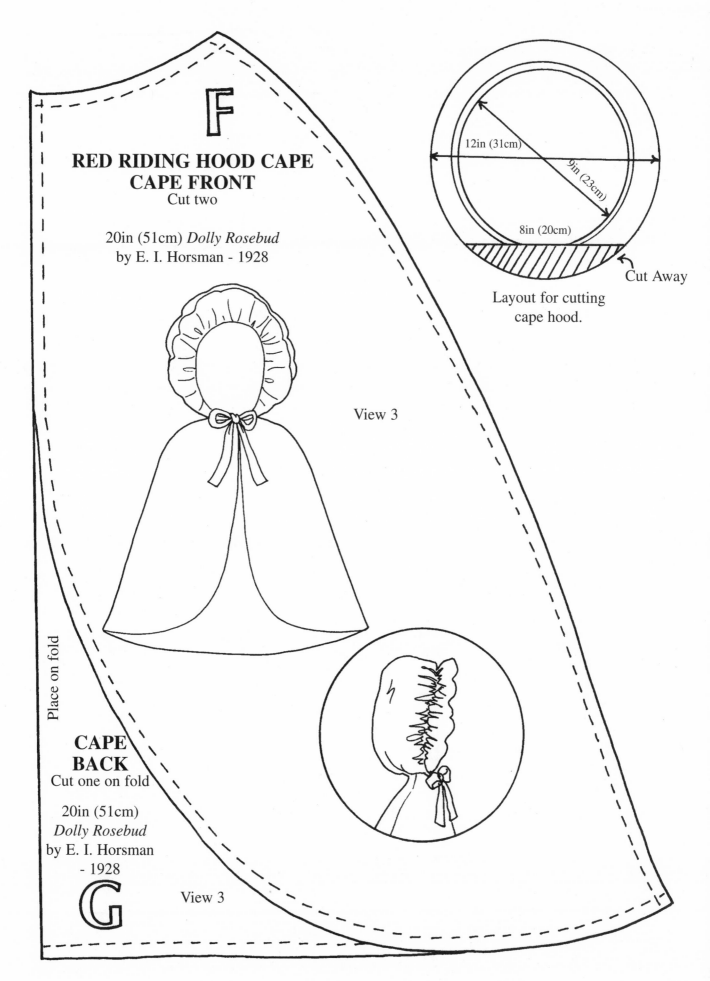

F

RED RIDING HOOD CAPE
CAPE FRONT
Cut two

20in (51cm) *Dolly Rosebud*
by E. I. Horsman - 1928

View 3

12in (31cm)

9in (23cm)

8in (20cm)

Cut Away

Layout for cutting
cape hood.

Place on fold

**CAPE
BACK**
Cut one on fold

20in (51cm)
Dolly Rosebud
by E. I. Horsman
- 1928

G

View 3

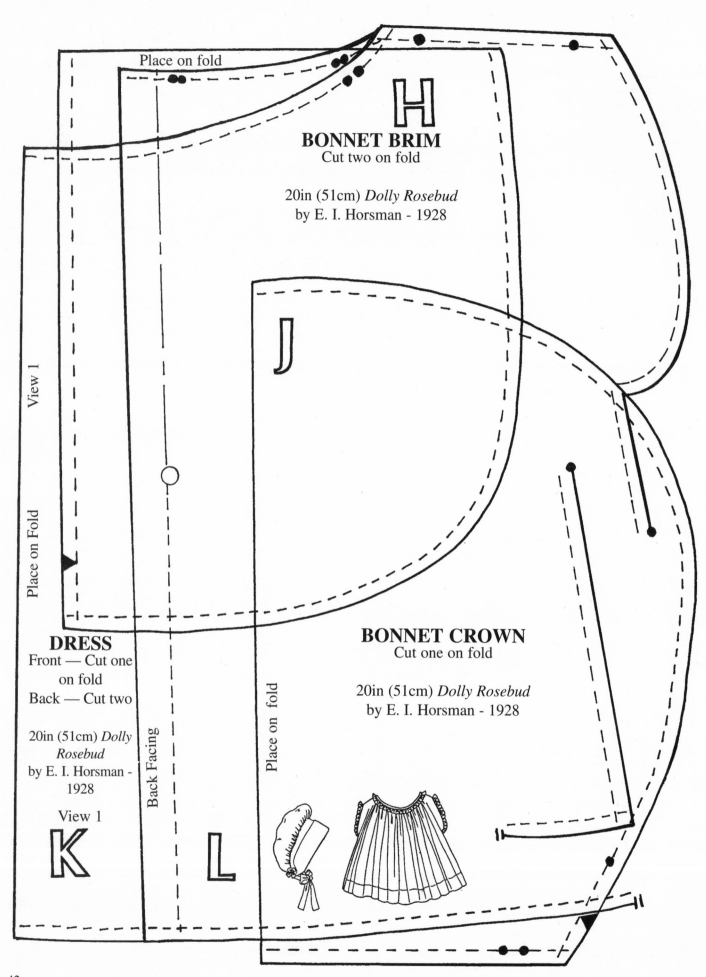

H

BONNET BRIM
Cut two on fold

20in (51cm) *Dolly Rosebud*
by E. I. Horsman - 1928

Place on fold

View 1

Place on Fold

J

DRESS
Front — Cut one
on fold
Back — Cut two

20in (51cm) *Dolly
Rosebud*
by E. I. Horsman -
1928

View 1

K

Back Facing

L

Place on fold

BONNET CROWN
Cut one on fold

20in (51cm) *Dolly Rosebud*
by E. I. Horsman - 1928

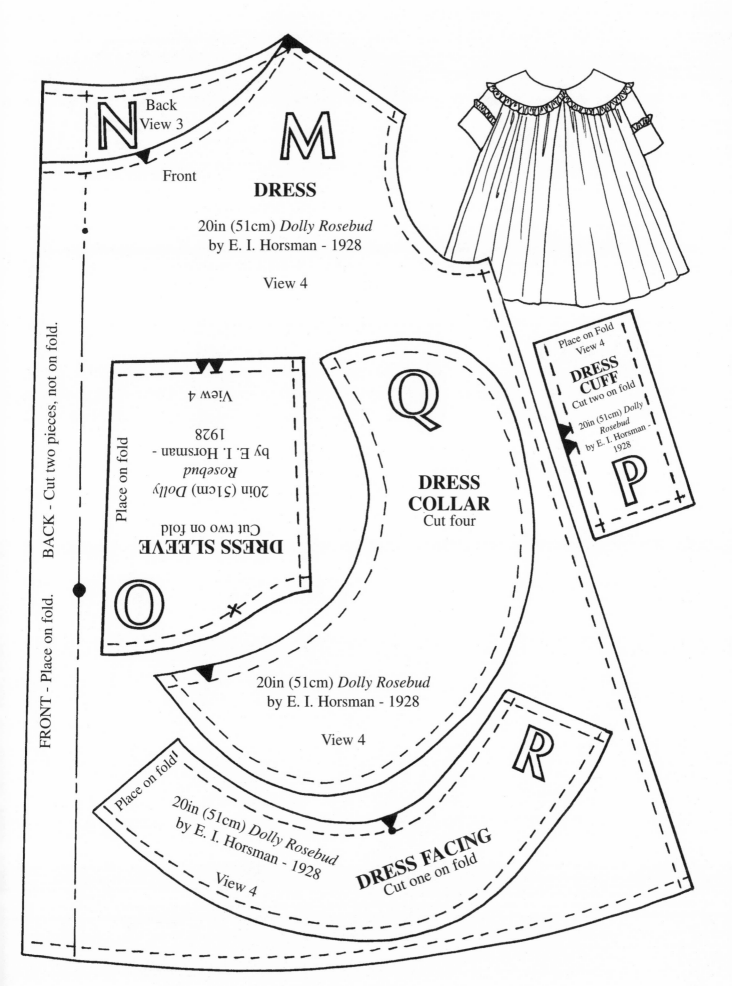

N Back
View 3

Front

M

DRESS

20in (51cm) *Dolly Rosebud*
by E. I. Horsman - 1928

View 4

BACK - Cut two pieces, not on fold.

FRONT - Place on fold.

DRESS SLEEVE
Cut two on fold

20in (51cm) *Dolly Rosebud* by E. I. Horsman - 1928

View 4

Place on fold

O

Q

DRESS COLLAR
Cut four

20in (51cm) *Dolly Rosebud*
by E. I. Horsman - 1928

View 4

Place on Fold
View 4

DRESS CUFF
Cut two on fold

20in (51cm) *Dolly Rosebud*
by E. I. Horsman - 1928

P

R

Place on fold

20in (51cm) *Dolly Rosebud*
by E. I. Horsman - 1928

View 4

DRESS FACING
Cut one on fold

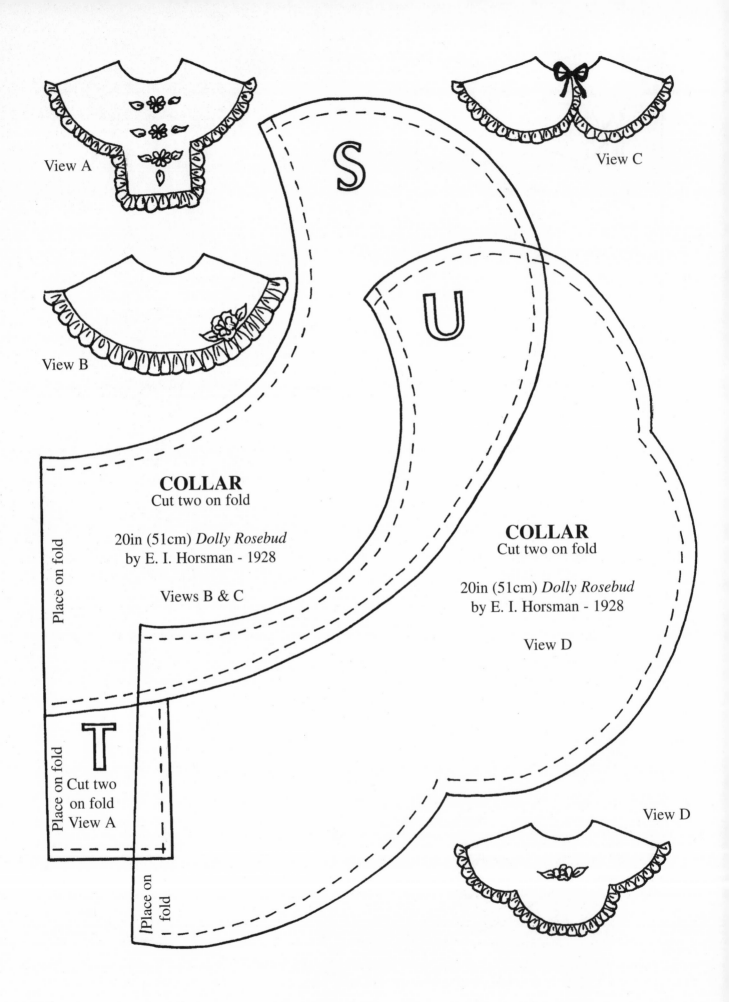

View A

View C

View B

COLLAR
Cut two on fold

20in (51cm) *Dolly Rosebud*
by E. I. Horsman - 1928

Views B & C

S

U

COLLAR
Cut two on fold

20in (51cm) *Dolly Rosebud*
by E. I. Horsman - 1928

View D

Place on fold

Place on fold

T

Cut two
on fold
View A

Place on
fold

View D

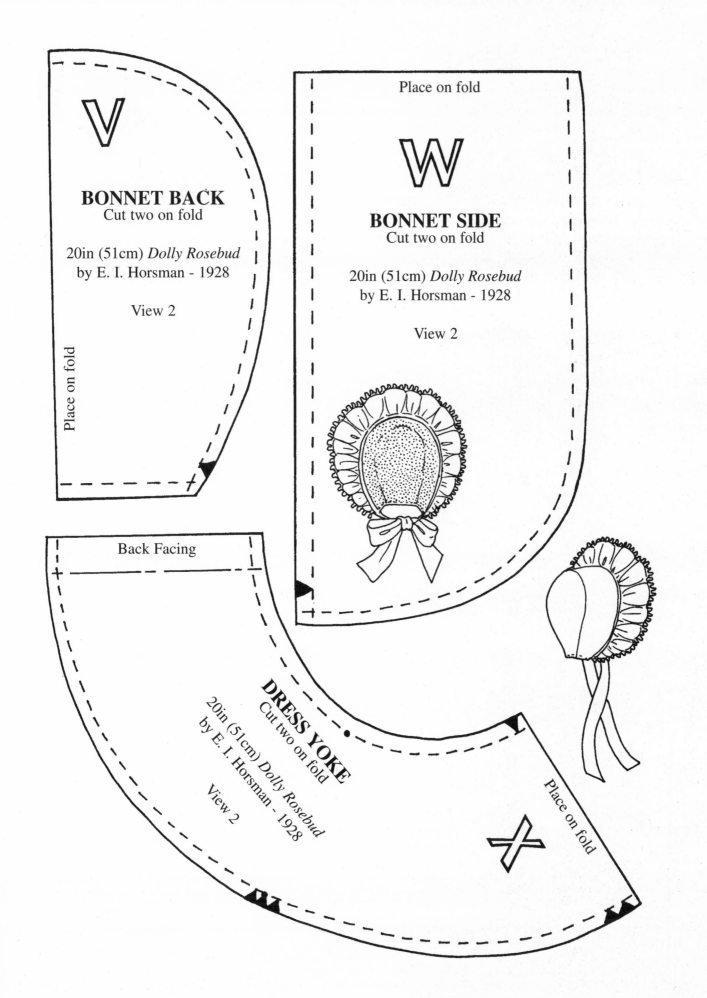

V

BONNET BACK
Cut two on fold

20in (51cm) *Dolly Rosebud*
by E. I. Horsman - 1928

View 2

Place on fold

Place on fold

W

BONNET SIDE
Cut two on fold

20in (51cm) *Dolly Rosebud*
by E. I. Horsman - 1928

View 2

Back Facing

DRESS YOKE
Cut two on fold
20in (51cm) Dolly Rosebud
by E. I. Horsman - 1928

View 2

Place on fold

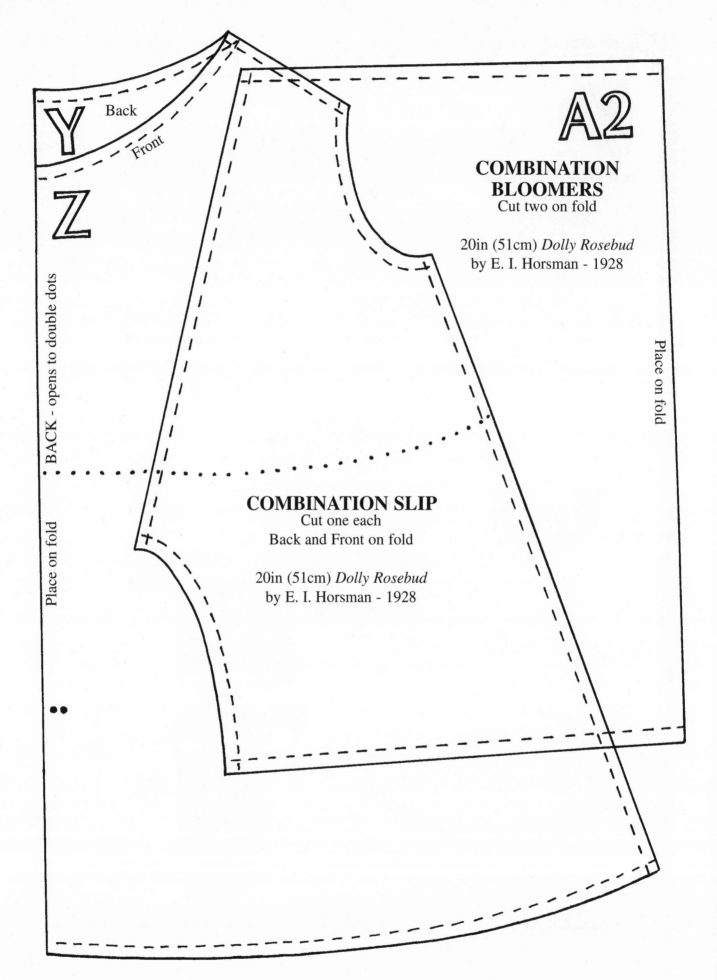

Y

Back

Front

Z

A2

**COMBINATION
BLOOMERS**
Cut two on fold

*20in (51cm) Dolly Rosebud
by E. I. Horsman - 1928*

BACK - opens to double dots

Place on fold

Place on fold

COMBINATION SLIP
Cut one each
Back and Front on fold

*20in (51cm) Dolly Rosebud
by E. I. Horsman - 1928*

View 2

Costumes for
20in (51cm)

BABY PEGGY
1923

View 1

View 5

View 4

View 3

20in
(51cm)
Doll by
Amberg
1923

COSTUMES FOR 20in (51cm) BABY PEGGY
by Amberg, 1923

A little creative sleuthing helped bring these outfits together. Views 1, 3, and 5 are shown in the *Baby Peggy* paper doll in the June 1925 issue of *Woman's Home Companion* and represent costumes worn in her films. Views 2 and 4 are from studio publicity stills; View 2 was subsequently confirmed as a film costume by the star. Baby Peggy Jean Montgomery went on to become a writer known as Diana Serra Carey. Through a mutual friend, Billie Nelson Tyrell, I was fortunate to be able to verify the titles and dates of films as well as the production companies involved.

In her article, "The 'Baby Peggy' Portrait Dolls" (*Doll Reader®*, April/May 1979), Patricia N. Schoonmaker describes the costume of the first "Baby Peggy" doll as a dress with "a scalloped hem and several rows of lace on the dress, sleeves, and collar," which would seem to have been similar to one of the *Dolly Rosebud* dresses. She also shows a dress, hat, and bloomers similar to but slightly different from View 3. Doubtless there were other original on-the-doll outfits.

Left: "Baby Peggy" wearing the View 4 dress in a studio still.

View 1
Costume for JACK AND THE BEANSTALK
Pattern Pieces L, M, N, U, V, X

This costume was worn by the child star in "Jack and the Beanstalk," a Century Pictures film of 1922.

Jerken - Turquoise blue cotton with sewn-in sleeves of golden yellow and turquoise striped knit. Sleeve pattern is the longest narrow sleeve in the layout.

Short Pants - Golden yellow satin with sewn-on stripes of turquoise satin ribbon.

Turquoise Felt Hat - Trimmed with a yellow feather.

Belt - Cut 2in (5cm) wide from black imitation leather, add gold buckle.

Shoes - Black felt is trimmed with golden yellow pompons. Remember to check the fit of the shoe pattern against your doll's foot before cutting the felt. Sizes may vary from doll to doll.

Ruff - Cut a piece of fabric 6in (15cm) x 24in (61cm). Sew short ends together, fold in half lengthwise, stitch a casing along the fold line, run elastic. Be sure elastic is long enough to pass over the doll's head.

Hose - Long turquoise knit stockings, doll-size leotards or tights complete the outfit.

View 2
Romper Dress from THE LITTLE FLOWER GIRL
Pattern Pieces A, B, O, P, S, W

This romper dress was drafted from a 1922 Century Pictures 8x10 publicity still advertising their latest release, a 2-reel film, "The Little Flower Girl." The outfit for the *Baby Peggy* doll came in peach or violet, with black trim.

Dress - Make this dress of lightweight wool serge or plain cotton and trim with contrasting bias binding. Use the shortest wide sleeve.

Bloomers - Cut from same fabric as dress and bind to match.

Beret-Type Hat - Cut two 8in (20cm) diameter circles of dress fabric for crown. (See illustration.) Cut a circle from one of the 8in (20cm) circles to fit doll's head. For head band cut a 4in (10cm) wide piece of fabric as long as the doll's head measurement plus 1in (3cm) for seam. Sew short sides together, turn and press. Fold band in half lengthwise and pin into the cutout of one 8in (20cm) circle. Baste bias trim around outer edge of one 8in (20cm) circle, with raw edges turned to outer edge of circle. Baste both 8in (20cm) circles right sides together (check that band seam will be on inside when turned), seam, and turn.

View 3
Toddie's Dress from "HELEN'S BABIES"
Pattern Pieces G, H, J, K, O, Q, S

From the Sal Lesser hit, "Helen's Babies" (Principal Pictures-Universal), this outfit was also recreated for the *Baby Peggy* dolls. Diana Serra Carey remembers it as a pink outfit; the dolls wore the pink as well as a soft, medium green voile, smocked and top-stitched with dark green.

Skirt - Cut a piece of dress fabric 7in (18cm) by 36in (91cm). Turn up a 2in (5cm) hem. Dress opens down the back to within 3in (8cm) of bottom edge. A decorative hand-stitching follows the upper edge of the hem.

Collar and **Cuffs** - These are of white organdy trimmed with tiny star-shaped buttons.

Ankle Socks - Use the dark green embroidery thread to work a design on the tops of a pair of white ankle socks to complete the outfit.

Dress From the Publicity Still
Pattern Pieces C, D, E, F, O

The publicity still of the child actress wearing this dress appeared in a movie magazine of the time. Child stars were required to spend large amounts of time before the cameras in dozens of different costumes. Like many others, this one has been lost to memory so there is only our supposition of what the fabric may have been, based on the photograph. Satin seems the most probable choice, based on the heavy use of the fabric in the 1920s. Barely discernible in the photograph is the wide lace trim around the skirt which appears to be black over a dark blue, green, or even red satin. There is no mistaking the white organdy used for collar and sash.

Dress - Use the satin or a soft voile or fine crepe for the dress. Construct bodice first. For skirt, cut a piece of dress fabric 9in (23cm) x 20in (51cm). Sew back seam of skirt so that back seam is open to within 5in (13cm) of bottom edge. Turn up a 2in (5cm) hem. Baste 1in (3cm) flat lace on right side over hem stitching. Machine stitch the lace along both edges, matching thread to the lace. Attach skirt to completed bodice.

Sash, Cuffs, Collar - These parts of the dress are of crisp white organdy. Use self bias binding instead of facing when attaching collar and cuffs. Sash also may be cut of dress fabric or of very wide matching satin ribbon.

Bloomers - Use leg band pattern from View 2 or bind legs with wide self bias.

View 5
Harlequin Outfit from "LITTLE MISS HOLLYWOOD"
Pattern Pieces T, U, R

"Little Miss Hollywood" was a Century Pictures film of about 1923 or possibly a little later, according to the star.

Harlequin Suit - This is a study in alternating black and white. Cut one right and one left from each of two colors. Cut one sleeve from each of two colors. Sew a casing on wrong side along dotted lines and run narrow elastic to make the ankle ruffle.

Stars, moons, and circles may be painted on with ballpoint fabric paints or appliquéd from scraps of fabric. The white hat and sleeves were allowed to remain undecorated.

Shoes - Cut two pieces from each of the two colors. In the original, a black shoe was worn on the left foot and a white shoe on the right foot.

Ruff - Cut one piece each measuring 6in (15cm) x 12in (31cm) from black and white organdy. Seam ends together and finish as for "Jack and the Beanstalk" costume.

Hat - Cut from white felt, seam, turn, fold up a narrow brim, crush point to hang down.

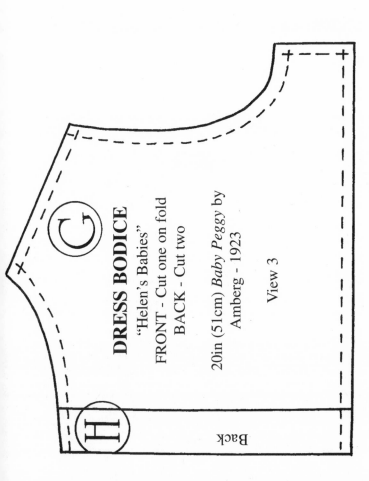

DRESS BODICE
"Helen's Babies"
FRONT - Cut one on fold
BACK - Cut two
20in (51cm) Baby Peggy by Amberg - 1923
View 3

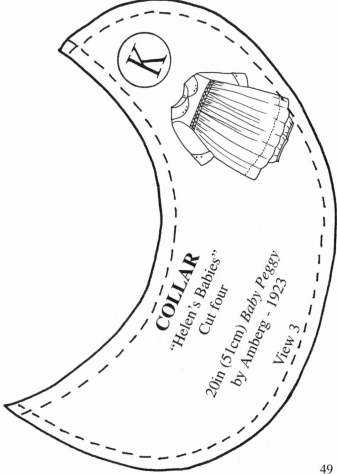

COLLAR
"Helen's Babies"
Cut four
20in (51cm) Baby Peggy by Amberg - 1923
View 3

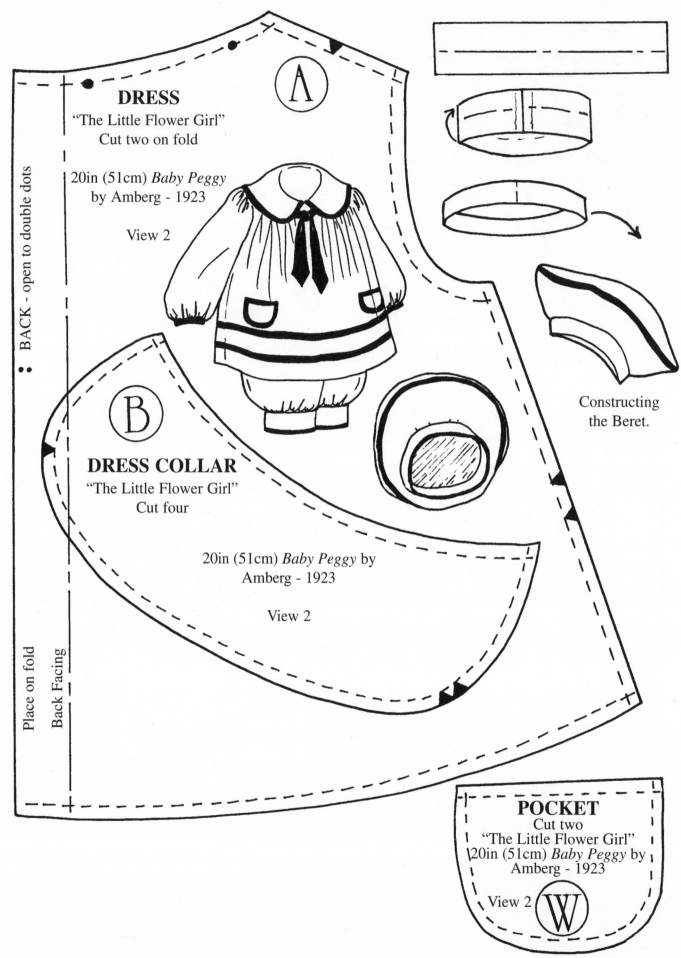

DRESS
"The Little Flower Girl"
Cut two on fold

20in (51cm) *Baby Peggy*
by Amberg - 1923

View 2

A

BACK - open to double dots

DRESS COLLAR
"The Little Flower Girl"
Cut four

20in (51cm) *Baby Peggy* by
Amberg - 1923

View 2

B

Place on fold

Back Facing

Constructing
the Beret.

POCKET
Cut two
"The Little Flower Girl"
20in (51cm) *Baby Peggy* by
Amberg - 1923

View 2

W

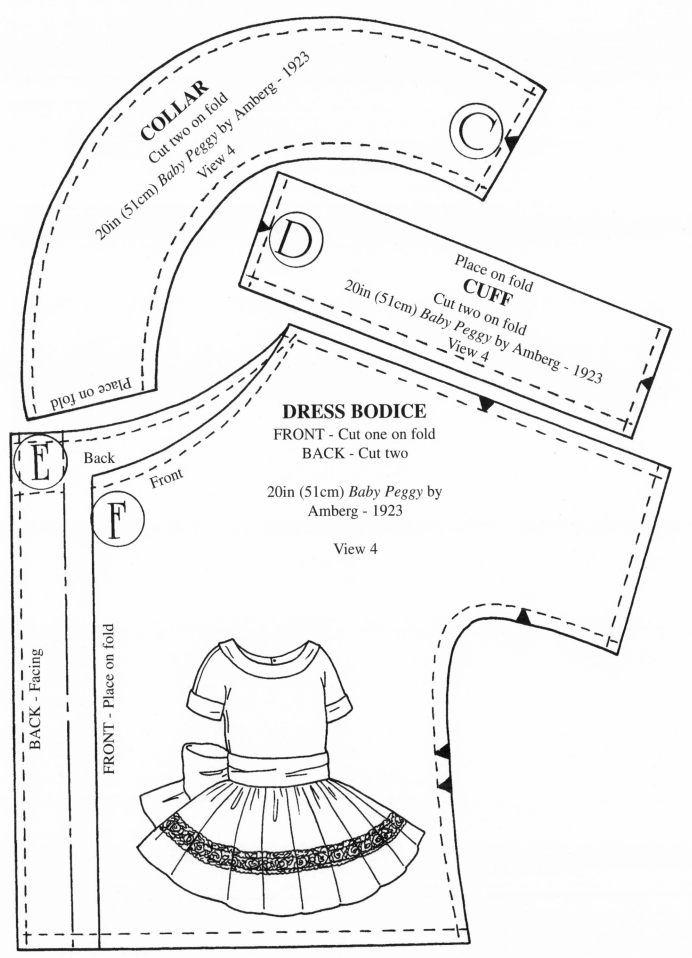

COLLAR
Cut two on fold
20in (51cm) *Baby Peggy by Amberg - 1923*
View 4

C

D

Place on fold
CUFF
Cut two on fold
20in (51cm) *Baby Peggy by Amberg - 1923*
View 4

DRESS BODICE
FRONT - Cut one on fold
BACK - Cut two

20in (51cm) *Baby Peggy* by
Amberg - 1923

View 4

E

Back

Front

F

Place on fold

BACK - Facing

FRONT - Place on fold

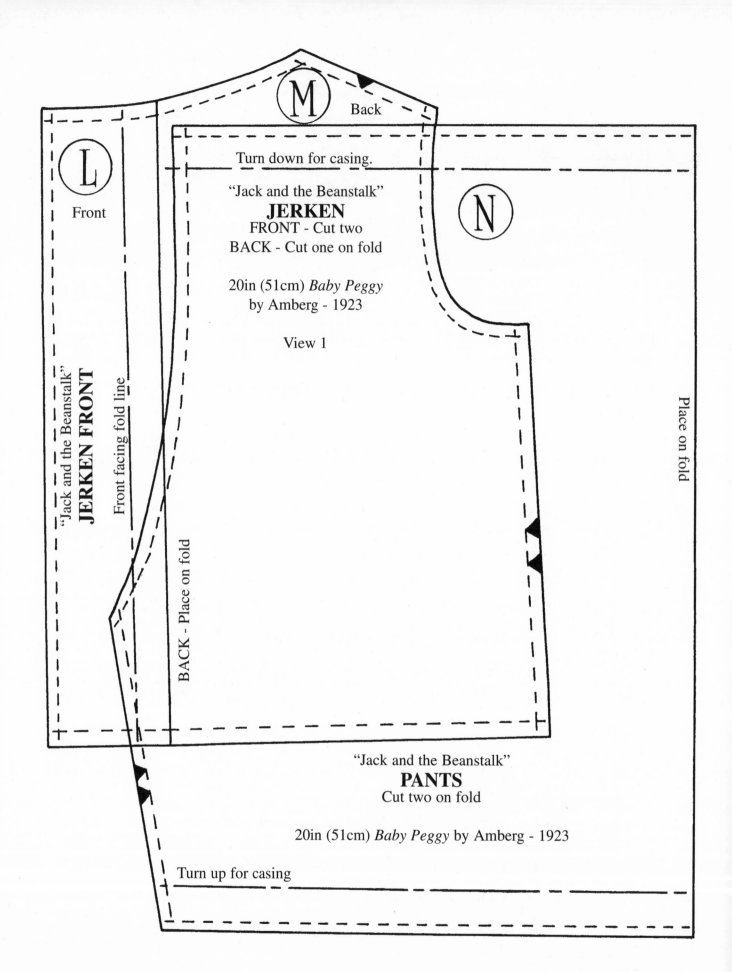

M Back

L Front

Turn down for casing.

"Jack and the Beanstalk"
JERKEN
FRONT - Cut two
BACK - Cut one on fold

20in (51cm) *Baby Peggy*
by Amberg - 1923

View 1

N

"Jack and the Beanstalk"
JERKEN FRONT

Front facing fold line

BACK - Place on fold

Place on fold

"Jack and the Beanstalk"
PANTS
Cut two on fold

20in (51cm) *Baby Peggy* by Amberg - 1923

Turn up for casing

52

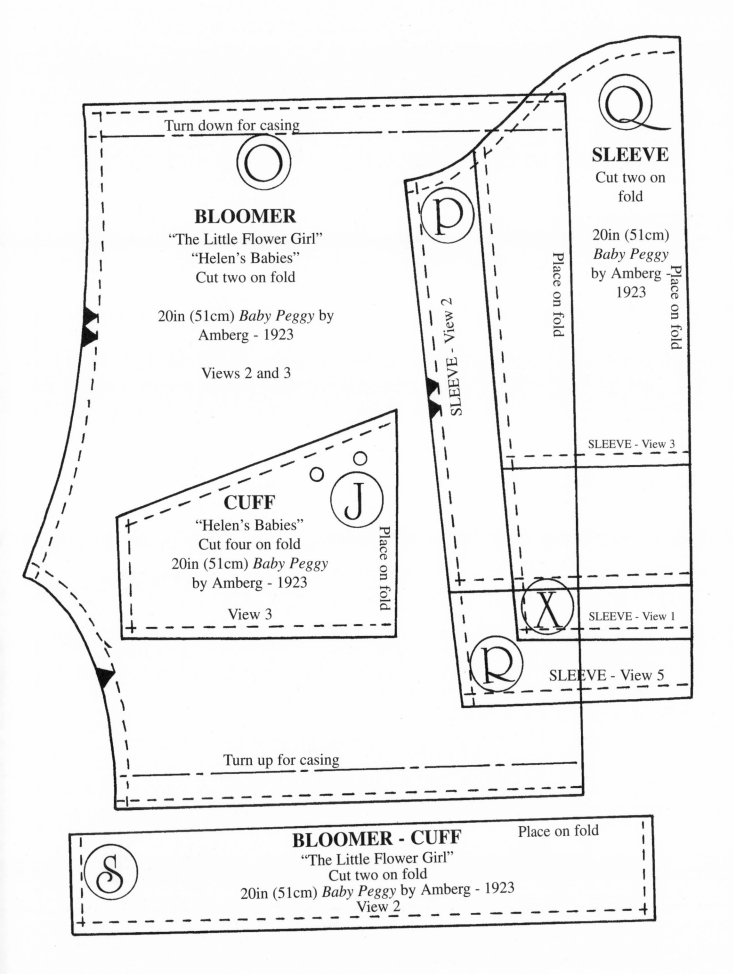

Turn down for casing

O

BLOOMER
"The Little Flower Girl"
"Helen's Babies"
Cut two on fold

20in (51cm) *Baby Peggy* by
Amberg - 1923

Views 2 and 3

Q

SLEEVE
Cut two on fold

20in (51cm)
Baby Peggy
by Amberg
1923

Place on fold

P

SLEEVE - View 2

Place on fold

CUFF
"Helen's Babies"
Cut four on fold
20in (51cm) *Baby Peggy*
by Amberg - 1923

View 3

J

Place on fold

SLEEVE - View 3

X

SLEEVE - View 1

R

SLEEVE - View 5

Turn up for casing

BLOOMER - CUFF
"The Little Flower Girl"
Cut two on fold
20in (51cm) *Baby Peggy* by Amberg - 1923
View 2

Place on fold

S

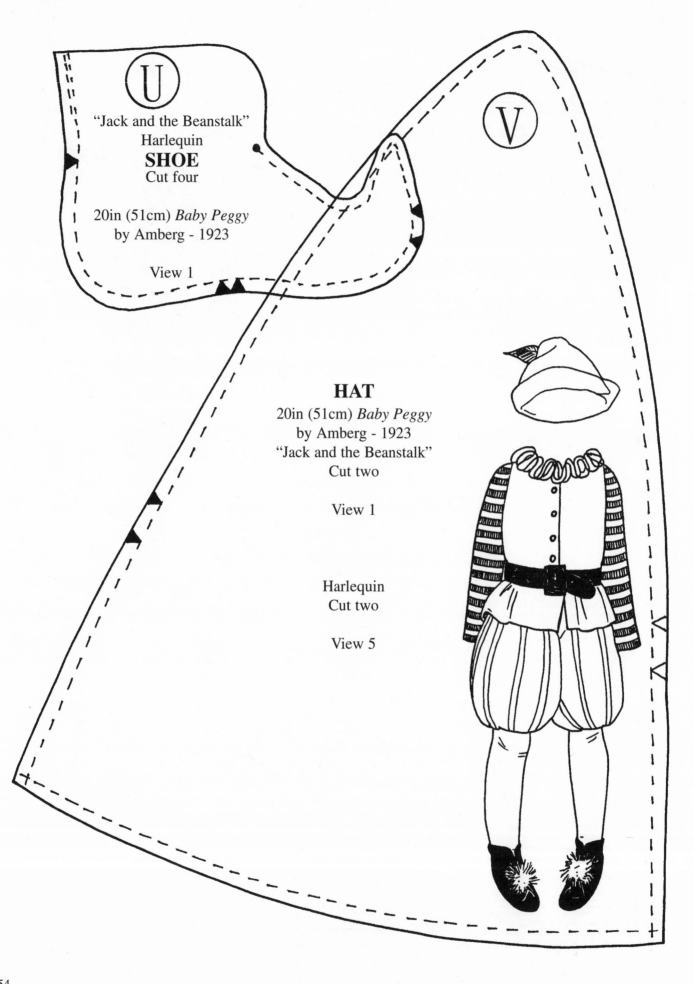

U

"Jack and the Beanstalk"
Harlequin
SHOE
Cut four

20in (51cm) *Baby Peggy*
by Amberg - 1923

View 1

V

HAT
20in (51cm) *Baby Peggy*
by Amberg - 1923
"Jack and the Beanstalk"
Cut two

View 1

Harlequin
Cut two

View 5

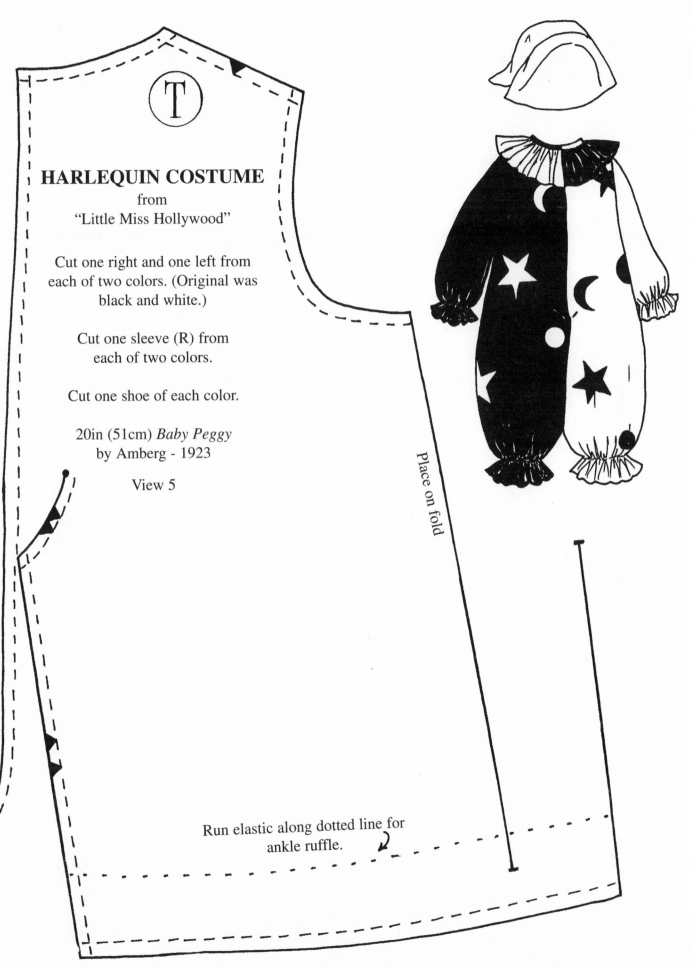

HARLEQUIN COSTUME

from
"Little Miss Hollywood"

Cut one right and one left from
each of two colors. (Original was
black and white.)

Cut one sleeve (R) from
each of two colors.

Cut one shoe of each color.

20in (51cm) *Baby Peggy*
by Amberg - 1923

View 5

Place on fold

Run elastic along dotted line for
ankle ruffle.

View 1

View A

View D

View 2

View 3

Wardrobe for 9in (23cm)
Patsyette and
Baby Patsyette
by Effanbee - 1920s

View 4

View 5

View 7

View B

View C

View 6

WARDROBE FOR A 9in (23cm) PATSYETTE
by Effanbee, 1920s

These patterns were drafted from original outfits found with a doll and its trunk.

View 1
YELLOW SILK DRESS
Pattern Pieces L, M, N, Q, S

Dress - The fabric of the original dress has a tiny all-over Art Deco print of pink, green, and black. The front is trimmed with "smocking" of yellow, green, and black.

To make the faux smocking, use widest stitch setting and loosen machine tension slightly. Run machine stitching along the five rows of dashed lines between dots. Pull all five threads at once, gathering evenly. Tie off each row firmly on back. With embroidery thread, work a row of cross-stitch between each row of gathering stitches. Add embroidered daisies, leaves, and French knots if desired. Tie off firmly. Finish neckline with 1in (3cm) self-bias.

Hat - View A is of the same silk. See Hats for construction details.

View 2
PALE YELLOW COTTON DIMITY DRESS
Pattern Pieces H, K, Q, S, U

Dress - This dress, although of cotton, would be charming done in silk. The yoke is finished with a fine trim. Gather dress between dots. Seam one piece of yoke to dress, right side of yoke to wrong side of dress, matching arrows. Baste self-ruffle or lace on long edge of other piece of yoke. Seam two pieces of yoke right sides together along ends and neckline; turn. Turn under raw edges of ruffle and yoke; blindstitch to dress under ruffle. Topstitch neckline close to edge.

Hat - View A - Make the hat of dress fabric either plain or trimmed with lace or ruffle as desired. See Hats for construction details.

Hat - View D - If the dress is made up as a sundress, this open-crown hat may be made of matching fabric and trimmed as desired. See Hats for construction details.

View 3
SUNSUIT OR UNDERSUIT
Pattern Pieces T, U

Sunsuit - Make this sunsuit of any cotton, either plain or printed with a tiny design. Suit opens down the back to dot on pattern. Bind armholes and neck with matching or contrasting bias tape or self bias.

Undersuit - This pattern may be used to make combinations by attaching a short, gathered skirt just under the bottom armhole line. Bottom of the skirt should reveal gathered legs of suit.

Closed Crown Sun Hat - View C - See Hats for construction details.

Open Crown Sun Hat - View D - See Hats for construction details.

View 4
SUNSUIT OR SWIMSUIT
Pattern Pieces U, V

Suit - The original sunsuit was made of dusty rose percale with medium light blue bias edging, trimmed with blue embroidered fish motif (see illustration).

Open Crown Sun Hat - View D - Cut of the same fabric as suit.

View 5
COTTON PRINT PAJAMA
Pattern Pieces B, C, D

Pajama - This "pajama" is actually another playsuit, not sleepers. The style was very popular in the 1920s and 1930s and was considered a rather daring fashion for little girls of the 1920s when it was introduced. Dimity, very light weight cotton print, gingham, plissé, or seersucker are suitable. Trim with matching or contrasting bias.

Hat - Make a hat of choice to match, views C or D. See Hats for construction details.

View 6
COTTON PRINT-AND-PLAIN DRESS & HAT
Pattern Pieces E, F, G, O, P

Dress - The front bodice and skirt panel are of solid-color fabric; the remainder of dress is of print fabric.

Hat - View C - In this application the hat has a print crown and plain brim. See Hats for construction details.

View 7
PINK FLANNEL SLEEPERS
Pattern Piece A

Sleepers - These sleepers are trimmed with blue bias tape. The front opening may be fastened with buttons, snaps, narrow zipper, or gripper fasteners.

View A
HAT
Pattern Pieces Q, S

Hat - I have found this hat on many of the Patsy Family dolls. Be sure to check pattern against your doll's head size. The pattern may have to be enlarged to accommodate a wigged head.

If the hat is made of a very thin fabric such as silk, it is advisable to make it completely double. In which case, construct the two crowns, baste them together around bottom edge, then attach to finished brim. For a nautical look in a cotton hat, rows of stitching may be added to the brim and crown as in View C. Tiny silk flowers will add interest on a silk or light cotton hat.

View B
BERET
Pattern Piece R

Beret - Make of felt or of dress fabric. Cut two circles from pattern. Cut out a circle the size of the doll's head from one of the circles. For felt beret, machine stay-stitch all around edge of this opening. For cotton beret, bind inner circle opening with commercial bias tape. Stitch two circles together all around, turn. Add loop of felt or bias tape at center top as shown in illustrations.

For a variation, baste contrasting folded bias tape to outer edge of one circle with fold toward center. Sew circles right sides together, turn. About 1/16in (.15cm) of bias trim should be visible around edge.

View C
SUN HAT
Pattern Piece U

Hat - Brim is cut double, assembled and finished with several rows of topstitching or a single row of stitching around edge of brim as shown in illustration. Stitching may also be added to crown. Before sewing crown to brim, press seams open. Turn to right side and stitch along both sides of each seam. An alternative approach is to make crown double, creating a reversible hat.

View D
OPEN-CROWN SUN HAT
Pattern Piece R

Sun Hat - Cut double of same fabric as suit, stitch right sides together, turn, close opening. Brim may be stitched in parallel rows for a nautical look, in which case the suit might be trimmed with an anchor or sea shell design. Attach ribbon ties at dots.

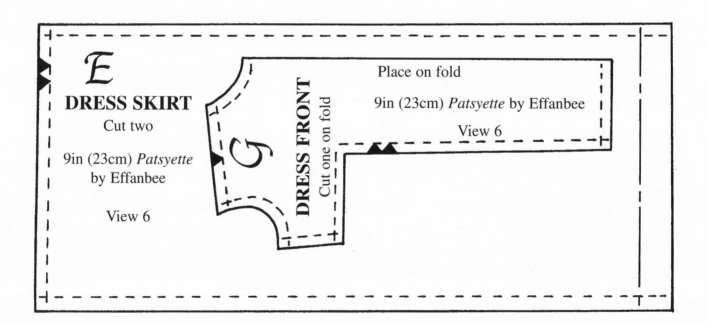

E

DRESS SKIRT
Cut two

9in (23cm) *Patsyette*
by Effanbee

View 6

G

DRESS FRONT
Cut one on fold

Place on fold

9in (23cm) *Patsyette* by Effanbee

View 6

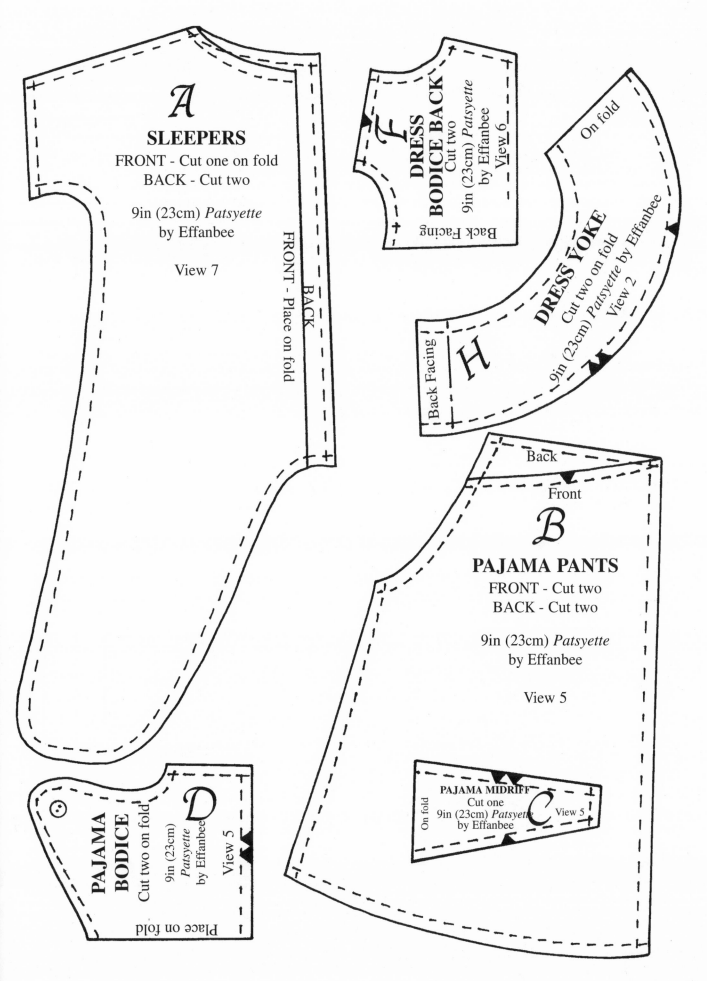

A
SLEEPERS
FRONT - Cut one on fold
BACK - Cut two

9in (23cm) *Patsyette*
by Effanbee

View 7

FRONT - Place on fold

BACK

F
DRESS BODICE BACK
Cut two
9in (23cm) *Patsyette*
by Effanbee
View 6

Back Facing

DRESS YOKE
Cut two on fold
9in (23cm) *Patsyette* by Effanbee
View 2

On fold

Back Facing

H

B
PAJAMA PANTS
FRONT - Cut two
BACK - Cut two

9in (23cm) *Patsyette*
by Effanbee

View 5

Back

Front

D
PAJAMA BODICE
Cut two on fold
9in (23cm)
Patsyette
by Effanbee
View 5

Place on fold

PAJAMA MIDRIFF
Cut one
9in (23cm) *Patsyette*
by Effanbee

On fold

C
View 5

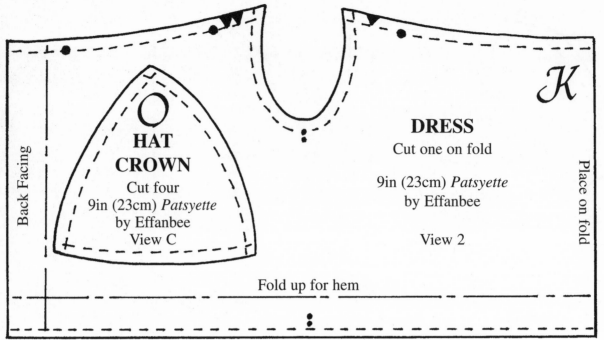

HAT CROWN
Cut four
9in (23cm) *Patsyette*
by Effanbee
View C

Back Facing

K

DRESS
Cut one on fold

9in (23cm) *Patsyette*
by Effanbee

View 2

Place on fold

Fold up for hem

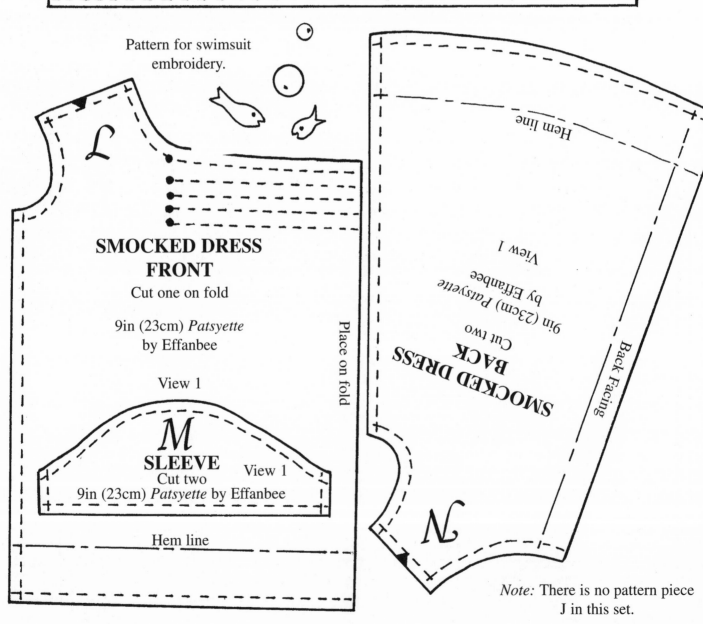

Pattern for swimsuit embroidery.

L

SMOCKED DRESS FRONT

Cut one on fold

9in (23cm) *Patsyette*
by Effanbee

View 1

Place on fold

M
SLEEVE View 1
Cut two
9in (23cm) *Patsyette* by Effanbee

Hem line

Hem line

Back Facing

View 1

9in (23cm) *Patsyette*
by Effanbee

Cut two

SMOCKED DRESS BACK

N

Note: There is no pattern piece J in this set.

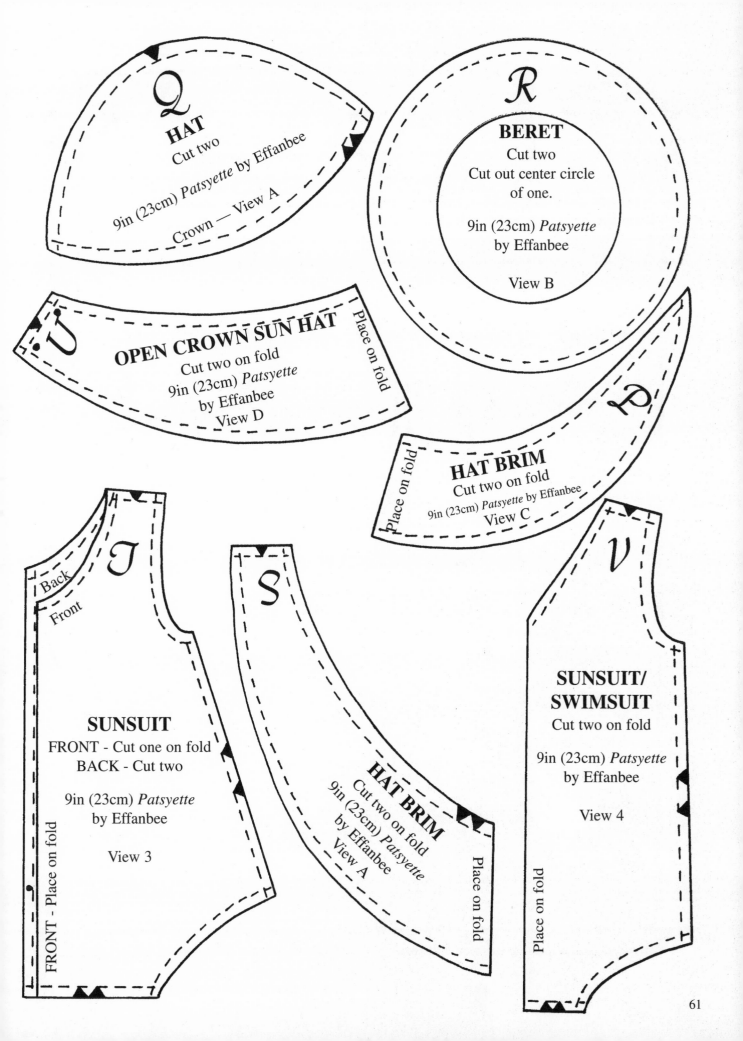

Q

HAT
Cut two

9in (23cm) *Patsyette* by Effanbee

Crown — View A

R

BERET
Cut two
Cut out center circle
of one.

9in (23cm) *Patsyette*
by Effanbee

View B

U

OPEN CROWN SUN HAT
Cut two on fold
9in (23cm) *Patsyette*
by Effanbee
View D

Place on fold

P

Place on fold

HAT BRIM
Cut two on fold
9in (23cm) *Patsyette* by Effanbee
View C

T

Back

Front

SUNSUIT
FRONT - Cut one on fold
BACK - Cut two

9in (23cm) *Patsyette*
by Effanbee

View 3

FRONT - Place on fold

S

HAT BRIM
Cut two on fold
9in (23cm) *Patsyette*
by Effanbee
View A

Place on fold

V

**SUNSUIT/
SWIMSUIT**
Cut two on fold

9in (23cm) *Patsyette*
by Effanbee

View 4

Place on fold

61

View 1

Wardrobe for
12in (31cm) Patsy and
14in (36cm) Patricia
by Effanbee
1934

View 2

View 5

View 7

View 3

View 4

View 8

View 6

View 6

WARDROBE FOR A 12in (31cm) PATSY and 14in (36cm) PATRICIA
by Effanbee, 1934

These clothes, apparently handmade from a commercial pattern, were found with a composition 1930s *Patsy* in an old Effanbee doll trunk. *Patsy* — Views 1 – 7; *Patricia* — View 8.

View 1
SUNDRESS & MATCHING SUN HAT
Pattern Pieces B, C, F-2

Sundress - Make this dress of any tiny print, check, or striped cotton, gingham, dimity, etc. Finish neck and armhole edges and skirt with narrow eyelet.

For skirt, cut a piece of dress fabric measuring 4-3/4in (12cm) by 10in (20cm). Proceed with usual methods for plain, gathered skirt. Dress is open in back to 2in (5cm) from finished bottom edge. Turn up a 1in (3cm) hem and machine stitch, then sew eyelet trim on right side over stitch line.

Sun Hat - For crown, cut a piece of dress fabric measuring 9-1/2in (24cm) by 2-1/4in (6cm). Turn down a casing on one long side. Sew ends together, leaving an opening for casing.

Sew the two pieces of brim F-2 right sides together along outer curve, turn, and press edge flat. Open piece and match double arrows. Sew one seam across both pieces. Press seam open. Pin, baste, and stitch one section of brim to crown, right sides together.

Turn to wrong side of crown. Tack brim together along outer edge. Baste inner edge to wrong side of crown, turning under 1/8in (.31cm) to cover seam. Blind stitch all around. Alternatively, instead of turning under the edge, cover seam with bias tape.

Run a ribbon through casing, gather casing into tight circle to form crown and tie off with double knot and bow.

View 2
SUN TOP & SHORTS
Pattern Pieces J, L

Make this simple little sun outfit of gingham, chambray, or print cotton. Trim with matching or contrasting bias. Top is open in back and fastens with one or two snap fasteners. Pull-on shorts have casing with narrow elastic around waist.

Variations: Solid-color shorts with print top or solid-color top with striped or checked shorts, etc. Try making bias tape from a print to trim the solid-color garment and solid-color bias to trim the print garment.

View 3
COLLAR or FISCHU
Pattern Piece G

A collar like this was very popular during the period. It may be made separate or sewn into a garment. Somewhat widened, it becomes a capelet, especially attractive trimmed with fine lace over a dress of silk or velvet.

View 4
COMBINATIONS

Here is an exercise in adapting patterns. Using the sunsuit/swimsuit and bloomer pattern pieces K and A, create a pattern for the combinations. You may also borrow a slip/panty combination pattern from elsewhere in this book. *Patsy* was dressed in both styles as well as in bloomers and a separate slip.

View 5
SWIMSUIT/SUNSUIT
Pattern Piece K

Use a nice knit fabric (wool, cotton, or silk jersey) for the swimsuit. See the 1920s *Patsyette* section for fish designs. Cut the sunsuit of cotton seersucker or plissé, dimity or cotton organdy. Make a sun hat of the same fabric. Have fun and use your imagination, but always work within the parameters of the time period.

View 6
SLIP, PANTIES & BLOOMERS
Pattern Pieces A, H, L

Make *Patsy's* undergarments from fine, soft cottons such as lawn or batiste. Or cut them from good sections of a well-worn 100% cotton shirt.

Remember: No synthetics for this 1930s composition doll. Keep laces to a minimum; this was a child of the Great Depression; her garments were simple and basic, though always dainty.

View 7
SUNDAY SCHOOL DRESS, BLOOMERS & BONNET
Pattern Pieces A, E, F, M-R

Bloomers - These undergarments were designed long enough to just peek from beneath the bottom of the dress. They were also designed for modesty and often were made of the dress fabric. Fold down casings for waist and legs. Run narrow elastic to fit doll.

Dress - This dress is made of organdy trimmed with a woven, flower design ribbon, making it a special dress. Depending on fabric used, the pattern would do well as a school dress. Try gingham, plaid, or a flower print cotton.

Bonnet - Make this bonnet of the dress fabric, or for a special look, cut it single layer of felt and trim with silk ribbon roses and streamers.

Seam center back of bonnet side D, matching arrows. With right sides together, sew crown E into bonnet side D. Run gathering stitches along outer edge of bonnet assembly. Set aside.

With right sides together, sew the two pieces of brim F along outer curved edge. Open and seam together along short sides. Press seam open and fold over with seams to inside.

Pin crown assembly into brim, pulling gathers evenly to fit opening. Cover seam edges with self bias. Add ribbon ties if desired.

View 8
Complete Outfit for
14in (36cm) PATRICIA
Pattern Pieces S through Z-1

This pattern is from an all-original doll in fine condition. The dress is white polished cotton with embossed pink roses. The bodice and sleeves are of pink organdy. Sleeves, collar, and slip are trimmed with the same 1/2in (1cm) fine cotton lace. Straps of the cotton are sewn into the shoulder seams of the bodice and two pink buttons finish the effect in front. Long ties which make up into a large bow in back are sewn into the side seams of the bodice.

Prepare the following before sewing the bodice:

Bodice straps - Cut 2 pieces of 2-1/2in (4cm) x 1in (3cm) of the cotton. Seam right sides together on long sides and turn. Press so that seam is centered; sew into shoulder seams with seam inside. Tack other end inside over-bodice at points. Finish with the buttons. Baste in place on front of bodice at shoulder seam.

Ties - Cut two pieces 2in (5cm) x 12in (31cm) of the cotton. Put a narrow handkerchief hem down both sides. With right sides together, sew a point on one end of each tie. Make a tiny tuck in remaining short ends and sew into side seams of bodice. (Be sure right side of points will be on outside when ties are pulled to the back.)

Over-bodice - Cut two of pattern piece V. Seam right sides together along top edge. Trim seam and turn. Make sure points are completely turned, then press. Baste to bodice front at waistline.

Collar - Carefully baste lace along seam line ABC on two of the four collar pieces. Turn lace toward center of piece and baste so it does not get involved in the seam. With right sides together, seam collars along line ABC (lace will be inside). Trim seam and turn. Press collar and baste along AC to hold in place. Baste in place on bodice after sewing shoulder seams.

Now you are ready to assemble the sleeves and bodice.

Skirt and Half-slip - For skirt cut a piece 26in (66cm) x 5in (13cm) of the embossed cotton. Turn up a 1-1/4in (3cm) hem and machine stitch to finish, using small stitches. For half-slip, cut a piece 26in (66cm) x 3-1/4in (8cm) of fine white cotton such as lawn or batiste. Turn up 1/8in (.31cm) hem and press. Oversew with 5/8in (2cm) lace. Pin to skirt along unfinished long side. Run double gathering threads to within 1in (3cm) of each end. Pull gathers to fit finished bodice and tie off securely. Seam together. Sew back seam up 1-3/4in (5m) from bottom of hem. Turn back facing of bodice inside and make buttonholes and sew on buttons at waist and neckline.

Bonnet - The bonnet is of polished cotton trimmed with a pink satin ribbon bow just off-center along the crown/brim seam with ties of the same ribbon ending at the same seam on each side in a bow. Follow guide marks on pattern to assemble, sewing pattern pieces X and Y as indicated. For brim pattern piece U, sew right sides together, trim seam, turn and press. Attach brim to crown as indicated on pattern.

Underpants - Underpants are white knit with pink machine binding.

Shoes and Sox - The stockings are pink and white and shoes are black leather buckle strap Mary Janes.

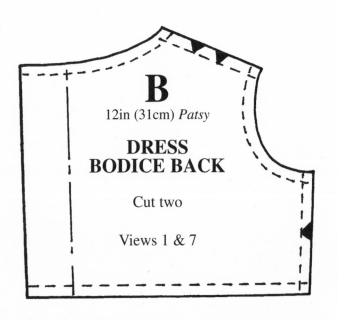

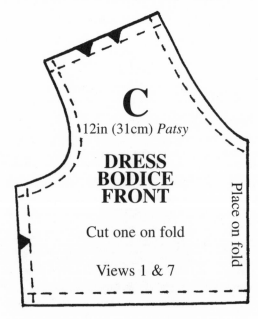

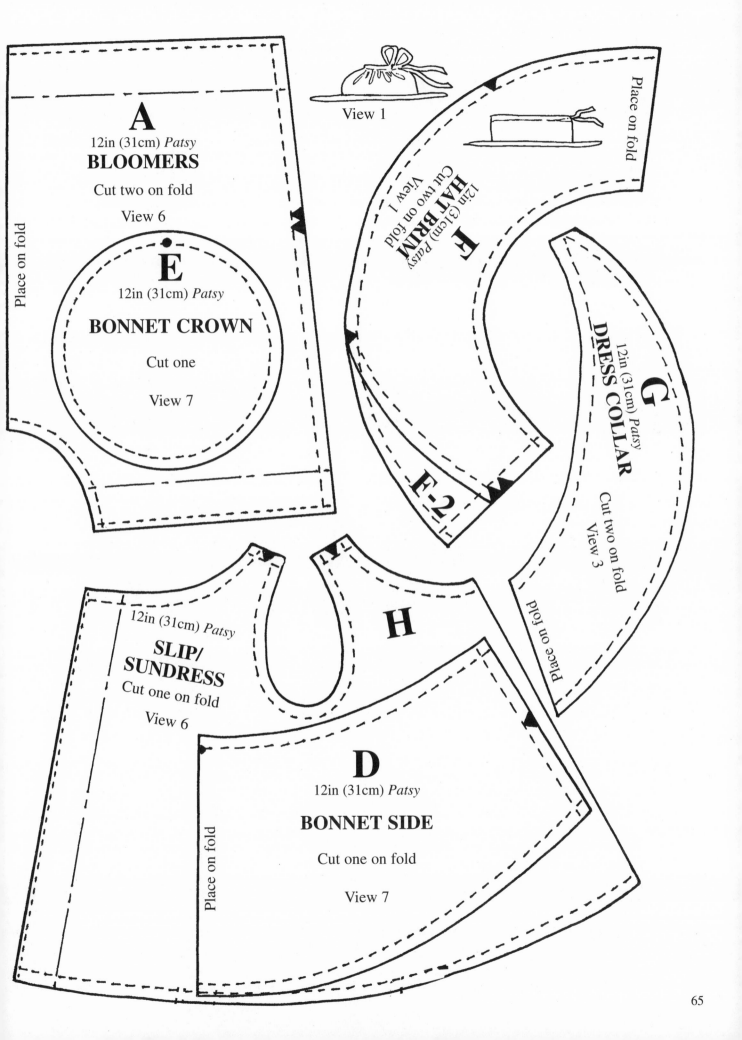

A

12in (31cm) *Patsy*

BLOOMERS

Cut two on fold

View 6

E

12in (31cm) *Patsy*

BONNET CROWN

Cut one

View 7

Place on fold

View 1

F

12in (31cm) *Patsy*

HAT BRIM

Cut two on fold

View 1

F-2

Place on fold

G

12in (31cm) *Patsy*

DRESS COLLAR

Cut two on fold

View 3

Place on fold

H

12in (31cm) *Patsy*

SLIP/ SUNDRESS

Cut one on fold

View 6

Place on fold

D

12in (31cm) *Patsy*

BONNET SIDE

Cut one on fold

View 7

65

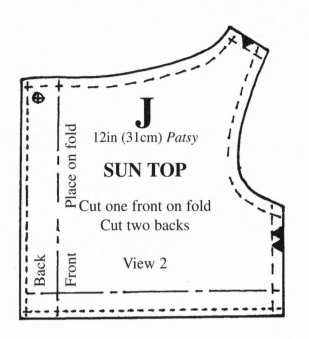

J

12in (31cm) *Patsy*

SUN TOP

Cut one front on fold
Cut two backs

View 2

Place on fold

Back   Front

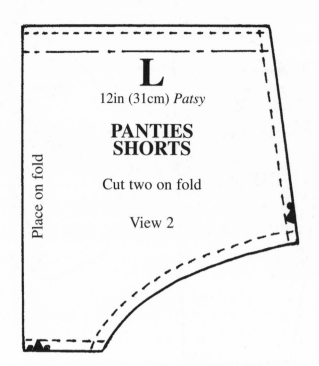

L

12in (31cm) *Patsy*

**PANTIES
SHORTS**

Cut two on fold

View 2

Place on fold

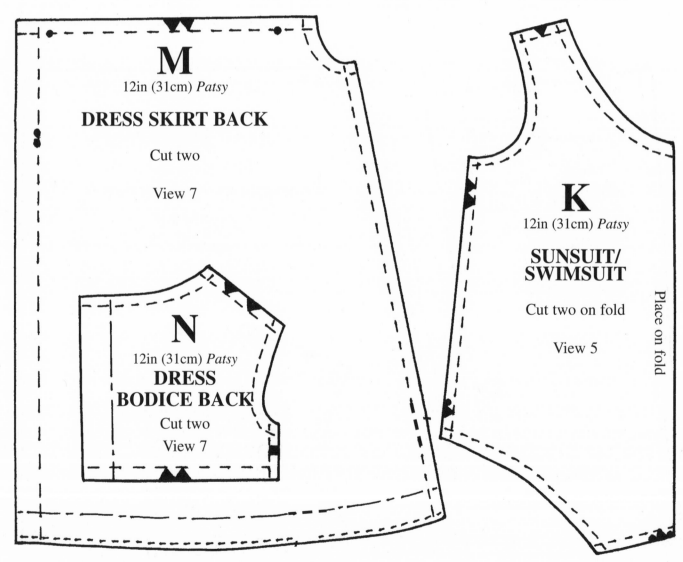

M

12in (31cm) *Patsy*

DRESS SKIRT BACK

Cut two

View 7

N

12in (31cm) *Patsy*
**DRESS
BODICE BACK**

Cut two

View 7

K

12in (31cm) *Patsy*

**SUNSUIT/
SWIMSUIT**

Cut two on fold

View 5

Place on fold

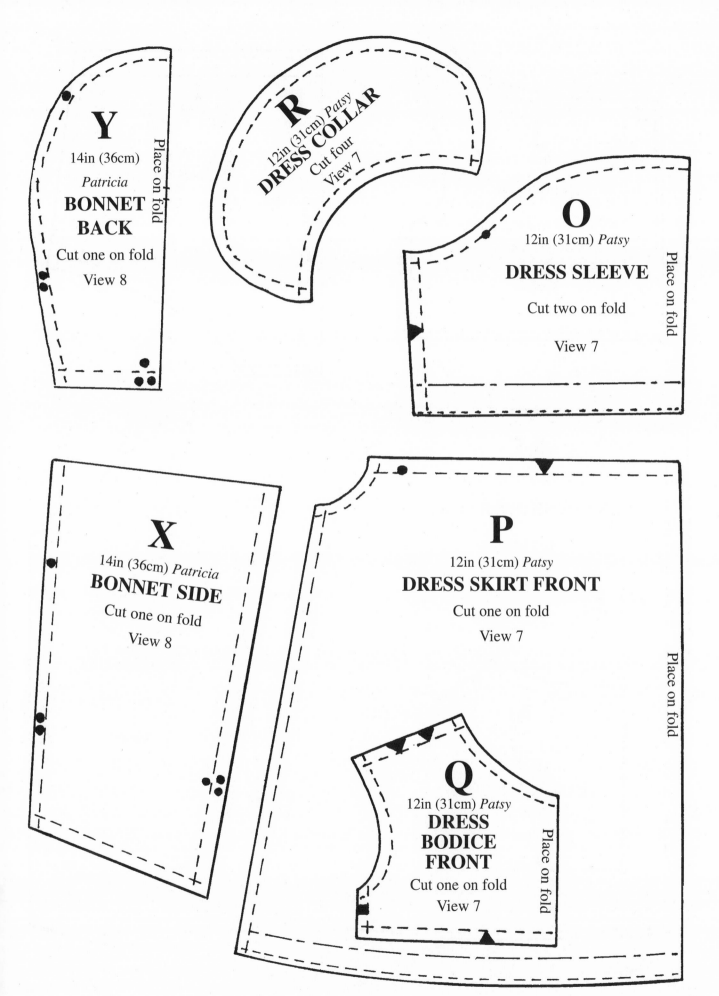

Y

14in (36cm)

Patricia

BONNET BACK

Cut one on fold

View 8

R

12in (31cm) *Patsy*

DRESS COLLAR

Cut four

View 7

O

12in (31cm) *Patsy*

DRESS SLEEVE

Cut two on fold

View 7

Place on fold

X

14in (36cm) *Patricia*

BONNET SIDE

Cut one on fold

View 8

P

12in (31cm) *Patsy*

DRESS SKIRT FRONT

Cut one on fold

View 7

Place on fold

Q

12in (31cm) *Patsy*

DRESS BODICE FRONT

Cut one on fold

View 7

Place on fold

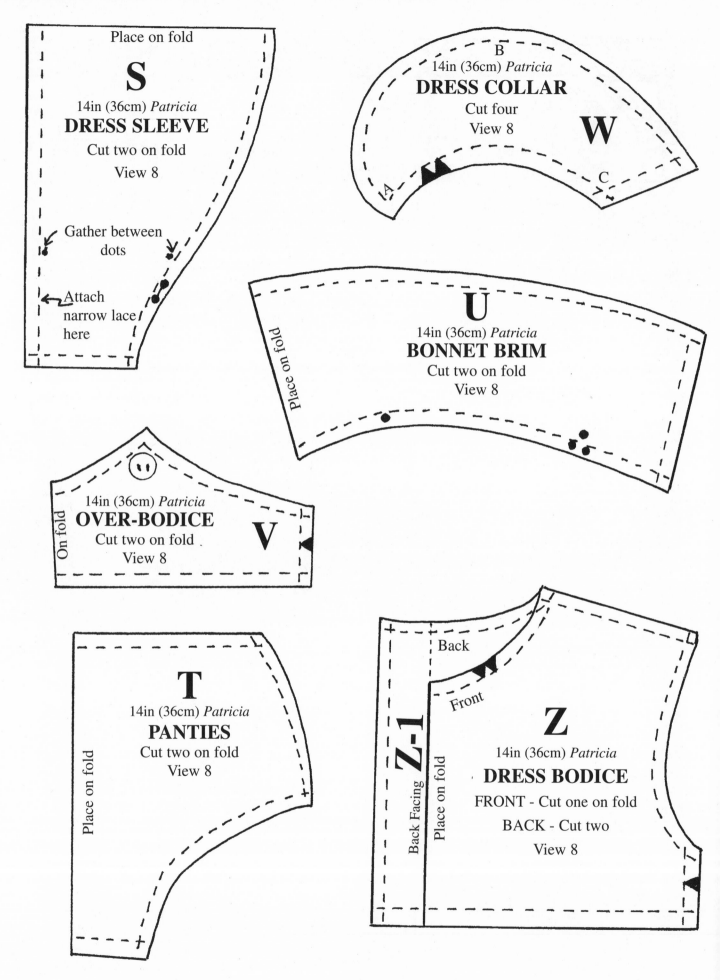

S

14in (36cm) *Patricia*
DRESS SLEEVE
Cut two on fold
View 8

Place on fold

Gather between dots

Attach narrow lace here

W

B

14in (36cm) *Patricia*
DRESS COLLAR
Cut four
View 8

A

C

U

14in (36cm) *Patricia*
BONNET BRIM
Cut two on fold
View 8

Place on fold

V

14in (36cm) *Patricia*
OVER-BODICE
Cut two on fold
View 8

On fold

T

14in (36cm) *Patricia*
PANTIES
Cut two on fold
View 8

Place on fold

Z-1

Back

Front

Back Facing

Place on fold

Z

14in (36cm) *Patricia*
DRESS BODICE
FRONT - Cut one on fold
BACK - Cut two
View 8

A Wardrobe for
7-1/2in (19in) - 8in (20cm)
Dionne Quintuplets
by Madame Alexander
1937

View 3a

View 1

View 2

View 3

View 4

View 5

View 6

View 4

ORIGINAL WARDROBE FOR 7-1/2in (19cm) - 8in (20cm) COMPOSITION DIONNES
by Madame Alexander, 1937

These patterns, as with most of the patterns in this book, were drafted from the originals. Each Dionne was dressed in a different pastel color - lavender, green, pink, blue, or yellow. The colors carried through the entire wardrobe with two exceptions, the plain white flannel nightgowns and the thick, white flannel blankets printed in pink with four lambs and Little Jack Horner. The pastel dotted Swiss dresses and bonnets were still fastened to the lid of the gift hamper when I examined the set and drew the patterns in 1992. The set had been obtained from the original owner by the dealer who so generously shared the treasure trove with the author.

Imagine - under the tree that Christmas morning of 1937 were the five little dolls in pink, yellow, blue, green, and lavender pastel voile dresses and bonnets. Then there was the huge hamper, stuffed with five sets of clothes. And last, but not least, the marvelous five-place, peachy-pink enameled chair. Lucky child.

The original owner remarked that her father had purchased everything he could buy to go with the dolls. She remembers the price of the dolls was $3.98. Five dolls for $3.98! But that was in 1937, in the depths of the Great Depression and was much more than it seems today. The original price of 59 cents is still visible on the bottom of the chair, written in pencil.

View 1
SUNSUIT & SUNBONNET
Pattern Pieces A, D, F, G

Sunsuit - The fabric of these sunsuits is a tiny print in the five pastels on thin white cotton, trimmed with a very narrow white loop edging. Collars are double, cut of organdy, finished with the same loop edging. The backs are open to the dot at lower back center on pattern.

Sunbonnet - The sunbonnet is cut of same fabric as sunsuit. The brim is a single piece of print fabric with a plain white cotton lining, bound with white bias tape. Ties are narrow white satin ribbon.

View 2
VOILE DRESS & BONNET
Pattern Pieces B, C, F, G

Again there are the five pastel shades, this time in fine voile. Dress is sleeveless and opens back center to dot, has a 1/2in (1cm) hem, and is finished with very narrow lace on edges (but not down back opening). The square collar is cut from dress fabric and has same lace trim. Matching bonnet uses sunbonnet pattern.

View 3
DOTTED SWISS DRESS & BONNET
Pattern Pieces P, F, G

Sewing this dress can be a bit tricky. Cut one bodice from dotted Swiss and one from white organdy for lining. Pin right sides together. Baste along seam A-AA. Baste armholes B-BB and turn right side out. If all is well, turn back to wrong side and machine-stitch the basted seams. Turn and press. Baste remaining edges together.

For skirt, cut a piece of dotted Swiss measuring 16in (41cm) x 3in (8cm). Skirt may be lined with organdy if desired, sewing both layers as one at back seam and waist.

Turn up a 1/2in (1cm) hem on one long side of piece (and separately on lining) and machine stitch. On outside sew loop trim over stitching line of hem. Run gathers on remaining long side to within 1/2in (1cm) of either end. Do not pull gathers. Turn under 1/4in (.65cm) of back edges of skirt from waist to bottom and blindstitch for back facing. (Back of skirt will be open.)

Tack bottom edges of armholes together. Pull gathering threads of skirt (and lining as one) to fit bodice and seam together. Finish armholes and neckline with loop edging trim. Sew on snap fasteners at waist and neckline.

Use bottom of combinations pattern to make matching panties. These may be lined with organdy if desired.

Use sunbonnet pattern, cut from dotted Swiss and trimmed to match dress.

View 3a
DRESS WITH PUFFED SLEEVES
Pattern Pieces P, P-1

Use these pattern pieces to create yet another dress. Follow direction of View 3 for the skirt. Another variation: Round out the neckline and borrow a collar pattern, either round or square from elsewhere in the book.

View 4
SLIP & COMBINATION SUIT
Pattern Pieces E, S, T

Slip - Cut these underthings of fine white cotton such as lawn. Turn and blindstitch neck edge and armholes. Check length of garment in relation to dress. Turn up hem and edge bottom with very narrow lace.

Combination Suit - Using pattern pieces S and T, construct garment, turning under narrow handkerchief hem all around.

For skirt of suit, cut a piece of fabric 2-1/4in (6cm) x 12in (31cm). Hem one long edge with very narrow lace or loop trim. Run double gathering thread on remaining long side. Seam two short sides together. Pull gathering threads and seam to suit along dotted line on pattern.

WHITE FLANNEL NIGHTIE
Pattern Piece U

The 1937 models were made of very heavy white wool flannel. Any modern flannel will do. Follow pattern, turn under plain hems all around.

WHITE FLANNEL BLANKET

Each doll has her own printed flannel blanket measuring 9-1/2in (24cm) x 13-1/2in (34cm), finished. The material is very thick. Corners are rounded and blanket is machine bound. For thickness, cut two of ordinary flannel for each blanket, baste together, then bind with buttonhole stitching all around or use a machine binding stitch. Print is of four lambs, one at each corner, and a Little Jack Horner design in the center, all printed in pink.

WOOL COAT, LEGGINGS & BONNET
Pattern Pieces H through O

This set is my favorite in the wardrobe. The dealer who shared this group with me states this is the only snowsuit set he has seen, although he has viewed several identical hampers loaded with Dionne outfits. Again we have the five pastels in a soft wool which has miraculously survived the dangers of moths, dust and time. All three pieces may be lined with a thin, soft rayon or silk, but will be perfectly presentable and authentic left unlined.

Hems are top-stitched by machine. A bias binding covers the seam where collar is attached to neck edge of coat. A single button fastens the coat. You may bind a buttonhole if you like, or construct a thread button loop.

Setting in sleeves in small garments is easier if you do so before the side seams are sewn. It is also a good idea to hem each sleeve before setting. (The purist, however, will want to complete this step last for a neater finish.) Then stitch sleeve and side seams as one. Be sure to check pattern against size of doll's hand, allowing for seams.

The leggings or snow pants of this set have an unusual feature. Bottoms of legs are rounded, sides are slit open, then faced, and closed with three tiny fasteners. The originals actually have covered buttons, these fastening with white thread loops. The pants have a nicer, more finished appearance if lined. Waist is turned down and narrow flat elastic or small round elastic run through the casing.

For bonnet follow construction details on pattern.

Pajamas may be constructed from this pattern by squaring off the bottom of the snow pants pattern and omitting the lining.

Shoes - Use pattern given and refer to general instructions for shoes in Volume I.

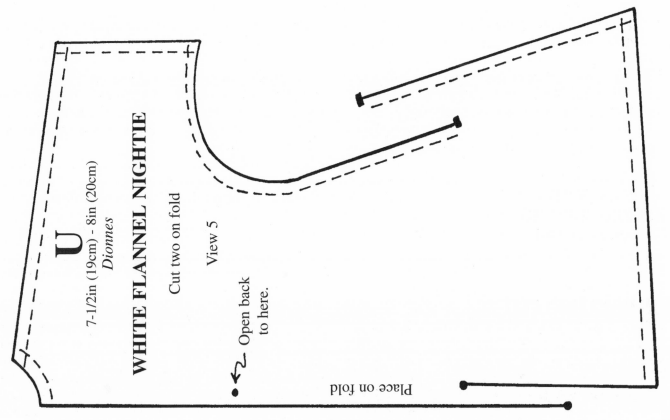

U

7-1/2in (19cm) - 8in (20cm)
Dionnes

WHITE FLANNEL NIGHTIE

Cut two on fold

View 5

Open back to here.

Place on fold

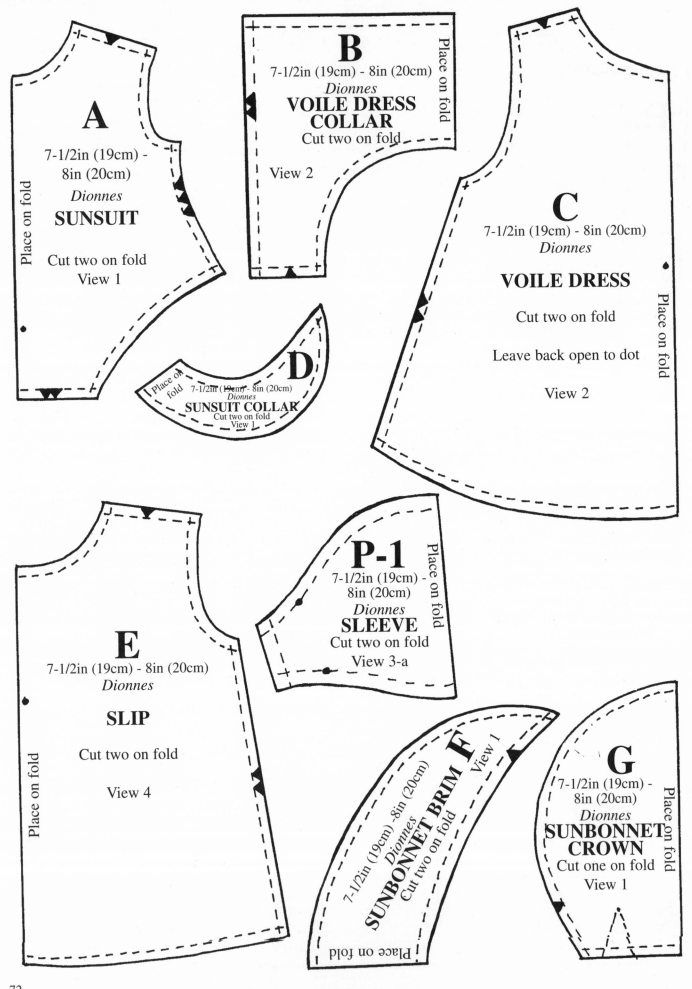

A

7-1/2in (19cm) -
8in (20cm)

Dionnes

SUNSUIT

Place on fold

Cut two on fold
View 1

B

7-1/2in (19cm) - 8in (20cm)

Dionnes

**VOILE DRESS
COLLAR**

Cut two on fold

Place on fold

View 2

C

7-1/2in (19cm) - 8in (20cm)

Dionnes

VOILE DRESS

Cut two on fold

Leave back open to dot

View 2

Place on fold

D

Place on fold

7-1/2in (19cm) - 8in (20cm)
Dionnes
SUNSUIT COLLAR
Cut two on fold
View 1

E

7-1/2in (19cm) - 8in (20cm)
Dionnes

SLIP

Place on fold

Cut two on fold

View 4

P-1

7-1/2in (19cm) -
8in (20cm)

Dionnes
SLEEVE
Cut two on fold

View 3-a

Place on fold

F

7-1/2in (19cm) - 8in (20cm)
Dionnes
SUNBONNET BRIM
Cut two on fold

View 1

Place on fold

G

7-1/2in (19cm) -
8in (20cm)
Dionnes
**SUNBONNET
CROWN**
Cut one on fold
View 1

Place on fold

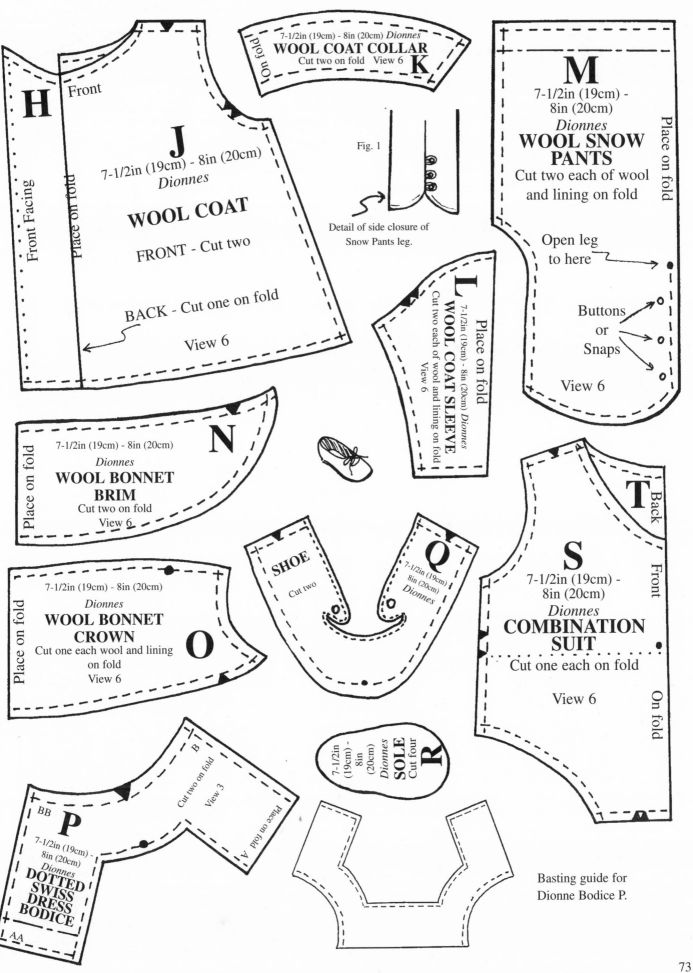

H

J
7-1/2in (19cm) - 8in (20cm)
Dionnes
WOOL COAT
FRONT - Cut two
BACK - Cut one on fold
View 6

Front

Front Facing

Place on fold

On fold

K
7-1/2in (19cm) - 8in (20cm) *Dionnes*
WOOL COAT COLLAR
Cut two on fold   View 6

Fig. 1

Detail of side closure of Snow Pants leg.

M
7-1/2in (19cm) - 8in (20cm)
Dionnes
WOOL SNOW PANTS
Cut two each of wool and lining on fold

Place on fold

Open leg to here

Buttons or Snaps

View 6

L
7-1/2in (19cm) - 8in (20cm) *Dionnes*
WOOL COAT SLEEVE
Cut two each of wool and lining on fold
View 6

Place on fold

N
7-1/2in (19cm) - 8in (20cm)
Dionnes
WOOL BONNET BRIM
Cut two on fold
View 6

Place on fold

O
7-1/2in (19cm) - 8in (20cm)
Dionnes
WOOL BONNET CROWN
Cut one each wool and lining on fold
View 6

Place on fold

SHOE
Cut two

Q
7-1/2in (19cm) - 8in (20cm)
Dionnes

T
Back

S
7-1/2in (19cm) - 8in (20cm)
Dionnes
COMBINATION SUIT
Cut one each on fold
View 6

Front

On fold

R
7-1/2in (19cm) - 8in (20cm) *Dionnes*
SOLE
Cut four

P
7-1/2in (19cm) - 8in (20cm)
Dionnes
DOTTED SWISS DRESS BODICE

BB

B

AA

A

Cut two on fold

View 3

Place on fold

Basting guide for Dionne Bodice P.

View 4

Wardrobe for 13in (33cm)

Shirley Temple

and other 13in (33cm)

Composition Dolls of the 1930s

View 1

View 5

View 2

View 3

View 5

View 6

WARDROBE FOR SHIRLEY TEMPLE AND OTHER 13in (33cm) COMPOSITION DOLLS OF THE 1930S

This set of patterns is representative of the fashions in which many 1930s composition dolls were dressed. They are presented here sized for 13in (33cm) dolls; however, enlargement figures are given below to fit dolls up to 25in (64cm) tall.

Fabrics were simple - cotton prints, organdy, chambray, flannel, batiste, and lawn are all acceptable choices.

Many dresses were made with combinations of two or more fabrics. View 4, for example, may be made up in a miniature print with organdy collar.

Most of the patterns in this set are self-explanatory. Remember to use very narrow laces and bias tape for the smaller-sized dolls such as the 13in (33cm) and 15in (38cm).

View 1 **PANEL FRONT DRESS** Pattern Pieces A through F

This dress may be made of a solid color cotton with a contrasting color or white used for the upper bodice and skirt front panel. Another combination might be a cotton print with contrasting solid color or white. The collar may be cut of dress fabric or organdy. The entire dress in organdy would also be quite appropriate.

View 2 **COMBINATIONS** Pattern Pieces G, H

Fine, soft lawn or batiste is recommended for this garment. Always make the underclothes first and fit outer garments over them. If this pattern is enlarged for taller dolls, check the waistline.

Toddlers and younger children have shorter bodies, therefore higher waistlines. Adjust the waistline/skirt attachment line to fit the doll.

Always trim underthings with the very narrowest lace unless otherwise specified or the doll's size requires wider trim.

View 3 **PLAY PAJAMAS** Pattern Pieces L, M, N

These pajamas were among the earliest of then new lines of "play clothes," a very modern innovation in dress for little girls of the 1920s and 1930s. Such designs were created in direct reaction to earlier extravagantly ruffled and pleated styles forced on children by a society that expected children always to present themselves in perfect decorum and attire. For the first time, little girls in particular were allowed the freedom to run and play in comfortable clothing.

With right sides together, stitch side seams of bodice. Cut back bodice facing following the lines of pattern piece N; front bodice facing follows pattern piece M. For back, with right sides together, stitch along line from X to O, trim, turn, and press. For front, with right sides together, stitch facing to bodice along neck, shoulder, and armhole edges. Trim seam, turn and press.

Attach bodice to pants, leaving back open to dot on back seam. Put garment on doll and mark position of buttons. Sew buttons on through all thicknesses.

View 4 **SLEEVELESS DRESS & BONNET** Pattern Pieces J, K, O, P, Q

Dress - Again, there is a wide choice of fabrics, although it is always important to choose a fabric in keeping with the period of the doll. Lace may be used to trim the collar, or dress fabric may be used to make a ruffle. Do not skimp on the length of fabric for the tie belt. To get an idea of what it takes to make a bow, use a piece of bias or ribbon, tie a bow, mark the ribbon, untie and measure. Add waist measurement and allow for lengths to hang down. The same is true for bonnet ties.

Bonnet - The bonnet crown may be a single thickness or doubled, which is almost a necessity for a thin fabric such as organdy. The brim must be double thickness to retain its shape. Edge of brim may be left plain or trimmed with lace or a narrow ruffle.

Views 5 & 6 **DRESS & "FUR" COAT, BERET & MUFF** Pattern Pieces Q through V

This pattern was drafted from the original coat and beret worn by the author's childhood doll. The doll is unmarked, although there is little doubt it is an Ideal doll. Her wig, long gone, was dark brown and short; her eyes are a golden brown. The dress and muff were lost in time and another collector came to the rescue with sketches and dimensions from her own recently acquired identical doll, another proof of the generosity of readers.

Coat - The original coat, muff, and beret (which we called a "tam") were of white pile "fur." Note that seam allowances for this pattern are drawn somewhat wider than for other patterns in the book. This has been done to allow for the thickness of the fabric and for the difficulty of working with the "fur." Where necessary, extra seam allowances may be trimmed to eliminate bulk. The pile may also be clipped from the seam allowance area with nail scissors if desired.

Draw full paper patterns for the collar, sleeve, and back so they may be laid out flat to cut. Never try to cut pile fabric on the fold.

Baste pieces together, turn, and check that pile is not

caught improperly in the seam. Use a large needle to "pick" out any caught pile. Ease fullness of sleeves into armhole; do not gather.

Beret - Make two patterns of 5in (13cm) circles using a compass. With the compass point in the same center hole of one of the patterns, draw another circle 3-3/4in (10cm) in diameter. Cut out and discard the smaller circle. Check the size of the hole made in the 5in (13cm) circle on the doll's head and make any necessary adjustments. Sew same color bias tape all around inner circle. Again try the piece on the doll. If fit is right, turn bias tape to inside and blindstitch being careful not to stitch through the fur.

With right sides together, baste the two circles together. Turn and check the pile; pick out any caught threads. Turn to inside and machine stitch all around.

Muff - Cut a piece of pile fabric 4-1/2in (12cm) x 2-1/2in (6cm). This allows for 1/4in (.65cm) seams. Finished size of muff will be 2in (5cm) x 2in (5cm). Sew same color bias tape to both long sides of piece. Seam short sides together. Fold bias to wrong side and blindstitch, being careful not to go through the pile. Attach a ribbon wrist strap at one end.

Dress - This dress, though not exactly like the original lost dress, is contemporary to the period. It is of rose pink organdy with a double square collar and a single tuck on the skirt. (My original was of blue cotton, but there is evidence that the doll came in several dress colors with the white fur outfit.)

Use pattern piece Q for the bodice and pattern piece V for the collar. For the skirt cut a piece of fabric 32in (81cm) x 6-3/4in (17cm). Finished length of skirt will be 3-3/4in (10cm), giving 1/4in (.65cm) for seam allowance at waistline and 1-1/4in (3cm) to be turned under to make a 1in (3cm) hem, plus 1-1/2in (4cm) for a finished 3/4in (2cm) tuck all around. This skirt will be quite full and is gathered very tightly, thus it is essential that the double gathering thread method be used. Finish the skirt before doing the gathering. Leave a back opening to within 2in (5cm) of bottom of skirt.

The bodice is finished with a snap at the neckline and a hook and eye at the waistline.

Enlarge the above patterns as follows:

15in (38cm) — 115%
18in (46cm) — 140%
25in (64cm) — 195%

For panties and half-slip, see patterns elsewhere in the book.

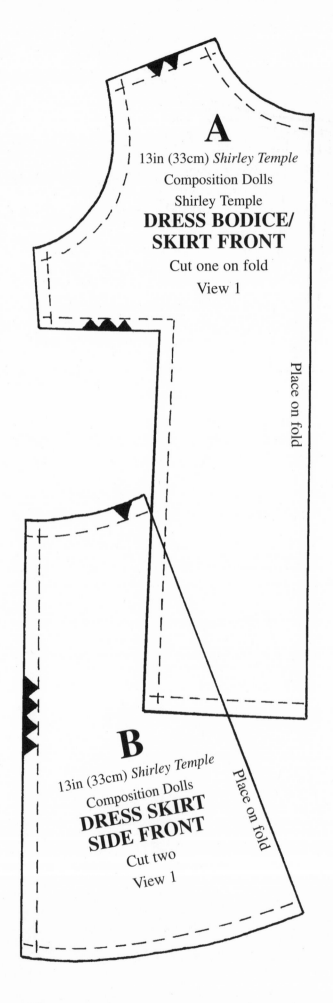

A

13in (33cm) *Shirley Temple*
Composition Dolls
Shirley Temple
**DRESS BODICE/
SKIRT FRONT**
Cut one on fold
View 1

Place on fold

B

13in (33cm) *Shirley Temple*
Composition Dolls
**DRESS SKIRT
SIDE FRONT**
Cut two
View 1

Place on fold

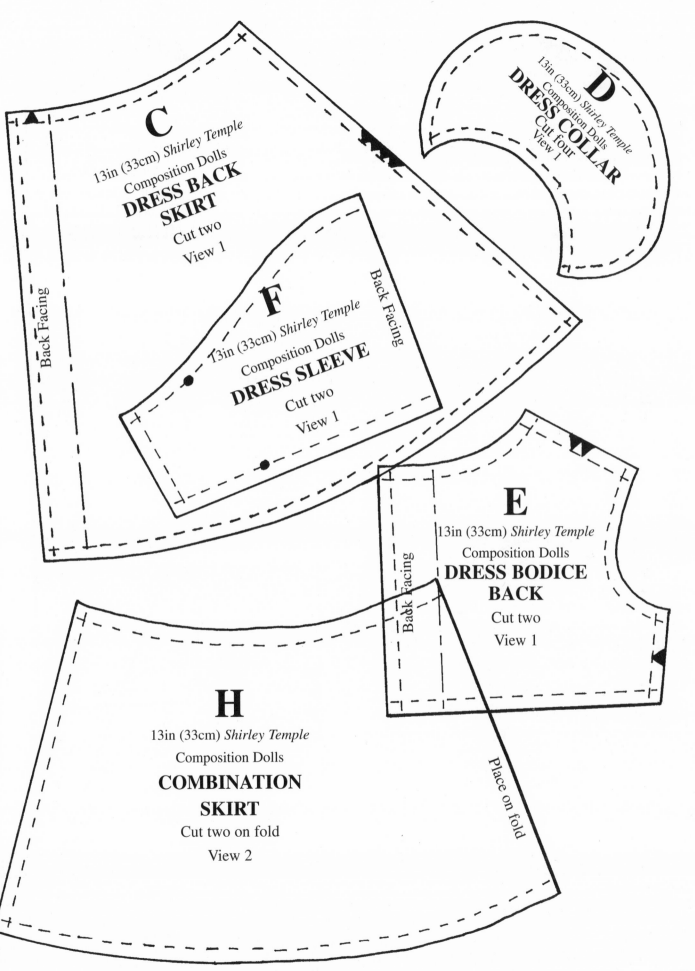

C

13in (33cm) *Shirley Temple*

Composition Dolls

DRESS BACK SKIRT

Cut two

View 1

Back Facing

D

13in (33cm) *Shirley Temple*

Composition Dolls

DRESS COLLAR

Cut four

View 1

F

13in (33cm) *Shirley Temple*

Composition Dolls

DRESS SLEEVE

Cut two

View 1

Back Facing

E

13in (33cm) *Shirley Temple*

Composition Dolls

DRESS BODICE BACK

Cut two

View 1

Back Facing

H

13in (33cm) *Shirley Temple*

Composition Dolls

COMBINATION SKIRT

Cut two on fold

View 2

Place on fold

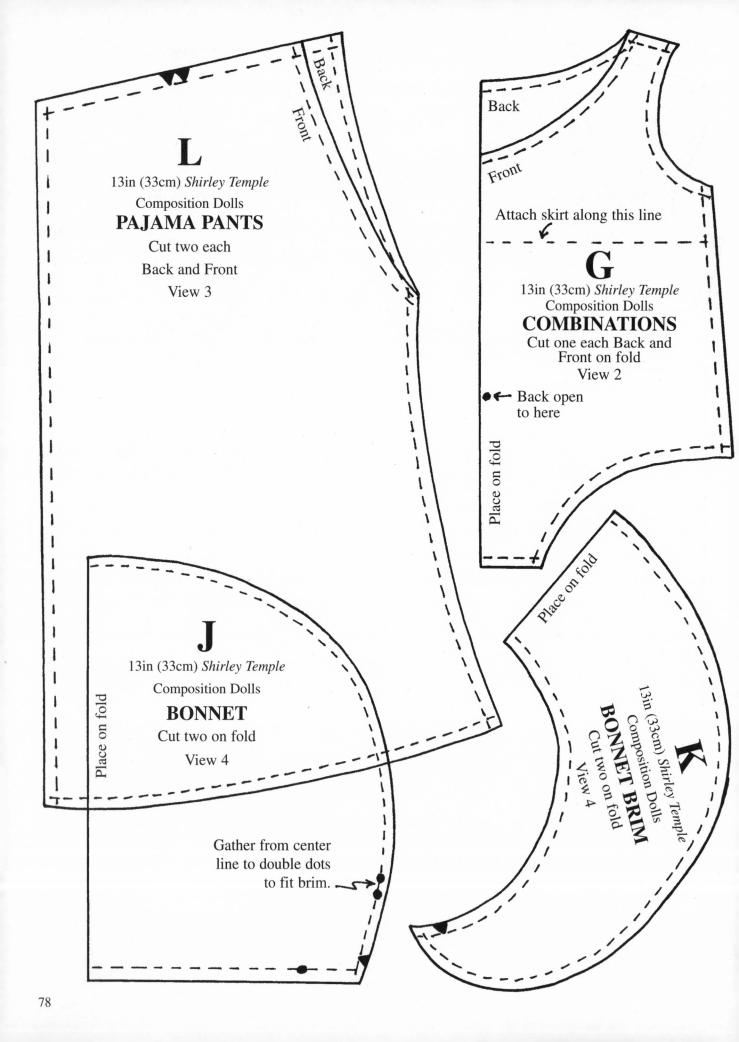

L

13in (33cm) *Shirley Temple*
Composition Dolls
PAJAMA PANTS
Cut two each
Back and Front
View 3

Back

Front

Back

Front

Attach skirt along this line

G

13in (33cm) *Shirley Temple*
Composition Dolls
COMBINATIONS
Cut one each Back and
Front on fold
View 2

◆ ← Back open
to here

Place on fold

Place on fold

J

13in (33cm) *Shirley Temple*
Composition Dolls
BONNET
Cut two on fold
View 4

Place on fold

Gather from center
line to double dots
to fit brim.

Place on fold

13in (33cm) *Shirley Temple*
Composition Dolls
BONNET BRIM
Cut two on fold
View 4

K

78

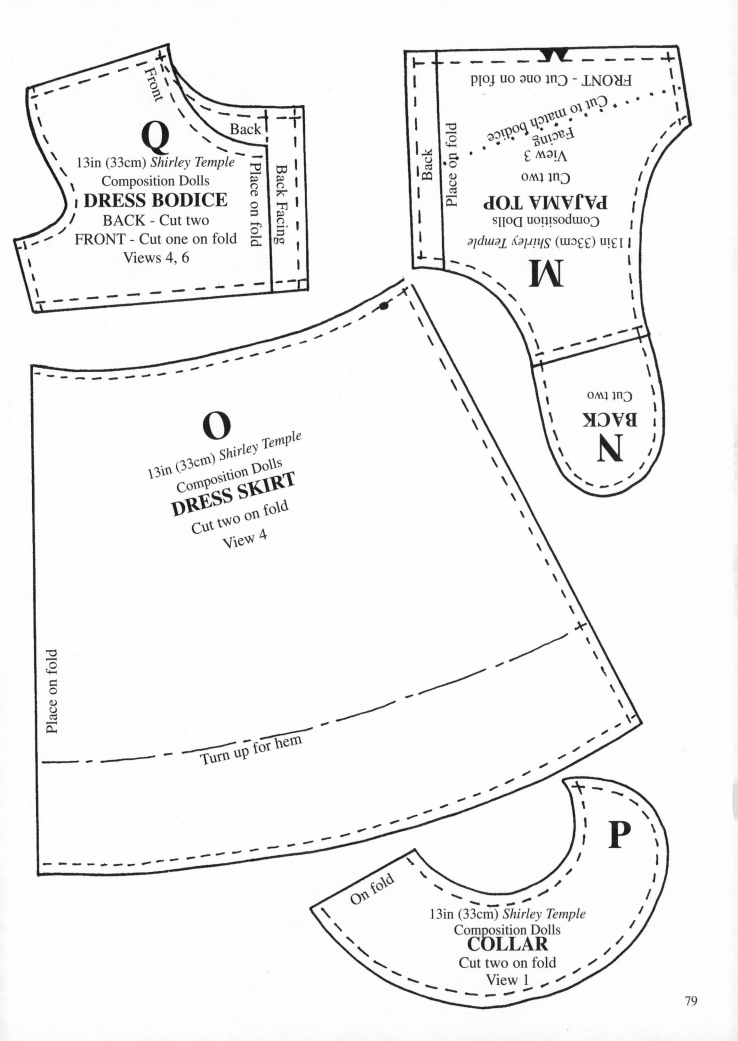

Q

13in (33cm) *Shirley Temple*
Composition Dolls
DRESS BODICE
BACK - Cut two
FRONT - Cut one on fold
Views 4, 6

Front

Back

Place on fold

Back Facing

M

FRONT - Cut one on fold

Cut to match bodice

Facing
View 3
Cut two
PAJAMA TOP
Composition Dolls
13in (33cm) *Shirley Temple*

Back

Place on fold

N
BACK
Cut two

O

13in (33cm) *Shirley Temple*
Composition Dolls
DRESS SKIRT
Cut two on fold
View 4

Place on fold

Turn up for hem

P

On fold

13in (33cm) *Shirley Temple*
Composition Dolls
COLLAR
Cut two on fold
View 1

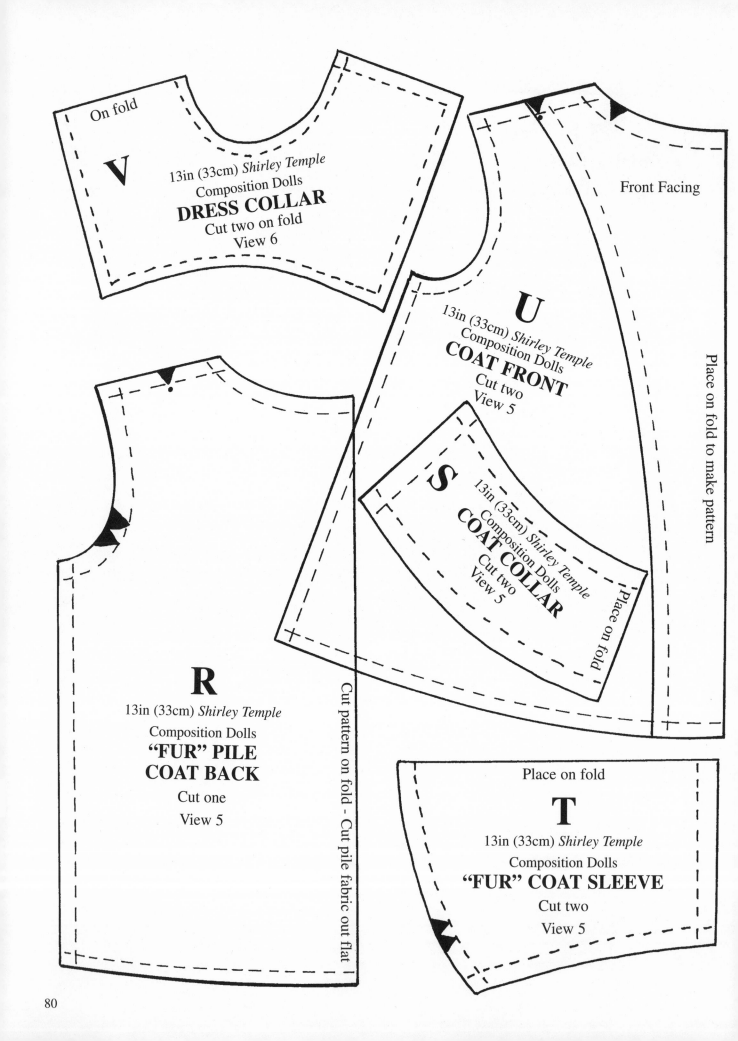

On fold

V

13in (33cm) *Shirley Temple*
Composition Dolls
DRESS COLLAR
Cut two on fold
View 6

Front Facing

U

13in (33cm) *Shirley Temple*
Composition Dolls
COAT FRONT
Cut two
View 5

Place on fold to make pattern

S

13in (33cm) *Shirley Temple*
Composition Dolls
COAT COLLAR
Cut two
View 5

Place on fold

R

13in (33cm) *Shirley Temple*
Composition Dolls
**"FUR" PILE
COAT BACK**
Cut one
View 5

Cut pattern on fold - Cut pile fabric out flat

Place on fold

T

13in (33cm) *Shirley Temple*
Composition Dolls
"FUR" COAT SLEEVE
Cut two
View 5

View 1

View 2

View 4

View 5

Wardrobe for
22in (56cm) Saucy Walker,
24in (61cm) Magic Lips,
and other
Ideal Dolls of the 1950s

View 3

View 6

Based on original dresses found on Saucy Walker, Toni, Betty Jane, and other Ideal dolls, these patterns may be used to create a wide variety of outfits, including outfits for Miss Curity and Harriet Hubbard Ayer dolls.

A 16in (41cm) P-91 Toni wore a dress identical to View 1. Apparently Ideal re-used styles from doll to doll and size to size as well as decade to decade. Note the 1930s dress on page 140 of the first volume of this work. This dress, found original on a composition doll with cloth body, is very similar to that shown in View 1.

When reducing or enlarging patterns, remember that height is not the only consideration in fitting a pattern. Always check your new pattern against your doll. Magic Lips, for example, is chubbier than Saucy Walker since the doll represents a much younger child. Thus Toni has a much more slender figure than Saucy Walker because she represents an older girl. Refer to the reduction and enlargement equations given elsewhere in the book for assistance in calculating changes in patterns.

View 1
22in (56cm) SAUCY WALKER DRESS WITH V DICKEY
Pattern Pieces A through F

This dress is of good quality plaid rayon taffeta trimmed with regular-size ric rac around the pointed dickey front and in two rows on the skirt. As noted above, the design is an old one. An earlier version, which was found on a 1930s composition, is shown in the first volume of this work.

Bodice - Make a lining for the bodice of fine cotton and sew as one with bodice pieces.

Cut sleeves and collar of white rayon. Sleeves are unlined.

The V-dickey is a single thickness of the dress fabric, trimmed with ric rac, then sewn into bodice seams as one with bodice pieces.

There are three buttons and worked buttonholes from neckline to waist on bodice back.

Skirt - Cut a piece of taffeta 7in (18cm) x 36in (91cm) including a 1in (3cm) hem.

Half-slip - This is a piece of white cotton 5in (13cm) x 24in (61cm), hemmed with narrow lace edging. Sew half-slip and skirt to bodice as one along with waistband.

Waistband - Cut a piece of dress fabric 2in (5cm) x 12in (31cm), fold in half lengthwise, sew raw long edges into waist seam. Turn up waistband, sew ends into back facings, then sew button at front center over V-dickey and waistband (see illustration).

View 2
22in (56cm) SAUCY WALKER SQUARE-NECK DRESS
Pattern Pieces G through L

This dress is made of pink cotton with pale pink polka dots. It has a sewn-in half-slip as in View 1, and basic construction is the same.

Bodice - The over-the-shoulder strap effect measures 2-1/2in (5cm) x 9in (23cm). To construct bodice, sew shoulder seams, press, and lay out flat. Turn under edges of pointed center panel and pin in place. Turn under edges of each strap and pin in place, overlapping sides of center panel. Do not stitch any of this at this time.

Construct shoulder ruffles: Put a narrow handkerchief hem on long straight edges of each ruffle. Run gathering threads along curved long side. Lay ruffle out flat on bodice and pull gathers to fit. Short ends of ruffle are sewn into waist seam front and back; gathered side fits under edge of strap. Baste down all pieces, then top stitch with small stitches by machine.

Half-slip - Cut a piece of white cotton 6in (15cm) x 36" 91cm). Trim bottom edge of slip with 1/2in (1cm) flat lace.

Skirt - Cut a piece of dress fabric 8in (20cm) x 44in (112cm). Continue as in View 1.

View 3
22in (56cm) SAUCY WALKER PRINT DRESS
Pattern Pieces P through T

This dress has a double bodice; the underbodice and sleeves are of organdy; the overbodice is cut from the same print material as the skirt. The fabric is a cream-color embossed cotton with orange, pink, and gold fruit print and moss-green leaves. Ric rac is a matching green. Narrow lace is white.

Bodice - Cut out all pieces. Attach double row of narrow lace down front of organdy underbodice along dotted lines. Matching points, sew organdy underbodice shoulder seams. Matching points, sew overbodice shoulder seams.

Turn under necklines of both bodices and attach ric rac all around on wrong side with single points showing above edge on right side. Sew side seams of each unit. Slip print unit over organdy unit and baste together at armholes and waist.

Sleeves - Lay pieces out flat and attach double row of narrow lace along dotted lines. Turn 1/8in (20cm) of lower edge of sleeve to right side and baste; topstitch narrow lace over turned-back edge. Run gathering stitches between dots at top and bottom of sleeve, but do not pull gathers. Sew underarm seam and press open.

Insert sleeve into armhole and baste underarms between dots. Pull gathering threads to fit and stitch seam. Pull gathering threads along lower sleeve to fit doll's arm and machine stitch to stay them. Be sure sleeve will fit over hand before making final stitches.

Petticoat - Cut one piece 6in (15cm) x 40in (101cm) from white lawn or other fine cotton. Turn back 1/8in (.31cm) along one long side, baste, then sew on narrow lace. Run gathering thread along other long side but do not gather.

Skirt - Cut one piece 8in (20cm) x 48in (122cm) from dress fabric. Turn up 1/8in (.31cm) along one long side and press, then turn up a 1-3/8in (3cm) hem and machine stitch.

Run gathering thread along remaining long side but do not gather.

Pin petticoat and skirt together along gathering edge at four equidistant points. Pull both gathering threads at once, keeping both pieces evenly gathered. Baste petticoat and skirt together along gathered waist. Pin and baste skirt assembly to bodice waistline, then machine stitch. Press entire thickness of seam upward over lower edge of bodice. Baste, then machine stitch a double row of ricrac along waistline of bodice over raw edges (see illustration).

Seam back of petticoat and back of skirt separately. Turn back facings along back opening. Work buttonholes on right back of bodice and sew buttons on left side.

Views 4 & 5
22in (56cm) *SAUCY WALKER* **SLIP & PANTIES**
Pattern Pieces M, N, O

Make these undies from fine lawn or soft old cotton from discarded garments. Make skirt of slip same as petticoat in View 3 above; attach to slip bodice. Trim slip and panties with narrow cotton lace or eyelet.

View 6
24in (61cm) *MAGIC LIPS* **DRESS WITH RUFFLED OVERBLOUSE & BLOOMERS**
Pattern Pieces U through Y

This original outfit was found on a 24in (61cm) *Magic Lips*. The dress and sash are of pink organdy with a flocked flower pattern. The overblouse is of white embossed cotton and the underthings are of rayon. (Lacking a fine rayon fabric, use fine cotton such as lawn or batiste.)

Dress - The entire dress is of embossed cotton with an overblouse of white embossed cotton.

To construct overblouse, pin and baste lace on right side of one piece with the finished edge facing inward. Pin remaining overblouse piece, right sides together, to this assembly; baste and stitch. Trim seam if needed. Turn and press. Baste overblouse assembly to bodice front.

For sash, cut a piece 2-1/2in (5cm) x 54in (138cm) and make a narrow hem all around, pointing the ends. To attach sash into the side seams, fold the sash in half and put a pin in the center. Pin sash to center of bodice front, over completed overblouse, and draw both ends of sash around to sides of bodice front and baste in place, then fold back toward center and baste again. When sewing bodice front and backs together, be sure that sash is to the front and ends are not caught in side seam.

Complete bodice construction with a stand-up collar of bias cut from dress fabric. Cut bias 2in (5cm) wide to make a collar 3/4in (2cm) wide when finished.

For skirt cut a piece of dress fabric measuring 12in (31cm) x 60in (152cm). Finished length of skirt will be 9in (23cm), allowing for a 2in (5cm) hem plus 1/2in (1cm) turned under on hem for finished edge, and 1/2in (1cm) for gathering and waist seam. Sew back seam before hemming, allowing for back opening to within 5in (13cm) of finished bottom hem. Run double gathering threads along waist, pull to fit bodice. Set aside and construct half-slip.

Half-slip - cut a piece of fabric measuring 8in (20cm) x 54in (138cm). Slip will be sewn as one with dress skirt, but should be gathered separately, then basted to gathered skirt before stitching to bodice. Hem is finished with narrow lace. Bodice back fastens with three evenly spaced buttonholes and buttons.

Bloomers - These have casings at waist and lower legs for narrow elastic. Edges of legs are trimmed with narrow lace.

Variations - The 24in (61cm) *Posie* of 1954 wears this basic dress trimmed in stand-up lace around neck and a V-shaped wider flat lace trim on the bodice. There is a wide band of the same lace midway around the skirt. The flat lace is sewn to dress along both edges. Fabric of this dress also appears to be embossed cotton. (See *Twentieth Century Dolls*, p. 256.)

Magic Lips of 1957 also wore this style with cotton lace or eyelet trim. (See *Twentieth Century Dolls*, p. 257.)

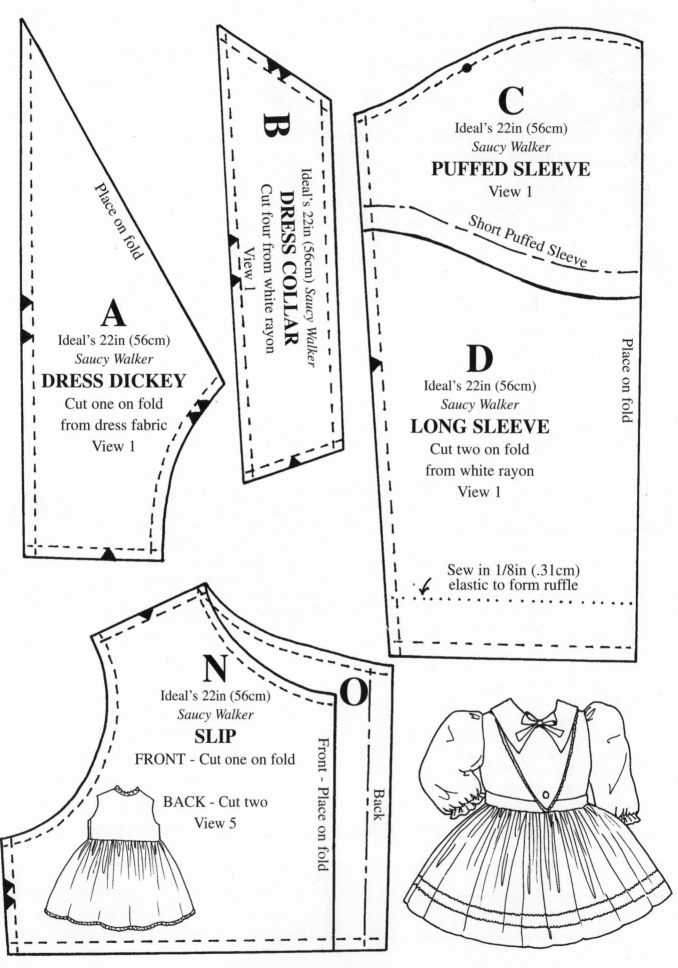

A

Ideal's 22in (56cm)
Saucy Walker
DRESS DICKEY
Cut one on fold
from dress fabric
View 1

Place on fold

B

Ideal's 22in (56cm) *Saucy Walker*
DRESS COLLAR
Cut four from white rayon

View 1

C

Ideal's 22in (56cm)
Saucy Walker
PUFFED SLEEVE
View 1

Short Puffed Sleeve

Place on fold

D

Ideal's 22in (56cm)
Saucy Walker
LONG SLEEVE
Cut two on fold
from white rayon
View 1

Sew in 1/8in (.31cm)
elastic to form ruffle

N

Ideal's 22in (56cm)
Saucy Walker
SLIP
FRONT - Cut one on fold

BACK - Cut two
View 5

O

Front - Place on fold

Back

84

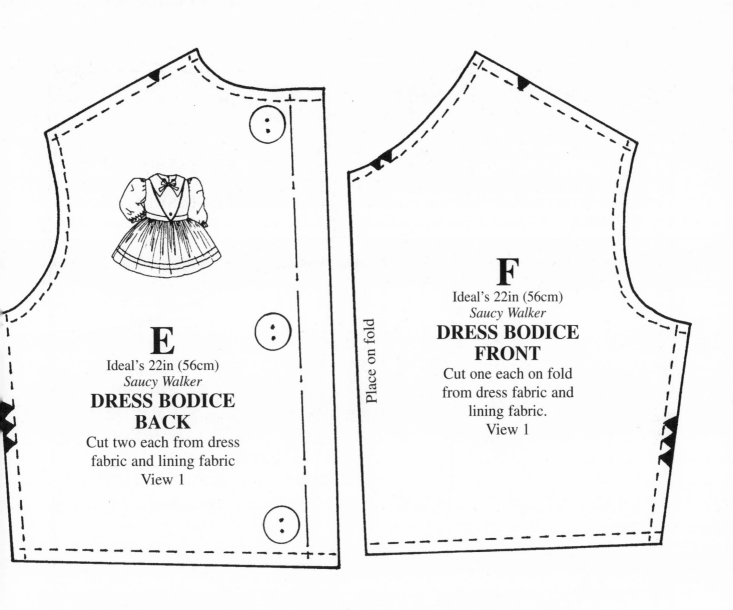

E

Ideal's 22in (56cm)
Saucy Walker
**DRESS BODICE
BACK**

Cut two each from dress
fabric and lining fabric
View 1

Place on fold

F

Ideal's 22in (56cm)
Saucy Walker
**DRESS BODICE
FRONT**

Cut one each on fold
from dress fabric and
lining fabric.
View 1

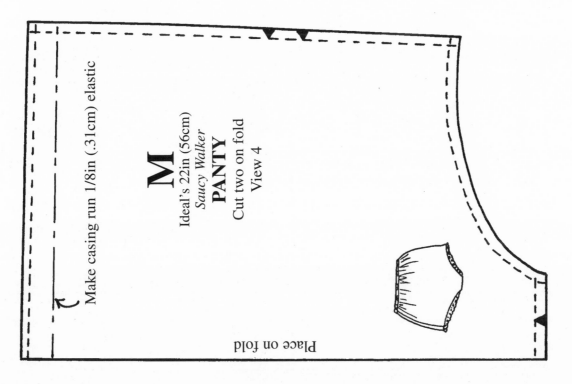

Make casing run 1/8in (.31cm) elastic

M

Ideal's 22in (56cm)
Saucy Walker
PANTY
Cut two on fold
View 4

Place on fold

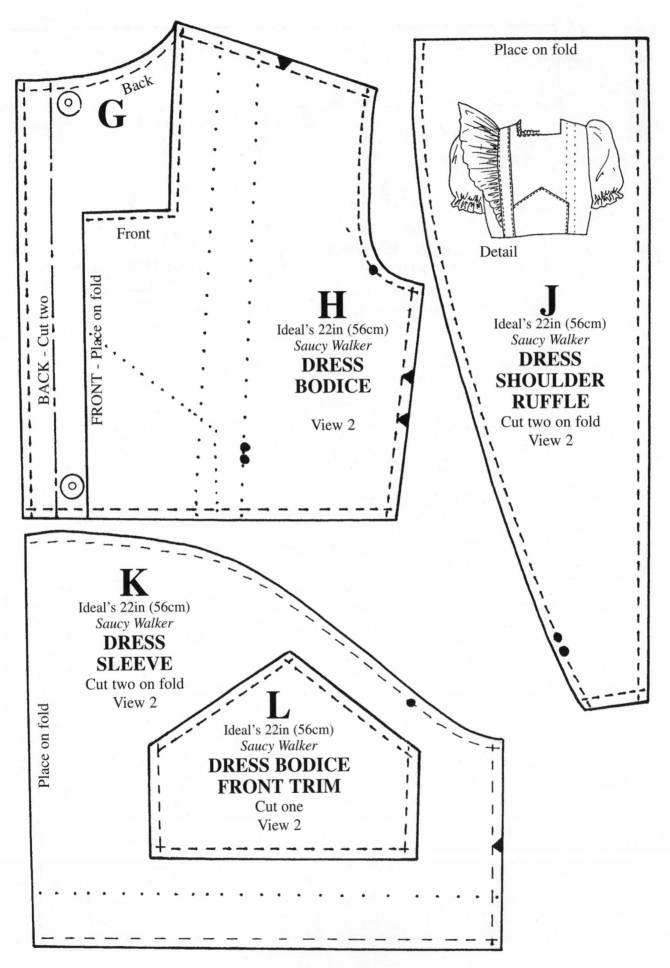

G

Back

Front

BACK - Cut two

FRONT - Place on fold

H

Ideal's 22in (56cm)
Saucy Walker
**DRESS
BODICE**

View 2

Place on fold

Detail

J

Ideal's 22in (56cm)
Saucy Walker
**DRESS
SHOULDER
RUFFLE**

Cut two on fold
View 2

K

Ideal's 22in (56cm)
Saucy Walker
**DRESS
SLEEVE**

Cut two on fold
View 2

Place on fold

L

Ideal's 22in (56cm)
Saucy Walker
**DRESS BODICE
FRONT TRIM**

Cut one
View 2

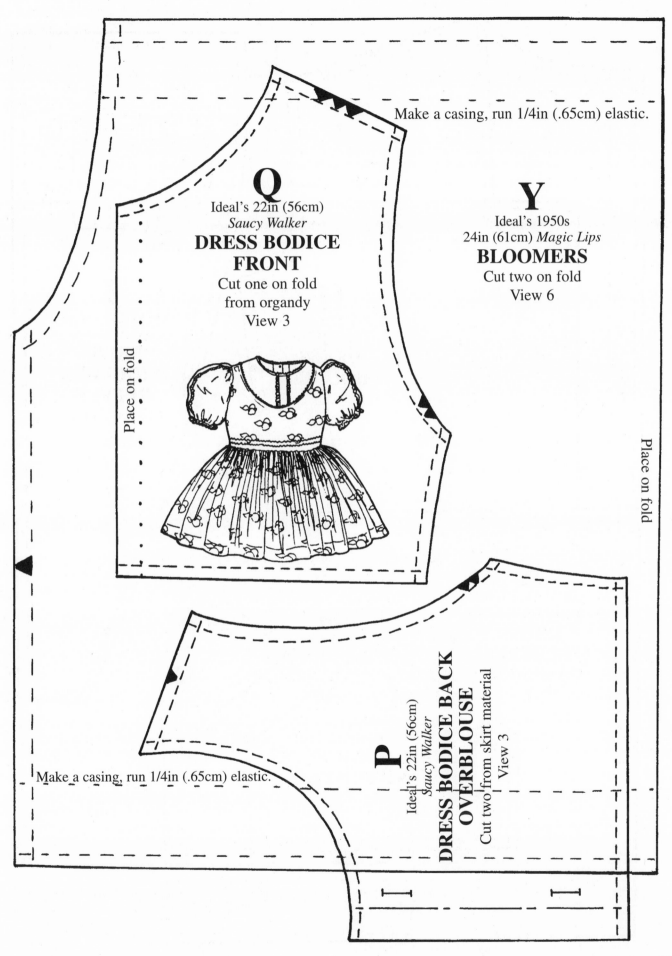

Q

Ideal's 22in (56cm)
Saucy Walker
**DRESS BODICE
FRONT**
Cut one on fold
from organdy
View 3

Place on fold

Make a casing, run 1/4in (.65cm) elastic.

Y

Ideal's 1950s
24in (61cm) *Magic Lips*
BLOOMERS
Cut two on fold
View 6

Place on fold

P

Ideal's 22in (56cm)
Saucy Walker
**DRESS BODICE BACK
OVERBLOUSE**
Cut two from skirt material
View 3

Make a casing, run 1/4in (.65cm) elastic.

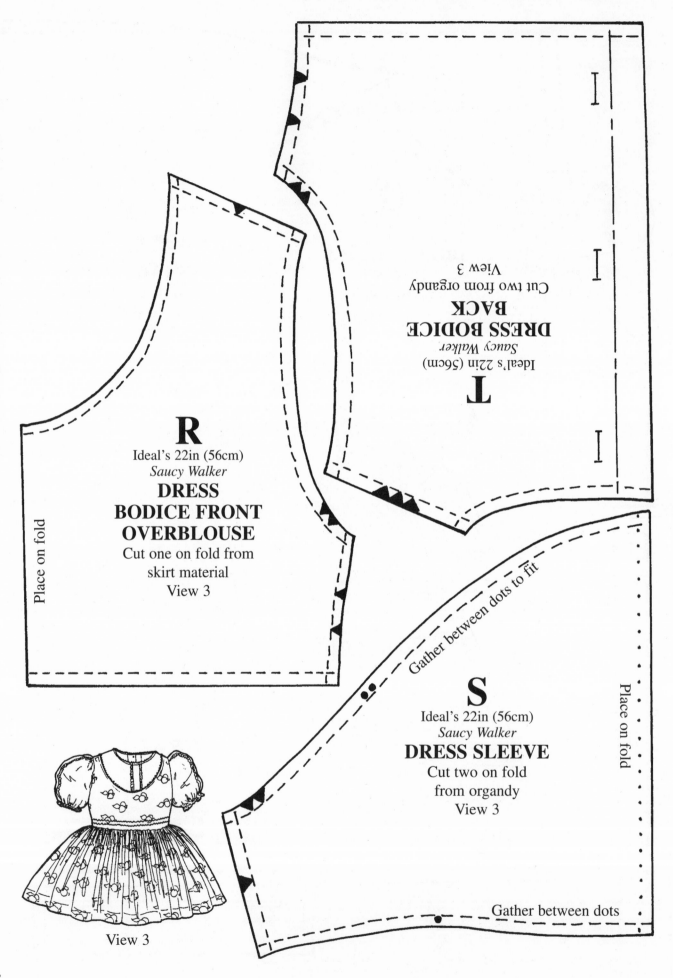

R

Ideal's 22in (56cm)
Saucy Walker
**DRESS
BODICE FRONT
OVERBLOUSE**
Cut one on fold from
skirt material
View 3

Place on fold

T

Ideal's 22in (56cm)
Saucy Walker
**DRESS BODICE
BACK**
Cut two from organdy
View 3

S

Ideal's 22in (56cm)
Saucy Walker
DRESS SLEEVE
Cut two on fold
from organdy
View 3

Gather between dots to fit

Place on fold

Gather between dots

View 3

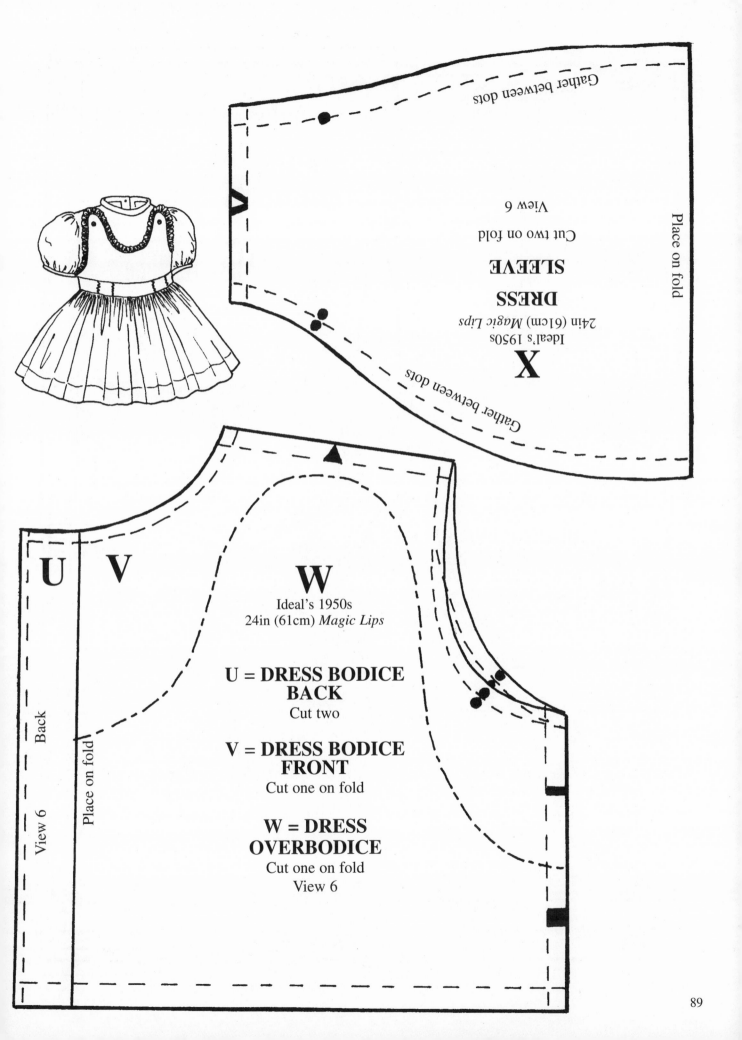

X

Ideal's 1950s
24in (61cm) *Magic Lips*

**DRESS
SLEEVE**

Cut two on fold
View 6

Gather between dots

Gather between dots

Place on fold

W

Ideal's 1950s
24in (61cm) *Magic Lips*

**U = DRESS BODICE
BACK**

Cut two

**V = DRESS BODICE
FRONT**

Cut one on fold

**W = DRESS
OVERBODICE**

Cut one on fold
View 6

U **V**

Back

View 6

Place on fold

Wardrobe for 1950s
14in (36cm) - 18in (46cm)
Hard Plastic Dolls
Various Manufacturers
Including Ideal's **Mary Hartline**

View 1

View 2

View 3

View 5

View 4

View 4

View 4

Views 1 & 4

WARDROBE FOR 1950s 14in (36cm)-18in (46cm) HARD PLASTIC GIRL DOLLS
Various Manufacturers

The first four dolls in this section show strong evidence of having come from the studio of Bernard Leipfert, perhaps the most prolific sculptor of dolls for several decades. It is well known that Leipfert worked freelance and created dolls for nearly all the doll companies of the period. The two 17in (43cm) and 18in (46cm) dolls, in particular, show a marked resemblance to the *Shirley Temple* doll in their profiles and chin lines, although the body styling is that of an older child

than the *Shirley* doll represents. These two, however, are completely different dolls both in face and body as well as height.

The 14in (36cm) dolls are almost identical and call to mind some Mary Hoyer dolls, Alexanders, R&Bs and others. All four are in all-original outfits in excellent condition. There is no doubt, of course, that Leipfert created the fifth doll, Ideal's *Toni*, which in this case masquerades as *Mary Hartline*.

View 1
Outfit for a 17in (43cm) UNMARKED HARD PLASTIC GIRL
Pattern Pieces A through G

This quality doll, though unmarked, closely resembles a Madame Alexander of the period. Her well-made dress is of pink cotton and white organdy trimmed with white lace and eyelet.

Bodice - The bodice is cut from a single thickness of pink cotton fabric. Baste lace to each bodice side front A along joining seam with center front B. Pin and baste side fronts to center front and stitch. Press with lace toward sides. Topstitch along edges of center front. Sew shoulder and side seams.

Construct and insert white organdy sleeves C and collar G. Sleeves are finished with very narrow elastic. Collar has lace all around.

Skirt - Cut a piece of pink cotton 30in (76cm) x 6-1/2in (17cm) which allows for a 1in (3cm) hem and 1/4in

(.65cm) turned under. Gather to fit bodice. Leave open in back to 2in (5cm) below waist seam. Turn under bodice back facing and finish with two buttons and buttonholes. Note that back skirt seam allowance turns under to form facing for skirt opening.

Sash - This is a loose sash. Cut a piece of white organdy 32in (81cm) x 2in (5cm). Make a narrow hem all around ending with a center point at each end (see fig. 2).

Slip - For skirt cut a piece of white cotton 22in (56cm) x 5-3/4in (15cm). Make a 1/2in (1cm) hem finished with 1/2in (1cm) white lace on one long side. Run double gathering threads on remaining long side. Gather to fit finished bodice E/F, turning back sufficient facing width on skirt to match back facing of bodice. Slip is open to hem with two snaps on bodice back. Tack facing at hem.

Panties - Use panties pattern for 14in (36cm) hard plastic doll. Be sure to check size against your doll; often the panties fit several height sizes.

View 2
SLEEVELESS TOP & PANTS for a 14in (36cm) UNMARKED HARD PLASTIC GIRL
Pattern Pieces H, J

Another quality doll in excellent condition and all-original. She could be an unmarked doll from any one of several well-known companies. Her top is white cotton with olive green bias trim at the armholes and around neckline and down the open back which fastens with one gripper snap. A fringed yellow, green, and white braid trims the

bodice front. Pants are of white background cotton with a geometric print of olive, brown, and gold. Olive bias finishes the pants legs.

Top - Lay fabric out flat and baste front trim across before sewing side seams. Bind sleeves, sew side seams, bind all around, install one gripper snap at back neckline.

Pants - Sew bias on bottoms of legs before sewing the seams. Finish waist with narrow casing, run narrow elastic. Try pants on doll before tying off elastic, paying particular attention to hip width.

View 3
BLOUSE & FULL SKIRT for a 14in (36cm) MARKED HARD PLASTIC GIRL
Pattern Pieces K through N

This doll is almost identical to the View 2 doll, differing only in hairstyle. Also, she is marked 14 on the head and MADE IN U.S.A. on the back. Her clothing is also quite well made. The cotton skirt has a red background with yellow and black print, trimmed with yellow bias tape and red ricrac. The blouse is quality white cotton trimmed with a red ribbon bow.

Skirt - Yellow bias tape opened out makes the stripe

around the skirt, with topstitching on both sides of bias. Press bias open before applying to skirt. After bias is sewn to skirt, sew 1/8in (.31cm) ricrac down the center of the bias tape. Do this before sewing the back seam.

Blouse - For collar ruffle, cut a piece of white cotton 8in (20cm) x 1-1/4in (3cm). Stitch extremely narrow hem on one long side; turn back 1/4in (.65cm) facing on each end. Double gather remaining long side and pull to fit neck opening.

Turn under narrow hem on sleeve edge. Before sewing sleeve seams, lay pieces out flat and stitch 1/16in (.15cm) elastic on a line 3/4in (2cm) from lower sleeve edge. Gather sleeves into openings and sew side and sleeve seams as one.

FIRST COMMUNION DRESS & VEIL for an 18in (46cm) UNMARKED HARD PLASTIC GIRL

Pattern Pieces O through R

Our little First Communion doll is a blonde dressed all in white and looks positively angelic. Her dress is of organdy lined with white cotton and trimmed in white lace and lace medallions. This dress has a fitted bodice, large round collar, and the sleeves hang loose and wide, rather than being gathered at the cuff. Three oval lace medallions trim the center front. Panties are of white cotton, also lace-trimmed. The veil is of a micro-mesh nylon net trimmed in lace and white satin ribbon.

Bodice - Cut pattern pieces Q and R from organdy and white cotton. Baste front pieces together, baste darts and try on your doll, make any necessary adjustments, and stitch. Baste back pieces together, then sew to front bodice.

Collar and sleeves are single thicknesses of organdy, trimmed with lace. Bodice fastens at back with snaps at neckline and waistline.

Skirt - Cut a piece of organdy measuring 23in (58cm) x 5in (13cm). Sew 1in (3cm) fine cotton lace to one long side.

For underskirt cut a piece of cotton 23in (58cm) x 4-1/2in (12cm). Sew 1/2in (1cm) lace to one long side.

Sew both pieces together on short ends within 2in (5cm) of top. Baste skirt and underskirt together along remaining long sides. Run double gathering stitch to within 3/4in (2cm) of each end. Gather, pin, and baste to finished bodice. Machine stitch carefully.

Veil - Cut a 16in (41cm) square of micro-mesh nylon net and trim the corners as shown in fig. 3. Finish all edges with 1/2in (1cm) lace. Measure 3-1/2in (9cm) from center of one rounded corner, but not from edge of lace. Run a double gathering thread across corner as indicated in fig. 4, line A-B.

Place on doll's head with gathers at top front to frame face and pull to fit; tie off gathering threads. Sew lace ruffle along gathering line to stand up. While veil is on doll's head, tack a piece of white satin ribbon at point A, carry it across back of neck to point B and fasten. This contours the veil to the shape of the doll's head. Add ribbon bows at points A and B and sew securely.

Panties - For panties, use pattern for 14in (36cm) hard plastic doll. Be sure to check size against your doll; often the panties fit several height sizes.

15in (38cm) MARY HARTLINE ORIGINAL COSTUME

Pattern Pieces S, T, U

Mary Hartline was a popular performer in the 50s and several companies made dolls representing her before Ideal bought the rights to the doll (see *Twentieth Century Dolls* p. 317). Ideal soon began marketing their P- series dolls in replicas of the star's costumes. To give an idea of the variety of colors and fabrics used for these costumes, here is a list of what I have seen and what has been reported to me:

16in (41cm) dolls in white, red, or green all-cotton costumes (see *Twentieth Century Dolls* p. 318)

16in (41cm) doll in white satin-look rayon

22in (56cm) doll with a shiny red dress

23in (58cm) doll with rayon dress very much like Mary's stage costume

23in (58cm) doll in red polished cotton, but with no music motifs or signature

23in (58cm) doll in red polished cotton with music motifs, signature, and heart on bodice (see *Hard Plastic Dolls II,* Judd, p. 137)

Note that dolls listed above as being 22in (56cm) and 23in (58cm) tall are listed variously in several reference books as measuring 22in (56cm), 22-1/2in (57cm), and 23in (58cm).

Trims were also varied. I have noted gold trim, bias trim in both red and white, and ric rac on the neckline and sleeves. Usually the skirt had the music staff and notes printed on it with a replica of Mary's signature above it. The bodice featured the heart symbol with "Mary" printed on it and a heart-shaped neckline.

This pattern was taken from a P-91 15in (38cm) doll wearing a red cotton dress with all the appropriate markings in white. The skirt is very tightly gathered and the bodice is lined.

Bodice - Use red cotton for dress and white cotton for lining. Note that sleeves are unlined. Lay out front bodice piece and pin flat to blotter paper or use an embroidery hoop to keep fabric taut. Using white fabric paint on the red cloth, apply the heart symbol (fig. 5).

Construct bodice using ricrac around neckline with only points showing on outside (see fig. 9). Run double gathering threads at top of sleeve, finish bottoms of sleeves by pressing under a 1/8in (.31cm) fold, tack red ricrac on inside of sleeve so that points only show on right side (see fig. 9) and top-stitch on outside by machine. Sew underarm seams. Insert sleeves, gathering to fit armhole openings.

Skirt - Cut a piece of red cotton measuring 34in (86cm) x 5-1/4in (13cm). Turn under and press 1/4in (.65cm) on one long side, then fold under and press a 1in (3cm) hem. Machine stitch.

Run double gathering stitches on remaining long side to within 1in (3cm) of ends and pull to fit bodice but do not cut threads. Even out gathers and place against bodice to determine center front of skirt. Mark center line of skirt, location of signature, and music motifs with white sewing pencil (see figs. 6, 7, 8). Let gathers out so skirt fabric is flat as above.

Repeat painting technique with music staff, notes, and signature (figs. 6, 7, 8) on the skirt, positioning the lower part of design at the 1in (3cm) hem seam, being careful to line up the signature to the left front of the skirt.

When paint is thoroughly dry and set (follow directions on paint container), stitch back seam to 2in (5cm) below waistline; tack seam allowance under for back skirt facing or face with self-bias if preferred. Pull skirt gathering threads to fit bodice; pin, baste, and stitch waist seam. Make two buttonholes on back bodice and sew on buttons.

Half-slip - Cut a piece of white cotton measuring 24in (61cm) x 4-3/4in (12cm). Make a plain narrow hem on one long side. Add narrow lace if desired. Cut a waistband to fit your doll. Gather remaining long side of skirt to fit waistband, leaving back open to 2in (5cm) below waistline. Sew a snap on waistband.

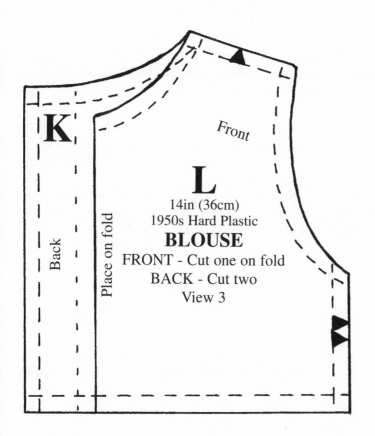

K

Front

L

14in (36cm)

1950s Hard Plastic

BLOUSE

FRONT - Cut one on fold

BACK - Cut two

View 3

Back

Place on fold

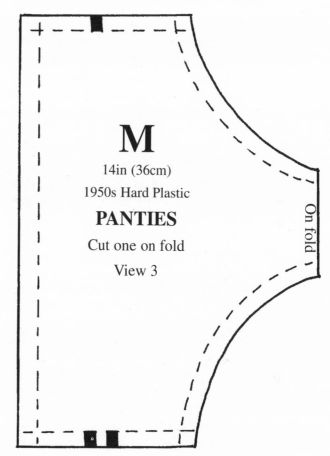

M

14in (36cm)

1950s Hard Plastic

PANTIES

Cut one on fold

View 3

On fold

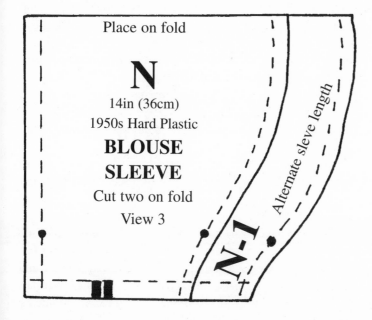

Place on fold

N

14in (36cm)

1950s Hard Plastic

**BLOUSE
SLEEVE**

Cut two on fold

View 3

N-1

Alternate sleeve length

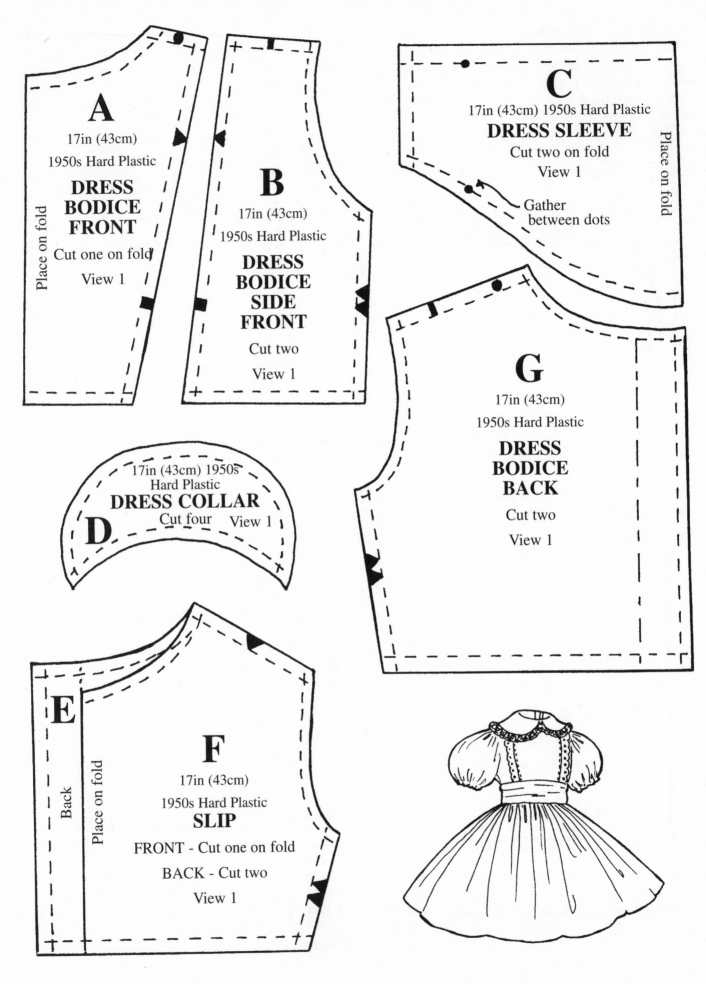

A

17in (43cm)

1950s Hard Plastic

DRESS BODICE FRONT

Cut one on fold

View 1

Place on fold

B

17in (43cm)

1950s Hard Plastic

DRESS BODICE SIDE FRONT

Cut two

View 1

C

17in (43cm) 1950s Hard Plastic

DRESS SLEEVE

Cut two on fold

View 1

Gather between dots

Place on fold

G

17in (43cm)

1950s Hard Plastic

DRESS BODICE BACK

Cut two

View 1

D

17in (43cm) 1950s Hard Plastic

DRESS COLLAR

Cut four   View 1

E

Back

F

17in (43cm)

1950s Hard Plastic

SLIP

FRONT - Cut one on fold

BACK - Cut two

View 1

Place on fold

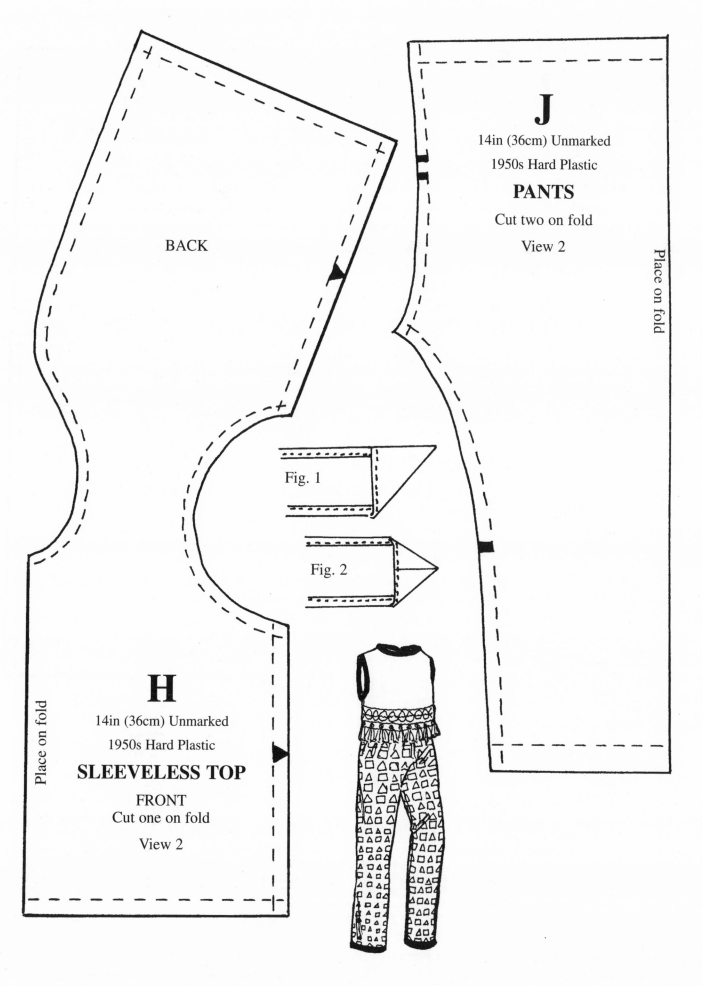

BACK

J

14in (36cm) Unmarked

1950s Hard Plastic

PANTS

Cut two on fold

View 2

Place on fold

Fig. 1

Fig. 2

Place on fold

H

14in (36cm) Unmarked

1950s Hard Plastic

SLEEVELESS TOP

FRONT
Cut one on fold

View 2

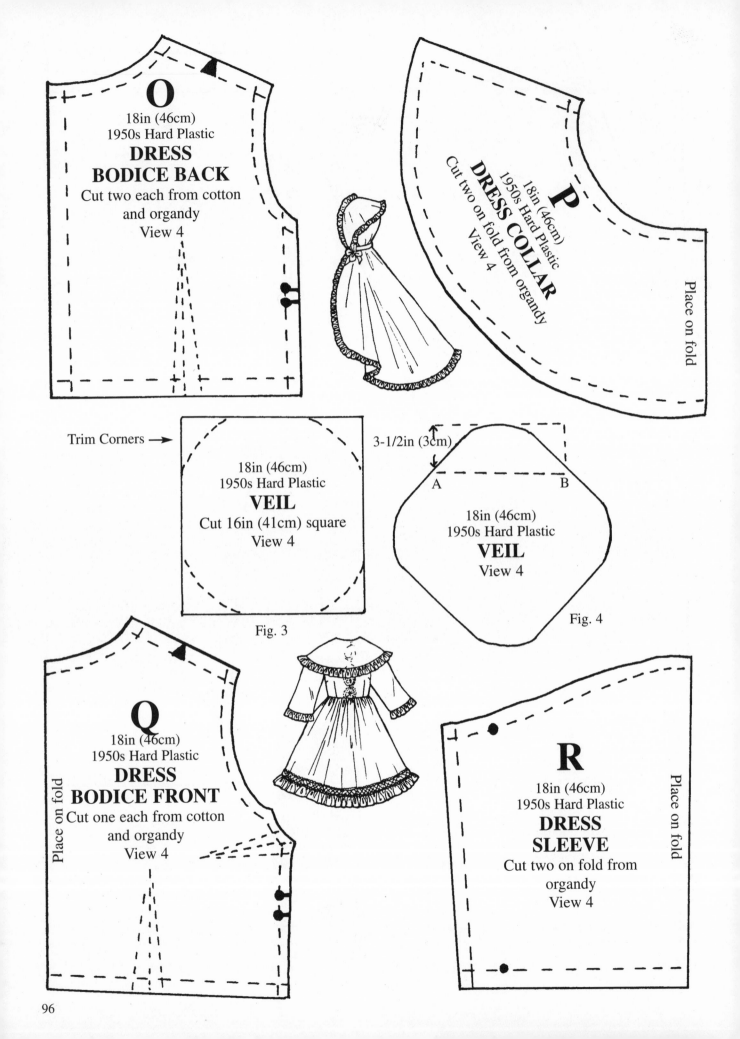

O

18in (46cm)
1950s Hard Plastic
**DRESS
BODICE BACK**
Cut two each from cotton
and organdy
View 4

P

18in (46cm)
1950s Hard Plastic
DRESS COLLAR
Cut two on fold from organdy
View 4

Place on fold

Trim Corners →

18in (46cm)
1950s Hard Plastic
VEIL
Cut 16in (41cm) square
View 4

Fig. 3

3-1/2in (3cm)

A   B

18in (46cm)
1950s Hard Plastic
VEIL
View 4

Fig. 4

Q

18in (46cm)
1950s Hard Plastic
**DRESS
BODICE FRONT**
Cut one each from cotton
and organdy
View 4

Place on fold

R

18in (46cm)
1950s Hard Plastic
**DRESS
SLEEVE**
Cut two on fold from
organdy
View 4

Place on fold

96

T

Bodice Back facing

Place on fold

Front

S

15in (38cm)
1950s *Mary Hartline*
DRESS BODICE
FRONT - Cut two on fold
BACK - Cut four
View 5

Gather between dots

U

15in (38cm)
1950s *Mary Hartline*
DRESS SLEEVE
Cut two on fold
View 5

Place on fold

Mary Hartline

Fig. 6

Fig. 7

Fig. 9

Mary

Fig. 5

Fig. 8

Wardrobe for 1950s

18in (46cm) - 21in (53cm)

Hard Plastic Dolls

18in (46cm) Ideal Miss Revlon

20in (51cm) Madame Alexander

Cissy

21in (53cm) Arranbee Nanette

View 1

View 2

View 3

View 5

View 6

View 4

WARDROBE FOR A GROUP OF 1950s 18in (46cm)-21in (53cm) HARD PLASTIC DOLLS
Various Manufacturers

This group of dolls represents girls somewhat older than the Dionnes and Shirley Temples, therefore the clothes are more sophisticated, though not quite adult in style.

The first four patterns, Views 1 through 4, are for a 21in (53cm) R&B (Arranbee), View 5 is for an 18in (46cm) Ideal *Miss Revlon*, and View 6 is for the 20in (51cm) Madame Alexander *Cissy*. Although there is a range of sizes represented, any of the patterns may be adjusted to fit any of the other dolls by means of reduction or enlargement with a photocopy machine.

View 1
21in (53cm)
ARRANBEE FORMAL
Pattern Pieces A, B, D, E

The light blue taffeta of this original dress has now faded to lavender. The net overdress is of very fine soft net. The sleeves of the taffeta dress and the skirt of the net overdress are trimmed with clear sequins centered with tiny turquoise beads. The bodice is accented with three of these decorations and fastened with two small snaps at back opening.

Bodice and Overbodice
Cut bodice A and B and sleeve D from taffeta.
Cut neckline facing as indicated by dotted lines on patterns.
Cut overbodice using E and B.

Sew side seams and shoulder seams of taffeta bodice and net overbodice separately. Sew in neckline facing on taffeta piece, clip seam, turn, press, and tack to bodice. Whipstitch neckline edge of net overbodice. Sew on sequins and beads as indicated in illustration. Assemble net and taffeta bodices with net on outside. Pin or tack at seams.

Lay sleeves out flat and apply sequins and beads. Run double row of gathering threads between dots as indicated on pattern. Sew underarm seams. Pull gathers carefully and evenly to fit sleeve openings and sew into bodice. Pull bottom edge gathers to fit doll's arm and finish edges of sleeves with self-bias band.

Skirt and Overskirt
Cut a piece of taffeta dress fabric measuring
12in (31cm) x 40in (101cm).
Cut a piece of very fine matching color net
14in (36cm) x 56in (101cm).
Make a narrow handkerchief hem on one long side of the taffeta piece (or for a nicer finish, hem this skirt after back seam is sewn). Set aside.

Whip a staystitch edge on one long side of the net piece; do not hem in usual way. Lay out flat and sew on sequins and beads.

Place both skirts together out flat with net on top, sequins and beads up. Pin two skirts together all around and baste together firmly along waistline. Run double gathering threads through both thicknesses. Pull gathers evenly and carefully to fit bodice.

Pin skirt to bodice, adjusting gathers if necessary. Firmly baste bodice and skirt together at waist, then machine stitch. Sew fancy silver braid and sequins over waist seam.

Finally, stitch back seam of skirt construction to 2in (5cm) below waist. Finish back opening and sew in fasteners.

View 2
21in (53cm)
ARRANBEE TOREADOR PANTS & TOP
Pattern Pieces B, E, G, R

Top - Cut all pattern pieces from knit fabric. Lengthen bodice pattern as desired for this top. Sleeve should be cut using narrow form of sleeve as indicated on pattern. (Wider sleeve may be gathered for use with a dress pattern.)

Pants - Cut pants from same or contrasting plain or patterned knit. Use Crissy pattern piece R; be sure to check fit. *Note:* Same pattern may also be used for panties, shorts, and clam diggers for this 21in (3cm) doll.

View 3
ARRANBEE COTTON EVERYDAY DRESS
Pattern Pieces F & H

This original dress is of red and blue print of tiny apples and leaves on white cotton piqué. Red bias tape trim is sewn between each of the three skirt tiers and at waist. Neckline and sleeves are bound with same tape. When binding neckline, leave enough tape at either end to form ties at back opening.

Bodice - Cut from cotton dress fabric pattern pieces F and H. Construct bodice following pattern, illustration, and description above.

Skirt - Cut from cotton dress fabric one piece each:
First tier, 2-1/2in (6cm) x 13in (33cm)
Second tier, 2-1/2in (6cm) x 18in (46cm)
Third tier, 2-1/2in (6cm) x 30in (76cm)

Run double row of gathering stitches along one long side of each piece, but do not pull.

Pull gathers on third tier to fit long edge of second tier. Pin and baste, then machine stitch together, with folded bias tape between pieces (see illustration).

Pull gathers on second tier to fit long edge of first tier. Pin together with bias trim, baste, machine stitch together.

Pull gathers on first tier to fit bottom edge of bodice. Pin together with bias trim, baste, machine stitch together.

Sew back skirt seam to within 2in (4cm) of waistline. Finish back opening; bias tape ties at top and one button at waistline. Hem skirt with very narrow machine-stitched hem.

Finish with two red buttons sewn to bodice center front as shown in illustration. Buttons should be proportioned to size of doll.

21in (53cm) ARRANBEE PUFFED SLEEVE DRESS
Pattern Pieces A, B, C, D

Bodice - Cut and assemble bodice as in View 1, eliminating overbodice. Assemble collar and sew to bodice, finishing with self-bias instead of facing as in View 1.

Finish bottoms of sleeves with a band cut from dress fabric. Measure around doll's arm and add 1-1/2in (4cm). Cut band to this length by 2in (5cm) wide.

Skirt - Cut a piece of dress fabric 10in (25cm) x 40in (101cm). Construct skirt as in View 1. Close back opening with two snap fasteners or two buttons and buttonholes.

Finish dress with gathered lace ruffle around sleeves, collar, and bottom of hem. (You may hem dress and apply lace ruffle in one step, if you wish.)

18in (46cm) *MISS REVLON* ORIGINAL DRESS
Pattern Pieces H through N

The pattern and description of this 18in (46cm) *Miss Revlon* dress with 3/8in (.9cm) alternating stripes of pink and white polished cotton was sent to me by a reader, which again points up the generosity of doll collectors.

A 20in (51cm) *Miss Revlon* wearing this dress in blue and white stripes was the cover girl for *Doll Reader*® magazine's October 1993 issue. The fashionable *Miss Revlon* had enough outfits to make a book of patterns for her alone. This basic dress was made with a red velvet bodice and white skirt, also with slightly longer sleeves and a huge round collar, and with full-length sleeves and a Peter Pan collar. Many of her outfits may be created by using the alternatives suggested here.

Bodice - Cut with the stripes horizontal and line with fine cotton. Before sewing lining and bodice together, construct the bow tab.

For tab, cut pattern piece M so stripes run vertically. With right sides together, stitch a seam from A to B, trim seam, turn and press. Center open end of tab on bodice front and baste. Then baste bodice and lining together.

For bow, cut pattern piece N with stripes running vertically. With right sides together, sew a narrow seam leaving room to turn. Clip seams especially at points, turn, press and close opening. Lift tab and center the bow under it, bunch center to form bow (fig. 1), and sew securely to bodice. Pull tab down over bow and secure with a couple of tiny stitches. Cover stitches with pronged rhinestone stud. Complete bodice.

Skirt - Cut a piece of dress fabric 7in (18cm) x 28in (71cm) with stripes running vertically. Run double gathering threads on one long side to within 3/4in (2cm) of ends. Pull gathers to fit completed bodice and tie off firmly. Sew back seam to within 2in (5cm) of waistline. Seam allowance on back should match back facing width. Turn up a 1-1/2in (4cm) hem. Sew three snaps to close bodice back.

Half-slip - The original half-slip is made of stiff white nylon. To hem, turn under 1/8in (.31cm) and topstitch over pink ricrac. Narrow elastic is used at the waist and a ruffle of fine white nylon net adds additional "pouf" to the garment. For ruffle, cut a piece of net 2-1/2in (6cm) x 36in (91cm). Bind one long edge with narrow pink bias tape. Gather remaining long edge to fit at dash line on pattern.

Note: Patterns for *Miss Revlon "Queen of Diamonds,"* as well as numerous patterns for *Little Miss Revlon*, may be found in the first volume of this work, pp. 190-193.

20in (51cm) MADAME ALEXANDER *CISSY* ORIGINAL OUTFIT
Pattern Pieces O through Y

This tall, leggy doll wears tight "toreador" pants of medium blue ribbed cotton with attached sun top. Under this is a light blue tie blouse of lightweight rayon which fastens with three front snaps. Completing the outfit is a light pink jacket of heavy cotton with an attached double-buttoned belt which has a unique fastener. One end of the belt slips through large buttonholed slash in the opposite end and both ends button to complete the closure. She also wears black high-heeled sandals and sheer seamed hose.

Blouse - Although this blouse closes in front with hidden snaps, small, attractive buttons may be sewn on the outside over the snaps. Sew shoulder seams and turn front facings right sides together with 1/8in (.31cm) turned under for smooth edge, press. Set aside.

Sleeves are cuffed by turning the fabric on the fold indicated by the dot-dash lines. Lay sleeve out flat and turn up and press a 1/8in (.31cm) hem to the outside. Then turn up again to the outside on the second dot-dash line and topstitch for completed cuff. Run double gathering threads from dot to dot on sleeve, but do not pull. Set aside.

For tie, cut a piece of blouse fabric measuring 22in (56cm) x 1-1/2in (4cm). With right sides together, seam all around, making square ends. Leave a centered opening for turning equal to measurement of dot to dot on neckline. (This section of tie forms the narrow stand-up collar.) Clip seam, turn, press, and attach to neckline.

Pull gathers in sleeves to fit armholes, pin, and baste in place. Sew sleeve and side seams as one, stitch front darts, make a narrow bottom hem. Sew snaps in place.

For a second outfit, make a typical '50s full skirt to be worn with this blouse. Use a print with a touch of blue to pick up the color of the blouse. Look through patterns for other '50s dolls or make a swing skirt from the *Cissy* pattern in the first volume of this work.

Jacket - Style often equates with complicated construction as is somewhat the case with this jacket. Taken step by step, however, there should be little problem.

First sew the shoulder seams and lay the piece out flat. Turn under 1/8in (.31cm) on each sleeve and press. Next turn under the dot-dash line marked 1 and topstitch on the machine. (This will be on the wrong side of fabric.) Finally, on dot-dash line marked 2, turn up a cuff to the outside and press.

Pin and baste collar pieces together, then seam. Clip seams, especially on curves. Turn and press. Topstitch along entire outer edge, using small stitches and taking care not to stretch fabric. Attach to jacket, centering at back neckline.

Sew side seams of jacket starting at cuff to ensure that cuff seams are even. Press and turn back collar at waistline just far enough that seam doesn't show on front. Tack in place. Run double gathering threads from dot to dot around bottom of jacket, pull gathers to fit belt. Centering belt at back, attach belt to waist, then run a topstitch all around belt. Put garment on doll and mark belt for 2 buttonholes and belt slash. Work these three openings using narrow buttonhole stitch. Sew on buttons (on original garment the buttons are medium blue).

Pants and bodice - Construction of the pants is simple. Note that back is left open to dot on back seam line. With a piece of pant fabric, cut a bias strip for facing. Topstitch the finished edge on right-hand side of opening and set aside.

Bodice is lined with same fabric. For straps, cut two pieces of pants fabric measuring 5in (13cm) x 3/4in (2cm). Turn back 1/8in (.31cm) on each long side and press. Fold piece in half lengthwise, pin, press, and baste. Topstitch along full length. Construct two bodices, pattern pieces Q, S, T. Pin straps in place on one, with straps on right side of fabric. Pin and baste the two bodice constructions with right sides together, then seam. Clip seams as needed, turn and press. Attach to pants, sew two snaps at bodice back opening.

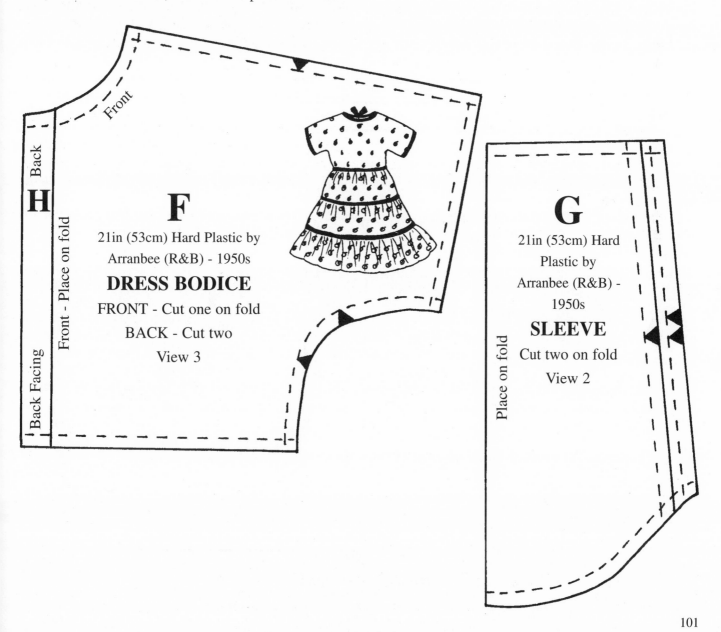

H
Back

Back Facing

Front - Place on fold

F

Front

21in (53cm) Hard Plastic by Arranbee (R&B) - 1950s

DRESS BODICE

FRONT - Cut one on fold

BACK - Cut two

View 3

G

Place on fold

21in (53cm) Hard Plastic by Arranbee (R&B) - 1950s

SLEEVE

Cut two on fold

View 2

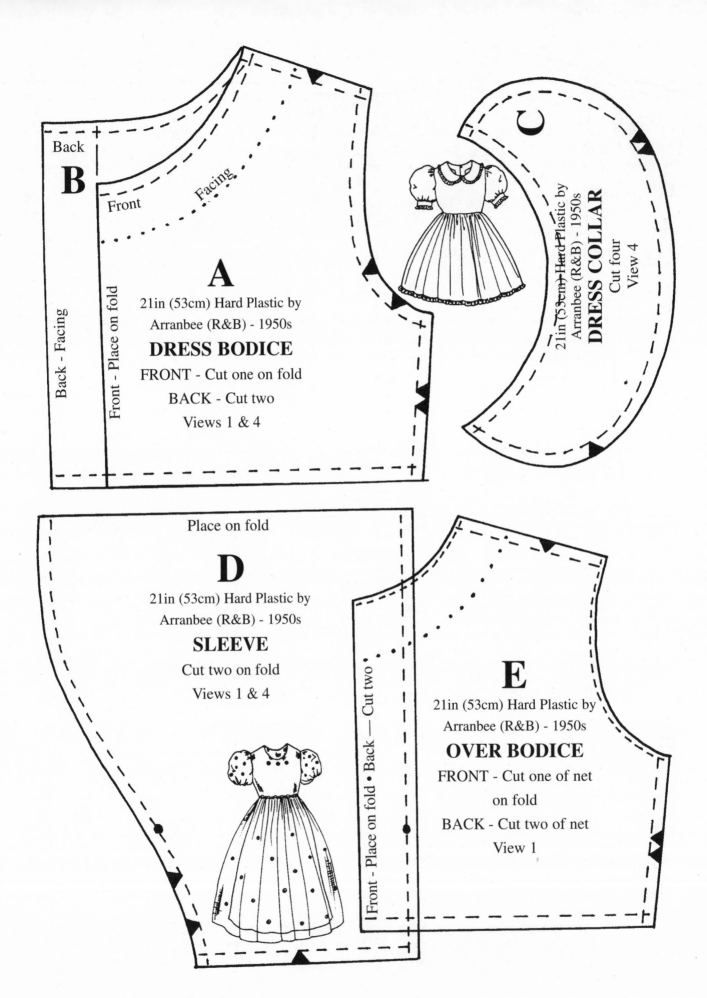

B

Back

Front

Facing

Back - Facing

Front - Place on fold

A

21in (53cm) Hard Plastic by
Arranbee (R&B) - 1950s

DRESS BODICE

FRONT - Cut one on fold

BACK - Cut two

Views 1 & 4

C

21in (53cm) Hard Plastic by
Arranbee (R&B) - 1950s

DRESS COLLAR

Cut four

View 4

Place on fold

D

21in (53cm) Hard Plastic by
Arranbee (R&B) - 1950s

SLEEVE

Cut two on fold

Views 1 & 4

Front - Place on fold • Back — Cut two

E

21in (53cm) Hard Plastic by
Arranbee (R&B) - 1950s

OVER BODICE

FRONT - Cut one of net
on fold

BACK - Cut two of net

View 1

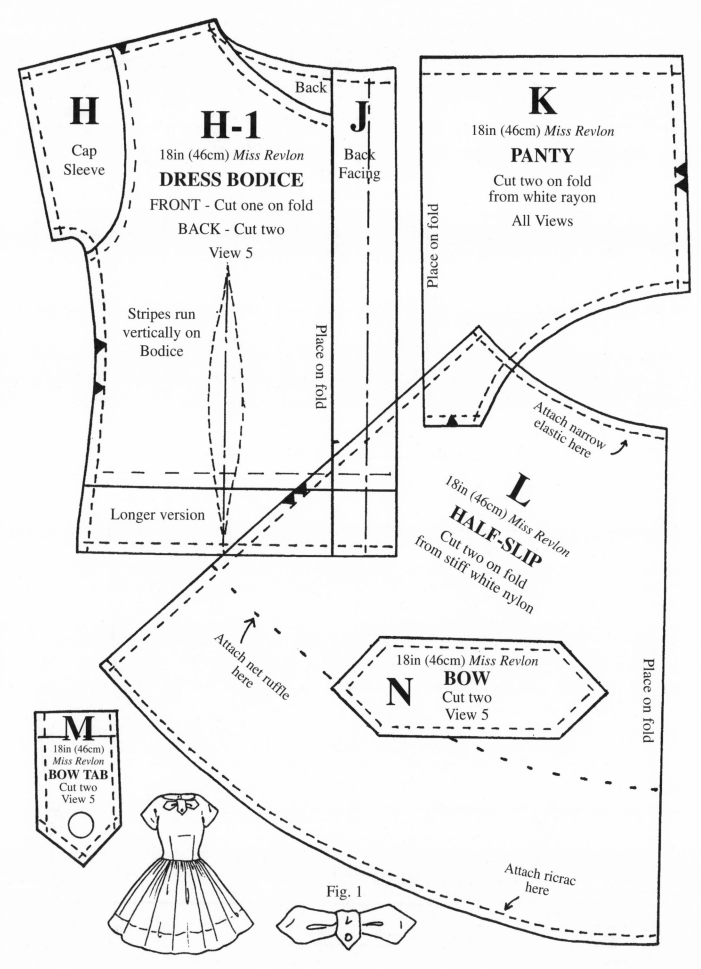

H

Cap
Sleeve

H-1

18in (46cm) *Miss Revlon*

DRESS BODICE

FRONT - Cut one on fold

BACK - Cut two

View 5

Stripes run
vertically on
Bodice

Longer version

Back

J

Back
Facing

Place on fold

K

18in (46cm) *Miss Revlon*

PANTY

Cut two on fold
from white rayon

All Views

Place on fold

Attach narrow
elastic here

L

18in (46cm) *Miss Revlon*

HALF-SLIP

Cut two on fold
from stiff white nylon

Attach net ruffle
here

N

18in (46cm) *Miss Revlon*

BOW
Cut two
View 5

Place on fold

M

18in (46cm)
Miss Revlon

BOW TAB
Cut two
View 5

Fig. 1

Attach ricrac
here

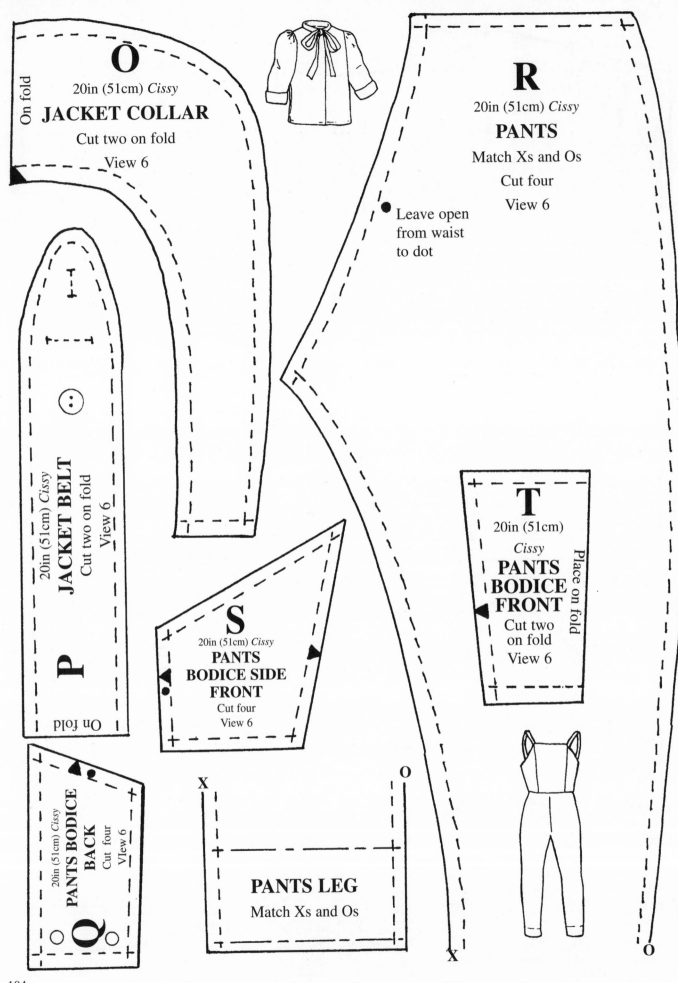

O

On fold

20in (51cm) *Cissy*

JACKET COLLAR

Cut two on fold

View 6

R

20in (51cm) *Cissy*

PANTS

Match Xs and Os

Cut four

View 6

● Leave open
from waist
to dot

P

20in (51cm) *Cissy*

JACKET BELT

Cut two on fold

View 6

On fold

S

20in (51cm) *Cissy*

**PANTS
BODICE SIDE
FRONT**

Cut four

View 6

T

20in (51cm)

Cissy

**PANTS
BODICE
FRONT**

Cut two
on fold

View 6

Place on fold

Q

20in (51cm) *Cissy*

**PANTS BODICE
BACK**

Cut four

View 6

X

PANTS LEG

Match Xs and Os

O

X

O

104

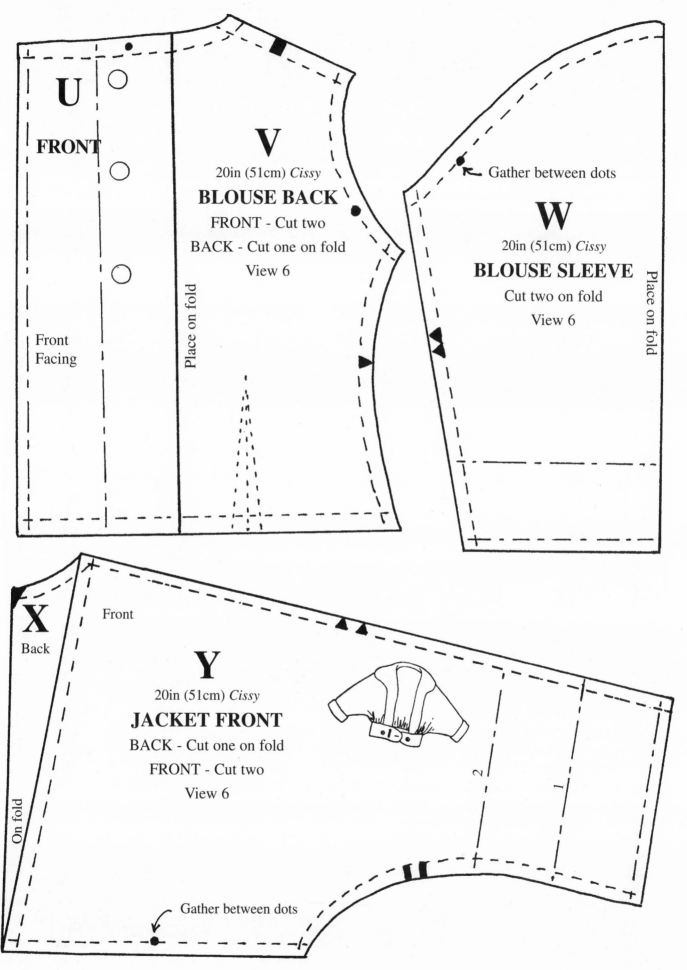

U

FRONT

FRONT

Front Facing

V

20in (51cm) *Cissy*

BLOUSE BACK

FRONT - Cut two

BACK - Cut one on fold

View 6

Place on fold

W

Gather between dots

20in (51cm) *Cissy*

BLOUSE SLEEVE

Cut two on fold

View 6

Place on fold

X

Front

Back

On fold

Y

20in (51cm) *Cissy*

JACKET FRONT

BACK - Cut one on fold

FRONT - Cut two

View 6

2

1

Gather between dots

MADAME ALEXANDER'S FASHIONS for DOLLS

#133. Polished pique dress trimmed with tiny buttons and a belt. White and assorted soft colors.

#106. Polished cotton pinafore trimmed with Rick-Rack. Red only. Looks very gay with plain dress.

#107. Two piece bra-top bathing suit of gay sunshine colors in asst. prints. Lace trimmed. Just the thing for an afternoon at the wading pool or beach.

#132. Housecoat of embossed rayon satin trimmed with Swiss embroidery. Pink or White.

#105. Nightie of softest rayon tricot with lace yoke. Pink only.

#136. Basic dress of taffeta goes well with a number of things. Simply styled. Button trim and a belt.
Red
White
Blue and White check
Red and White check

#134. White organdie pinafore.

#137. Perennial favorite of dolls and little girls. Dress of flowered or checked cotton in asst. colors. White organdie collar, cuffs and sash.

#218. Imported organdie dress trimmed with tucks and val lace. Satin ribbon sash. Very cool for a hot afternoon.

Asst. pastel shades.

#138D. Every well dressed doll needs a slacks outfit. Slacks of denim in asst colors. Shirt of contrasting checked cotton.

#139. Pure wool cardigan in Jelly Bean colors.

#211. What could be sweeter than this rain coat and hat of waterproof taffeta! Looks very smart over summer dresses.

Red and White

Green and White

Blue and White

#217. Bolero dress of finest polished cotton with self dot. White blouse top.

Capri Blue

Camellia Pink

Annabelle

This appealing little girl doll was inspired by Kate Smith's "Stories of Annabelle".

She is made of unbreakable plastic. She is fully jointed for more play value. She has a lovely woven wig which you can wash, comb and curl, and is charmingly dressed. She has her own beauty kit.

Select additional clothes for Annabelle or any of Madame Alexander's girl dolls from this booklet.

#216. Three piece playsuit of cotton quilteen. Shirt, shorts and flare skirt.

Aqua or Bittersweet.

#274. Flannel coat with velvet Beret.

Navy lined white taffeta.

Gray lined red taffeta.

Especially smart worn with dress #136.

#271. Really elegant outfit. Red Taffeta redingote over sleeveless dress of white taffeta. Rhinestone buttons. Very dressy and most becoming to your doll. Red only.

#275. A favorite with all the dolls. Swing skirt of beautiful flowered cotton trimmed with rhinestones to wear with the white lace trimmed organdie blouse.

Skirts—asst. prints

Blouse—White

#138T. For the doll who prefers dressier slacks for casual wear choose a clan Tartan with white shirt. Red predominating.

#214. Dotted Swiss suspender dress. Simple and in good taste. Trimmed with Swiss embroidery. White organdie blouse.

Copen with red dots

Sky blue with pink dots

#103. Sweet little nightie of cotton, either plain white or printed, trimmed with beading and ribbon.

#131. Practical bath robe of fine terry cloth with rayon satin collar and pocket. Asst. pastel shades.

#423. What could be newer than a poodle cloth coat with matching beret for your doll! Every well-dressed doll should own one. Bittersweet or Sky Blue. Lined with taffeta.

Annabelle and her costumes were available in three sizes: 15in (38cm), 18in (46cm), and 23in (58cm). This catalog is dated 1952.

#212. Plaid gingham. Pleated skirt. White pique shirt top, trimmed with tiny buttons.

#273. Ruffles, edged with val lace trim this lovely party dress of imported organdie. Asst. pastel shades.

#272. Three-tier skirt of lace trimmed organdie with low neck blouse makes this sweet dress. Any doll would love to have it. Asst. pastel shades.

#541. To have a bridal outfit is every doll's secret hope. Four piece bridal outfit complete with bouquet. White satin gown, lace edged starched net veil. Slip and panties. White only.

#213. Jumper dress of fine pique. Can be worn with or without blouse.

Lilac pique dress

Yellow organdie blouse

21in (53cm)
Whimsies
by American Character Doll Co.
1960

ORIGINAL COSTUME FOR 21in (53cm) WHIMSIES
by American Doll & Toy Corporation (American Character) 1960

These big, heavy, stuffed-vinyl dolls are so goofy looking they are adorable, and the costumes are fun to sew. Perhaps because they were considered novelty dolls, the clothing was not of high quality. I have given little or no directions since the simple designs require a minimum of sewing skills. A bonus - because of their size and the simplicity of the designs - the task goes quickly.

View 1 **BESSIE THE BASHFUL BRIDE** Pattern Pieces G, J, Q

For dress, use white cotton or satin, trim with lace ruffles. Cut skirt desired length (full length or just below knees) plus a 1in (3cm) hem by 36in (91cm). Construct gathered skirt and attach to bottom edge of bodice G. Make a sash by cutting a piece of dress fabric 4in (10cm) x 30in (76cm). Hem all around with handkerchief hem.

For veil, cut a circle of net 24in (61cm) in diameter. Following diagram, attach veil to circle of silk flowers.

For sandals, use white ties for this bride. Instructions for making sandals are given at end of this section.

View 2 **FREDDIE THE FRIAR** Pattern Pieces M, X, Q

Freddie's hooded robe was made of light brown wool felt tied at the waist with heavy cord from which hung a 1-1/2in (5cm) brass bell. The robe is open 7in (18cm) down the front. He also wore light brown cotton underpants and brown sandals. Most of the other dolls in the series also wore sandals.

View 3 **TILLIE THE TALKER** Pattern Pieces K, L, Q

Tillie wears red cotton pedal pushers. Her top is red and white diamond print flannel, bound with white bias tape.

View 4 **FANNY ANGEL** Pattern Pieces E, K, Q

White cotton or even a shiny or sheer white fabric may be used. Use pattern piece K; lay out on fabric and extend side seams to length desired (short, medium, full-length). Make a belt from same fabric: Cut a piece 2in (5cm) wide by 36in (91cm) long, fold, seam, turn.

Make halo of gilt ribbon stiffened with fine wire or pipe cleaner, or check the craft shops for other ideas.

Wings may be constructed in several ways. One method is to make a coated wire frame following the pattern outline, then glue on a paper or sheer fabric covering. For sheer whimsy (for a Whimsie angel - sorry) you may want to cut four pieces from sheer fabric, pad lightly between with a thin layer of batting, whip edges, then lightly quilt the entire wing. Single thicknesses of white plastic (bleach bottle, etc.) would also work. Use your imagination for this one. Not recommended, but wings are often available in craft shops.

Views 5, 6, & 7 **LENA THE CLEANER** Pattern Pieces L, Y, Z, A2, B2, Q

Lena's apron pockets contained, according to my catalog illustrations, a knife, fork, and spoon and something that looks like a box of cereal. Inexplicably, she wore a tag that read, "Lena the Cleaner's frisky and bright. She looks pretty good for a gal that cleans day and night." This rhyme would seem to indicate she should be carrying cleaning tools. Perhaps she was so busy she had to carry a snack in her apron - no time for lunch.

The apron is white cotton bound in red bias and trimmed with red ricrac. Bias binding on neckline extends on both sides at back to form ties. Three snap fasteners are evenly spaced down the back of the apron. Pockets are shown with dotted lines.

Lena's undersuit is made of blue and white striped cotton bound with white bias tape. Note the stripes run horizontally on the top and vertically on the pants. Leave back seam of pants open to 4in (10cm) below waist. Use the long sleeve for this garment.

View 8 **ZACK THE SACK** Pattern Pieces A, B

Zack's original nightshirt and nightcap were made of red and white wide-striped flannel. Follow cutting directions on pattern pieces. Finish robe with shirttail hem; bind sleeves and neck opening with bias tape. Trim tip of nightcap with a red pompon.

View 9 **WHEELER THE DEALER** Pattern Pieces H, O, U, V, W, A2, C2

Wheeler wears a white shirt, black cotton slacks, a debonair vest and black string tie with a "gold" watch hanging on a short "gold" chain from his vest pocket.

Use A2 bodice pattern cut from black felt, velour, or

satin, Cut along dotted armhole. Extend front to allow closing with buttons and buttonholes; cut back on fold. Cut shoes from black felt shoes. Make eyeshade from a green plastic two-litre soft drink bottle. Attach black elastic at one corner, measure around head, pulling on the elastic; allow 1in (3cm) for tying off.

View 10 **RAGGIE** Pattern Piece A2	

Raggie's character is defined by her pigtail hairstyle, her headscarf and apron, and by her corncob pipe. Construct her plain cotton dress using A2 bodice with long sleeves, attached to a gathered skirt.

For scarf, cut an 18in (46cm) square of pattern paper. Draw a line from one corner to the opposite corner to make pattern for triangular scarf. Cut from plaid fabric. Make a narrow hanky hem all around.

Make the apron of same fabric, by cutting an 8in (20cm) x 12in (31cm) rectangle, gathering it on one long edge and hanky hemming other three sides. For belt, cut a piece of plaid fabric 3in (8cm) x 24in (61cm); sew to apron.

View 11 **MISS TAKE** Pattern Piece D	

Cut one each on fold and construct the classic swimsuit. Make a 3in (8cm) wide award ribbon 12in (31cm) long.

Using fabric paint or ball-point pen, write Miss Take on ribbon. Attach ribbon from right shoulder to left hip of suit.

View 12 **SIMON THE GRADUATE** Pattern Pieces O, P, R, S, T, U, V, W, A2	

Simon's robe is of black velour, open in front with two snap fasteners. His mortar board is of black felt with a gold tassel on top and a black elastic band under his chin to hold it on his head. His slacks are black cotton, and his shirt is white cotton with a collar of white velour. *Please note:* When cutting shirt (A2), extend length to allow for tucking into slacks.

Simon's shoes are of black felt bound all around with black bias tape.

View 13 **SUSIE SNOOZER** Pattern Pieces F, J	

Cut the full-length nightgown with long sleeves from cozy rosebud-sprigged flannel. Make skirt of gown by cutting a rectangle measuring 12in (31cm) by 30in (76cm); gather along one long side; hem other long side. Attach to bodice F. Trim neckline with narrow gathered cotton eyelet ruffle.

Gather sleeve J between dots for puffed sleeve; add gathered eyelet edge. Because she is so sleepy, *Susie* is barefoot and ready for bed.

View 14 **POLLY THE LOLLY** Pattern Pieces A2, Q	

Polly is an enigma. In one of my catalogs she is called *Dixie the Pixie*; outfit and hairstyle are the same and both illustrations show the doll holding a "lollipop," which makes me think *Polly the Lolly* is actually the correct name, that there has been a mistake made in the other catalog. Since I have brochures from both 1960 and 1961, it is possible the name was changed from one year to the next. For now we will call her "*Polly*."

Polly's hairstyle is very short and curly except for her surprised-looking twin pigtails which are shooting straight up from her head. She wears a pastel cotton dress trimmed with white ricrac, and the ubiquitous sandals on her feet.

Cut bodice A2 with the curved sleeve and sew to a short gathered skirt. Trim with ricrac as indicated in the illustration, View 14.

View 15 **ZERO THE FOOTBALL PLAYER** Pattern Pieces C, A2, V, W	

Zero's football pants are of a canvas-like cotton. Top of pants are faced, using pants pattern, cutting across dotted lines.

His jersey is cotton knit or sweatshirt fabric using long sleeves of the pattern. A felt letter of your choice may be appliquéd to the front.

Striped socks may be constructed from an old pair of children's or adult's socks, or a new pair in appropriate size may be found at a nearby discount store. Shoes are constructed as for Wheeler and Simon.

For a helmet, find a plastic bottle or jug that will fit over the doll's head. Cut it off to the length of measurement from top of doll's head to shoulder. Place over doll's head and draw with a marker around the face area, then curve around to the sides and across back of head at what would be base of skull. Trim off excess and use this plastic piece as your base for applying imitation leather or felt to build a helmet. If you are acquainted with the art of papier mache, you could build a good helmet of the material over the plastic bottle. When papier maché has dried, the plastic is pulled out and the helmet painted as desired.

Add a school pennant of felt with felt letters attached to a dowel for a complete football picture.

View 16 **SAMSON THE STRONGMAN** Pattern Piece D	Using swimsuit pattern, cut raggedly across the body in front and use the pattern line in back.	Run strap of same fabric across one shoulder to back. The rougher, the better. No shoes, of course.
Not Shown **HEDDA GET BEDDA**	*Hedda* gets Bedda tucked in her bed in her warm flannel nightie. See Susie the Snoozie for *Hedda*'s night-	gown. A fake plastic thermometer (no real ones, please), fake medicine, and a spoon complete this little invalid's outfit. And perhaps some fuzzy slippers?
Not Shown **LITTLE GIRL DEVIL** Pattern Pieces K, U	The name of this little girl has escaped me; strangely, she is not named in the brochures I have. She	wears a short red cotton top (K) with a white collar (U). Red leotards and a "pitchfork" complete her outfit.

MAKING THE SANDAL
Pattern Piece Q

Cut sandals (Q) from leather or imitation leather, or glue two or three layers of cardboard together. Place a weight on cardboard until completely dry. When dry, cut sole and punch holes according to pattern. Paint sole with acrylic artist paints.

Ties are a pair of 24in (61cm) shoestrings; you may choose white, brown, black, or a color to match the costume.

Stringing the sandals: Run shoestring from top of sole to underside through one of the holes at A, then back to top through other hole. Pull shoestring up so both sides are equal. Take a string back on each side to the B hole nearest the toes, run down through first hole and back up through second hole. Repeat with second string.

Place doll's foot in sandal, draw strings up around heel to back and cross. Bring forward around ankle and tie.

Illustrations from American Character brochures packaged with *Whimsie* dolls in 1960 and 1961.

From *More Twentieth Century Dolls*, Athena, p. 575.

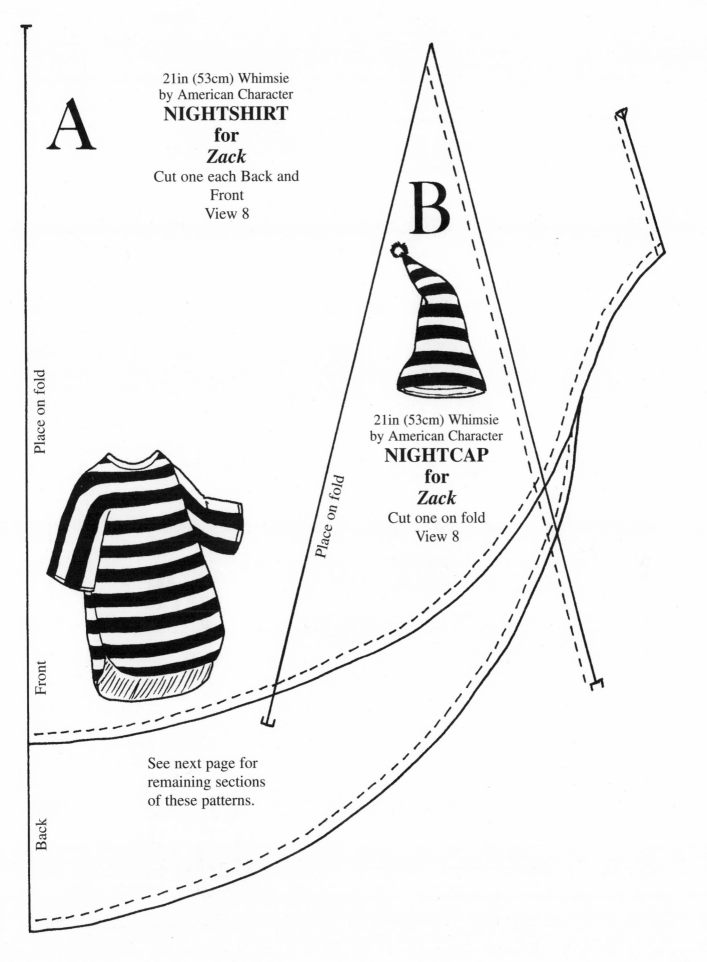

A

21in (53cm) Whimsie
by American Character
NIGHTSHIRT
for
Zack
Cut one each Back and
Front
View 8

Place on fold

Front

Back

See next page for
remaining sections
of these patterns.

B

21in (53cm) Whimsie
by American Character
NIGHTCAP
for
Zack
Cut one on fold
View 8

Place on fold

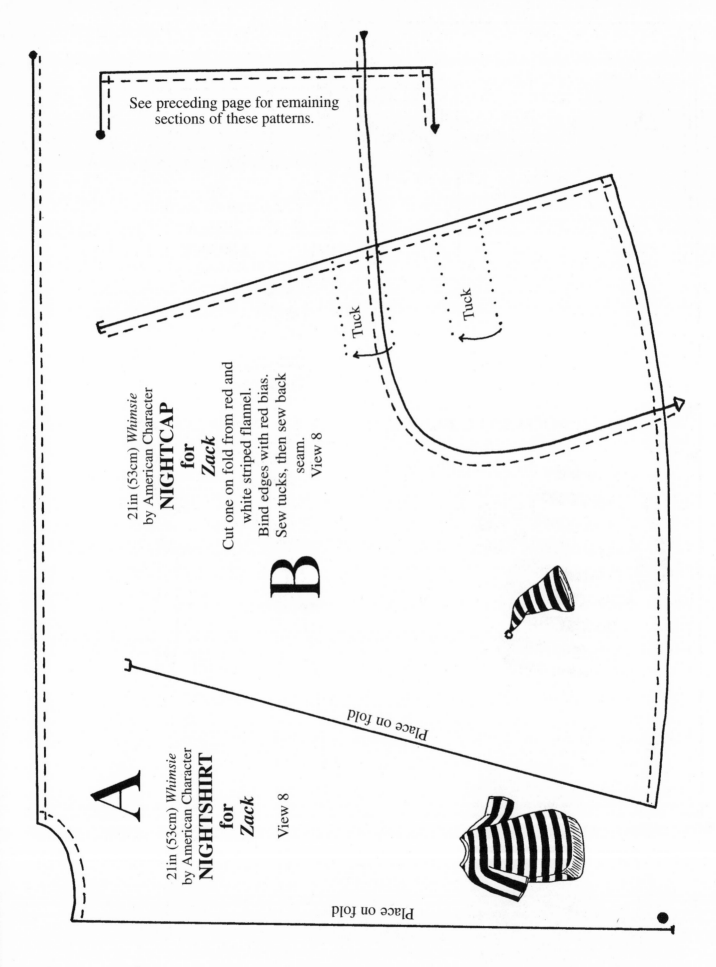

See preceding page for remaining sections of these patterns.

B

21in (53cm) *Whimsie*
by American Character
NIGHTCAP
for
Zack

Cut one on fold from red and
white striped flannel.
Bind edges with red bias.
Sew tucks, then sew back
seam.
View 8

Tuck

Tuck

A

21in (53cm) *Whimsie*
by American Character
NIGHTSHIRT
for
Zack

View 8

Place on fold

Place on fold

114

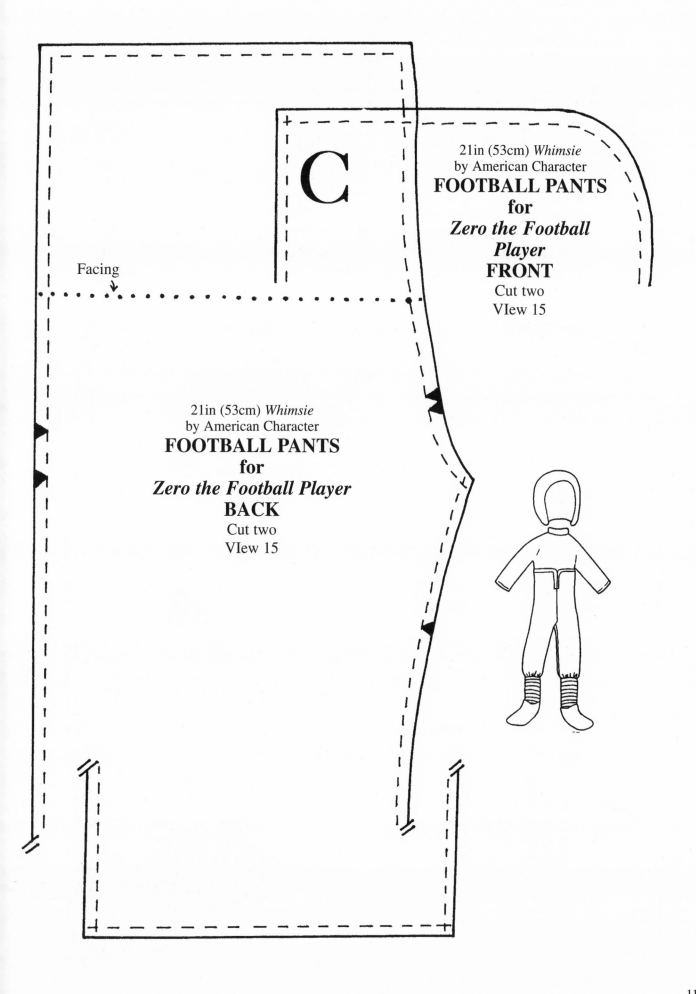

C

Facing

21in (53cm) *Whimsie*
by American Character
FOOTBALL PANTS
for
Zero the Football
Player
FRONT
Cut two
VIew 15

21in (53cm) *Whimsie*
by American Character
FOOTBALL PANTS
for
Zero the Football Player
BACK
Cut two
VIew 15

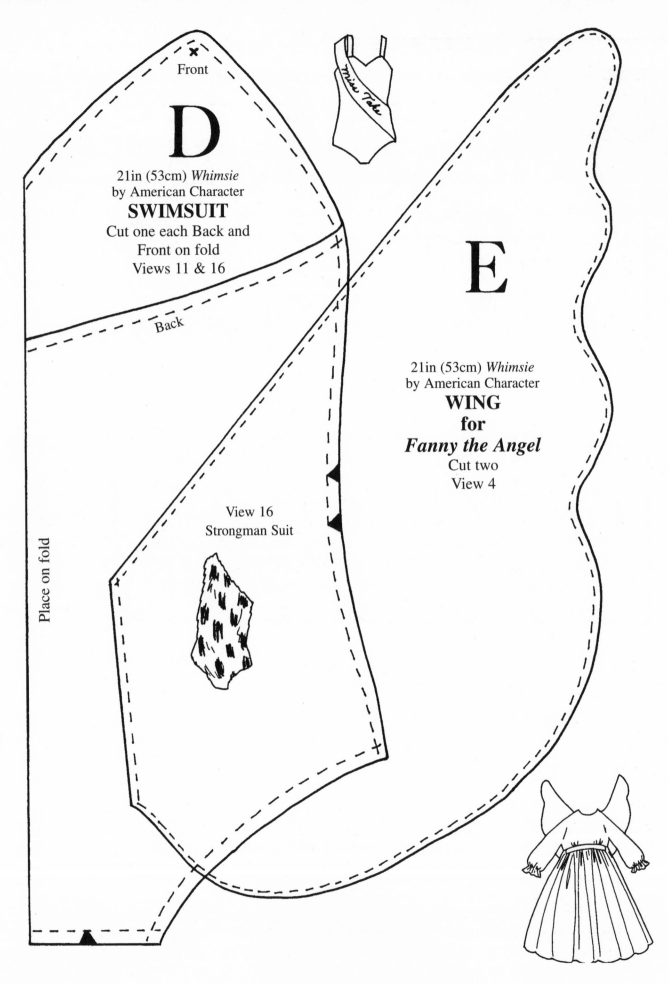

Front

D

21in (53cm) *Whimsie*
by American Character
SWIMSUIT
Cut one each Back and
Front on fold
Views 11 & 16

Back

Place on fold

E

21in (53cm) *Whimsie*
by American Character
WING
for
Fanny the Angel
Cut two
View 4

View 16
Strongman Suit

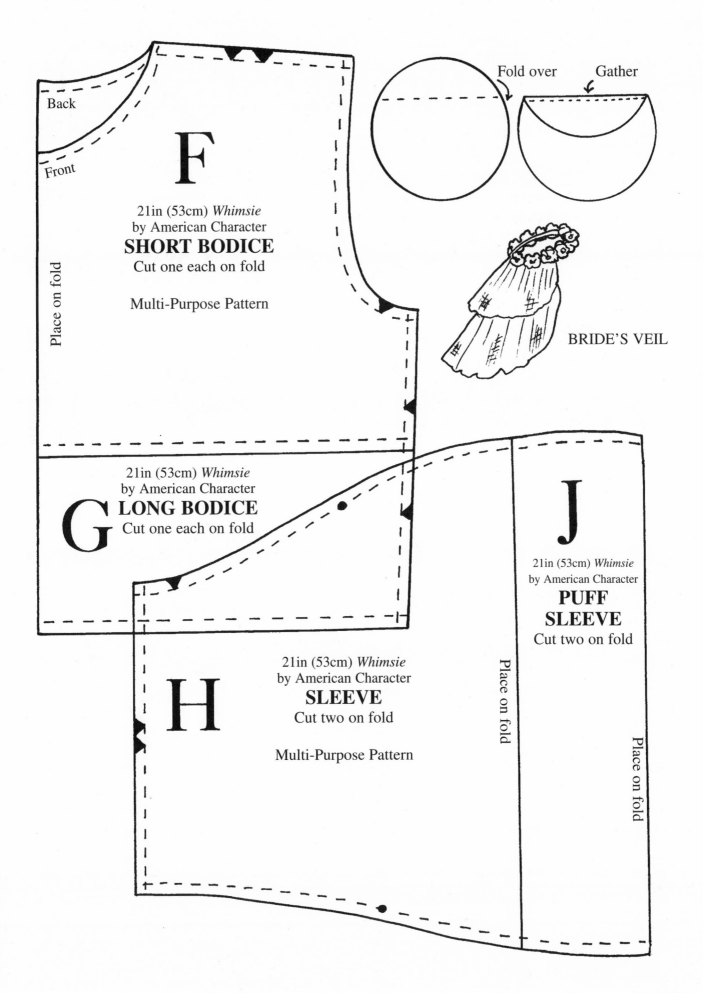

Back

Front

Place on fold

F

21in (53cm) *Whimsie*
by American Character
SHORT BODICE
Cut one each on fold

Multi-Purpose Pattern

Fold over   Gather

BRIDE'S VEIL

21in (53cm) *Whimsie*
by American Character
G LONG BODICE
Cut one each on fold

J

21in (53cm) *Whimsie*
by American Character
**PUFF
SLEEVE**
Cut two on fold

Place on fold

Place on fold

H

21in (53cm) *Whimsie*
by American Character
SLEEVE
Cut two on fold

Multi-Purpose Pattern

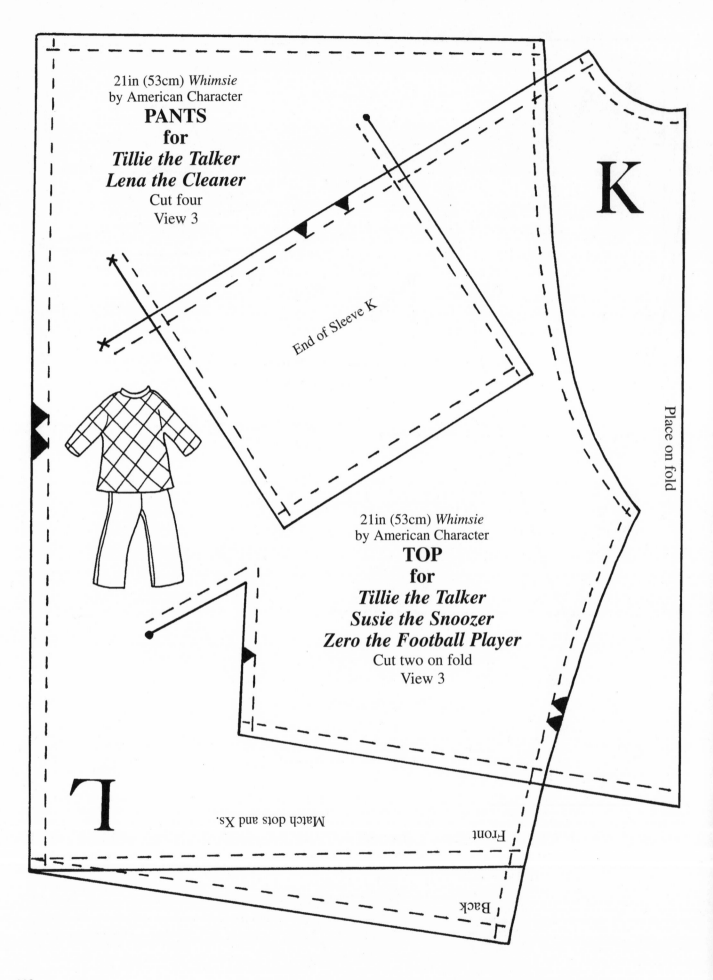

K

21in (53cm) *Whimsie*
by American Character
PANTS
for
Tillie the Talker
Lena the Cleaner
Cut four
View 3

End of Sleeve K

Place on fold

21in (53cm) *Whimsie*
by American Character
TOP
for
Tillie the Talker
Susie the Snoozer
Zero the Football Player
Cut two on fold
View 3

L

Match dots and Xs.

Front

Back

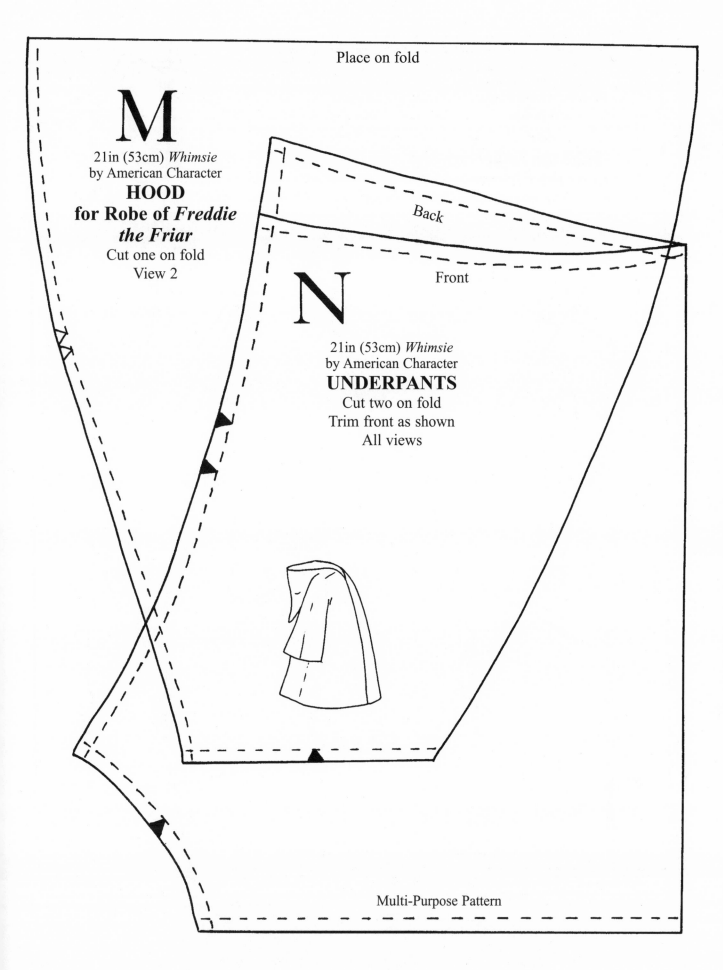

Place on fold

M

21in (53cm) *Whimsie*
by American Character
**HOOD
for Robe of *Freddie
the Friar***
Cut one on fold
View 2

Back

Front

N

21in (53cm) *Whimsie*
by American Character
UNDERPANTS
Cut two on fold
Trim front as shown
All views

Multi-Purpose Pattern

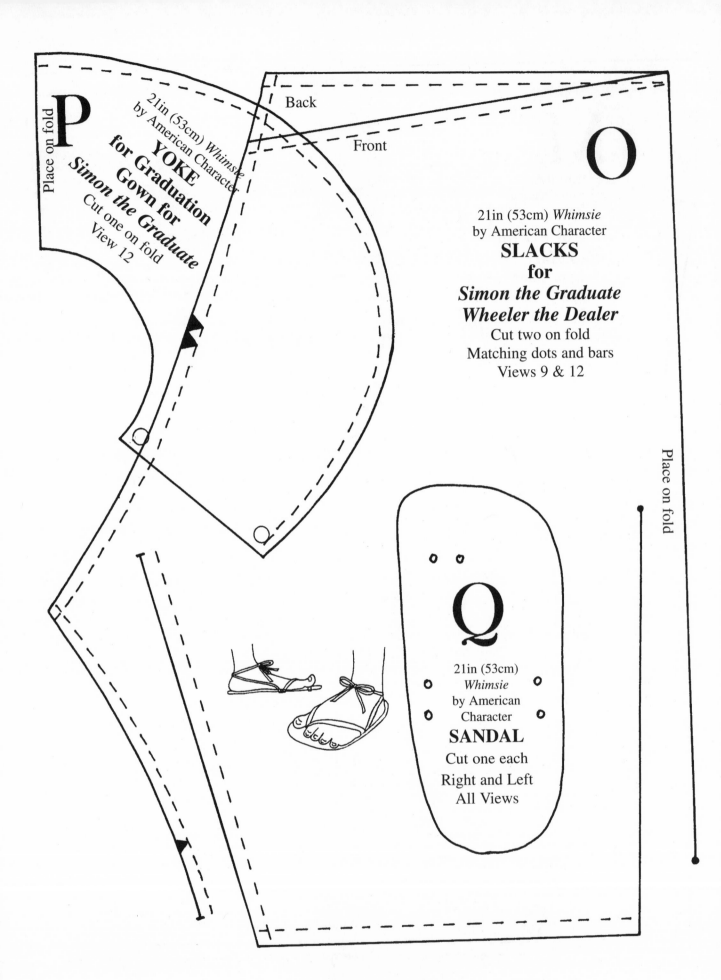

P

Place on fold

21in (53cm) *Whimsie*
by American Character
YOKE
for Graduation
Gown for
Simon the Graduate
Cut one on fold
View 12

Back

Front

O

21in (53cm) *Whimsie*
by American Character
SLACKS
for
Simon the Graduate
Wheeler the Dealer
Cut two on fold
Matching dots and bars
Views 9 & 12

Place on fold

Q

21in (53cm)
Whimsie
by American
Character
SANDAL
Cut one each
Right and Left
All Views

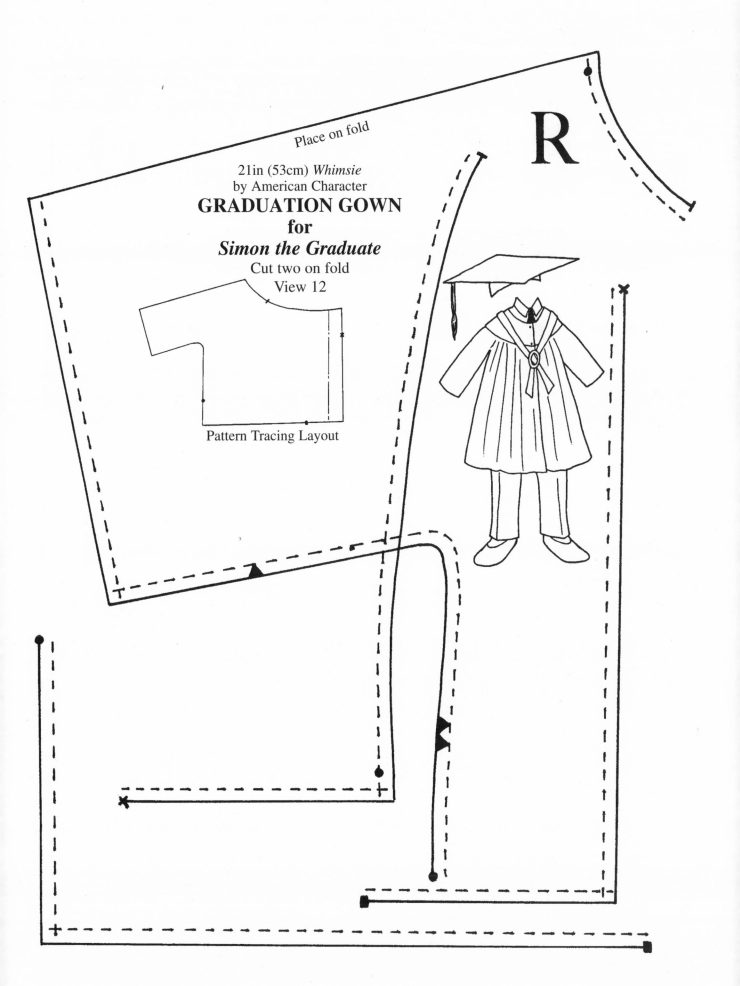

Place on fold

21in (53cm) *Whimsie*
by American Character
GRADUATION GOWN
for
Simon the Graduate
Cut two on fold
View 12

Pattern Tracing Layout

R

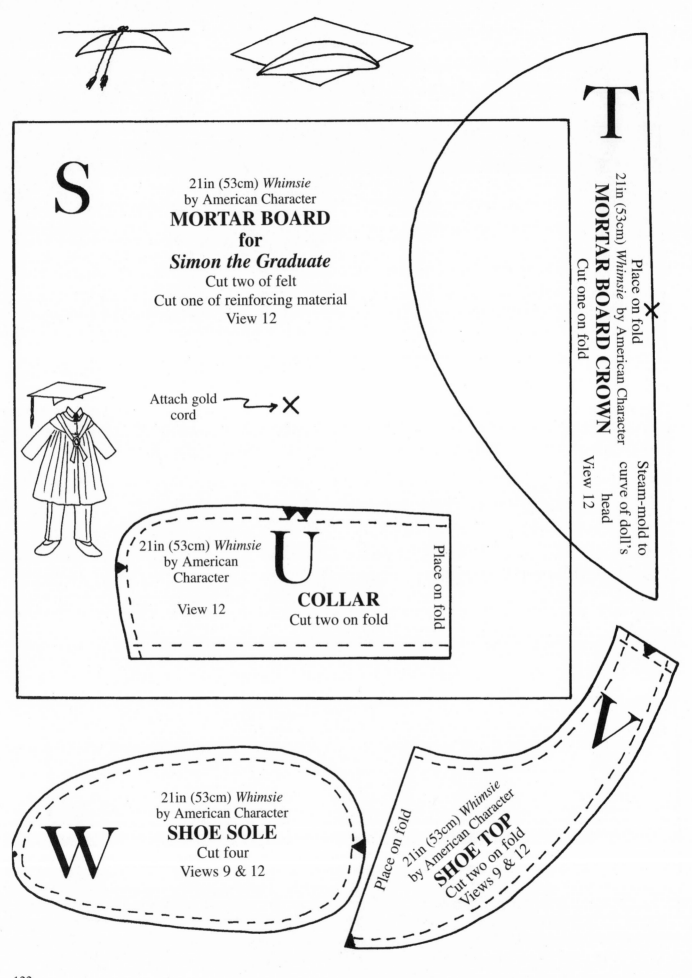

S

21in (53cm) *Whimsie*
by American Character
MORTAR BOARD
for
Simon the Graduate
Cut two of felt
Cut one of reinforcing material
View 12

Attach gold
cord ⟶ ✗

T

21in (53cm) *Whimsie* by American Character
MORTAR BOARD CROWN
Cut one on fold
View 12

Place on fold ✗

Steam-mold to
curve of doll's
head
View 12

U

21in (53cm) *Whimsie*
by American
Character

View 12

COLLAR
Cut two on fold

Place on fold

V

Place on fold

21in (53cm) *Whimsie*
by American Character
SHOE TOP
Cut two on fold
Views 9 & 12

W

21in (53cm) *Whimsie*
by American Character
SHOE SOLE
Cut four
Views 9 & 12

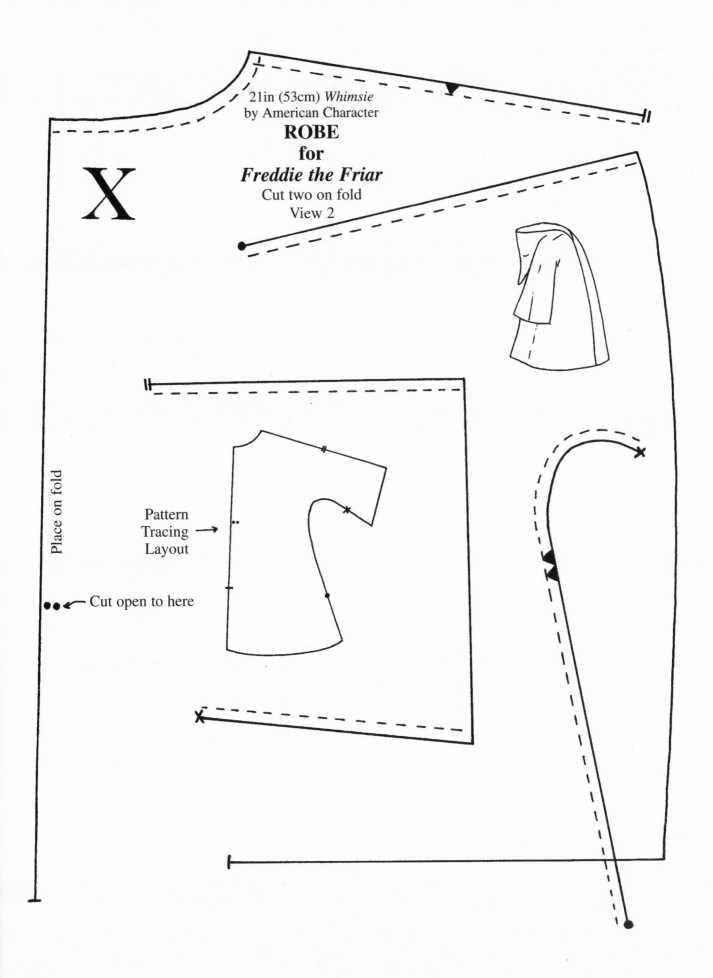

X

21in (53cm) *Whimsie*
by American Character
ROBE
for
Freddie the Friar
Cut two on fold
View 2

Place on fold

Pattern
Tracing
Layout →

←•• Cut open to here

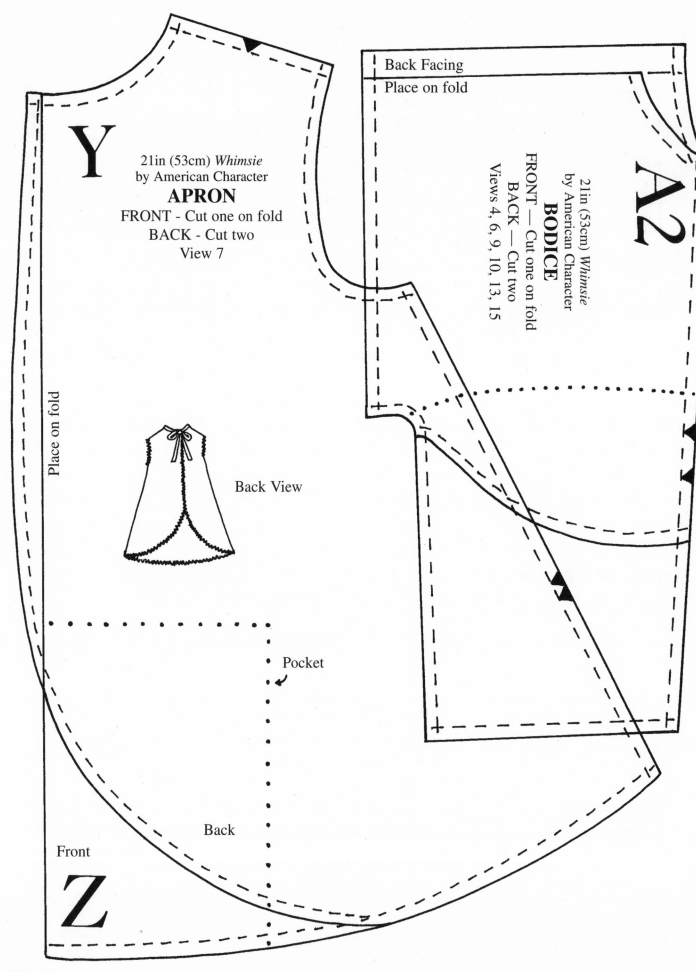

Y

21in (53cm) *Whimsie*
by American Character
APRON
FRONT - Cut one on fold
BACK - Cut two
View 7

Place on fold

Back View

Pocket

Back

Front

Z

Back Facing
Place on fold

A2

21in (53cm) *Whimsie*
by American Character
BODICE
FRONT — Cut one on fold
BACK — Cut two
Views 4, 6, 9, 10, 13, 15

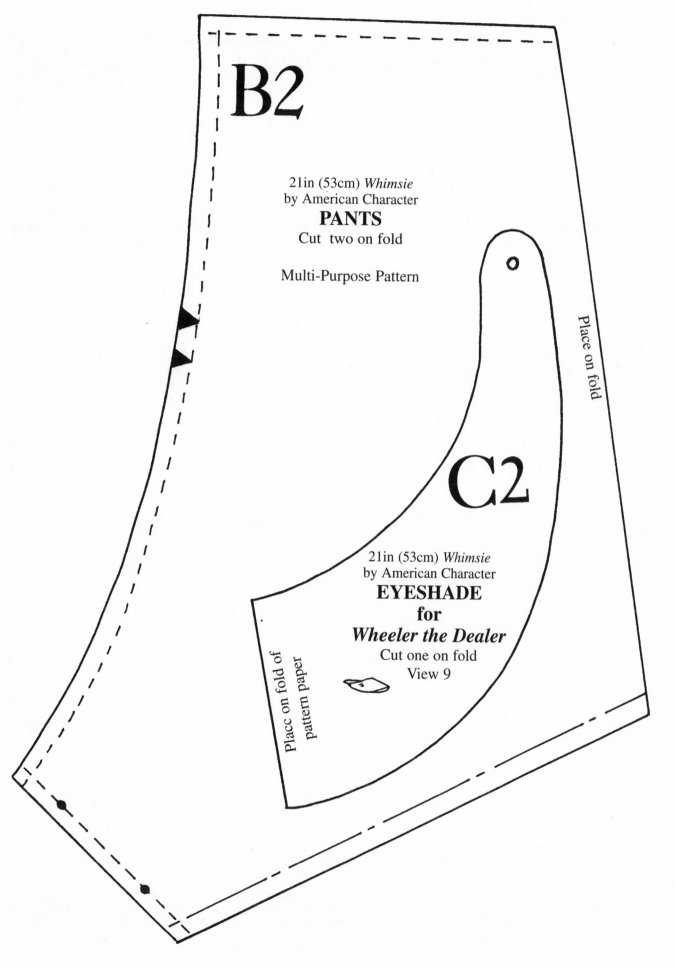

B2

21in (53cm) *Whimsie*
by American Character
PANTS
Cut two on fold

Multi-Purpose Pattern

C2

21in (53cm) *Whimsie*
by American Character
EYESHADE
for
Wheeler the Dealer
Cut one on fold
View 9

Place on fold

Place on fold of
pattern paper

The
Littlechap Family

Remco, 1963

15in (38cm) Father John
14in (36cm) Mother Lisa
13-1/4in (34cm) Daughter Judy
10-1/2in (27cm) Daughter Libby

View 1

View 2

View 4

View 6

View 6

View 5

View 7

View 3

OUTFITS FOR THE LITTLECHAP FAMILY
by Remco, 1963

There were four dolls in this "family": 15in (13cm) **Dr. John**, the father; 14in (36cm) *Lisa*, the mother; 13-1/4in (34cm) *Judy*, the older sister; and 10-1/2in (27cm) *Libby*, the youngest girl. *Judy*'s resemblance to Jacqueline Kennedy Onassis has been noted by many collectors. The family was supposed to typify the average upper middle-class American family of the '60s.

Patterns for the majority of their outfits were given in *Sewing for Twentieth Century Dolls, Volume I*. These dolls and their wardrobes are not in abundant supply; therefore, it was necessary to work with what was available. At the time the first volume was released, I knew there were items missing; since then I have come across the additional pieces shown here.

The dolls were Remco's attempt to meet Mattel's *BARBIE®* in the marketplace, therefore the clothing in this line is of exceptional quality. As did the early *BARBIE®* outfits, the *Littlechap* styles followed then current couture.

Fine fabrics and correctly proportioned patterns, trims, and fasteners were used; quality snaps and other closures were sewn in by hand. Garments were lined and seaming was impeccable, a challenge to the seamstress who wishes to recreate the outfits today. Trim seams carefully to avoid bulkiness.

Most but not all garments had sewn-in cloth labels. In the *Libby* pajama set I have examined, the label was sewn into the bottom hem of the pajama top; however my *Judy* pajama set is not labeled, although in mint, never-played-with condition in the original package.

In my opinion, the only mistake Remco made with regard to the *Littlechaps* was in the size of the dolls. If they had been sized to wear *BARBIE®* and *Ken®* clothes, they would have lasted longer than the one short year they were produced. Alas, they were on "close-out" the second season in stores across the country.

THE BASICS

View 1
DR. JOHN'S TERRY ROBE
Pattern Pieces D, E

John's robe is of bright blue and white striped terry cloth bound with white bias tape and has a white belt. He is shown in the *Littlechap* booklet wearing this robe with a white terry towel wrapped around his neck, but the towel is not listed as an accessory. Follow guides on pattern to assemble this robe. Make a towel for him if it suits you.

View 2
THE *LITTLECHAP* LADIES' WRAP-AROUND BATH SARONGS
Pattern Pieces A, B, C

Lisa's sarong is of red and white striped terry cloth; *Judy*'s is a pale bluish-pink and white; and *Libby*'s is bright yellow and white. The stripes are about 1/2in (5cm) wide.

Place patterns on fabric so the stripes are diagonal on finished garments (see illustration). Bind elliptical edge with white bias tape. Turn up 3/8in (20cm) hem around bottom; machine stitch. Sew fasteners at points indicated. Note that one section of the fastener will be sewn on right side of fabric, the other part on the wrong side. Attach one piece, then try on garment to check positioning of fastener and to determine correct side of fabric.

THE PACKAGED OUTFITS

View 3
LIBBY'S YA YA DRESS
Pattern Pieces F, G, H, J

This red velvet dress has a 4-1/2in (12cm) back zipper. The skirt is lined with orange rayon and the belt is made of the same fabric.

For belt, cut a piece 3/4in (2cm) wide and 10in (25cm) long. Fold lengthwise, right sides together and stitch long side. Turn (this will be a test of your patience). Set aside.

Cut back of skirt and lining from waist to hem. Stitch a seam up back of each piece from hem to dot. Pin, baste, stitch skirt and lining right sides together along hem. Turn and press lightly all around bottom edge, taking care not to mark velvet. Baste waist edges together. Set aside.

Stitch shoulder seams, matching single arrows. Lay out flat and set in sleeves. Stitch underarm seams and side seams. Turn up lower edges of sleeves and blindstitch. Bind neck edge with orange bias to inside.

Pin, then baste bodice to skirt, velvet right sides together. Install zipper in back.

Beginning at right side of back, pin orange belt around waistline. Clip off excess, leaving 1/2in (5cm) at left side and 1/4in (.65cm) on right side. Turn under and sew snap fastener to close over zipper. (See detail sketch.) Use remaining length of belt to make a bow at center front.

JUDY'S PAJAMAS
Pattern Pieces O, P, Q, R, S

Tailored two-piece pajamas with solid orange pants. The top is orange and white striped with solid orange pockets, cuffs and front band. These lined garments are made of a very fine, soft cotton chambray or gingham that hangs nicely despite the two thicknesses.

Accessories: White mules, comb, brush, mirror, French poodle.

To make the paper pattern, place the coat back and front patterns shoulder to shoulder, matching points, and overlapping to seam lines. Tape them together carefully. You now have a one-piece pattern for the pajama coat. This step may be done as you trace the patterns, if desired. Place on fold of material as indicated, pin carefully, and cut one each from the plain and striped fabric. Trim off extra facing of striped piece along dot-dash lines on fronts and sleeves.

Set sleeves in each piece, stitch underarm seams from cuff to dot on side. Put constructions together, wrong sides facing and seam together along bottom edge, beginning at left front edge dot to side seam dot, across side seam, around back to side seam dot, across side seam, to right front edge dot. Turn to right side and press.

Construct pockets and install according to dotted guide on pattern. Open side will be toward center front. Fold front facing over striped fabric and pocket, turn under edges 1/8in (.31cm) down front and across bottom and baste carefully. Topstitch with small stitches. Finish neck edge to inside with narrow bias cut of the plain fabric.

Fold plain sleeve to outside over striped fabric for cuff. Fold under 1/8in (.31cm) and topstitch as for front.

Install snap fasteners as indicated on pattern.

Fold over top of pajama pants for casing. Run narrow elastic through casing to fit doll's waist. Bottom of pajama leg is finished with a turned up cuff at dot-dash line. Turn under 1/8in (.31cm) and topstitch as above.

JUDY'S FOOTBALL OUTFIT
Pattern Pieces K, L, M, N

This outfit consists of a beige corduroy car coat with attached hood, patch pockets, and gold buttons. It is lined with a tartan plaid of red, yellow and black. There is a black bulky knit v-neck sweater and matching plaid, tapered slacks.

Accessories: Matching plaid scarf, red leatherette mittens, golden football chrysanthemum, black boots, school pennant, gold neckchain with gold football.

Given here is the pattern for the coat only. Use the pattern for *Judy*'s pajama pants to make her plaid slacks. Construct sweater from man's heavy sock as shown in sketch. For the plaid scarf, cut a piece of fabric 12in (31cm) long and 3in (8cm) wide. Fold lengthwise with right sides together and seam long side. Turn, press with seam in center. Stitch across each end 1in (3cm) from end and pull threads to make fringe.

JUDY'S BATHING ENSEMBLE
Pattern Pieces Y, Z, AA, BB, CC, DD

Set consists of orange, blue, green, and yellow striped terry cloth poncho with attached hood. Hood lining and binding is bright orange. Two-piece orange stretch bathing suit is trimmed with orange and white braid.

Accessories - Straw hat with orange and blue ribbons, matching straw tote with orange and blue trim, orange-framed sunglasses, and white beach shoes.

Swimsuit - Make casing around top of pants. Run very narrow elastic; tie off and close opening. Bind legs with bias to inside. Bind bottom edge and back edges of suit top with bias to inside. Construct straps of orange and white braid. Attach at dots in front. Finish top edge with orange and white braid. Put on doll and mark where straps attach at back and for snap fasteners.

Hooded Beach Cape - With terry hood pieces right sides together, seam along curved edge. Repeat with solid color for lining. Set aside.

Slit front of cape down front to dot on pattern. Run gathers along bottom edges and hood pieces. Pin lining to inside of cape neck right side of lining to wrong side of terry, pull gathers to fit and tie off. Pin terry hood to outside of cape along neck edge, right sides together. Pull gathers to fit and tie off.

Bring terry hood and lining together. Pin and baste together along front edge. Bind front edge of hood and front opening of cape with solid color bias. Make small bow of bias to finish front opening.

Bind cape all around hem with solid color bias.

Beach Bag and Hat - These are of finely woven straw. A fine straw placemat would work well.

Cut a 5in (13cm) circle for hat and seal edges with white glue to prevent raveling of edges (glue will dry clear and nearly invisible). Prepare a slightly oval crown block 1-3/4in (5cm) by 1-1/2in (4cm) by 3/4in (2cm) tall.

To make a crown, steam piece over a boiling teakettle until quite damp and warm. Mold over crown block, keeping brim flat with weights if necessary. When dry, pull sides of hat up Aussie-style and fasten with one orange and one blue ribbon, tied on top of crown.

Cut one each bag bottom and side from woven straw. Glue ends together, matching arrows. Trim bottom as shown in sketch and turn under 1/4in (.65cm). Run a bead of glue all around inside top edge of bag, allow to set for two or three minutes, then turn down 1/4in (.65cm).

Put light glue bead on outside of turned bottom edge

and run a light bead of glue around edge of bottom piece. Allow to set, then glue bag to bottom. Finish with orange ribbon handles and blue ribbon center trim (see illustration).

<table>
<tr><td>

</td></tr>
</table>

This set consists of three-quarter-length pants of yellow print and an open-backed French smock top of bright blue cotton with bell-shaped sleeves, lined with the same print. Back edge of print lining is on the dot-dash line.

Pajamas - For pajama top sleeve: With right sides together of one plain and one print sleeve, stitch straight side. Lay out flat and press seam open. Fold entire piece and sew underarm seam of both fabrics. Turn and fold printed side in. Run gathering stitches through both fabrics between dots; do not pull gathers. Complete second sleeve and set aside.

Smock - For yoke: Seam print and plain pieces right sides together along neck and down back edges (back will be open). Trim seams, giving special attention to corners. Turn and press 1/8in (.31cm) under all around open edges. Set aside.

Bodice - Sew print and plain separately at side seams. With right sides together, sew together along bottom edge. Turn and press. Baste together along top edge. Run gathering stitches between dots, but do not pull gathers.

Turn plain material of back edges inside for facing. Turn under 1/8in (.31cm) and blindstitch (reverse of <u>Judy</u>'s pajama top fronts which are faced to outside).

Pin bodice center front to center front of yoke. Pin back edges of bodice to back edges of yoke. (Bodice will be inside the two layers of the yoke.) Pull gathers but do not tie off.

Insert finished sleeve and baste in place. Adjust bodice and sleeve gathers and tie off. Baste, then machine stitch. This seam may be covered with a narrow self-bias if desired.

Sew snap fasteners as indicated on pattern. Add buttons for decoration if desired.

Accessories - Red mules, diary, stuffed toy.

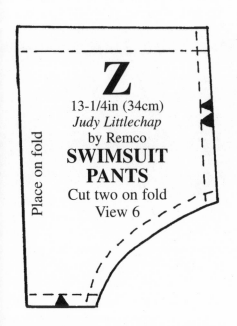

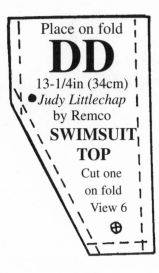

The *Littlechap* Ladies
by Remco
BATH SARONG
Cut one each of terry cloth

A = 14in (36cm) *Lisa*
B = 13-1/4in (34cm) *Judy*
C = 10-1/2in (27cm) *Libby*

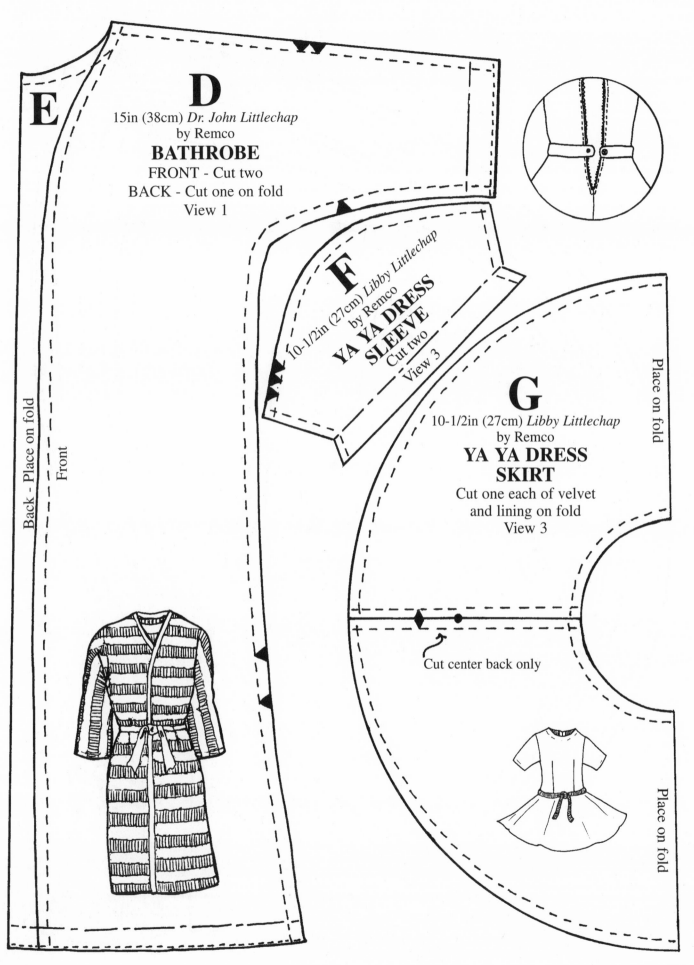

E

D

15in (38cm) *Dr. John Littlechap*
by Remco
BATHROBE
FRONT - Cut two
BACK - Cut one on fold
View 1

Back - Place on fold

Front

F

10-1/2in (27cm) *Libby Littlechap*
by Remco
**YA YA DRESS
SLEEVE**
Cut two
View 3

G

10-1/2in (27cm) *Libby Littlechap*
by Remco
**YA YA DRESS
SKIRT**
Cut one each of velvet
and lining on fold
View 3

Place on fold

Cut center back only

Place on fold

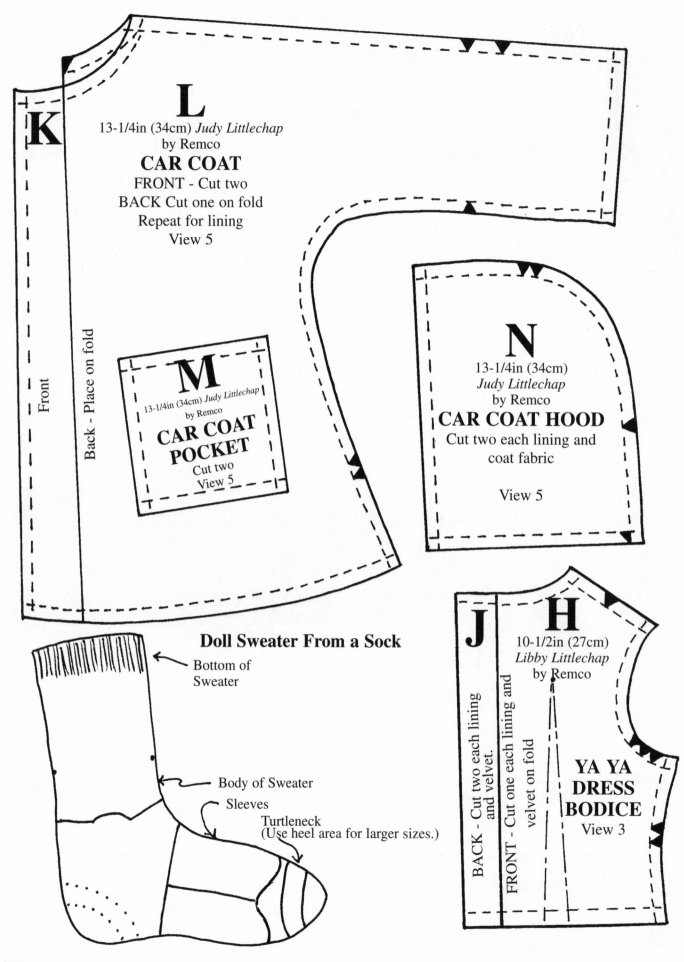

K

L

13-1/4in (34cm) *Judy Littlechap*
by Remco
CAR COAT
FRONT - Cut two
BACK Cut one on fold
Repeat for lining
View 5

Front

Back - Place on fold

M

13-1/4in (34cm) *Judy Littlechap*
by Remco
CAR COAT POCKET
Cut two
View 5

N

13-1/4in (34cm)
Judy Littlechap
by Remco
CAR COAT HOOD
Cut two each lining and
coat fabric

View 5

Doll Sweater From a Sock

Bottom of
Sweater

Body of Sweater

Sleeves

Turtleneck
(Use heel area for larger sizes.)

J

H

10-1/2in (27cm)
Libby Littlechap
by Remco

BACK - Cut two each lining
and velvet.

FRONT - Cut one each lining and
velvet on fold

**YA YA
DRESS
BODICE**
View 3

132

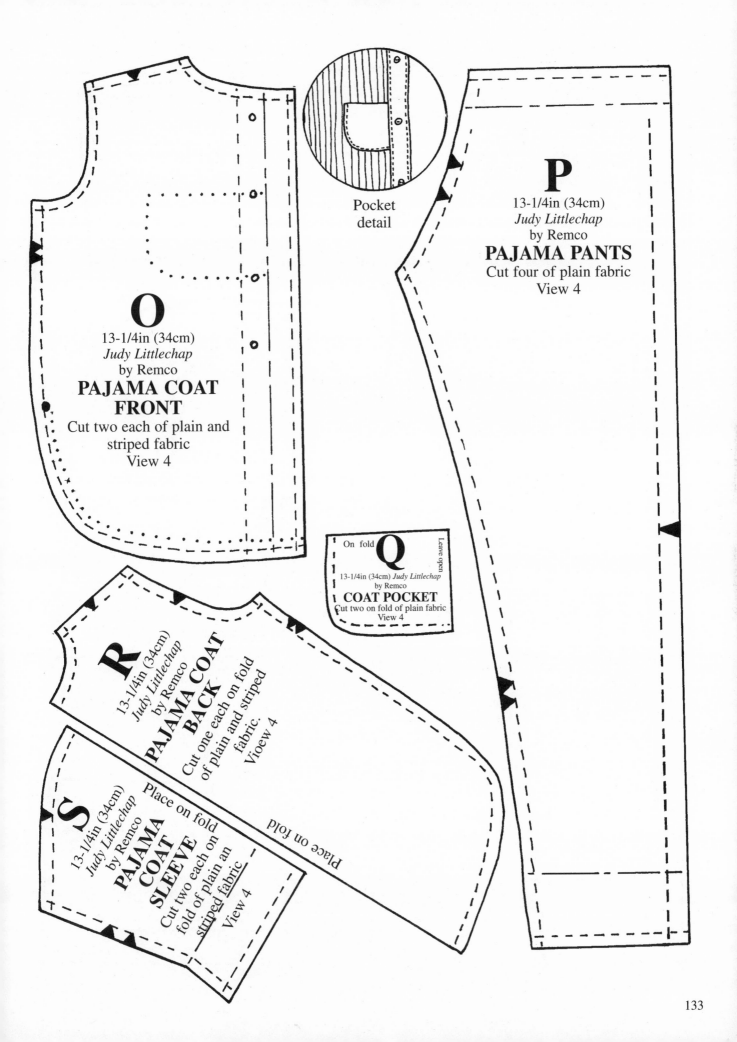

O

13-1/4in (34cm)
Judy Littlechap
by Remco
**PAJAMA COAT
FRONT**
Cut two each of plain and
striped fabric
View 4

Pocket
detail

P

13-1/4in (34cm)
Judy Littlechap
by Remco
PAJAMA PANTS
Cut four of plain fabric
View 4

On fold   **Q**   Leave open

13-1/4in (34cm) *Judy Littlechap*
by Remco
COAT POCKET
Cut two on fold of plain fabric
View 4

R

13-1/4in (34cm)
Judy Littlechap
by Remco
**PAJAMA COAT
BACK**
Cut one each on fold
of plain and striped
fabric.
Vioew 4

S

13-1/4in (34cm)
Judy Littlechap
by Remco
**PAJAMA
COAT
SLEEVE**
Cut two each on
fold of plain an
striped fabric
View 4

Place on fold

Place on fold

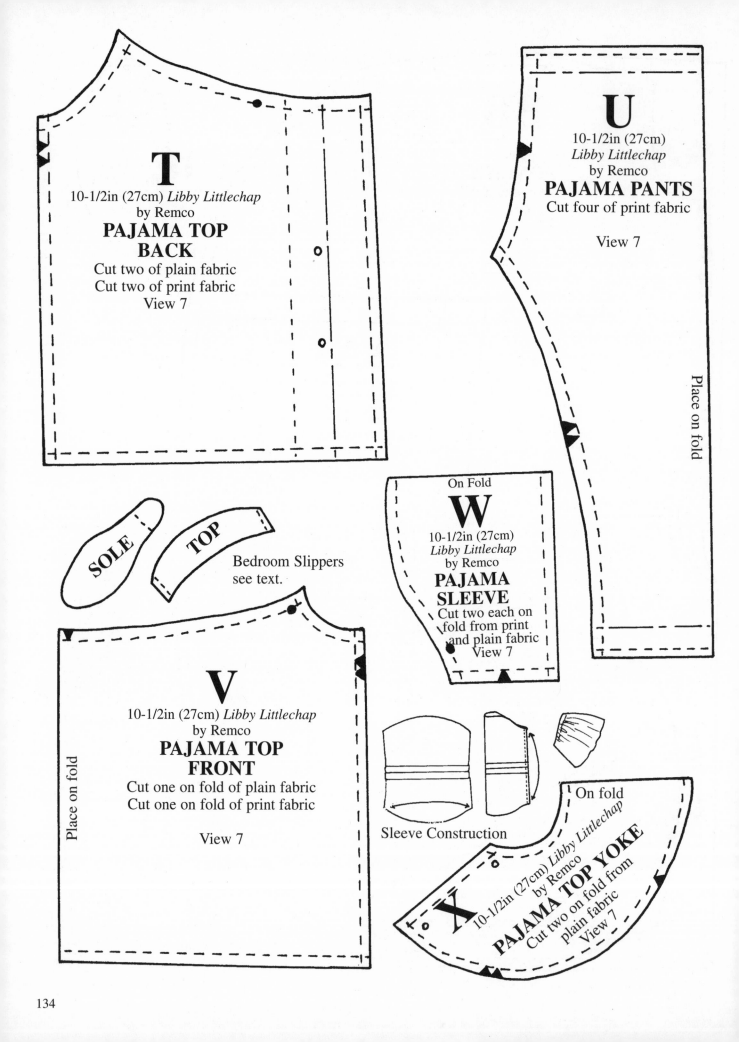

T

10-1/2in (27cm) *Libby Littlechap*
by Remco
**PAJAMA TOP
BACK**
Cut two of plain fabric
Cut two of print fabric
View 7

U

10-1/2in (27cm)
Libby Littlechap
by Remco
PAJAMA PANTS
Cut four of print fabric

View 7

Place on fold

SOLE

TOP

Bedroom Slippers
see text.

On Fold

W

10-1/2in (27cm)
Libby Littlechap
by Remco
**PAJAMA
SLEEVE**
Cut two each on
fold from print
and plain fabric
View 7

V

10-1/2in (27cm) *Libby Littlechap*
by Remco
**PAJAMA TOP
FRONT**
Cut one on fold of plain fabric
Cut one on fold of print fabric

View 7

Place on fold

Sleeve Construction

On fold

10-1/2in (27cm) *Libby Littlechap*
by Remco
PAJAMA TOP YOKE
Cut two on fold from
plain fabric
View 7

X

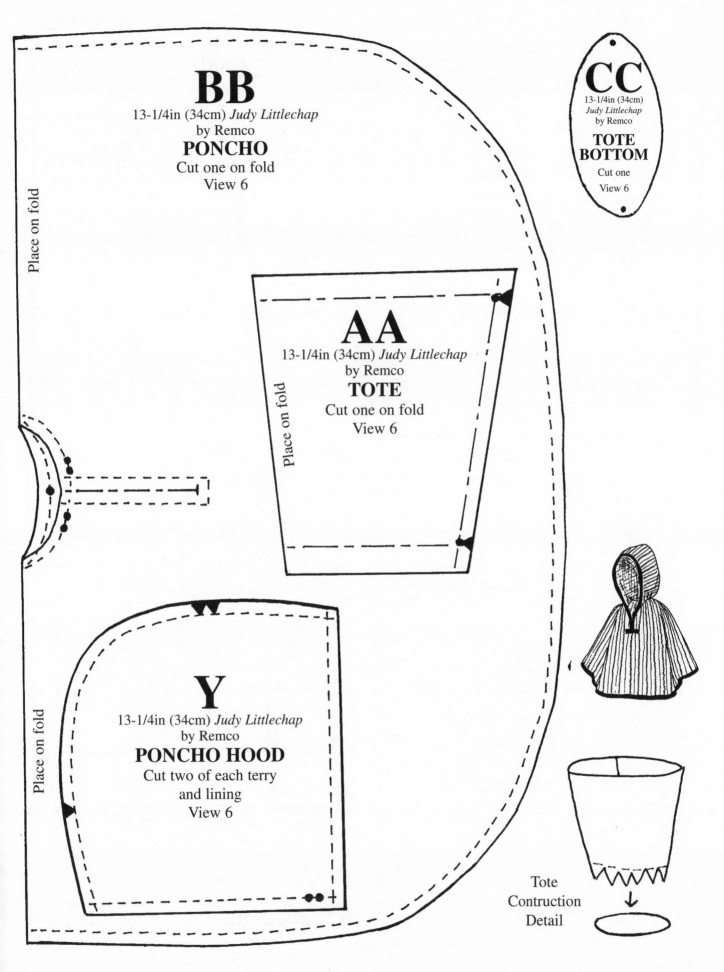

BB

13-1/4in (34cm) *Judy Littlechap*
by Remco
PONCHO
Cut one on fold
View 6

Place on fold

CC

13-1/4in (34cm)
Judy Littlechap
by Remco
**TOTE
BOTTOM**
Cut one
View 6

AA

13-1/4in (34cm) *Judy Littlechap*
by Remco
TOTE
Cut one on fold
View 6

Place on fold

Y

13-1/4in (34cm) *Judy Littlechap*
by Remco
PONCHO HOOD
Cut two of each terry
and lining
View 6

Place on fold

Tote
Contruction
Detail

135

Miss Seventeen... A Beauty Queen
Does your Miss Seventeen have all of these fashions?*

View 1

LOVELY NIGHT

Cloud-soft, cloud-white nylon peignoir with its matching Grecian-style gown makes Miss Seventeen feel so pretty and pampered! This sleepy-time fashion comes with a separate taffeta underslip, dainty white slippers and a comb and mirror boudoir set.
$3.98

View 2

AMERICAN A LA MODE

America's favorite casual fashion — the shirtwaist dress! This one is styled for Miss Seventeen in a cool cotton print with tiny pearl buttons. Dress comes with a separate net crinoline for that bouffant look, white sandals, an umbrella, a handbag, panties and sunglasses.
$1.98

View 3

RAGE OF PARIS

A sophisticated fashion for Miss Seventeen in smart black faille bedecked with a rose. The finishing touch? A hat and muff of scarlet velvet and a rope of pearls. Separate petticoat, panties, black sandals and a slim umbrella are also included.
$2.98

View 4

TURNABOUT

A three-way wonder! Black wool sheath is a stylish basic... so chic with just a string of pearls. Reversible cape adds a fashion flair. One side matches the dress, the other is a contrasting velvet. Matching velvet bag and hat, pearl necklace, panties and dainty black sandals also included.
$2.49

View 5

ON THE TOWN

The most elegant gown in our fair lady's wardrobe! It's a rich, gold lame sheath — reed-slim and strapless. Comes with a lavish evening cape of satin brocade, a satin clutch bag, long pearl necklace and gay red sandals.
$2.49

View 6

WEDDING BELLES

A breathtaking wedding gown of sleek white taffeta with an elegant lace train. Veil is of filmy net with a white floral crown. Comes with a lovely white bouquet, a dainty blue garter for luck and a necklace of pearls. White sandals, separate petticoat and panties also included.
$4.98

View 7

WEDDING BELLES BRIDESMAID

A fresh and pretty springtime look for the bridesmaids of Miss Seventeen! Pink embroidered bouffant dress with a face-framing picture hat to match and a separate net petticoat. Comes with a bouquet of multi-colored garden flowers, panties and a pair of white sandals.
$4.98

View 8

CHAMPAGNE WALTZ

A dress for dancing the evenings away! Pastel transparent nylon gown ties in back with a giant butterfly bow. Rustling taffeta underskirt is splashed with dainty white appliqued flowers. Comes with a long rope of glistening pearls, panties and a pair of white, light-footed sandals.
$2.98

View 9

BEACH BAIT

A polka-dot costume to catch all eyes! Red and white cotton skirt slips over her "Beauty Queen" bathing suit — has a great cartwheel sun hat to match. Comes with all these extras for a day at the beach; striped terry towel, carryall bag, sunglasses and a pair of red sandals.
$2.49

View 10

MATINEE

The "gracious lady" look for our Miss Seventeen. Smart black 2-piece fashion is just right for the theatre, especially when it's brightened with a red velvet muff and a gay flowered hat. Muff, hat, a pair of black sandals, a long pearl necklace and panties come with this fashion.
$3.98

View 11

DATE AT THE PLAZA

Straight from the pages of a fashion magazine... a 3-piece luxury costume! The front-belted coat of elegant velvet has a pencil-slim skirt to match. Soft silk blouse matches lining of coat. Also included: A hat, matching muff, panties and a pair of black sandals.
$3.98

View 12

ST. MORITZ

Snow bunny or expert, she's smart on the slopes in this cozy hooded ski jacket worn over a turtle-neck sweater and slim black pants. Also included are ski boots, mittens to keep her fingers warm, ski poles and a pair of sunglasses to cut the glare of the sun on the snow.
$2.98

ALL ABOVE FASHIONS FOR 18" MISS SEVENTEEN DOLL
* Materials and colors are subject according to the style treands without notice.

COMPLETE ORIGINAL WARDROBE FOR THE 18in (46cm) MISS SEVENTEEN BEAUTY QUEEN
by Louis Marx, 1961

Miss Seventeen looks very much like the first *BARBIE*® doll. She arrived in her black cotton knit one-piece swimsuit with her competition ribbon across her chest, wearing a lined satin cape, molded golden plastic crown, and packed with a folder illustrating her extensive, designer-look wardrobe. Patterns for the outfits shown on the feature page for this section were developed by the author from the small brochure enclosed with the doll.

These patterns may be used to develop fashions for *Super Size BARBIE*®, the "Wild Styles" dolls by Tiger Toys, Lady Luminous, and other dolls of the same type. If your *Miss Seventeen* is the 15in (38cm) size, photocopy these patterns at the 83% setting to reduce them to fit your doll.

ORIGINAL IN-BOX OUTFIT
Pattern Pieces A, B

Cape - Cut one piece measuring 10-1/2in (27cm) x 11in (28cm) from red satin and white satin lining. Sew right sides together, leaving one 10-1/2in (27cm) side open. Turn. Gather along open 10-1/2in (27cm) side, catching both cape and lining, Pull gathers to 3in (8cm) and stay-stitch on machine. Cut a piece of red satin 1in (3cm) x 3-1/2in (9cm), fold in both 1in (3cm) ends by 1/4in (.65cm) each and press, attach to neck opening of cape right side to lining side, turn to right side of cape and topstitch along length for stand-up collar.

Crown - First cut paper pattern on fold. Lay out flat; cut from plastic bleach jug or similar container. (Cover stock or card stock may also be used.) Overlap along dotted line and glue with plastic glue. (If using card, use white glue.) Spray with gold craft paint.

Ribbon - Cut a piece of 3/4in (2cm) ribbon 13in (33cm) long. Trace *Miss Seventeen* lettering from pattern page and fill in with ball-point fabric paint.

LINGERIE
(Not shown in brochure)
Pattern Pieces X, QQ

Crinoline Petticoat - Short: Cut a piece of nylon taffeta 6-1/2in (17cm) x 30in (76cm). Gather to fit waistband. Long: Cut a piece of nylon taffeta 9-1/2in (24cm) x 30in (76cm). Gather to fit waistband.

Panties and Bra - Use pattern pieces X and QQ to construct these undergarments. Cut from sheer lingerie fabric and overlay with lace or trim with embroidery as desired.

View 1
"LOVELY NIGHT"
Pattern Pieces C, D, N

Nightgown - For skirt, cut piece 10in (25cm) x 16in (41cm), gather to bodice. Attached wide lace straps at double dots on bodice N.

Peignoir - For collar, cut piece 5in (13cm) x 20in (51cm), fold in half lengthwise, stitch together along short ends, turn. Gather along long side opposite fold to fit neck opening. Finish neck opening with self bias cut long enough to make a bow in front. Sew two rows of 1in (3cm) ruffles at 3/4in (2cm) intervals as indicated by dots on pattern piece.

View 2
"AMERICAN A LA MODE"
Pattern Pieces E, F, G, H, M

Full Skirt - Cut a piece of dress fabric 7in (18cm) x 36in (91cm) (measurements include 1/2in [1cm] for hem allowance, 1/2in [1cm] facing each side of back, and 1/4in [.65cm] seam allowance at waist.) Gather to bodice, then fold over back facing.

Tie Belt - Cut a piece of dress fabric 2in (5cm) x 36in (91cm). Fold lengthwise, seam right sides together, leaving 1in (3cm) opening for turning. Turn and press; close opening.

Purse - Cut one piece of fold from purse fabric and one from lining fabric. Cut a 2in (5cm) slit along fold line of lining. Sew two purse pieces right sides together, turn through slit, and press. Whipstitch slit closed. Fold unit in half, matching corners, pin. Blindstitch along both sides from corners on fold to double dots. Purse straps may be of self-fabric, fine chain, or contrasting woven braid or cord. Fabric straps: Cut two pieces 1-1/2in (4cm) x 8in (20cm), fold in 1/8in (.31cm) each long side of strap and press. Fold entire strap lengthwise in half, press, then topstitch 1/16in (.15cm) from each edge full length. Attach straps at dots along top edge either side of top of purse.

View 3
"RAGE OF PARIS"
Pattern Pieces J, K, L, M, O, P, T

Dress - This elegant dress is completely lined and has a zipper down the back, allowing for better fit. Look for zippers designed for fine silk garments.

Turban - This pattern is used for both lined turbans shown. Cut one each velvet and lining measuring 3in (8cm) x 6-1/2in (17cm). Sew each piece together on short ends, creating two tubes. Place tubes right sides together and stitch together along one end of tube. Turn.

Cut circles from velvet and lining. Insert velvet circle in open end of velvet tube and stitch all around. Turn turban so that lining is out and velvet is on inside. Whipstitch lining circle in place, folding in all raw edges. Turn turban right side out.

Complete the "Rage of Paris" turban with three or four tiny stitches gathering about 3/4in (2cm) of the fabric on front right, pull tightly, and tie off. Cover these stitches with a decorative button or bit of costume jewelry such as a single earring from which the clip or screw has been removed. Be sure the piece compli-ments the ensemble.

Muff - Follow directions on pattern piece to construct muff.

Cummerbund - Follow directions on pattern piece. Use piece of velvet used on turban and muff to construct rose; attach to cummerbund with invisible stitches.

View 4
"TURNABOUT"
Pattern Pieces P, Q, R, BB, CC

Dress - This dress is constructed using the bodice patterns given and the short straight skirt pattern. Again, the dress is lined and zips down the back.

Turban - Follow directions for "Rage of Paris" turban, except this turban does not have the gathering and jewel at front right.

Purse - Purse is cut from velvet and lining and is con-structed much the same as the "American A La Mode" purse, except for the extra stitching at corners. These seams are done after purse is finished and on the wrong side, then turned, or may be omitted if preferred. Finish with self strap or chain.

Cape - This velvet cape is lined with the dress fabric and carefully constructed so that it may be worn either way. Sew both pieces right sides together leaving neckline open, turn, finger press, then blindstitch neckline closed. Attach decorative matching hook and eye.

View 5
"ON THE TOWN"
Pattern Pieces Q, S, U, AA, FF, GG

Dress - Construct this dress using strapless bodice pattern and long straight skirt pattern. For bodice back use pattern from "Champagne Waltz". Dress is completely lined and zipped down the back. Self-fabric rose is pinned at waist.

Long Cape - Cape has a "capelet" collar; both are com-pletely lined (see section on laying out large pattern pieces). Construct each section of cape separately, leaving necklines open. Turn and press each piece. Assemble with right side (cape fabric side) of capelet collar to lining side of cape. Stitch along neckline. Raw edges of seam should be on out-side of cape and under collar. Finish raw edge with narrow self bias of lining fabric.

Evening Bag - Follow directions on pattern piece.

View 6
"WEDDING BELLES BRIDE"
Pattern Pieces V, W, X, AA, QQ

Dress - Cut a long full skirt (see above); fold in half. Using template on pattern page, cut scallops at center front of skirt. Apply two rows of 1in (3cm) lace ruffles around bottom of skirt. Run gathering stitches around top of skirt, but do not pull gathers at this time.

Cut out and construct a crinoline (see above), run gather-ing stitches but do not pull at this time.

Follow tracing layout for "Wedding Dress" overskirt. Complete overskirt except do not pull gathers at this time.

Use wedding dress bodice front pattern and "Champagne Waltz" bodice back pattern. *Note:* Bodice is fully lined.

Turn bodice to wrong side. Pull gathers on overskirt and pin to waistline of bodice. Pull gathers on skirt and pin to waistline over overskirt. Pull gathers on crinoline and pin to waistline over skirt. Baste bodice and skirts together as one along waist seam. Turn and check that the three skirts are positioned so the raw seams will be on the inside when dress is completed. Machine stitch waist seam, using small stitches.

Make large bow (see pattern page) and stitch to center back waistline.

Veil - Cut a circle 18in (46cm) in diameter. Fold over not quite in half. Gather folded edge to headband of white flow-ers and satin ribbon rosebuds.

Bouquet - Use white flowers and satin ribbons. See instructions for bridesmaid's nosegay.

Underwear - Make a set of white satin panties and bra, trim with lace.

View 7
"WEDDING BELLES BRIDESMAID"
Pattern Pieces X, Y, QQ

Dress - Cut bodice from sheer pink embroidered nylon and line with fine pink silk lining. Make a short full skirt (see "American A La Mode") from the same fabric, lined with the silk, over a bouffant crinoline (see above). Cut a piece of satin ribbon long enough to go around waist, tie bow, and hang stream-ers down in back.

Hat - For crown: cut a 5in (13cm) circle each of dress and lining fabrics. Pin together. Run a gathering thread around circumference of circle and pull to fit doll's head. For brim: cut a piece of dress fabric 6in (15cm) x 24in (61cm). Seam the two 6in (15cm) sides together, turn, and press. Fold the loop in half lengthwise with seam on inside and run gathering stitches along the edge opposite fold.

Pull gathering thread of brim to fit gathered edge of crown. Stitch together with raw edges to outside of hat. Cover raw seam with matching satin ribbon, tie bow at back of hat, and allow ends to stream down back.

Underwear - Make a set of pink satin panties and bra with lace trim.

Nosegay - Insert bunch of small silk flowers in center of 4in (10cm) doily or piece of lace. Twist doily around stems and wire together. Cover wire with ribbon and allow to stream about 3in (8cm) to 4in (10cm).

| View 8 "CHAMPAGNE WALTZ" Pattern Pieces K, L, Z, AA | **Dress** - Cut bodice pieces from sheer nylon and matching taffeta. Cut a short full | skirt from sheer nylon and an underskirt using Rage of Paris peg-top skirt. Attach to bodice as one. Attach large bow of sheer nylon at center back waist. Embroider three flowers on nylon skirt, or attach purchased motifs. |

| View 9 "BEACH BAIT" Pattern Pieces JJ, KK | **Skirt** - Cut a short full skirt and pockets from bright cotton. Cut waistband 2in (5cm) x 5-1/2in (14cm) from same fabric.

Hat - Cut 8in (20cm) circle. From circle cut out a pie-shaped slice measuring 4in (10cm) on the circumference, from edge to center. Sew cut edges together. Finish edges with bias or fringe fabric. Hat can be cut from a fine-woven straw placemat if desired. Machine stay-stitch all around | edge to prevent raveling. Finish with multicolored pompon at peak of hat.

Beach Bag - Use crocheted cords, braided narrow ribbons (in colors to match skirt print), or twisted yarns to make straps for bag.

Towel - Cut piece of multi-colored striped terry toweling 5in (13cm) x 8in (20cm); run tight zigzag machine stitch all around to prevent raveling, or bind sides and fringe ends. |

| View 10 "MATINEE" Pattern Pieces M, Q, T, DD, EE | **Dress** - Cut a short straight skirt from dress fabric and another from lining fabric. Use bracelet length sleeve. Cut overskirt and peplum from matching satin; tie with same fabric.

Overskirt - Cut a piece of satin 5in (13cm) x 12in (31cm). Gather along one long side to fit doll's waist. Sew as one with peplum to tie belt. Sew front seam, leaving top 3in (8cm) open. Hem with blindstitch. | **Muff** - Cut of contrasting velvet. See pattern page for instructions for constructing muff.

Hat - Make a clip-on by cutting a 1in (3cm) section all around from a plastic bottle approximately the size of doll's head or from the neck of a larger bottle. Trim edges and shape to desired style. Cover with fabric to match the outfit and decorate with silk flowers, ribbons, and veiling as desired, but remain true to the fashion period of the doll. Flowers should match velvet muff in the "Matinee" outfit. |

| View 11 "DATE AT THE PLAZA" Pattern Pieces C, Q, R, T, HH | **Velvet Swing Coat** - Use peignoir pattern for velvet coat, cutting at top dot as hemline. Use coat sleeve pattern. Cut linings for coat body and sleeves from same silk as blouse and scarf.

Skirt and Blouse - Make short straight skirt of velvet. Make sleeveless blouse and scarf of coordinated silk print. | Scarf is 5in (13cm) x 12in (31cm) piece, folded, stitched, turned. Ends may be angled if desired.

Hat - Cut 2in (5cm) diameter crown and 2-1/4in (3cm) x 6-1/2in (17cm) sides from velvet or a short-fur synthetic. Line with silk print. Construct similar to turban.

Muff - Cut from velvet or short-fur synthetic and construct as above. *Note:* No lining; this construction results in furry inside and outside. |

| View 12 "ST. MORITZ" Pattern Pieces LL, MM, NN, OO, PP | **Turtleneck and Pants** - Simple instructions are found on pattern pieces.

Ski Jacket - Run header | around bottom of jacket and pull through a cord or self-tie. Tie at center front bottom of jacket.

Mittens - Cut of knit or furry fabric. Line if desired. |

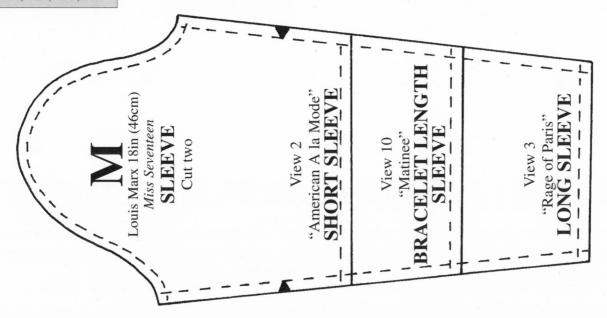

M

Louis Marx 18in (46cm)
Miss Seventeen
SLEEVE
Cut two

View 2
"American A la Mode"
SHORT SLEEVE

View 10
"Matinee"
BRACELET LENGTH SLEEVE

View 3
"Rage of Paris"
LONG SLEEVE

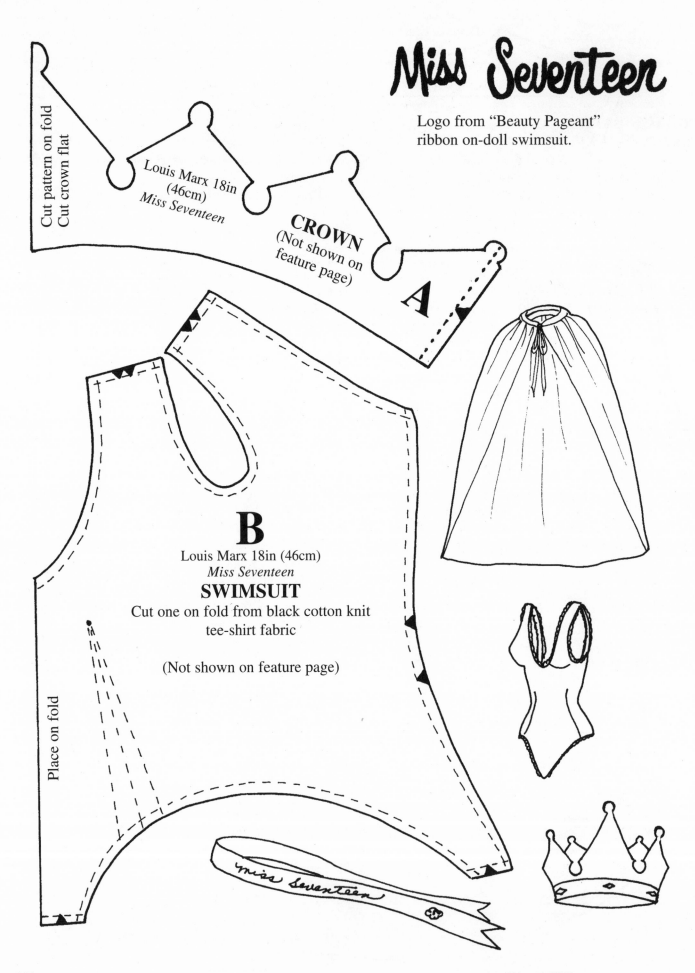

Miss Seventeen

Logo from "Beauty Pageant" ribbon on-doll swimsuit.

Cut pattern on fold
Cut crown flat

Louis Marx 18in (46cm)
Miss Seventeen

CROWN
(Not shown on feature page)

A

B
Louis Marx 18in (46cm)
Miss Seventeen
SWIMSUIT
Cut one on fold from black cotton knit tee-shirt fabric

(Not shown on feature page)

Place on fold

miss Seventeen

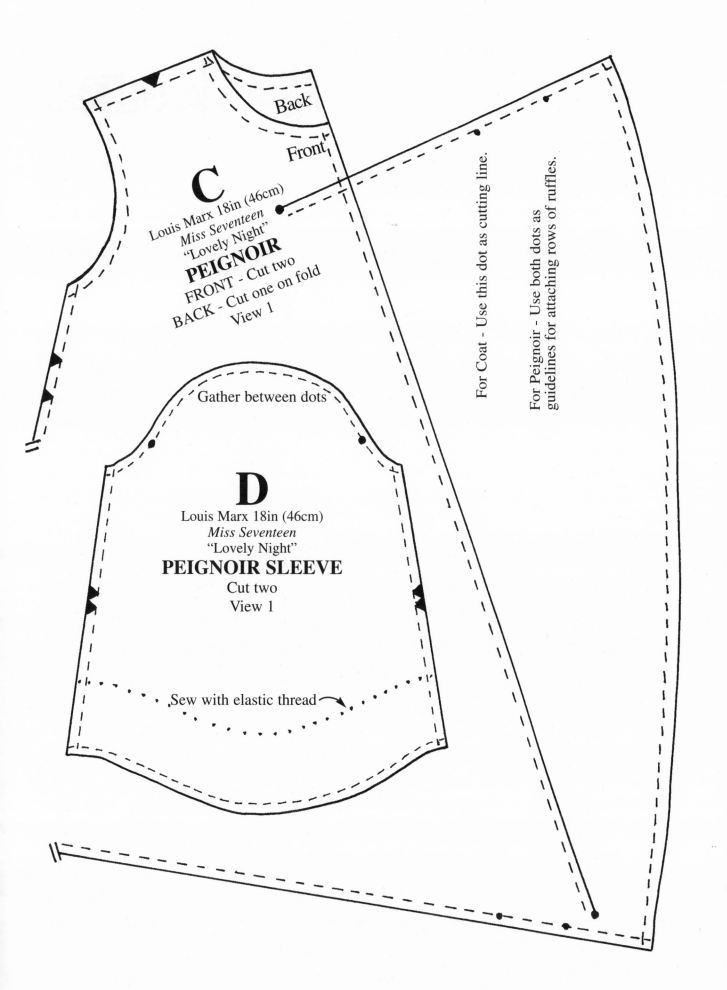

C

Louis Marx 18in (46cm)
Miss Seventeen
"Lovely Night"
PEIGNOIR
FRONT - Cut two
BACK - Cut one on fold
View 1

Back

Front

For Coat - Use this dot as cutting line.

For Peignoir - Use both dots as guidelines for attaching rows of ruffles.

Gather between dots

D

Louis Marx 18in (46cm)
Miss Seventeen
"Lovely Night"
PEIGNOIR SLEEVE
Cut two
View 1

Sew with elastic thread

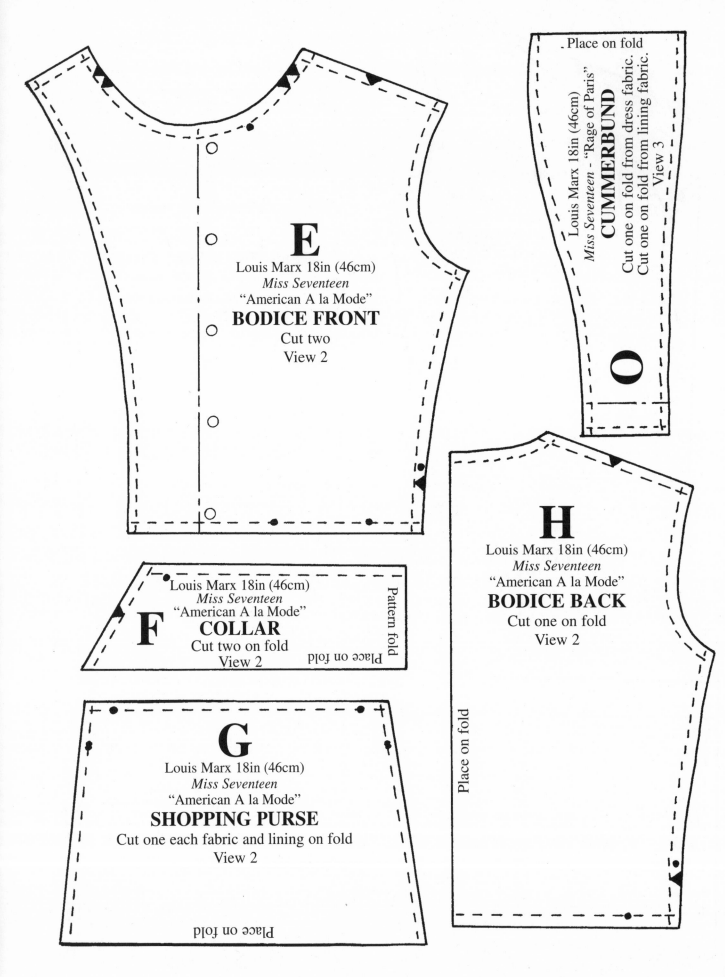

E

Louis Marx 18in (46cm)
Miss Seventeen
"American A la Mode"
BODICE FRONT
Cut two
View 2

Place on fold
Miss Seventeen - "Rage of Paris"
Louis Marx 18in (46cm)
CUMMERBUND
Cut one on fold from dress fabric.
Cut one on fold from lining fabric.
View 3

O

H

Louis Marx 18in (46cm)
Miss Seventeen
"American A la Mode"
BODICE BACK
Cut one on fold
View 2

Place on fold

F

Louis Marx 18in (46cm)
Miss Seventeen
"American A la Mode"
COLLAR
Cut two on fold
View 2

Pattern fold

Place on fold

G

Louis Marx 18in (46cm)
Miss Seventeen
"American A la Mode"
SHOPPING PURSE
Cut one each fabric and lining on fold
View 2

Place on fold

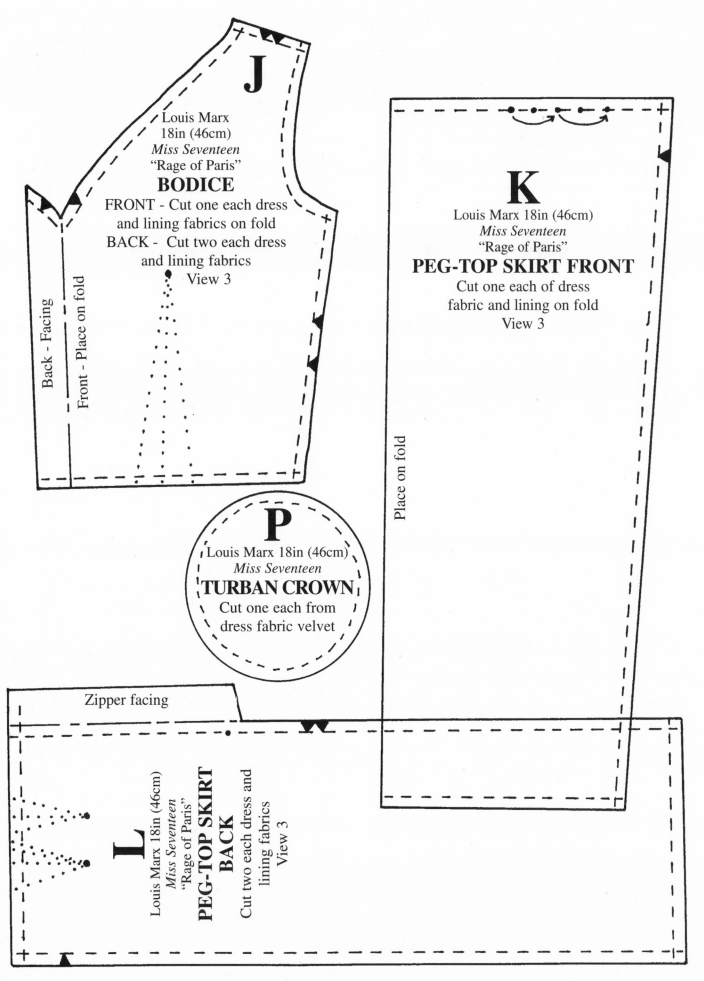

J

Louis Marx
18in (46cm)
Miss Seventeen
"Rage of Paris"
BODICE
FRONT - Cut one each dress
and lining fabrics on fold
BACK - Cut two each dress
and lining fabrics
View 3

Back - Facing

Front - Place on fold

K

Louis Marx 18in (46cm)
Miss Seventeen
"Rage of Paris"
PEG-TOP SKIRT FRONT
Cut one each of dress
fabric and lining on fold
View 3

Place on fold

P

Louis Marx 18in (46cm)
Miss Seventeen
TURBAN CROWN
Cut one each from
dress fabric velvet

Zipper facing

L

Louis Marx 18in (46cm)
Miss Seventeen
"Rage of Paris"
PEG-TOP SKIRT BACK
Cut two each dress and
lining fabrics
View 3

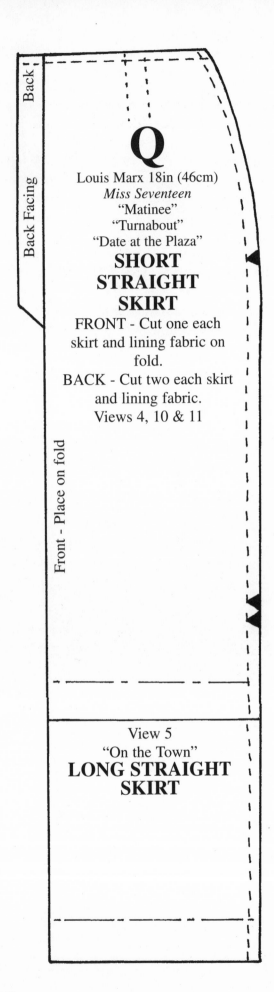

Q

Louis Marx 18in (46cm)
Miss Seventeen
"Matinee"
"Turnabout"
"Date at the Plaza"

SHORT STRAIGHT SKIRT

FRONT - Cut one each skirt and lining fabric on fold.
BACK - Cut two each skirt and lining fabric.
Views 4, 10 & 11

Back

Back Facing

Front - Place on fold

View 5
"On the Town"
LONG STRAIGHT SKIRT

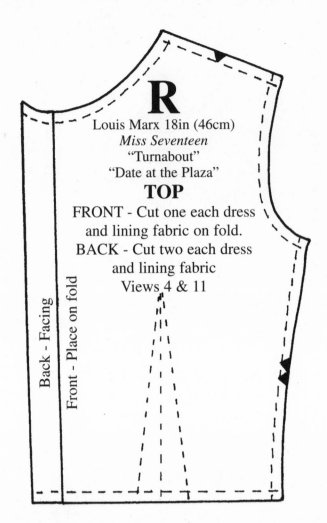

R

Louis Marx 18in (46cm)
Miss Seventeen
"Turnabout"
"Date at the Plaza"

TOP

FRONT - Cut one each dress and lining fabric on fold.
BACK - Cut two each dress and lining fabric
Views 4 & 11

Back - Facing

Front - Place on fold

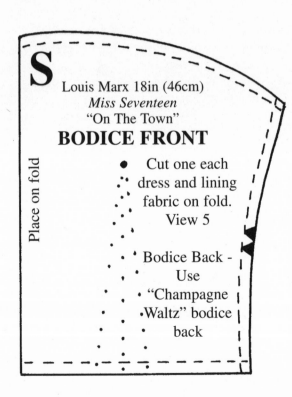

S

Louis Marx 18in (46cm)
Miss Seventeen
"On The Town"

BODICE FRONT

Place on fold

• Cut one each dress and lining fabric on fold.
View 5

• Bodice Back - Use
• "Champagne
•Waltz" bodice back

144

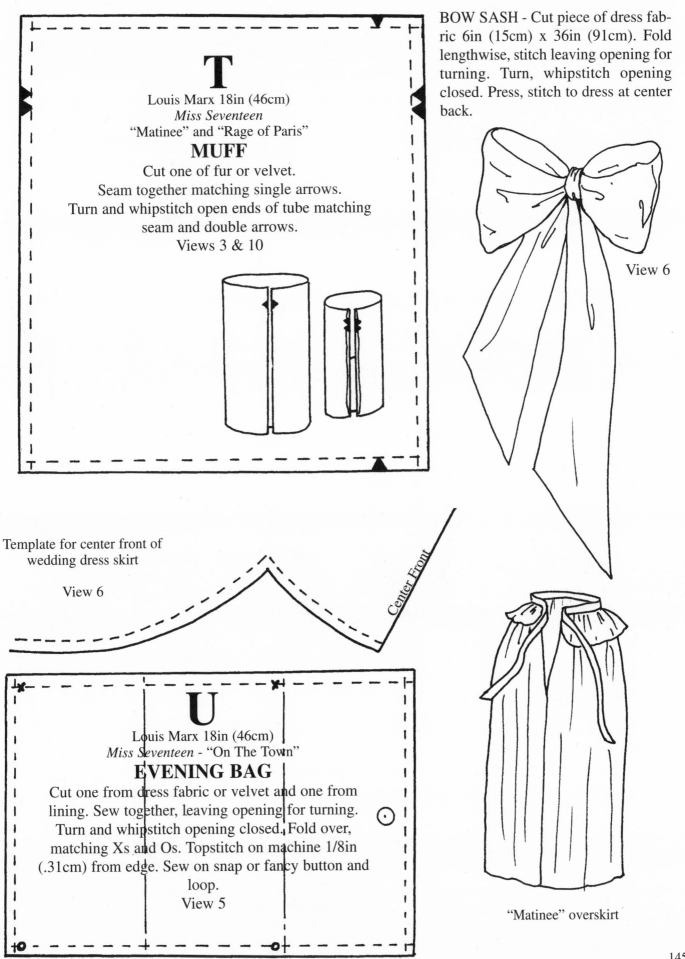

BOW SASH - Cut piece of dress fabric 6in (15cm) x 36in (91cm). Fold lengthwise, stitch leaving opening for turning. Turn, whipstitch opening closed. Press, stitch to dress at center back.

T

Louis Marx 18in (46cm)
Miss Seventeen
"Matinee" and "Rage of Paris"

MUFF

Cut one of fur or velvet.
Seam together matching single arrows.
Turn and whipstitch open ends of tube matching seam and double arrows.
Views 3 & 10

View 6

Template for center front of wedding dress skirt

View 6

Center Front

U

Louis Marx 18in (46cm)
Miss Seventeen - "On The Town"

EVENING BAG

Cut one from dress fabric or velvet and one from lining. Sew together, leaving opening for turning. Turn and whipstitch opening closed. Fold over, matching Xs and Os. Topstitch on machine 1/8in (.31cm) from edge. Sew on snap or fancy button and loop.
View 5

"Matinee" overskirt

145

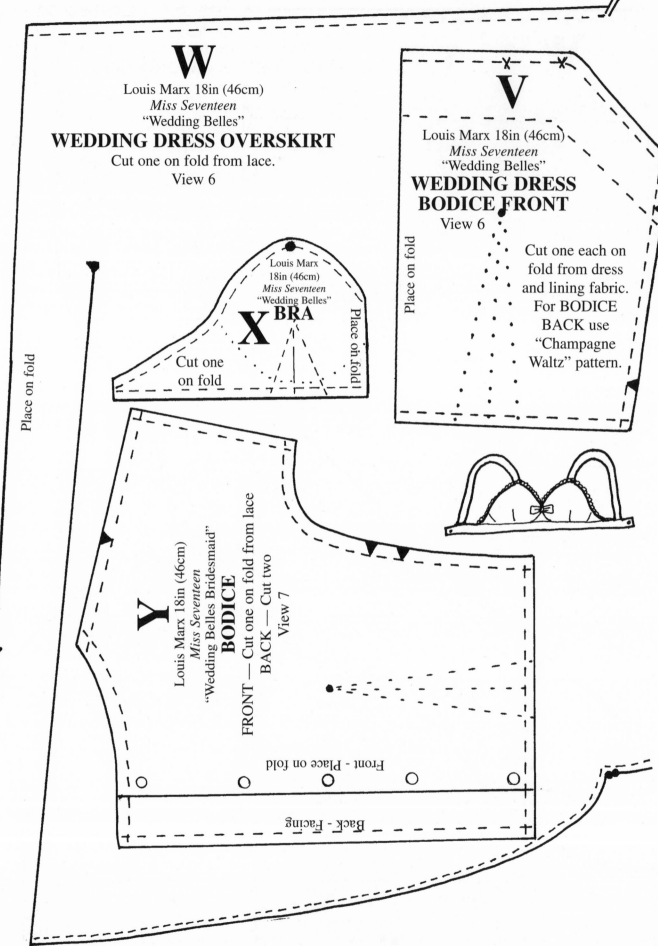

W

Louis Marx 18in (46cm)
Miss Seventeen
"Wedding Belles"
WEDDING DRESS OVERSKIRT
Cut one on fold from lace.
View 6

Place on fold

V

Louis Marx 18in (46cm)
Miss Seventeen
"Wedding Belles"
**WEDDING DRESS
BODICE FRONT**
View 6

Place on fold

Cut one each on
fold from dress
and lining fabric.
For BODICE
BACK use
"Champagne
Waltz" pattern.

Louis Marx
18in (46cm)
Miss Seventeen
"Wedding Belles"

X **BRA**

Cut one
on fold

Place on fold

Y

Louis Marx 18in (46cm)
Miss Seventeen
"Wedding Belles Bridesmaid"
BODICE
FRONT — Cut one on fold from lace
BACK — Cut two
View 7

Front - Place on fold

Back - Facing

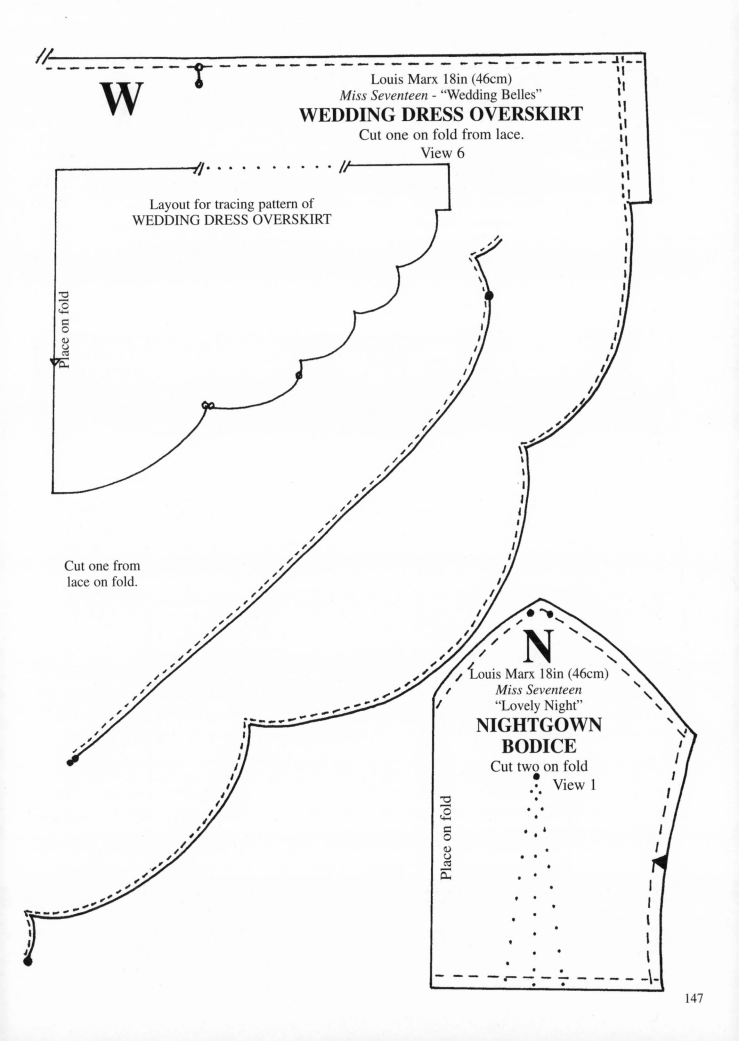

W

Louis Marx 18in (46cm)
Miss Seventeen - "Wedding Belles"
WEDDING DRESS OVERSKIRT
Cut one on fold from lace.
View 6

Layout for tracing pattern of
WEDDING DRESS OVERSKIRT

Place on fold

Cut one from
lace on fold.

N

Louis Marx 18in (46cm)
Miss Seventeen
"Lovely Night"
NIGHTGOWN
BODICE
Cut two on fold
View 1

Place on fold

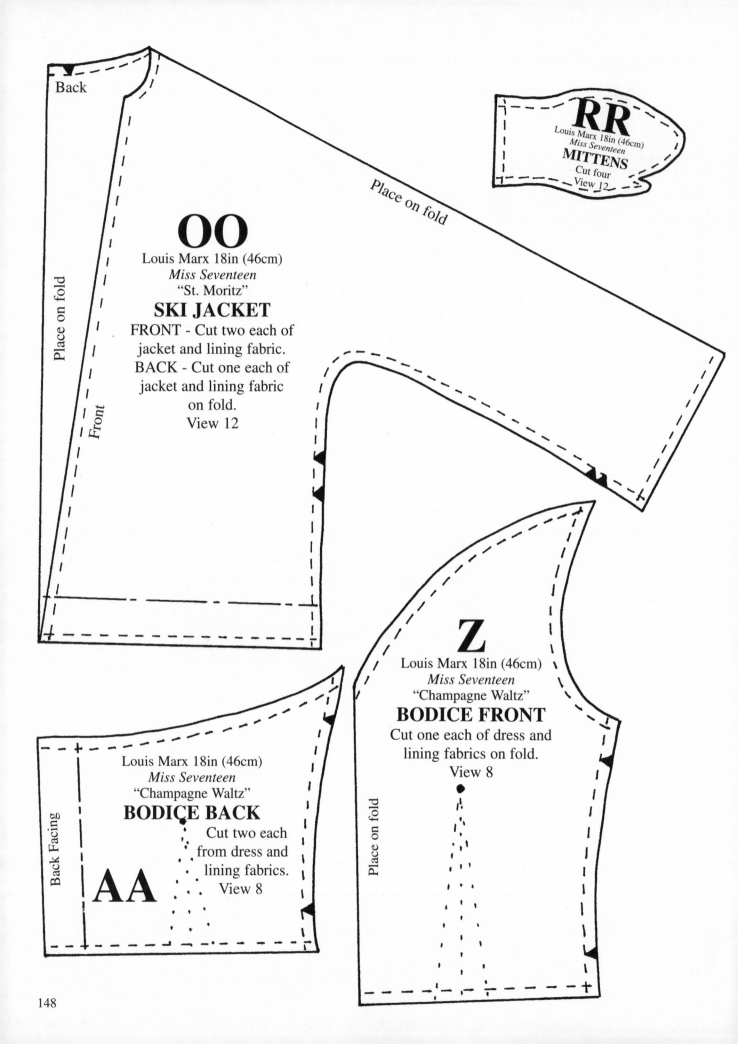

Back

Place on fold

Place on fold

Front

OO
Louis Marx 18in (46cm)
Miss Seventeen
"St. Moritz"
SKI JACKET
FRONT - Cut two each of
jacket and lining fabric.
BACK - Cut one each of
jacket and lining fabric
on fold.
View 12

Place on fold

RR
Louis Marx 18in (46cm)
Miss Seventeen
MITTENS
Cut four
View 12

Z
Louis Marx 18in (46cm)
Miss Seventeen
"Champagne Waltz"
BODICE FRONT
Cut one each of dress and
lining fabrics on fold.
View 8

Place on fold

AA
Louis Marx 18in (46cm)
Miss Seventeen
"Champagne Waltz"
BODICE BACK
Cut two each
from dress and
lining fabrics.
View 8

Back Facing

148

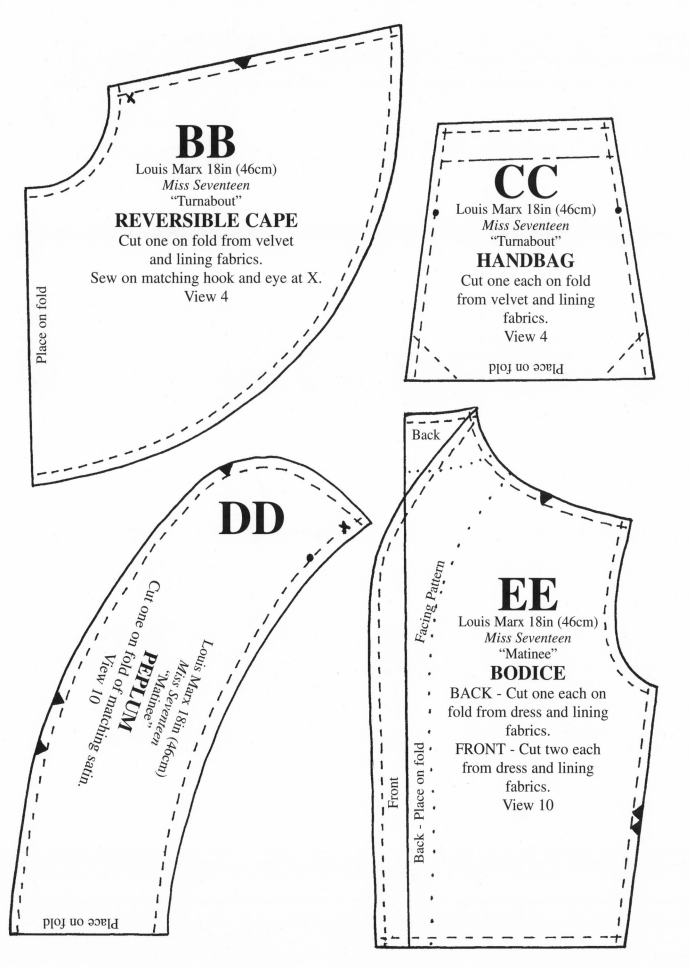

BB

Louis Marx 18in (46cm)
Miss Seventeen
"Turnabout"
REVERSIBLE CAPE
Cut one on fold from velvet
and lining fabrics.
Sew on matching hook and eye at X.
View 4

Place on fold

CC

Louis Marx 18in (46cm)
Miss Seventeen
"Turnabout"
HANDBAG
Cut one each on fold
from velvet and lining
fabrics.
View 4

Place on fold

DD

Louis Marx 18in (46cm)
Miss Seventeen
"Matinee"
PEPLUM
Cut one on fold of matching satin.
View 10

Place on fold

EE

Back

Facing Pattern

Front

Back - Place on fold

Louis Marx 18in (46cm)
Miss Seventeen
"Matinee"
BODICE
BACK - Cut one each on
fold from dress and lining
fabrics.
FRONT - Cut two each
from dress and lining
fabrics.
View 10

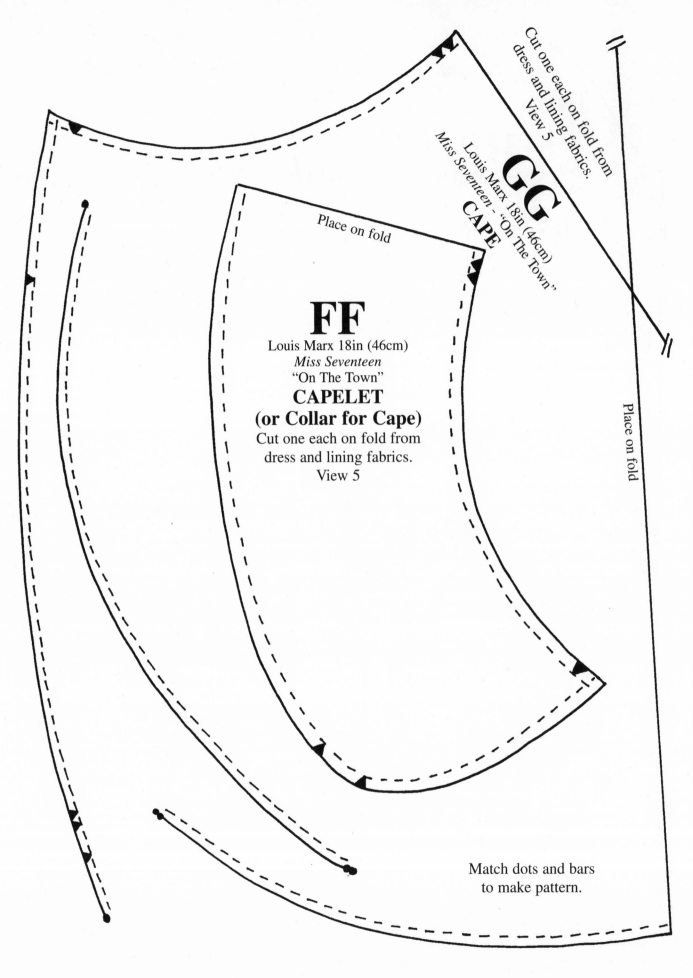

Cut one each on fold from dress and lining fabrics. View 5

GG
Louis Marx 18in (46cm)
Miss Seventeen - "On The Town"
CAPE

Place on fold

Place on fold

FF
Louis Marx 18in (46cm)
Miss Seventeen
"On The Town"
CAPELET
(or Collar for Cape)
Cut one each on fold from
dress and lining fabrics.
View 5

Match dots and bars
to make pattern.

HH

Louis Marx 18in (46cm)
Miss Seventeen
"Date at the Plaza"

COAT SLEEVE

Cut two each from coat
and lining fabrics.
Use Peignoir pattern for coat
body, using top dots as coat
hemline. Cut coat and lining.
View 11

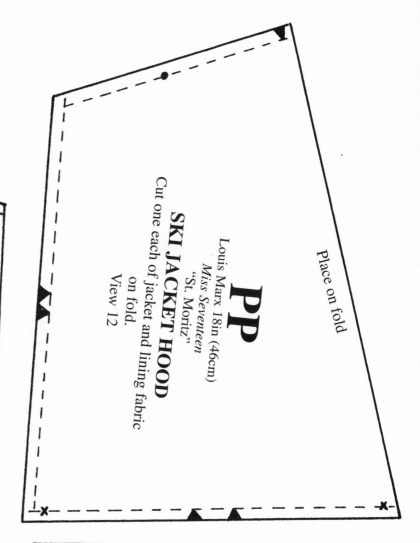

Place on fold

PP

Louis Marx 18in (46cm)
Miss Seventeen
"St. Moritz"

SKI JACKET HOOD

Cut one each of jacket and lining fabric
on fold.
View 12

Place on fold

JJ

Louis Marx 18in (46cm)
Miss Seventeen
"Beach Bait"

SKIRT POCKETS

Cut two each from skirt
fabric on fold.
View 9

KK

Louis Marx 18in (46cm)
Miss Seventeen
"Beach Bait"

BEACH BAG

Cut two each from outer fabric
and lining fabric.
View 9

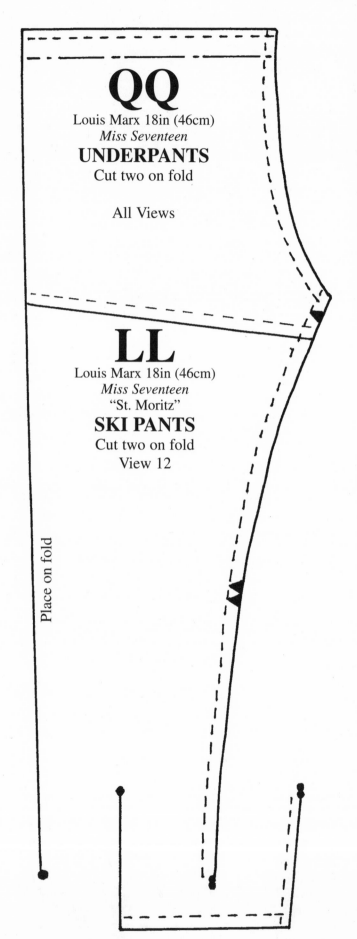

QQ

Louis Marx 18in (46cm)
Miss Seventeen
UNDERPANTS
Cut two on fold

All Views

LL

Louis Marx 18in (46cm)
Miss Seventeen
"St. Moritz"
SKI PANTS
Cut two on fold
View 12

Place on fold

MM

Louis Marx 18in (46cm)
Miss Seventeen
"St. Moritz"

**TURTLENECK
SWEATER COLLAR**
Cut one on fold
View 12

Place on fold

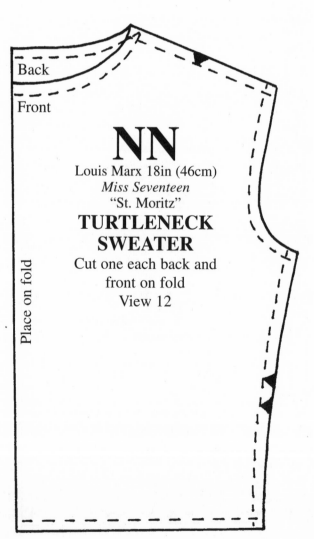

Back

Front

NN

Louis Marx 18in (46cm)
Miss Seventeen
"St. Moritz"
**TURTLENECK
SWEATER**
Cut one each back and
front on fold
View 12

Place on fold

24in (61cm)
"CHARMIN' CHATTY"
by
Mattel, Inc.
1962

View 1

View 5

View 2

View 4

View 2

View 3

WARDROBE FOR 24in (61cm) CHARMIN' CHATTY
by Mattel, Inc. - 1962

This doll's little girl looks, combined with her size, make her an excellent "learn-to-sew" doll for a favorite child.

View 1
"LETS TALK 'N TRAVEL IN FOREIGN LANDS"
Pattern Pieces A, C, E, L

Coat - The fabric is dark navy blue serge or very fine wool if you prefer. There are three brass buttons and a white pique collar. Patterns for sleeve, bodice, and collar are given. For skirt of coat, cut a piece of coat fabric 8in (20cm) x 25in (64cm). This includes 1/2in (1cm) for turning up hem and 3/4in (2cm) on either end for front facing.

Pleat skirt using illustration as guideline. Coat may be lined if desired. Note that sleeve seam is on top of arm.

Red Straw Hat - Finished brim measures 8in (20cm) in diameter. Cut a 12in (31cm) circle and steam into shape or sew braid round and round, beginning at center of crown and shaping as you sew. Trim with dark navy blue grosgrain ribbon, cut long enough to stream down back.

Dress Gloves - See View 3 instructions.

View 2
BLOUSE, SKIRT & POPOVER
Pattern Pieces B, D, F, G, H

Blouse - This garment is made of red cotton with tiny white dots. This sleeve is cut with top of sleeve on fold.

Skirt and Popover - These are cut from light blue chambray. Skirt is trimmed with a 1in (3cm) band of dotted fabric edged with mini ricrac on both sides, stitched so that only one row of points peeps out on either side of the dotted band. Popover is edged at neck and armholes with same red ricrac, sewn underneath so only a single row of points shows on right side.

View 3
ORIGINAL ON-THE-DOLL SAILOR DRESS
Pattern Pieces B, J, K, M through R, T

Skirt - The skirt is dark navy blue cotton with a striped dark navy blue and white cotton dickey attached. Dickey straps are cut from same fabric as skirt. Pleat skirt according to illustrations, fitting to doll.

Nautical Blouse - Fabric is white serge or other heavy cotton. Note how seaming at top of sleeve shapes sleeve to contour of shoulder. Collar is red cotton trimmed with white braid.

Dress Gloves - The pattern may look strange, but is exactly the shape of the original gloves. They are of unlined white stretch nylon.

Eyeglasses - These are fun to construct but require patience. Cut a paper pattern on the fold, then lay out flat and cut from heavy cardboard or plastic, or use the pattern as a template to make wire frames. Because the tracing was made around the outside edges of the original plastic glasses, the pattern given is slightly thicker than the actual glasses. Originals were black, so these may be sprayed with black craft paint.

Saddle Oxfords - Follow guidelines on pattern and refer to shoe-making chapter in first volume of this work. This pattern may be varied to make slippers and other styles.

View 4
"LET'S PLAY CINDERELLA"
Pattern Piece S

Dress - Cut of loosely woven, burlap-colored fabric, this dress is unhemmed and fringed along the jagged edge. Neckline and armhole edges are merely turned under and stitched on machine. Add a patch or two of varied prints for effect.

View 5
BIRTHDAY PARTY DRESS
Pattern Pieces U through Z

The bodice of this dress is red velvet with a white cotton broadcloth Peter Pan collar. Two inset bands of lace trim the white cotton broadcloth skirt. At the waist is a red ribbon sash. The underskirt is attached to the dress at the waist. On her feet are white nylon anklets and white "kid" slippers trimmed with embroidered roses and leaves.

Note: When cutting velvet, corduroy, or any napped fabric, be sure to lay out pattern so nap is all one way.

Bodice - The bodice is of simple construction with short, eased-in sleeves which were hemmed before sewing the sleeve and side seams as one. Construct the Peter Pan collar and baste into neck opening, turn back facings under and sew across collar and facings, turn. Finish neck opening with white bias tape. Set aside.

Skirt - Cut the following sections and pin a note to each with section letter:

Section a   1 strip white cotton 32in (8cm) x 2-1/2in (5cm)

Section b   2 strips white 3/4in (2cm) lace 32in (81cm) long

Section c   1 strip white cotton 32in (81cm) x 5-1/2in (14cm)

Section d   1 strip white cotton 32in (5cm) x 1-1/2in (4cm)

Underskirt - 1 piece white taffeta for underskirt 32in (81cm) x 5-1/2in (14cm)

Sash - 1 piece 3/4in (2cm) red satin ribbon 24in (61cm).

Prepare fabric as follows:

1. Fold section a in half lengthwise and press. The fold is the bottom edge of the skirt. Turn both long sides inside 1/4in (.65cm) and press. Set aside.

2. Press and sew four 1/4in (.65cm) tucks the length of section c. It's a good idea to mark these with a sewing pencil to ensure accuracy; mistakes will show. Press all four tucks facing same way; stitch line will be the "up" side, fold side is "down". Turn under 1/4in (.65cm) on each long edge of piece and press. Set aside.

3. Press under 1/4in (.65cm) on both long sides of section d.

4. Turn under and press 1/4in (.65cm) on both long sides of section c.

Assemble skirt as follows:

1. Open section a and seam one pressed edge to back of lace. Topstitch remaining edge to right side of lace.

2. Topstitch one long side of section c to remaining long side of same piece of lace.

3. Topstitch other long side of section c to second piece of lace.

4. Topstitch one long, folded-under side of section d to top edge of second piece of lace.

This makes the skirt read cotton-lace-cotton with tucks-lace-cotton.

Underskirt - Make a handkerchief hem on one long side of taffeta. Whipstitch short ends of taffeta and skirt construction together. Pin or baste unfinished long side of skirt and underskirt together. Run double gathering stitches as one along this side within 1in (3cm) of each end. Pull gathering stitches to fit bodice and seam right sides together, keeping gathers even. Turn back and press a 3/4in (2cm) facing on skirt and bodice and stay-stitch at waist seam on each side. Sew three snaps as indicated on pattern. (Skirt is open in back.)

Shoes - Cut two shoes and two soles on outside lines of pattern from white leatherette or kid leather. Sew back seam, then baste all around sole, easing as needed, and machine stitch, taking care to keep the toes rounded. Any slight squareness will be evident when turned to right side. Clip seam as needed.

Sew 1/8in (.31cm) white elastic across instep. Glue tiny embroidered rose and leaf motif on each toe. Cut two innersoles of stiff red fabric using inside line of pattern. Glue innersole in place after shoe is completed. Place a small plastic bag of loosely packed clean sand in each shoe to weight innersole till glue is completely dry.

Panties - See first volume of this work, pg. 237, for panty pattern, or borrow from another pattern in this volume.

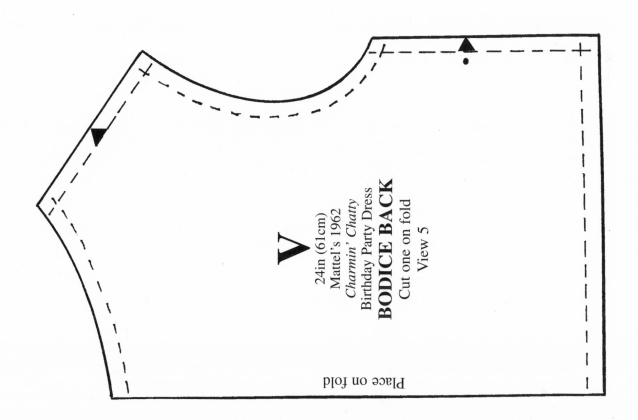

24in (61cm)
Mattel's 1962
Charmin' Chatty
Birthday Party Dress
BODICE BACK
Cut one on fold
View 5

Place on fold

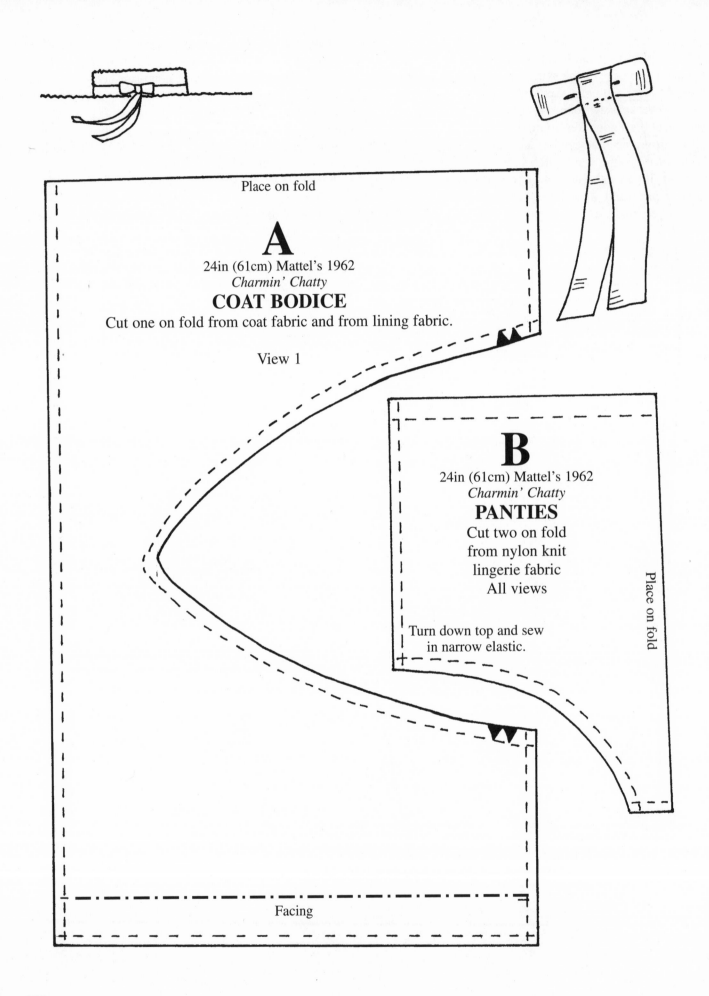

A

24in (61cm) Mattel's 1962
Charmin' Chatty
COAT BODICE
Cut one on fold from coat fabric and from lining fabric.

View 1

Place on fold

B

24in (61cm) Mattel's 1962
Charmin' Chatty
PANTIES
Cut two on fold
from nylon knit
lingerie fabric
All views

Turn down top and sew
in narrow elastic.

Place on fold

Facing

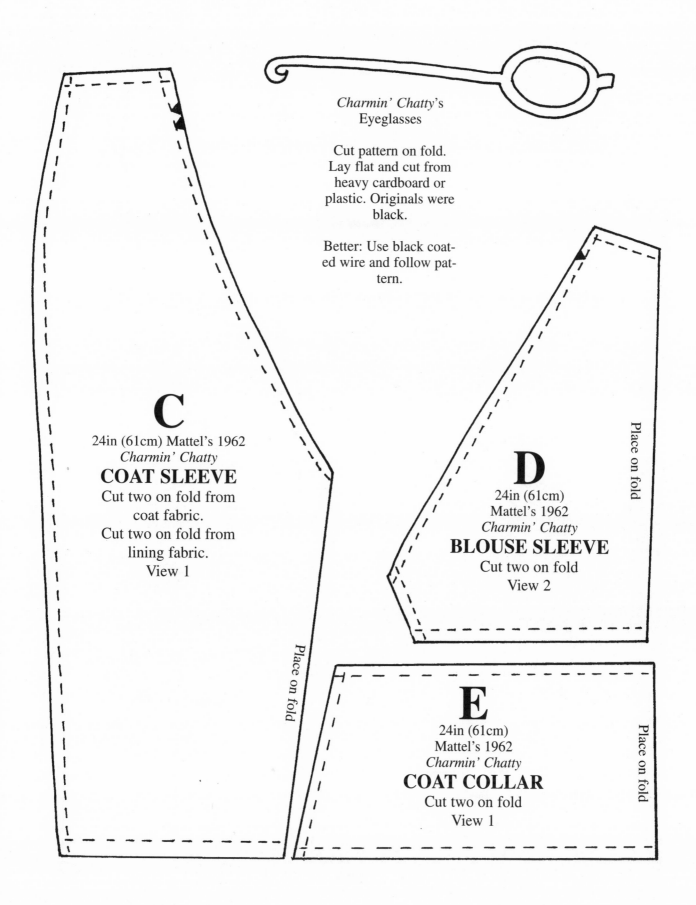

Charmin' Chatty's
Eyeglasses

Cut pattern on fold.
Lay flat and cut from
heavy cardboard or
plastic. Originals were
black.

Better: Use black coated wire and follow pattern.

C

24in (61cm) Mattel's 1962
Charmin' Chatty
COAT SLEEVE
Cut two on fold from
coat fabric.
Cut two on fold from
lining fabric.
View 1

Place on fold

D

24in (61cm)
Mattel's 1962
Charmin' Chatty
BLOUSE SLEEVE
Cut two on fold
View 2

Place on fold

E

24in (61cm)
Mattel's 1962
Charmin' Chatty
COAT COLLAR
Cut two on fold
View 1

Place on fold

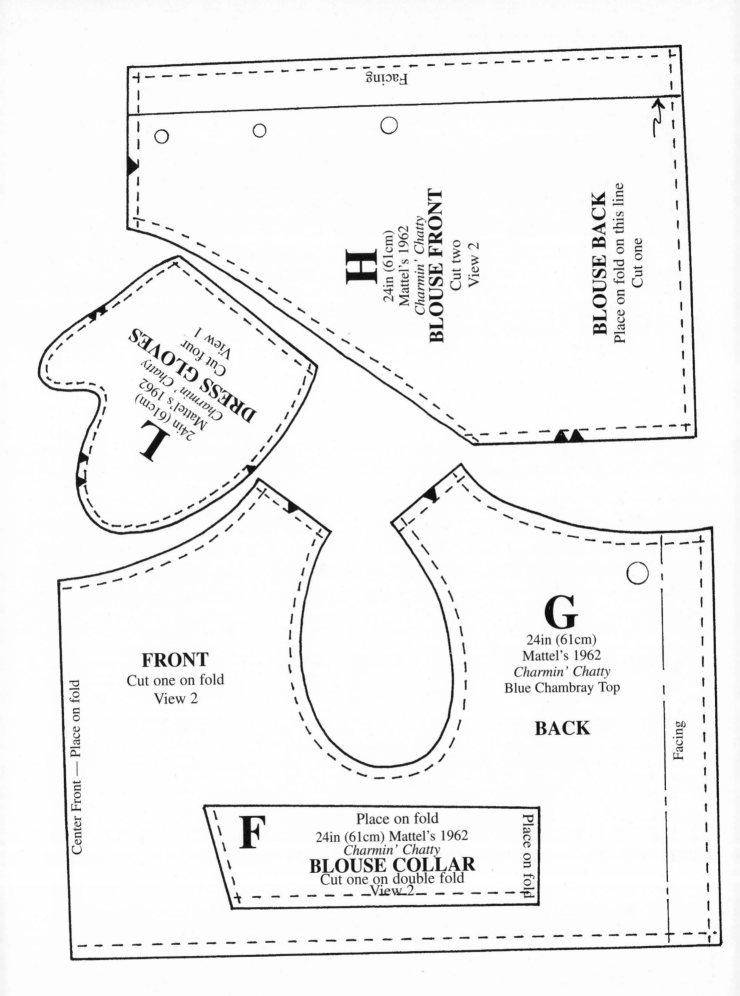

Facing

H
24in (61cm)
Mattel's 1962
Charmin' Chatty
BLOUSE FRONT
Cut two
View 2

BLOUSE BACK
Place on fold on this line
Cut one

DRESS GLOVES
Charmin' Chatty
Mattel's 1962
24in (61cm)
L
Cut four
View 1

FRONT
Cut one on fold
View 2

Center Front — Place on fold

G
24in (61cm)
Mattel's 1962
Charmin' Chatty
Blue Chambray Top

BACK

Facing

Place on fold

Place on fold
24in (61cm) Mattel's 1962
Charmin' Chatty
BLOUSE COLLAR
Cut one on double fold
View 2
F

Place on fold

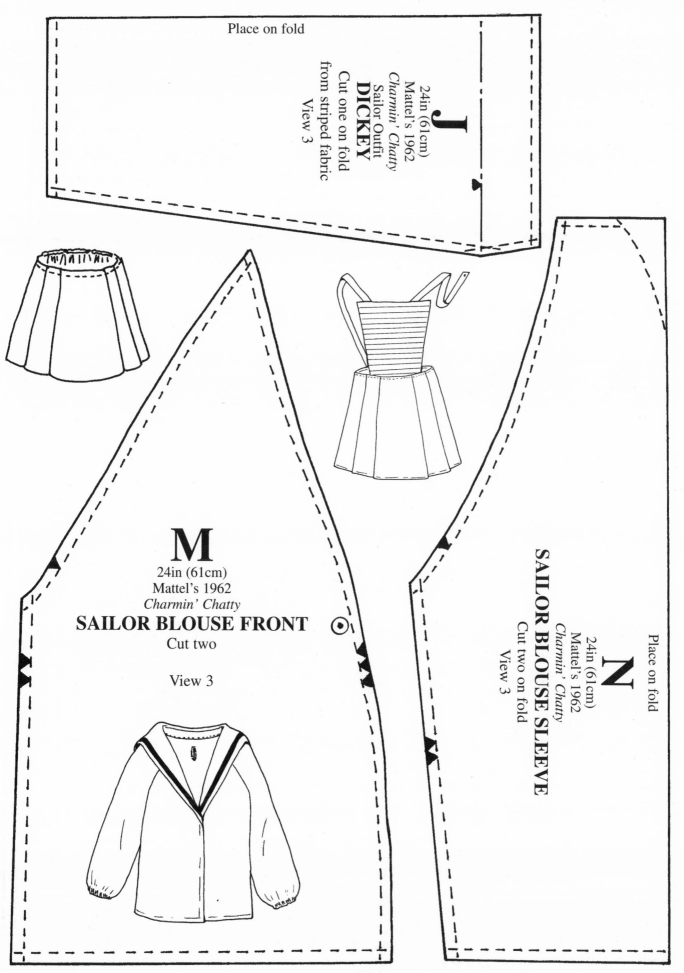

J

24in (61cm)
Mattel's 1962
Charmin' Chatty
Sailor Outfit
DICKEY
Cut one on fold
from striped fabric
View 3

Place on fold

M

24in (61cm)
Mattel's 1962
Charmin' Chatty
SAILOR BLOUSE FRONT
Cut two

View 3

N

24in (61cm)
Mattel's 1962
Charmin' Chatty
SAILOR BLOUSE SLEEVE
Cut two on fold
View 3

Place on fold

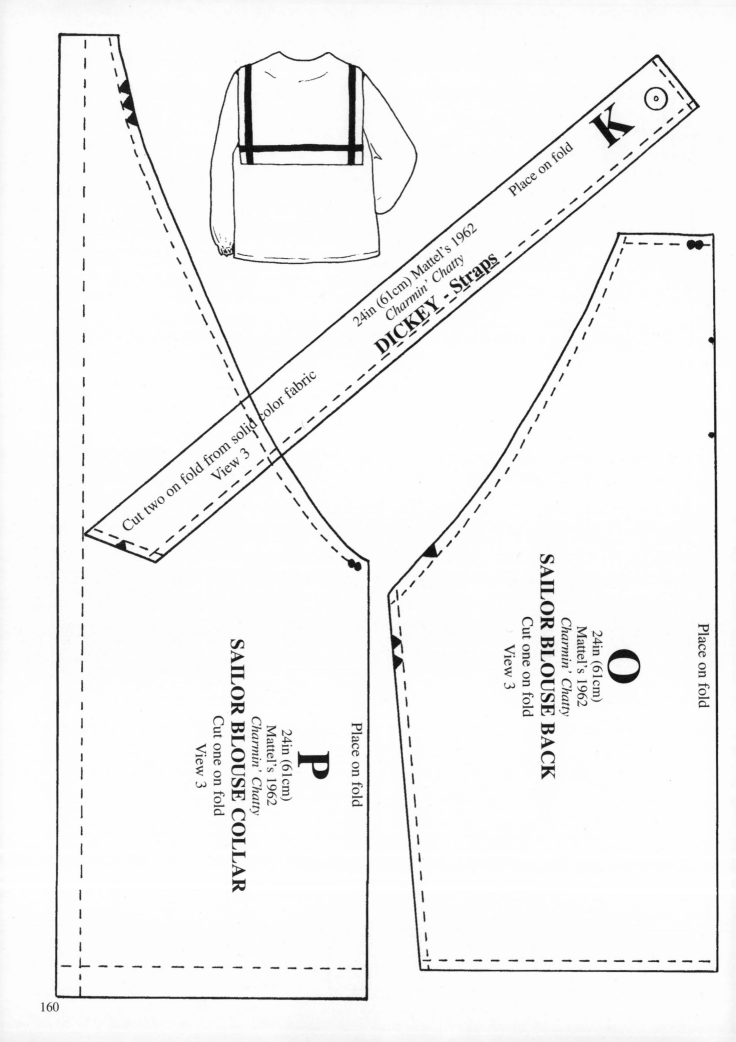

K

Place on fold

24in (61cm) Mattel's 1962
Charmin' Chatty
DICKEY - Straps

Cut two on fold from solid color fabric
View 3

O

24in (61cm)
Mattel's 1962
Charmin' Chatty
SAILOR BLOUSE BACK
Cut one on fold
View 3

Place on fold

P

24in (61cm)
Mattel's 1962
Charmin' Chatty
SAILOR BLOUSE COLLAR
Cut one on fold
View 3

Place on fold

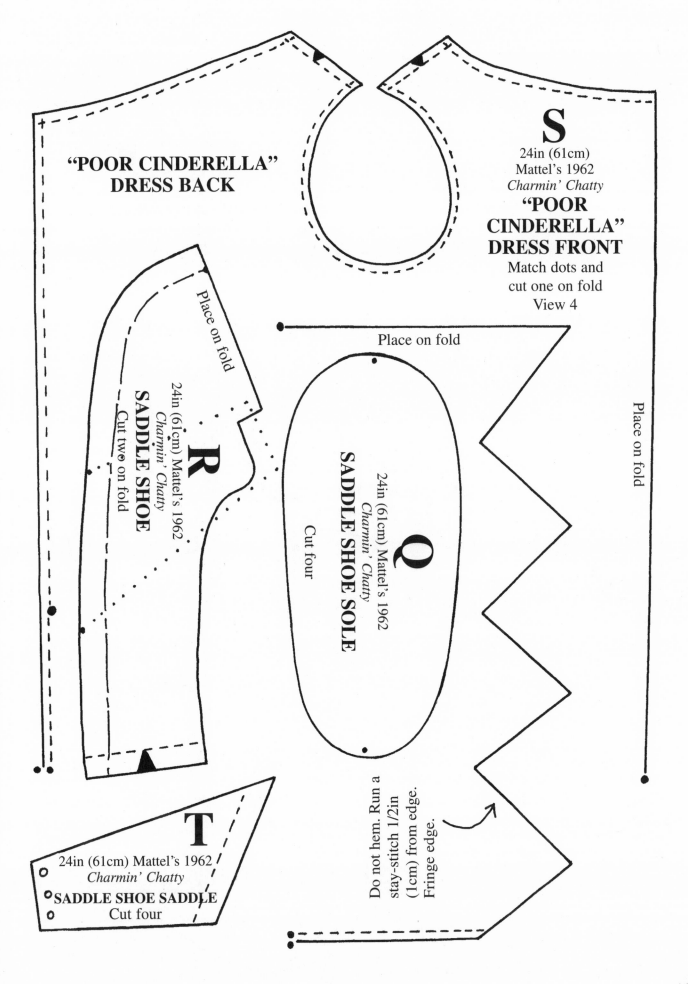

"POOR CINDERELLA"
DRESS BACK

S

24in (61cm)
Mattel's 1962
Charmin' Chatty
**"POOR
CINDERELLA"
DRESS FRONT**
Match dots and
cut one on fold
View 4

Place on fold

Place on fold

Place on fold

24in (61cm) Mattel's 1962
Charmin' Chatty
R
SADDLE SHOE
Cut two on fold

24in (61cm)
Charmin' Chatty
Q
SADDLE SHOE SOLE
Cut four

Do not hem. Run a
stay-stitch 1/2in
(1cm) from edge.
Fringe edge.

T

24in (61cm) Mattel's 1962
Charmin' Chatty
SADDLE SHOE SADDLE
Cut four

161

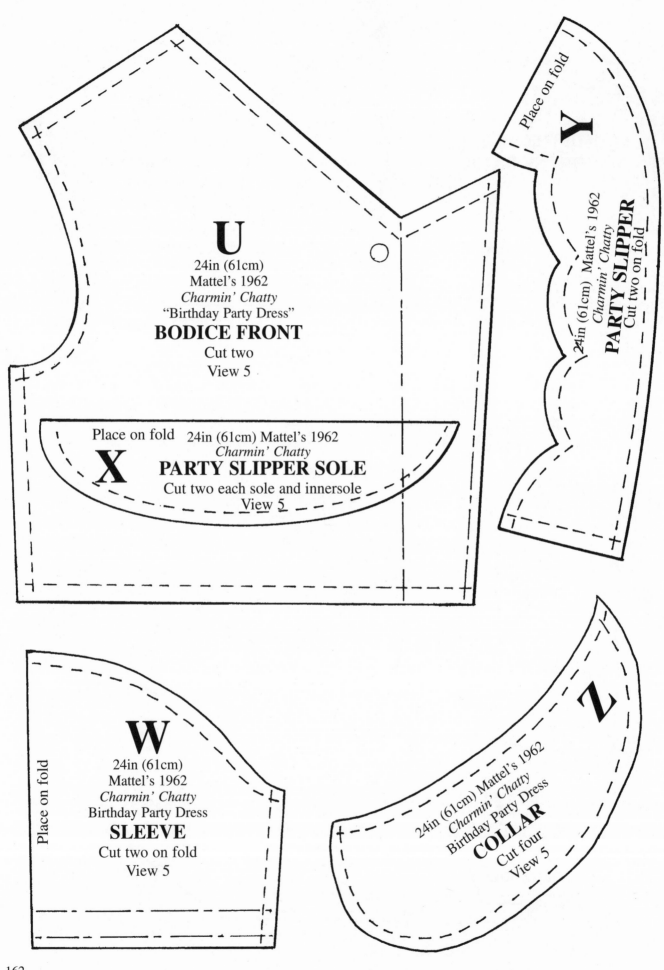

U

24in (61cm)
Mattel's 1962
Charmin' Chatty
"Birthday Party Dress"
BODICE FRONT
Cut two
View 5

Place on fold   24in (61cm) Mattel's 1962
Charmin' Chatty
X   **PARTY SLIPPER SOLE**
Cut two each sole and innersole
View 5

Place on fold

Y

24in (61cm) Mattel's 1962
Charmin' Chatty
PARTY SLIPPER
Cut two on fold

W

24in (61cm)
Mattel's 1962
Charmin' Chatty
Birthday Party Dress
SLEEVE
Cut two on fold
View 5

Place on fold

Z

24in (61cm) Mattel's 1962
Charmin' Chatty
Birthday Party Dress
COLLAR
Cut four
View 5

Original Styles
for the
1960s Chatty Family
by Mattel

View 3

View 1

20in (51cm) Chatty Cathy

18in (46cm) Chatty Baby

15in (38cm) Tiny Chatty Baby

17in (43cm) Singin' Chatty

View 2

View 9

View 4

View 5

View 6

View 8

View 7

ORIGINAL STYLES FOR THE 1960S CHATTY FAMILY
by Mattel, Inc.

20in (51cm) Chatty Cathy, 1960-1965

View 1
PINK & WHITE STRIPED DRESS & APRON
Pattern Pieces A through D

Many people do not remember (or never knew of) the stir caused by the introduction of *Chatty Cathy* in the 1960s. My next-door neighbor stood in line for hours trying to get one for her daughter that Christmas. On more than one occasion, that is. All across the nation, young mothers were determined to make Christmas perfect for their often spoiled daughters by providing this "doll of the moment."

Each day, the stores announced that another shipment was coming in on such and such a day. Dozens of mothers were waiting as the stores opened on the designated morning and only a lucky few took home that special talking doll. My neighbor, through sheer persistence, was one of them. Compared to the *Chatty Cathy* "riots", the early *Cabbage Patch Kids* mobs were a bunch of kindergartners waiting for snack time.

The following patterns are basic and, along with those shown in the first volume of this work, may be used to create nearly any style of outfit for *Chatty Cathy* and her family.

Dress - This is the dress I always think of when someone mentions *Chatty Cathy*. It is of soft cotton in pale pink and white stripes, with white cotton pique collar, worn with a white cotton eyelet-trimmed apron, white socks, and pink velour slippers. All this pink and white is perfect with the glossy dark hair and big brown eyes of the *Chatty* that stays at our house.

For the skirt of this dress cut a piece of fabric measuring 28in (71cm) x 7-1/4in (19cm). Make a 1-1/4in (3cm) hem plus 1/4in (.65cm) turned under. A piece of very fine, soft nylon net 3in (8cm) x 36in (91cm) is doubled, gathered and sewn in as the skirt is hemmed to add fullness.

Allow 1/4in (.65cm) at the top for seam. Run double gathers and pull to fit bodice. Dress is open in back with 1/2in (5cm) turned under for back facing. There are two gripper snaps sewn on bodice back.

White Cotton Eyelet Apron - To construct the apron, cut the following pieces:

1 Waistband - 6-1/2in (17cm) piece of 2in (5cm) wide eyelet
2 Ties - 12-1/2in (32cm) x 2in (5cm) pieces of cotton
2 Shoulder Straps - 3in (8cm) pieces of 2in (5cm) wide eyelet
1 Skirt - 8in (20cm) piece of 4in (10cm) wide eyelet with narrow border design

Turn back 1/2in (1cm) on each end of skirt piece for facing. Bottom will already be finished as part of eyelet. Run double gathering threads along remaining long side. Gather to fit waistband.

Hem ties on two long sides and make a center point on one short end on each. Sew unfinished ends of ties to ends of waistband. Sew shoulder straps at front and back of waistband/ties. Hint: Try apron on doll and mark for proper points of attachment.

View 2
WHITE COTTON SLIP & PANTIES
Pattern Pieces E, F

Slip - The slip is of white lawn or another lightweight cotton, with arm and neck openings finished with an overcast hem. The bottom hem has a 1/4in (.65cm) lace edging and one snap fastens the back at the top. Construction is fairly straightforward; follow the guidelines on the pattern.

Slip Variations - Extend the slip pattern 2in (5cm) to make a romper-type sunsuit. Cut out armholes and neck 1/2in (1cm) all around for a jumper or apron to be worn over a dress.

Panties - Use the shorts pattern pieces K and L, run elastic around the legs and waist, trimming, if desired, with 1/4in (.65cm) lace.

View 3
SUN TOP, SHORTS & HAT
Pattern Pieces G, H, J through N

To make this set you will need brightly colored cotton in chartreuse, light turquoise, and dark orange, almost a burnt orange. Save all the scraps to cut for bias binding.

Sun Top - The right side of this top is chartreuse, the left side is light turquoise, and it is bound all around with dark orange bias. The top fastens in back with one gripper snap. Cut seal appliqué (fig. 1) from dark orange cotton and blindstitch to right side front as indicated on pattern before sewing top.

Shorts - Use dark orange cotton, turn down a casing for elastic on the dot-dash line, and bind with aqua cotton bias.

Sun Hat - The center crown is chartreuse cotton, side sections are light turquoise, and the brim is dark orange. Make crown and set aside. Sew brim pieces together, trim seams, turn, and press. Sew six evenly spaced rows of stitching entire length of brim. Sew to crown and topstitch along crown at edge of seam.

ROSE-SPRIGGED FLANNEL PAJAMAS
Pattern Pieces O, P, Q

These snuggly PJs are white flannel with pink rosebuds and green leaves. Trim is 1/8in (.31cm) pink ricrac on neckline, around cuffs, over bodice/skirt seam and skirt/ruffle seam, as well as along the bottom edges of pants legs and around the brim of the "mob cap."

Bodice - Use the bodice pattern pieces A and B for these pajamas. Make narrow hems on sleeves, then sew elastic into sleeves on dot-dash line a. Gather sleeves between dots to fit armholes.

Cut a ruffle of flannel measuring 1-1/2in (4cm) x 32in (81cm). Turn under a 1/8in (.31cm) hem on one long side and sew ricrac over seam. Gather remaining long side to fit skirt of pajama top and attach to skirt. Sew ricrac over the seam. Attach skirt to bodice, using excess to make an inverted box pleat at center front. Sew ricrac over the seam.

Turn under a 1/2in (5cm) back facing and work four evenly spaced buttonholes from top to bottom, just above ruffle. Sew on four tiny white pearl buttons. Finish with a snap at extreme top and a small pink satin ribbon bow just above top buttonhole.

Bind neckline with self bias or shaped facing, complete ricrac trim.

Mob Cap - Cut a 12in (31cm) circle of flannel, turn and baste a 1/8in (.31cm) edge to right side. Cover with ricrac. Measure doll's head and cut a piece of 1/8in (.31cm) elastic that measurement plus 1/2in (5cm) for sewing. Over-stitch the elastic on a line 1in (3cm) in from outer edge of cap (fig. 2). Secure ends of elastic firmly.

18in (46cm) Chatty Baby, 1962-1964

RED DRESS
Pattern Pieces P, Q

This short, full dress is worn over the combinations in View 6. The dress is made of lightweight, bright red cotton, with a pocket on the front featuring the doll's name. Follow construction diagram (fig. 3) for joining dress sections.

Cut a 3in (8cm) square of red fabric for the pocket. Using white fabric paint pen, center and paint the design (fig. 4) on the pocket, following manufacturer's instructions. When paint is thoroughly dry, turn down 1/2in (1cm) for the top and 1/4in (.65cm) on other three sides. Topstitch to dress front at X's.

Sew side seams. Make a narrow handkerchief hem at bottom of dress and on armholes. Cut two 20in (51cm) pieces of ready-made red bias tape for ties. Gather dress top front and back to measure 4in (10cm) each. Center bias tape on each piece, pin, baste, stitch. Topstitch free sections of bias for shoulder ties.

COMBINATIONS
Pattern Pieces T, U

These are of white cotton, with narrow lace around neck, armholes, and leg openings. The skirt is trimmed with wider lace and the back closes with one gripper snap at top.

Construct bodice and panties separately, finishing edges with 1/8in (20cm) lace, and set aside.

For the skirt, cut a piece of white cotton measuring 20in (51cm) x 3in (8cm). Sew 1-1/4in (3cm) lace on one long side. Turn back 1/2in (1cm) on each short side for facing. Gather remaining long side to fit bodice.

Fit and stitch all three pieces as one to complete the garment. Install gripper snap.

AQUA POLKA DOT DRESS
Pattern Pieces R, S

Another short dress to be worn over the combinations of View 6, this dress is aqua with white dots. The neck is bound with self-bias, the armholes with white bias tape, and the remaining edge with a narrow handkerchief hem. White 2in (5cm) lace with an aqua detail forms a decorative "bib" effect. Sew this lace along dotted line. Install a gripper snap at top back to complete the garment.

15in (38cm) Tiny Chatty Baby, 1963-1964

AQUA ROMPER
Pattern Pieces V through Z

The top section of this romper suit is solid aqua cotton while the lower section is aqua and white pin-striped cotton. Armholes are bound with bias of the striped fabric, while the neckline is bound in white bias tape which extends to form back ties.

The personalized bib is edged with 1/2in (1cm) white lace as is the seam joining the top and bottom sections of the romper. Leg openings are finished with 1/8in (.31cm) elastic.

First, cut out the bib. Center and transfer the name pattern (fig. 5) to the fabric. Paint with aqua fabric paint pen and allow to dry thoroughly, following manufacturers instructions. Attach lace, then pin and baste bib to front of romper along neckline, using dotted lines on pattern as a guide. Note that bib is sewn to dress only at neckline.

Turn under and baste 1/8in (.31cm) on either side for back facings. Bind armholes and neckline, allowing 6in (15cm) extra at each end for ties. Lap right side over left side 1/2in (1cm) in back and tack. Set aside.

Sew crotch seam and back seam of lower section. Finish leg openings with narrow hem and elastic. Pin and baste white lace along top of this section with raw edge of lace up, along unfinished edge of section. Pin and baste bias of striped fabric with raw edges up and the fold down. Pin and baste top section, right sides together, to the lower assembly, easing if required. Machine stitch on wrong side.

17in (43cm) Singin' Chatty, 1965-1967

View 9
ORIGINAL RED DRESS & PANTIES
Pattern Pieces AA through FF

The original red cotton dress with white cotton collar and matching red panties was decorated in white with the doll's name and a band of music notes along the lower part of the skirt. The dress and panties that were available to me for study were part of a large quantity of such outfits found in original plastic bags purchased from a dealer. These may have been replacements or, since only the music notes were printed on the skirts, without the name, they may have been rejects. There was no question they originally were intended for *Singin' Chatty*; they matched exactly in size, color, and fabric all the marked originals I had seen.

Bodice - To make the dickey, turn under 1/8in (.31cm) around edge from A to B to C, then baste white ricrac on underside of dickey so one side of points shows from the right side. (There is no ricrac along neckline of dickey.) Open bodice front out flat and place dickey in center on right side; pin, baste, and topstitch to bodice. Complete bodice, attach collar, binding with white bias tape, sew two tiny buttons to dickey, and finish with a narrow red ribbon bow at center front.

Skirt - Cut a piece of red dress fabric 5-1/2in (14cm) x 30in (6cm) and put a 1in (3cm) hem on one long side. Run double gathering threads on remaining long side, but do not pull. Lay piece out flat, transfer and paint music design (fig. 2) with a white fabric paint pen. When paint is thoroughly dry (follow manufacturer's directions), turn back seam allowance under for back facing, pull gathers and attach to completed bodice. Original dress is open in back. Install two gripper snaps or buttons on bodice, as desired.

Panties - Use dress fabric to make matching panties. Bind leg openings with white bias tape; sew narrow elastic at waist.

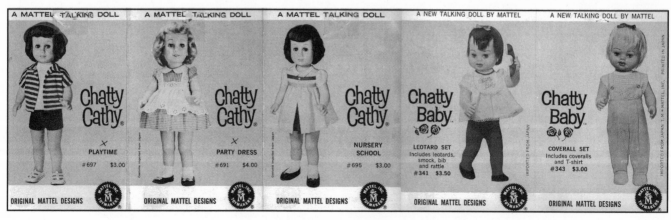

Illustrations from brochures included in the boxes with the *Chatty Family* dolls.

Chatty Cathy and *Chatty Baby* are registered trademarks of Mattel, Inc.

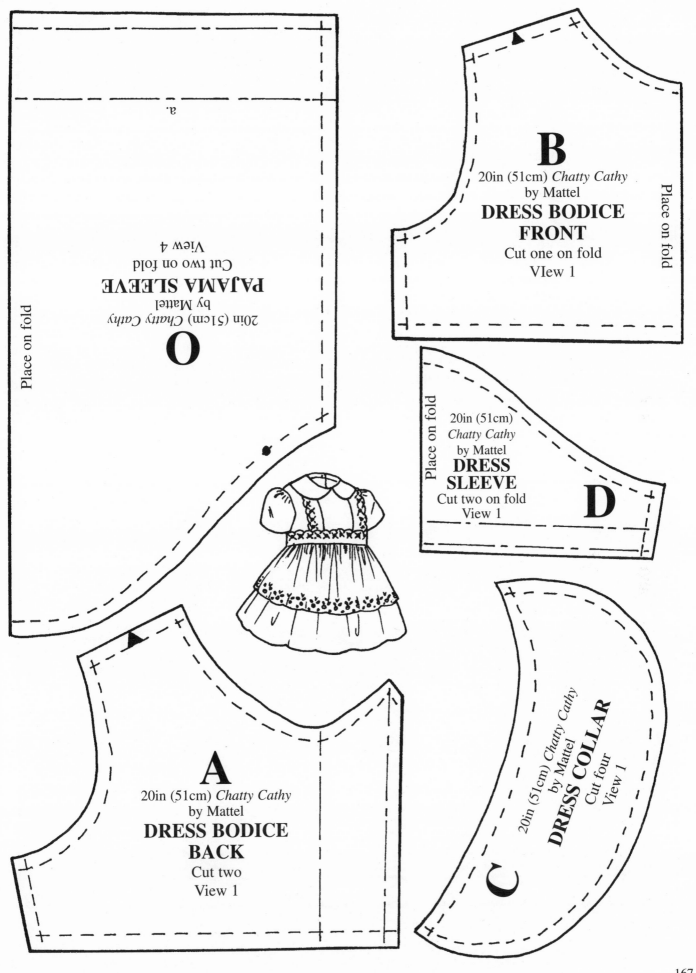

a.

PAJAMA SLEEVE
by Mattel
20in (51cm) *Chatty Cathy*
Cut two on fold
View 4

O

Place on fold

B

20in (51cm) *Chatty Cathy*
by Mattel
**DRESS BODICE
FRONT**
Cut one on fold
VIew 1

Place on fold

Place on fold

20in (51cm)
Chatty Cathy
by Mattel
**DRESS
SLEEVE**
Cut two on fold
View 1

D

A

20in (51cm) *Chatty Cathy*
by Mattel
**DRESS BODICE
BACK**
Cut two
View 1

20in (51cm) *Chatty Cathy*
by Mattel
DRESS COLLAR
Cut four
View 1

C

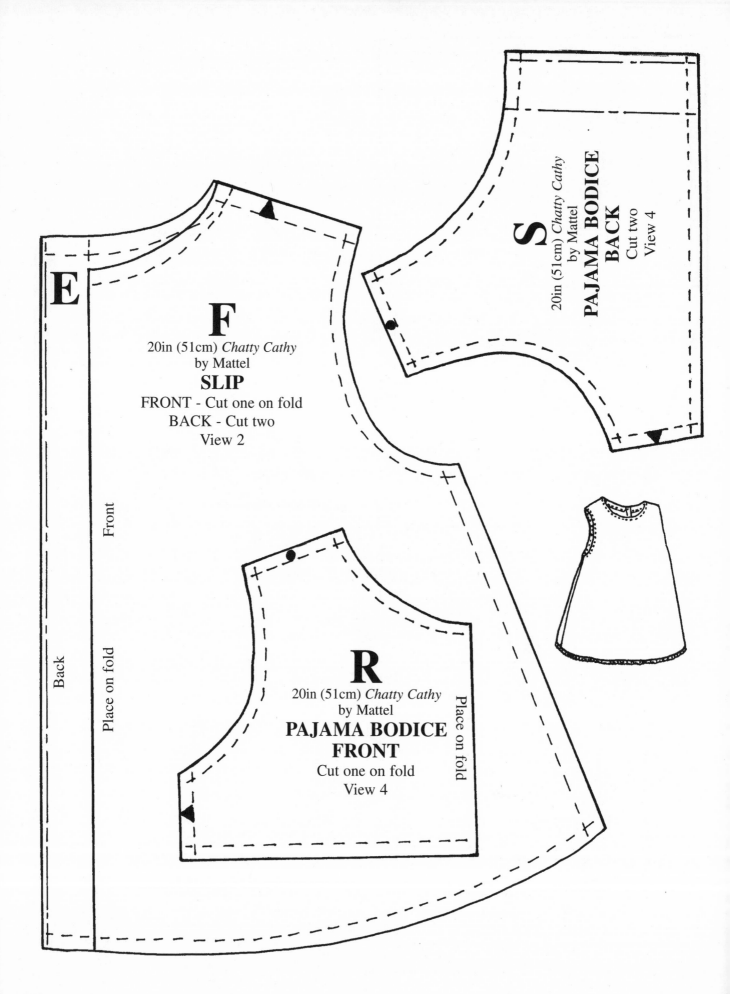

E

F

20in (51cm) *Chatty Cathy*
by Mattel
SLIP
FRONT - Cut one on fold
BACK - Cut two
View 2

Front

Back

Place on fold

S

20in (51cm) *Chatty Cathy*
by Mattel
**PAJAMA BODICE
BACK**
Cut two
View 4

R

20in (51cm) *Chatty Cathy*
by Mattel
**PAJAMA BODICE
FRONT**
Cut one on fold
View 4

Place on fold

168

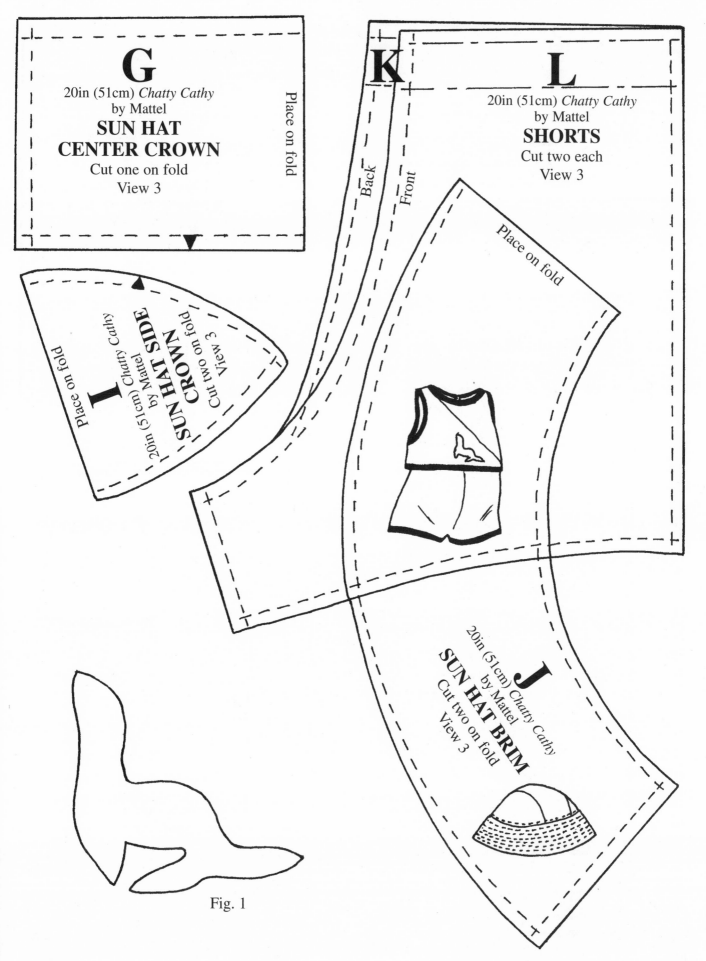

G

20in (51cm) *Chatty Cathy*
by Mattel
**SUN HAT
CENTER CROWN**
Cut one on fold
View 3

Place on fold

I

20in (51cm) *Chatty Cathy*
by Mattel
**SUN HAT SIDE
CROWN**
Cut two on fold
View 3

Place on fold

K

Back

Front

L

20in (51cm) *Chatty Cathy*
by Mattel
SHORTS
Cut two each
View 3

Place on fold

J

20in (51cm) *Chatty Cathy*
by Mattel
SUN HAT BRIM
Cut two on fold
View 3

Fig. 1

169

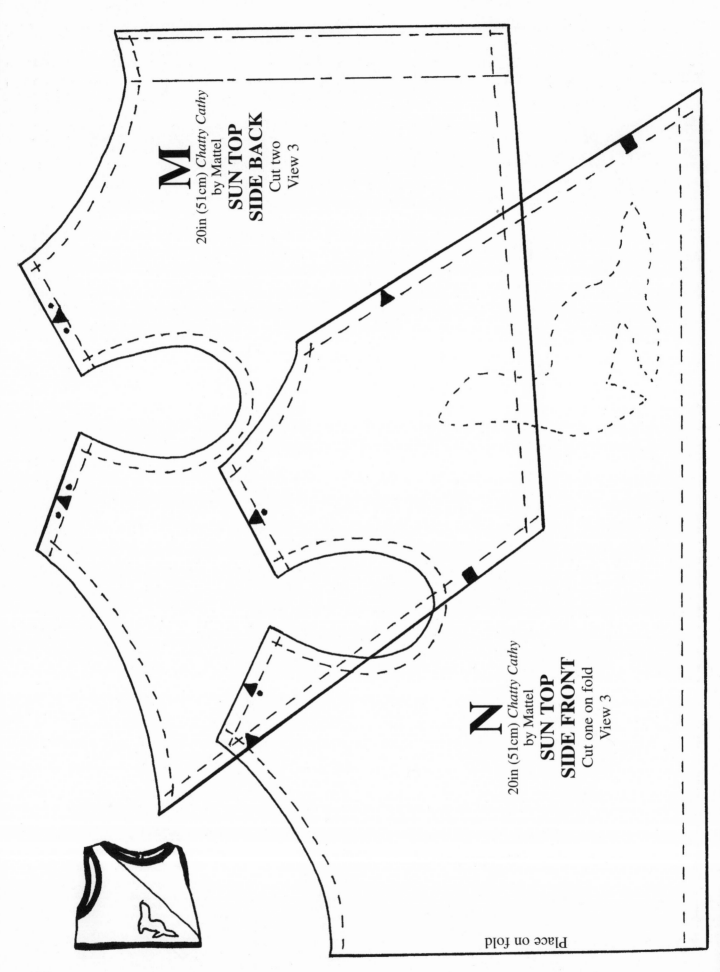

M

20in (51cm) *Chatty Cathy*
by Mattel
**SUN TOP
SIDE BACK**
Cut two
View 3

N

20in (51cm) *Chatty Cathy*
by Mattel
**SUN TOP
SIDE FRONT**
Cut one on fold
View 3

Place on fold

Place on fold

170

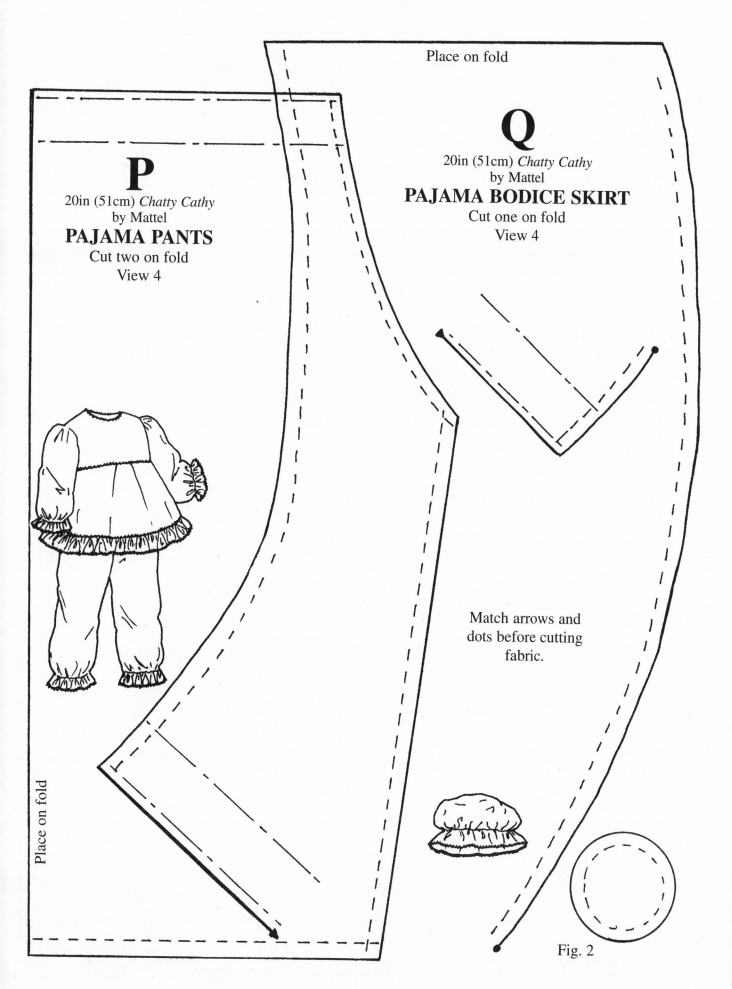

P

20in (51cm) *Chatty Cathy*
by Mattel
PAJAMA PANTS
Cut two on fold
View 4

Place on fold

Q

20in (51cm) *Chatty Cathy*
by Mattel
PAJAMA BODICE SKIRT
Cut one on fold
View 4

Place on fold

Match arrows and
dots before cutting
fabric.

Fig. 2

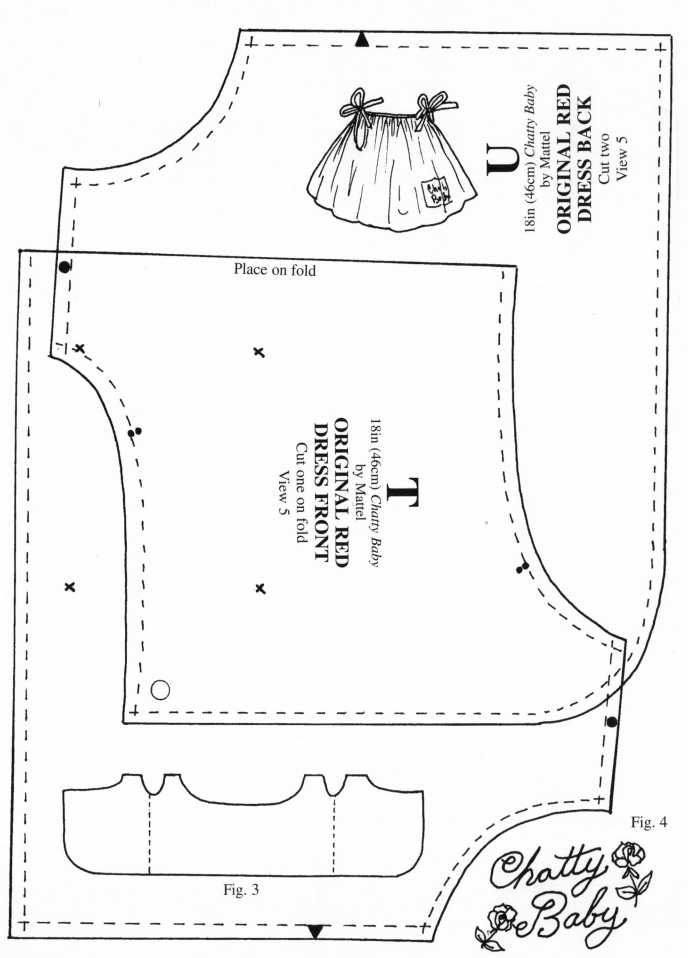

Place on fold

18in (46cm) *Chatty Baby*
by Mattel

T

**ORIGINAL RED
DRESS FRONT**

Cut one on fold
View 5

18in (46cm) *Chatty Baby*
by Mattel

U

**ORIGINAL RED
DRESS BACK**

Cut two
View 5

Fig. 4

Fig. 3

*Chatty
Baby*

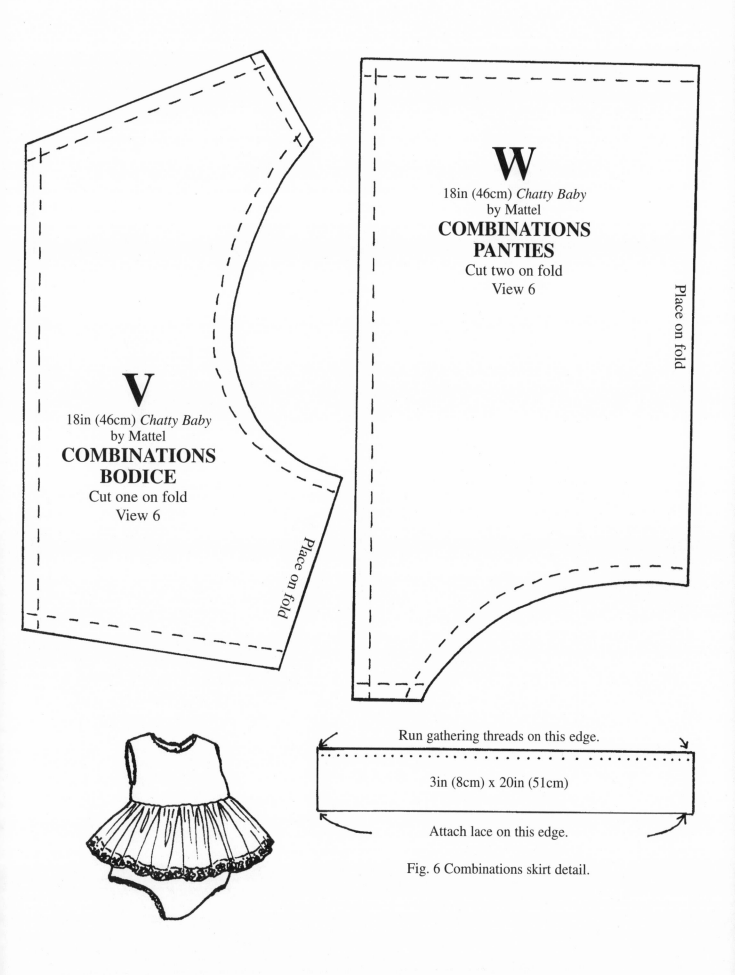

V

18in (46cm) *Chatty Baby*
by Mattel
**COMBINATIONS
BODICE**
Cut one on fold
View 6

Place on fold

W

18in (46cm) *Chatty Baby*
by Mattel
**COMBINATIONS
PANTIES**
Cut two on fold
View 6

Place on fold

Run gathering threads on this edge.

3in (8cm) x 20in (51cm)

Attach lace on this edge.

Fig. 6 Combinations skirt detail.

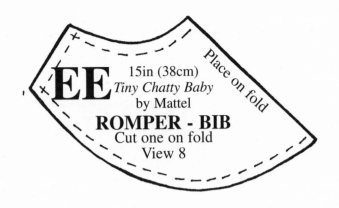

EE 15in (38cm) *Tiny Chatty Baby*
by Mattel
ROMPER - BIB
Cut one on fold
View 8

Place on fold

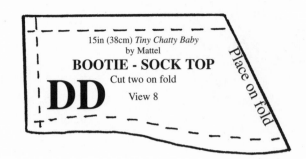

15in (38cm) *Tiny Chatty Baby*
by Mattel
BOOTIE - SOCK TOP
Cut two on fold
View 8

DD

Place on fold

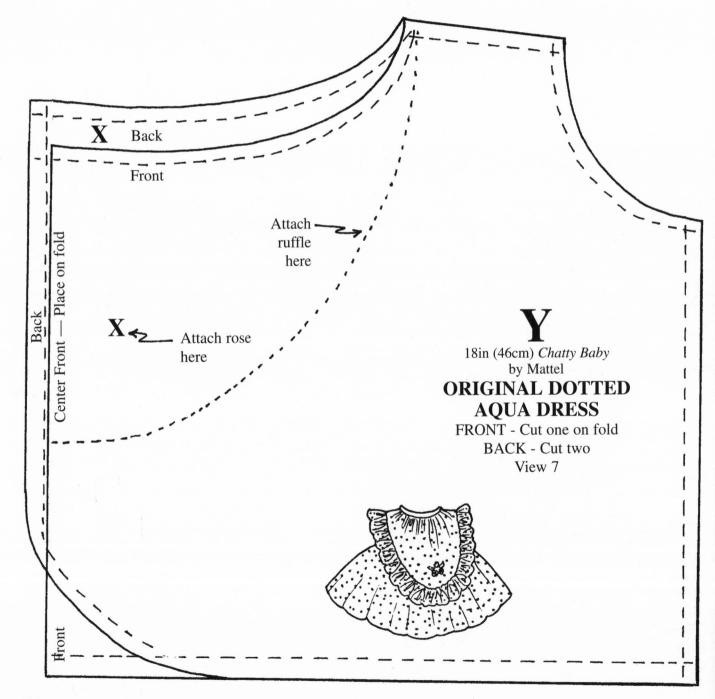

X Back

Front

Attach ruffle here

Back

Center Front — Place on fold

X Attach rose here

Y

18in (46cm) *Chatty Baby*
by Mattel
ORIGINAL DOTTED AQUA DRESS
FRONT - Cut one on fold
BACK - Cut two
View 7

Front

174

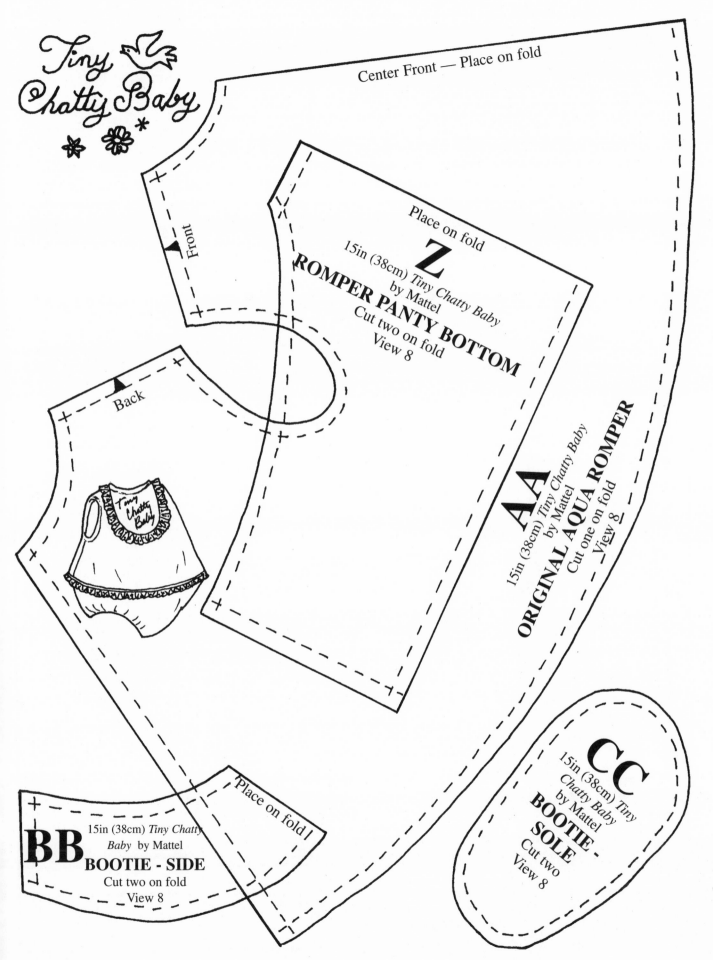

Tiny Chatty Baby

Center Front — Place on fold

Front

Back

Place on fold

Z
15in (38cm) *Tiny Chatty Baby*
by Mattel
ROMPER PANTY BOTTOM
Cut two on fold
View 8

AA
15in (38cm) *Tiny Chatty Baby*
by Mattel
ORIGINAL AQUA ROMPER
Cut one on fold
View 8

Place on fold

BB
15in (38cm) *Tiny Chatty Baby* by Mattel
BOOTIE - SIDE
Cut two on fold
View 8

CC
15in (38cm) *Tiny Chatty Baby*
by Mattel
BOOTIE - SOLE
Cut two
View 8

GG

17in (43cm) Singin' Chatty by Mattel

BODICE BACK

Cut two from red cotton fabric

View 9

Place on fold

HH

17in (43cm) Singin' Chatty by Mattel

BODICE FRONT

Cut two on fold from red cotton fabric

View 9

Fig. 2

FF

17in (43cm) Singin' Chatty by Mattel

DICKEY

Cut one from white cotton fabric

View 9

A   C

B

JJ

17in (43cm) Singin' Chatty by Mattel

COLLAR

Cut four from white cotton fabric

View 9

KK

17in (43cm) Singin' Chatty by Mattel

SLEEVE RUFFLE

Cut two on fold from red cotton fabric

View 9

Place on fold

Place on fold

Casing for 1/8in (.31cm) elastic.

LL

17in (43cm) Singin' Chatty by Mattel

UNDER PANTS

Cut two on fold from red cotton fabric

View 9

Bind leg openings with white bias.

1970s Original
On-The-Doll Fashions
Various Manufacturers

Laurie Partridge by *Remco*
Cynthia *by Mattel*
Sonny & Cher *by Mego*

Kewpie *by Cameo*
Dorothy Hamil *by Ideal*
Kristi McNichol *by Mego*

View 3

View 2

View 6

View 5

View 7

View 1

View 4

1970s ORIGINAL ON-THE-DOLL FASHIONS
Various Manufacturers

The term "on-the-doll fashion" is applied to any costume or fashion which was marketed on the doll in question in original packaging. These are usually the first outfits to be ruined in children's play. It is therefore desirable to have patterns and descriptions of such outfits for the use of the doll dressmaker. Always try to duplicate the described fabric as nearly as possible.

Views 1 & 2
Basic patterns for
SONNY & CHER
by Mego - 1976
Pattern Pieces A through J

Some of the most fabulous fashion designs of this period were created for *Sonny* and *Cher* dolls, mostly by top designers. A book devoted entirely to these two dolls would be needed to give patterns for duplicating all their original fashions. Patterns shown, therefore, are the clothes in which the dolls were originally packed. With these two patterns and the illustrations from the folder that came in the original box, the doll seamstress will be able to design dozens of ravishing outfits. Keep in mind that *Cher*, especially, favored "far-out" fashions.

Cher's first in-box outfit was a halter-top, pink polyester jersey dress with a body-hugging skirt and a wide-flared, bias-cut flounce. The halter is a cross-over style, fastened with a snap or button at the back of the neck. Later *Cher* dolls were issued in different outfits, including a killer black evening dress.

Sonny originally came in dark blue chambray jeans and a white long-sleeved, knit turtleneck top with black sewn-in dickey. He also wore a leather-like belt through jeans loops, and black shoes. His other doll-in-box outfits were equally uninteresting with only an occasional touch of sparkle. The *Cher* doll's designer outfits were the show-stoppers since they closely followed what the star was actually wearing on stage and television.

Use these two patterns and borrow other '70s patterns from elsewhere in the book to create a wide array of outfits. Use a copy machine to enlarge or reduce to the size you need. Follow the illustrations from the original *Sonny* and *Cher* in-box folder shown here to create duplicates of the additional costumes sold for the dolls.

For example, widen the leg of *Sonny*'s jeans pattern to make the wide-leg pants for *Cher*. Enlarge the 9in (23cm) male action figure patterns to fit *Sonny*. Some adjustments will be required, but that is a good exercise in working with patterns. Such experience will prove invaluable in working to adapt other patterns. All you need is the doll and a place to begin - in this case, the patterns in this book.

Feel free to let your imagination soar; become a high fashion designer. *Cher* has always been noted for her penchant for dramatic costumes. You will be following in the footsteps of some of the world's best-known fashion designers in creating an original, one-of-a-kind for your *Cher* doll. You may even decide to make *Sonny* a costume with a little more pizzazz!

View 3
Outfits for 19in (48cm)
LAURIE PARTRIDGE
by Remco - 1973
Pattern Pieces K through Q

This doll wore a hot pink stretch nylon, long-sleeved turtleneck top sewn at the waist to a pair of bell-bottom trousers. These jeans are of a dark blue rib-patterned denim and the bottoms are fringed, not hemmed. The back of this one-piece garment fastens with five snaps, one at waist, one on turtleneck collar, and the other three spaced out evenly down the back. There are two pockets on the front of the jeans, located by the square of four X's on the pattern. Sew pockets before assembling main pieces of garment.

Using this pattern along with other 1970s patterns in this book, you may create a large wardrobe for *Laurie* and other large dolls of this period.

View 4
Original ON-THE-DOLL
Dress for 19in (48cm)
CYNTHIA
by Mattel - 1971
Pattern Pieces R through W

Cynthia's dress is a soft pink cotton trimmed with woven braid of white background with blue roses and green leaves. The cummerbund, sewn to the dress only at the back facing on each side, is a soft blue velvet tied with white cord lacing. The dress is open down the back with three snap closures. The neck opening is trimmed with braid and narrow white eyelet. The same braid creates the Juliet-style feature of the sleeve. Lay sleeves out flat and attach braid before assembling the garment. Be sure the final measurement of the sleeve where braid is attached will allow the hand to pass through the sleeve. Remember seam allowances when making this measurement.

Dress & Panties for a 12in (31cm)-14in (36cm) Vinyl *KEWPIE*

Pattern Pieces X through AA

This pattern is based on a dress and panties sold by Sears in the early 1970s for vinyl *Kewpies*, packed in a plain brown cardboard box. It is of light blue nylon trimmed in white nylon lace at sleeve edges, around the white nylon collar, and along panty legs.

Bodice - Dress fastens with large white snap at top back and is open down the back. The collar is trimmed with pink ribbon roses and light green leaves at X's on pattern.

Skirt - Make an underarm template from a 3in (8cm) x 5in (13cm) file card, following the pattern. Cut a 4-1/2in (12cm) x 22in (56cm) piece of dress fabric for skirt. Fold length in half end to end. Center template for underarm on folded fabric and cut out following template. This is the lower section of the armhole. Turn back a 1in (3cm) hem; turn back 1/2in (1cm) facing at each end of piece. Gather to fit bodice.

Original Outfit for 11in (33cm) *DOROTHY HAMIL* by Ideal - 1976-77

Pattern Pieces BB, CC

The *Dorothy Hamil* doll, even without her original outfit, is easy to spot because the dark brown rooted wig is done in the special *Dorothy Hamil* flip. Her outfit is of red nylon tricot trimmed with gold braid.

The skirt is a 4in (10cm) circle of fabric with a cutout for the waist; panties are sewn into the skirt. Construct top, skirt, panties, and sew together at the waist. Neckline and sleeves are trimmed with gold braid.

She wears stretch tights, ice skates, and a "gold" medal with the Olympic symbols around her neck suspended on a red, white, and blue ribbon. On the obverse of the medal is WORLD CHAMPION 1976. She measures 11-1/2in (29cm) in her skates.

The pattern for the panties is far different from any other I have seen, but it works. Follow matching symbols on the pattern and leave the back open down to the dot.

Original Outfit for 9in (23cm) *KRISTI McNICHOL* by Mego - 1977

Pattern Pieces DD through GG

Kristi wears jeans made of faded blue chambray, with white topstitching, that close with one snap in back. Back opening is faced with self-bias. Her top is of white stretch knit, also with a back opening and one snap.

A colorful nylon windbreaker tops the outfit. Sleeves are medium blue, body is red, and jacket is trimmed with red, white, blue, and yellow knitted cuff material on bottom of jacket, sleeve cuffs, and around neck edge. There is also a yellow stripe down the top of the sleeve as indicated by the dotted line on pattern.

White plastic wedge oxfords complete the outfit.

Sonny and *Cher* Fashions. Folder was packaged with each doll in 1976. By Mego.

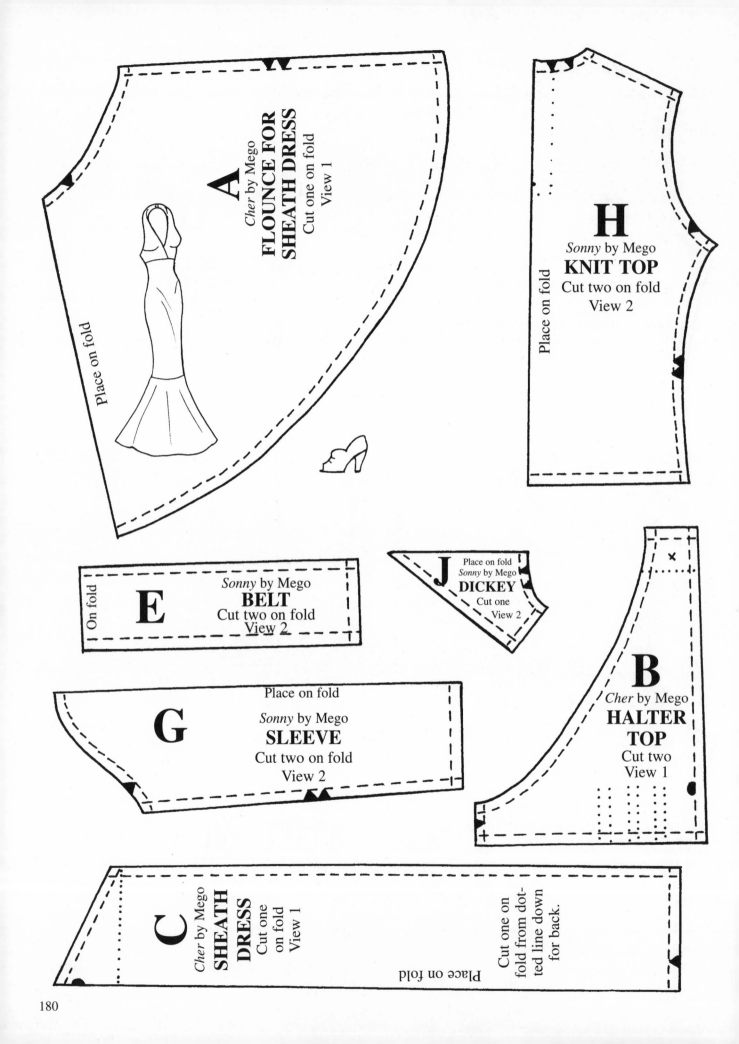

A

Cher by Mego
**FLOUNCE FOR
SHEATH DRESS**
Cut one on fold
View 1

Place on fold

H

Sonny by Mego
KNIT TOP
Cut two on fold
View 2

Place on fold

On fold

E

Sonny by Mego
BELT
Cut two on fold
View 2

J

Place on fold
Sonny by Mego
DICKEY
Cut one
View 2

B

Cher by Mego
**HALTER
TOP**
Cut two
View 1

Place on fold

G

Sonny by Mego
SLEEVE
Cut two on fold
View 2

C

Cher by Mego
**SHEATH
DRESS**
Cut one
on fold
View 1

Cut one on
fold from dot-
ted line down
for back.

Place on fold

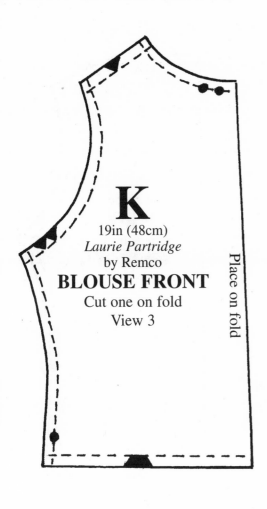

K

19in (48cm)
Laurie Partridge
by Remco
BLOUSE FRONT
Cut one on fold
View 3

Place on fold

F
COLLAR

Sonny by Mego

Cut one on fold   Place on fold

View 2

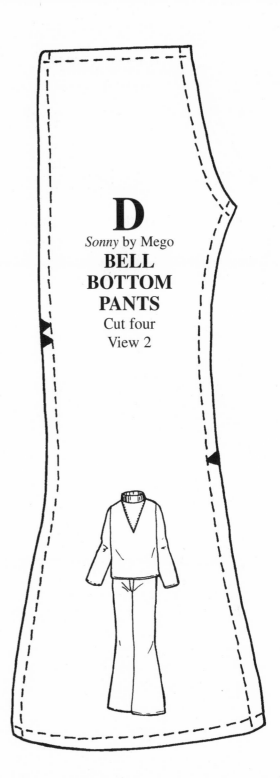

D

Sonny by Mego
**BELL
BOTTOM
PANTS**
Cut four
View 2

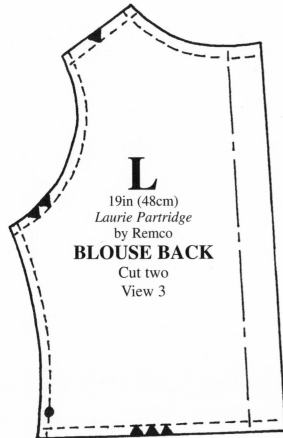

L

19in (48cm)
Laurie Partridge
by Remco
BLOUSE BACK
Cut two
View 3

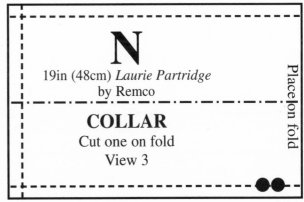

N

19in (48cm) *Laurie Partridge*
by Remco

COLLAR
Cut one on fold
View 3

Place on fold

181

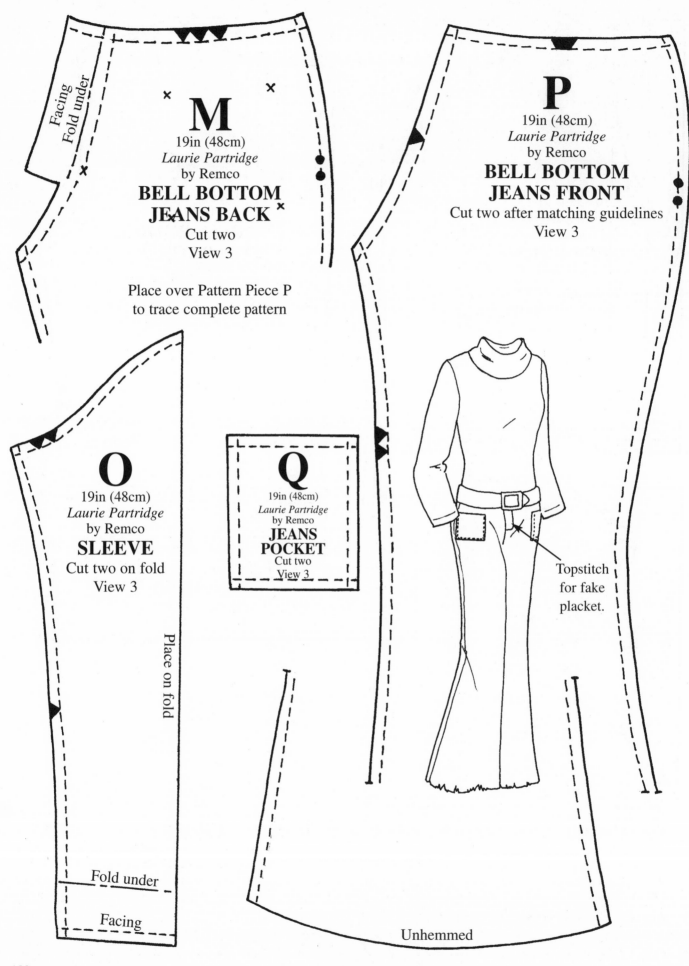

M

19in (48cm)
Laurie Partridge
by Remco
**BELL BOTTOM
JEANS BACK**
Cut two
View 3

Place over Pattern Piece P
to trace complete pattern

Facing
Fold under

P

19in (48cm)
Laurie Partridge
by Remco
**BELL BOTTOM
JEANS FRONT**
Cut two after matching guidelines
View 3

O

19in (48cm)
Laurie Partridge
by Remco
SLEEVE
Cut two on fold
View 3

Place on fold

Fold under

Facing

Q

19in (48cm)
Laurie Partridge
by Remco
**JEANS
POCKET**
Cut two
View 3

Topstitch
for fake
placket.

Unhemmed

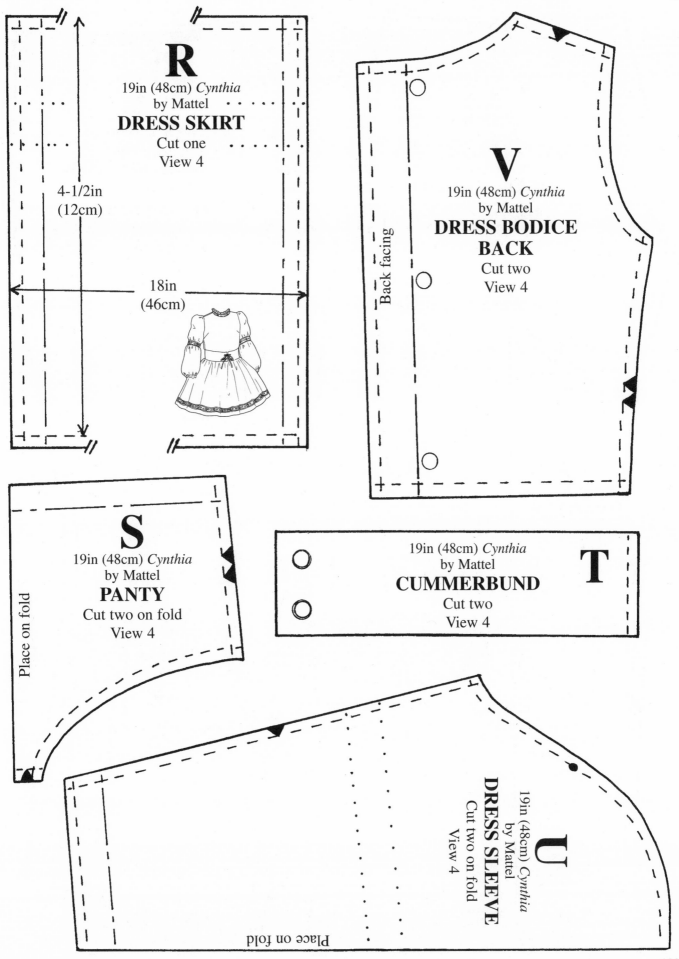

R

19in (48cm) *Cynthia*
by Mattel
DRESS SKIRT
Cut one
View 4

4-1/2in
(12cm)

18in
(46cm)

V

19in (48cm) *Cynthia*
by Mattel
**DRESS BODICE
BACK**
Cut two
View 4

Back facing

S

19in (48cm) *Cynthia*
by Mattel
PANTY
Cut two on fold
View 4

Place on fold

19in (48cm) *Cynthia*
by Mattel
CUMMERBUND
Cut two
View 4

T

U

19in (48cm) *Cynthia*
by Mattel
DRESS SLEEVE
Cut two on fold
View 4

Place on fold

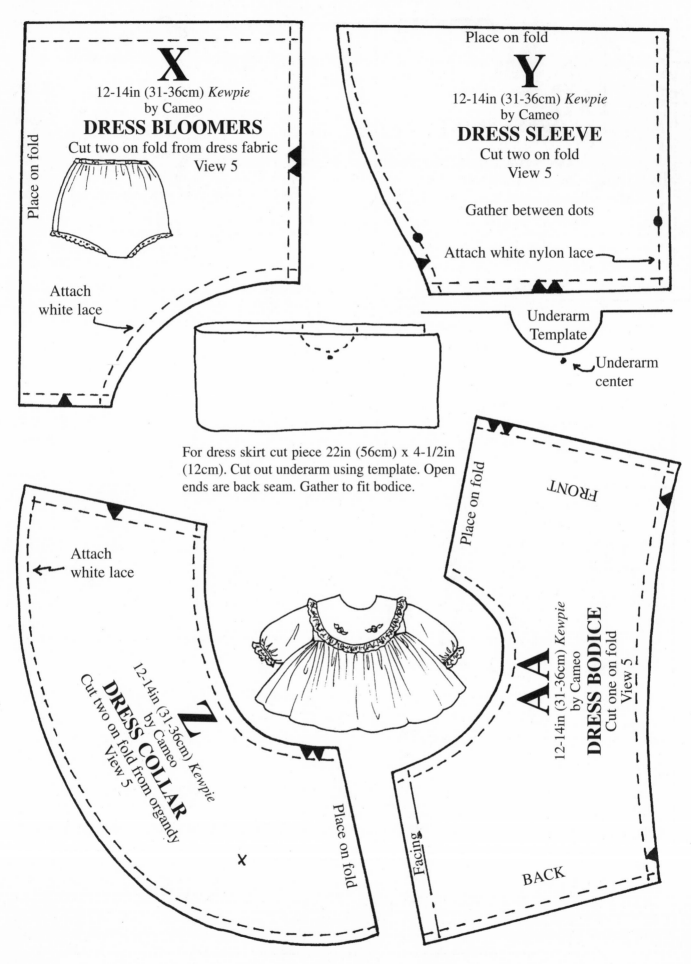

X

12-14in (31-36cm) *Kewpie*
by Cameo
DRESS BLOOMERS
Cut two on fold from dress fabric
View 5

Place on fold

Attach white lace

Y

Place on fold

12-14in (31-36cm) *Kewpie*
by Cameo
DRESS SLEEVE
Cut two on fold
View 5

Gather between dots

Attach white nylon lace →

Underarm Template

Underarm center

For dress skirt cut piece 22in (56cm) x 4-1/2in (12cm). Cut out underarm using template. Open ends are back seam. Gather to fit bodice.

Attach white lace

Z

12-14in (31-36cm) *Kewpie*
by Cameo
DRESS COLLAR
Cut two on fold from organdy
View 5

X

Place on fold

AA

Place on fold

FRONT

12-14in (31-36cm) *Kewpie*
by Cameo
DRESS BODICE
Cut one on fold
View 5

Facing

BACK

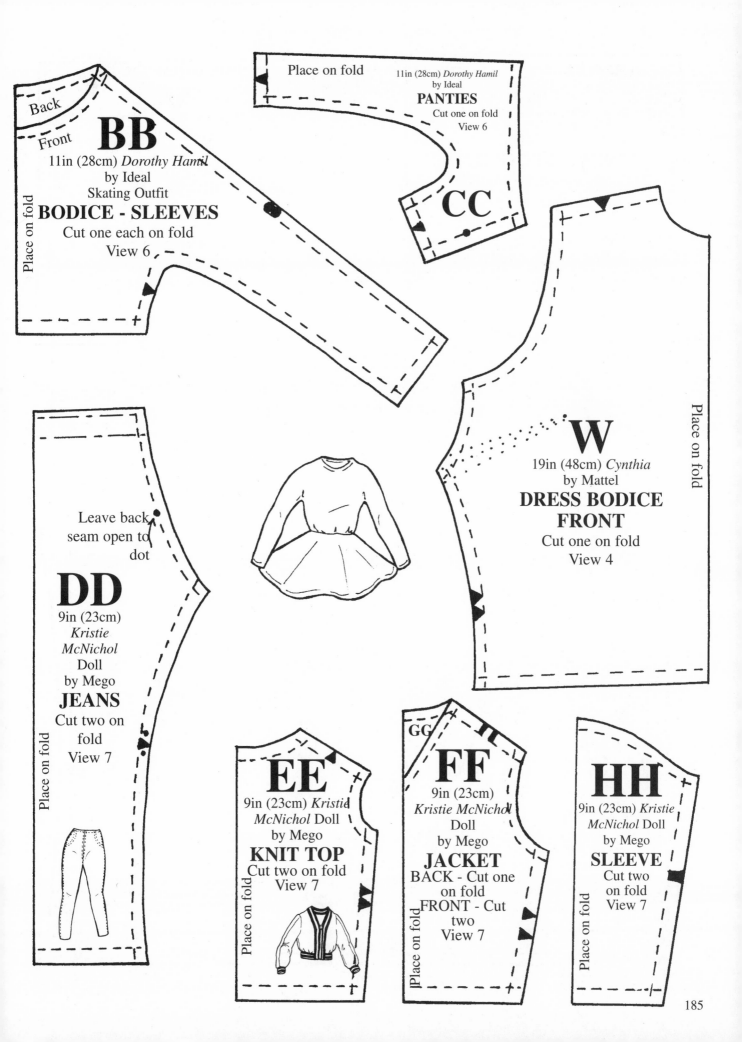

BB

Back

Front

11in (28cm) *Dorothy Hamil*
by Ideal
Skating Outfit
BODICE - SLEEVES
Cut one each on fold
View 6

Place on fold

Place on fold
11in (28cm) *Dorothy Hamil*
by Ideal
PANTIES
Cut one on fold
View 6

CC

W
19in (48cm) *Cynthia*
by Mattel
**DRESS BODICE
FRONT**
Cut one on fold
View 4

Place on fold

Leave back
seam open to
dot

DD
9in (23cm)
*Kristie
McNichol*
Doll
by Mego
JEANS
Cut two on
fold
View 7

Place on fold

EE
9in (23cm) *Kristie
McNichol* Doll
by Mego
KNIT TOP
Cut two on fold
View 7

Place on fold

GG

FF
9in (23cm)
Kristie McNichol
Doll
by Mego
JACKET
BACK - Cut one
on fold
FRONT - Cut
two
View 7

Place on fold

HH
9in (23cm) *Kristie
McNichol* Doll
by Mego
SLEEVE
Cut two
on fold
View 7

Place on fold

View 1

View 2

View 3

Wardrobe for

18-20in (46-51cm) Dolls of the 1970s

Fits Betsy McCall,
The My Friend Series,
and others

View 4

View 5

View 6

View 7

View 8

WARDROBE FOR 18-20in (46-51cm) DOLLS OF THE 1970s
Various Manufacturers

These patterns fit such dolls as *Betsy McCall*, Fisher-Price's *My Friend* series, and *Kimberly* by Tomy as well as many of the modern artist dolls. The size and shape of the 70s dolls make them easy to sew for and fun to dress. Use your imagination in creating '70s styles for these charmers.

Guide to Pattern Pieces

A-Back of coat or dress
B-Front of coat or dress
C-Back of jumper or slip
D-Front of jumper or slip
E-Armhole for slip
F-Back of high-necked dress

G-Short puffed sleeve
H-Long sleeve
J-Collar for blouse, robe, coat, dress
K-Short shorts, panties
L-Long shorts, shortie pajama pants
M-Pocket for robe, coat, shorts, pants

N-Tee shirt with sleeves
O-Sleeveless tee shirt
P-Blouse front
Q-Blouse back

View 1 **JUMPER** Pattern Pieces C, D

Check length of pattern for your doll before tracing pattern and make any necessary adjustments. Cut one back and one front on fold.

Bind edges with matching or self-bias to inside, or with contrasting bias to outside. Turn up 1/4in (.65cm) around bottom edge, then turn up appropriate hem for your doll.

Views 2 & 5 **TEE SHIRTS** Pattern Pieces N, O

Cut tee shirt in either style from the good parts of a worn or outgrown man's or boy's tee shirt, or from decorative tee shirt fabric. Bind edges with self-bias or turn neat hems. Extend sleeves of style B and cut from heavier knit for sweatshirt look. For turtlenecks, cut a piece 6in (15cm) x 1-3/4in 5cm). Fold in half lengthwise with right sides together, seam short sides together, turn, and fit to neck opening, stretching fabric as you sew. Be sure neck opening will go over doll's head.

Views 2 & 5 **SHORT SHORTS & LONG SHORTS** Pattern Pieces K, L

Given are guidelines for short shorts and long shorts. This pattern may be extended for clamdiggers or full-length jeans. For jeans, cut outside leg 1/4in (.65cm) wider and seam together. For a real "jeans" look, make a pocket following dotted lines on pattern and sew into outside leg seam. You may wish to allow extra length for a cuff on the jeans, in which case dress your doll in a tailored shirt and saddle oxfords for a real teenybopper look. Topstitching the jeans with contrasting thread adds authenticity to the styling.

Turn down casing around top and run narrow elastic. Add pockets as desired.

View 3 **DRESS** Pattern Pieces A, B, H

This dress has a high neckline and back opening to within 3in (8cm) of finished hem. Measure doll from back of neck and shoulder to length desired. Cut pattern pieces A and B accordingly. When tracing the pattern be sure to include back seam allowance.

Sew shoulder seams, insert long sleeves and cuffs. Sew side seams. Trim neck edge with lace or borrow a collar pattern from another pattern in this book. For sleeve cuff, measure around your doll's hand at widest point, add 3/4in (2cm) and cut two pieces that measurement by 1-1/4in (3cm). Trim dress with narrow ruffle or eyelet edging as desired.

For cummerbund, measure doll's waist and cut of contrasting fabric or felt, using "Cynthia" pattern from this book.

Variations: Follow guidelines on pattern to make a short-sleeved dress (view 8).

View 4 **UNDERWEAR** Pattern Pieces D, K

Slip - Cut two of pattern piece D from white lawn or other fine cotton. Trim all edges with 1/8in (.31cm) lace or eyelet, turn narrow handkerchief hems, or bind with self-bias.

Panties - Use short shorts pattern piece K. Make casings at waist and bottom of leg. Run 1/8in (.31cm) elastic. Trim as desired.

Not Shown **ROBE** Pattern Pieces A, B, H, J

Use pattern as shown or extend to desired length. Follow guidelines for coat. Make pockets same as for coat except omit lining. For robe tie, cut one piece 16in (41cm) x 2in (5cm), sew long seam and ends with right sides together, leaving 2in (5cm) opening in center for turning. Turn, close opening. Alternatively, seam long side only, turn and fringe ends. Chain crochet belt loops of matching yarn.

View 6
COAT
Pattern Pieces A, B, H, M, J (optional)

Follow guidelines on pattern. Back is cut on fold. Cut lining using same pattern. Sew shoulder seams and sides seams. Construct pockets and sew in place. Construct sleeves and pin in place, easing fullness between dots to fit.

Repeat above for lining. Insert lining into coat, wrong sides together. Fold front coat facings back. Trim away excess lining at fronts, turn under 1/4in (.65cm) of lining and blindstitch to facing.

For optional collar: With right sides together, sew collar seam. Clip seam, turn and press. Install collar.

If using "fur" trim, finish neck edge with facing of coat fabric. Using coat pattern cut a facing approximately 1in (3cm) wide. Pin, baste, stitch to neck edge right sides together. Clip and trim seam, turn down, press, and blindstitch facing to lining. Attach fur with stitching or sew on three snap fasteners. Repeat for cuffs.

This is attractive using white "fur" on red or royal blue velvet. Or try brown "mink" on green or blue wool. If larger collar is preferred, borrow from another pattern in this book or enlarge pattern piece J.

Turn under bottom edges of coat, sleeves, and lining. Blindstitch lining to coat.

View 7
LONG & SHORTIE NIGHTIES

Long version - Cut two pieces of flower-sprigged cotton 12in (31cm) x 11-1/2in (29cm). With right sides together, sew short sides together to within 3in (8cm) of top, taking full 1/2in (1cm) seam allowance. Turn back seam allowance and blindstitch for armholes. Run a double row of gathering stitches on each top edge to within 1in (3cm) of each end, but do not gather. Turn up a 1/4in (.65cm) hem.

Put garment on doll and pull gathers to fit. Tie off threads. Measure over shoulder to determine length of shoulder ties. Be sure to allow enough length for tying a bow. Cut four pieces of cotton 1-1/4in (3cm) wide by length of your measurement plus 1in (3cm). Fold each piece lengthwise right sides together and sew long side. Turn and press. Pin in place on gown. (Ribbon or bias tape may be substituted for these self-fabric ties.)

Cut a piece of ruffle or eyelet edging and bias tape to fit top of gown. Pin, then baste to gown. Machine stitch. Blindstitch bias to cover seam. Tack edging to shoulder straps.

Shortie Pajamas - Cut two pieces of fabric 18in (46cm) x 5-1/2in (5cm) for shortie pajama top and proceed as for nightie. Use long shorts pattern piece L for pajama bottoms. Make a casing along short shorts bottom line and run narrow elastic. Turn up bottom in narrow hem. Trim to match top.

Sundress Variation - Cut two pieces of fabric 20in (51cm) x 7in (18cm) for a sundress and proceed as for nightie.

Note: Fullness of long nightie, sundress, and shortie pajama top may be adjusted for more or less fullness as desired by changing the first measurement in each of the above.

View 8
LOW-NECKED BLOUSE
Pattern Pieces G, P, Q

Sew shoulder seams, press flat. Lay construction out flat, right side down. Turn back facings to inside. Finish neckline with bias tape.

On sleeves, gather between dots and pull to fit sleeve opening. Tie off gather threads and pin sleeves in place, baste, stitch. Sew underarm seams and side seams.

Measure widest part of doll's hand. Cut two sleeve cuffs the hand measurement plus 3/4in (2cm) and 2in (5cm) wide. Seam ends of cuff together, press seam open. Gather lower edge of sleeve to fit cuff. Pin right side of cuff to wrong side of sleeve, baste, and stitch.

Bring cuff to outside. Turn back 1/4in (.65cm) all around and press. Fold cuff up to cover gathers; pin, baste, and topstitch. Finish bottom edge with narrow handkerchief hem or machine topstitch.

View 8
SKIRT

Cut a piece of fabric 6-1/2in (17cm) wide and 24in (61cm) long. Run double gathering stitches on one long side to within 1in (3cm) each end. (Ends will be at center back seam.) Make a 1in (3cm) seam by sewing ends together to within 3in (8cm) of top. Baste upper seam allowances back to form facing.

For waistband: Measure doll's waist. Cut a piece of fabric the waist measurement plus 1in (3cm) and 2in (5cm) wide. With right sides together, sew short ends. Trim seam, turn and press.

Gather skirt to fit waistband, leaving 1/4in (.65cm) overlap of each end for snap fasteners (see detail sketch).

Turn bottom edge of skirt under 1/4in (.65cm) and press. Turn up 1/2in (1cm) hem and blindstitch.

Note: This pattern may be adjusted to make a one-piece dress with or without an inset belt, as desired.

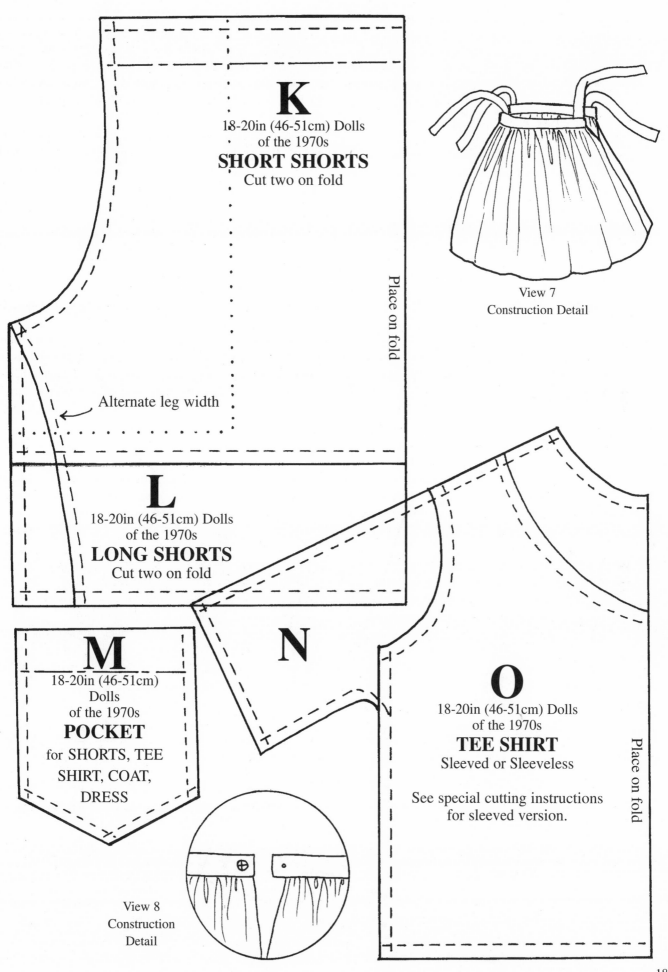

K

18-20in (46-51cm) Dolls
of the 1970s
SHORT SHORTS
Cut two on fold

Place on fold

View 7
Construction Detail

← Alternate leg width

L

18-20in (46-51cm) Dolls
of the 1970s
LONG SHORTS
Cut two on fold

M

18-20in (46-51cm)
Dolls
of the 1970s
POCKET
for SHORTS, TEE
SHIRT, COAT,
DRESS

N

O

18-20in (46-51cm) Dolls
of the 1970s
TEE SHIRT
Sleeved or Sleeveless

See special cutting instructions
for sleeved version.

Place on fold

View 8
Construction
Detail

189

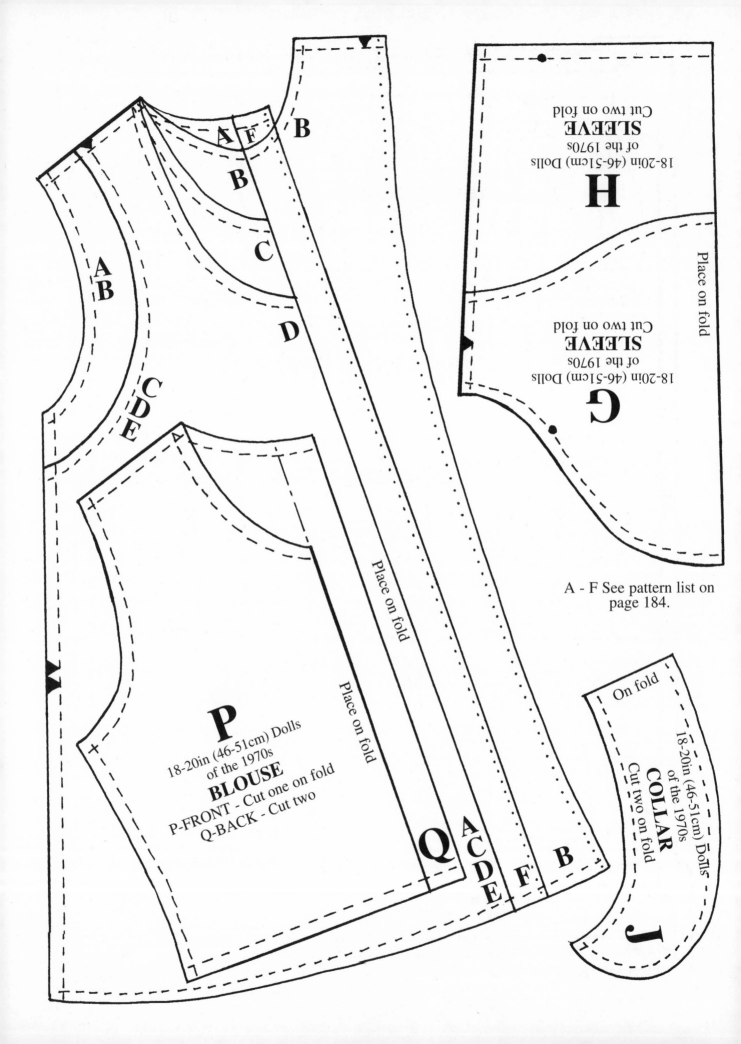

SLEEVE
Cut two on fold
of the 1970s
18-20in (46-51cm) Dolls

H

SLEEVE
Cut two on fold
of the 1970s
18-20in (46-51cm) Dolls

G

Place on fold

A - F See pattern list on
page 184.

A
F
B

B

B

C

A
B

D

C
D
E

Place on fold

Place on fold

P
18-20in (46-51cm) Dolls
of the 1970s
BLOUSE
P-FRONT - Cut one on fold
Q-BACK - Cut two

Q

A
C
D
E

A
C
D
E

F

B

On fold

18-20in (46-51cm) Dolls
of the 1970s
COLLAR
Cut two on fold

J

View 2

View 3

Wardrobe for 9in (23cm)
Male Action Figures
1970s
Fits: Kotter Cast Dolls,
Happy Days Cast Dolls, and others

View 1

View 7

View 4

View 5

View 6

WARDROBE FOR 9in (23cm) MALE ACTION FIGURES OF THE 1970s
by Various Manufacturers

This wardrobe consists of everything the young American male needed to be "cool" in the 1970s. Besides the standard sport coat, shirt, and slacks, there are jeans, car coat, motorcycle jacket, athletic jacket, sleeveless denim jacket, and "muscle" shirt.

Patterns will fit the "Kotter" figures (Mattel, 1973), the "Happy Days" boys (Mego, 1973), and others. Everything from pajamas to business suit to tuxedo, even Boy Scout uniforms for *Steve Scout* and *Bob Scout* (Kenner, 1974) and clothes for some of the *BARBIE®* Family boys may be created from these basic patterns. And remember: You can always use a copy machine to increase or reduce the patterns for the size you need.

View 1 **BROWN TWEED SPORT COAT, SPORT SLACKS, DRESS SHIRT** Pattern Pieces A through H	Make these pieces as tailored as possible. Use tiny buttons. Press shirt and	slacks crisply. Use collar H for sport jacket and shirt. Jacket is not lined. Suggested fabrics are lightweight wool for coat and slacks, cotton or blend for shirt. Alternate fabrics are wool-look cotton print or plain for coat and pants.
View 2 **SLEEVELESS DENIM JACKET** Pattern Pieces N, Q	This sleeveless jacket may be worn with View 5 knit shirt or with a "muscle" shirt or under-	shirt (not shown) using pattern pieces U, V. Cut this garment from an old undershirt; bind openings with bias or turn narrow hems.
View 3 **ATHLETIC JACKET** Pattern Pieces D, F, G	For this jacket, cut the pieces 1/4in (.65cm) larger than when cutting for shirt. Finish neck edge	and sleeves with narrow coordinating ribbed knit collar and cuffs. If such material is not available, construct band collar and cuffs cut on the bias of jacket material.
View 4 **CAR COAT** Pattern Pieces S, T, W	Make this unlined coat of corduroy, a heavy cotton poplin, or lightweight wool. Make plain	band cuffs of coat fabric. Add topstitching and pockets for a finished look.
View 5 **KNIT SHIRT** Pattern Pieces M, P, R	This shirt would ordinarily be a pull-over style, but for ease of dressing the dolls, the designer	made it to open in the back. Add two snap fasteners for closing.
View 6 **"LEATHER" MOTORCYCLE JACKET** Pattern Pieces X, Y	The black "leather" motorcycle jacket goes with everything. Very tiny top stitching adds style to this	jacket. Collar and cuffs are narrow knit ribbing. If by-the-yard ribbing is not available, make collar and cuffs of bias-cut tee shirt knit, dyed to match.
View 7 **JEANS** Pattern Pieces J, K, L, O	These jeans and the sleeveless denim jacket may be worn with any of the shirts or with	only the "muscle" shirt. Remember, for the most part, faded jeans were not fashionable in the '70s.

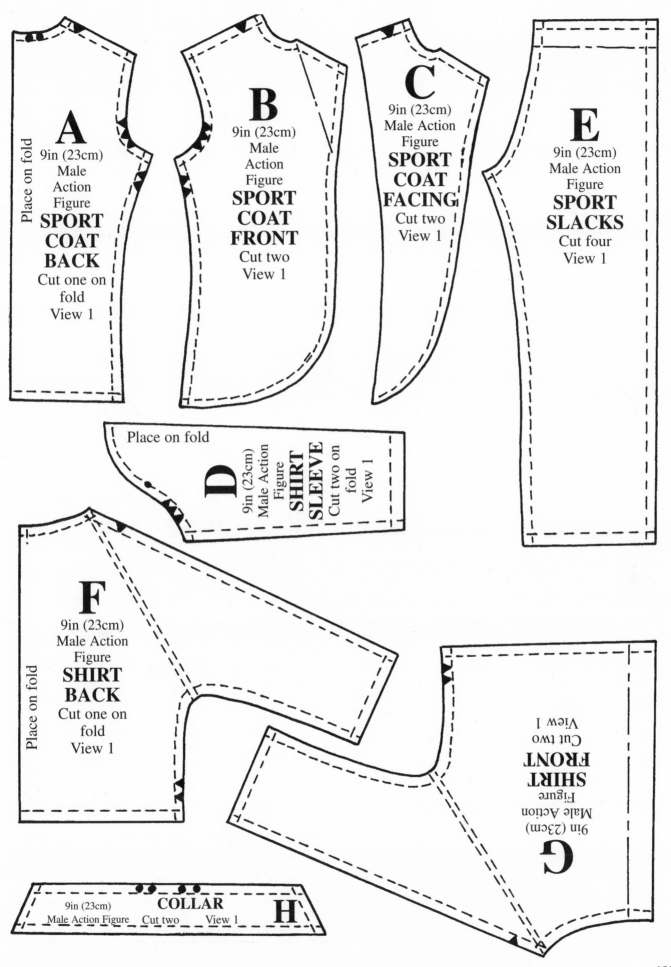

A
Place on fold
9in (23cm) Male Action Figure **SPORT COAT BACK** Cut one on fold View 1

B
9in (23cm) Male Action Figure **SPORT COAT FRONT** Cut two View 1

C
9in (23cm) Male Action Figure **SPORT COAT FACING** Cut two View 1

E
9in (23cm) Male Action Figure **SPORT SLACKS** Cut four View 1

D
Place on fold
9in (23cm) Male Action Figure **SHIRT SLEEVE** Cut two on fold View 1

F
Place on fold
9in (23cm) Male Action Figure **SHIRT BACK** Cut one on fold View 1

G
9in (23cm) Male Action Figure **SHIRT FRONT** Cut two View 1

H **COLLAR**
9in (23cm) Male Action Figure Cut two View 1

193

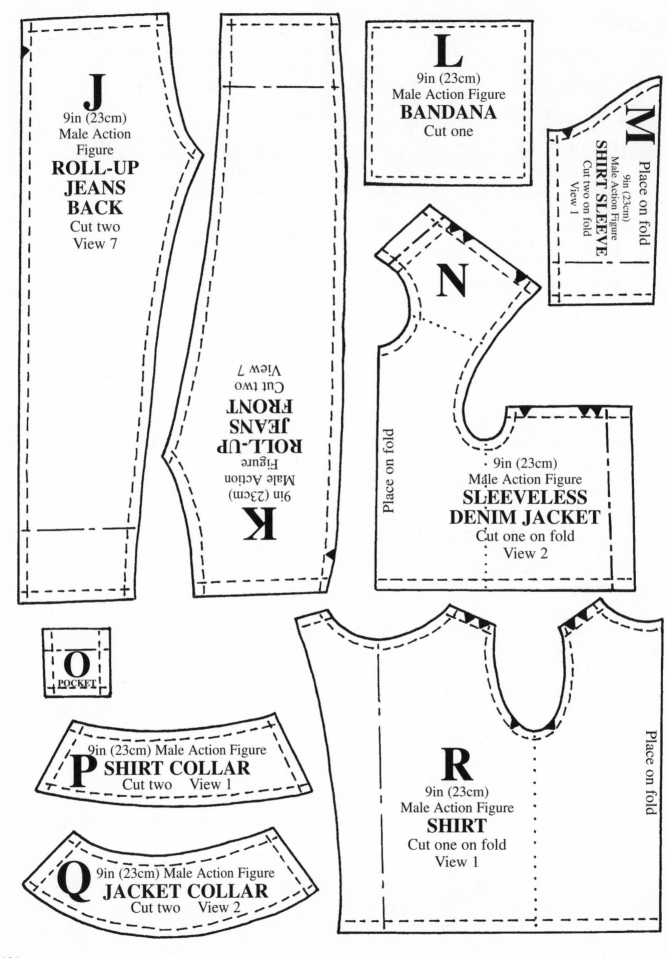

J
9in (23cm)
Male Action
Figure
**ROLL-UP
JEANS
BACK**
Cut two
View 7

K
9in (23cm)
Male Action
Figure
**ROLL-UP
JEANS
FRONT**
Cut two
View 7

L
9in (23cm)
Male Action Figure
BANDANA
Cut one

M
9in (23cm)
Male Action Figure
SHIRT SLEEVE
Cut two on fold
View 1

Place on fold

N

Place on fold

9in (23cm)
Male Action Figure
**SLEEVELESS
DENIM JACKET**
Cut one on fold
View 2

O
POCKET

P SHIRT COLLAR
9in (23cm) Male Action Figure
Cut two   View 1

Q JACKET COLLAR
9in (23cm) Male Action Figure
Cut two   View 2

R
9in (23cm)
Male Action Figure
SHIRT
Cut one on fold
View 1

Place on fold

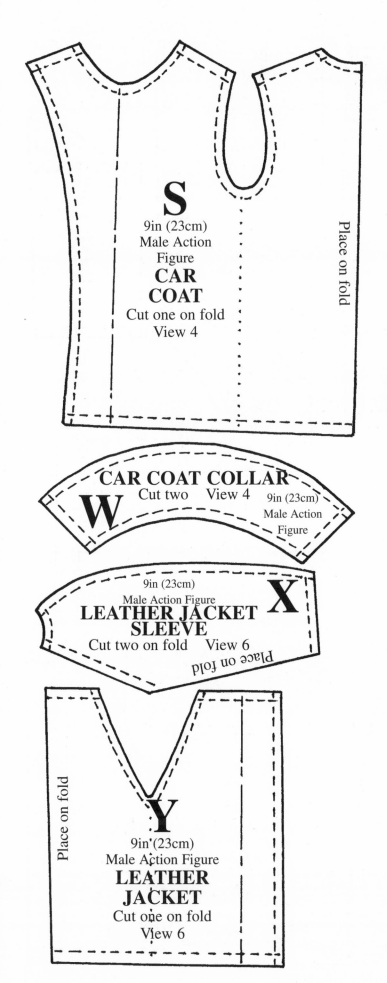
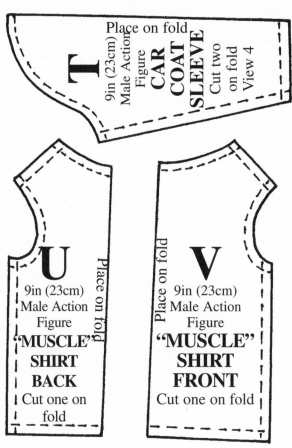

S

9in (23cm)
Male Action
Figure
**CAR
COAT**
Cut one on fold
View 4

Place on fold

T

Place on fold

9in (23cm)
Male Action
Figure
**CAR
COAT
SLEEVE**
Cut two
on fold
View 4

U

Place on fold

9in (23cm)
Male Action
Figure
**'MUSCLE'
SHIRT
BACK**
Cut one on
fold

V

Place on fold

9in (23cm)
Male Action
Figure
**"MUSCLE"
SHIRT
FRONT**
Cut one on fold

CAR COAT COLLAR
Cut two   View 4

W

9in (23cm)
Male Action
Figure

X

9in (23cm)
Male Action Figure
**LEATHER JACKET
SLEEVE**
Cut two on fold   View 6

Place on fold

Y

Place on fold

9in'(23cm)
Male Action Figure
**LEATHER
JACKET**
Cut one on fold
View 6

195

View 1

View 2

View 3

CRiSSY Hair

The
CRISSY FAMILY
by Ideal Doll Co. - 1970s

View 4

WARDROBE FOR THE CRISSY FAMILY
by Ideal Doll Corporation, 1970s

Patterns given here for *Crissy®* generally will fit *Tressy, Kerry, Brandi,* and others of the *Crissy®* family with the exception of the 24in (61cm) *Crissy® Baby*. Those given for *Velvet* fit *Mia* and *Dina* among others. Although the first group is approximately 18in (46cm) tall and the second group only about 15in (38cm) tall, their clothes are interchangeable with only a few minor adjustments to the patterns. *Velvet* patterns also may be downsized to fit the slightly smaller *Cinnamon*.

Given are patterns for five *Crissy* outfits and two Velvet outfits. A universal pattern designed by the author may be found in the first volume of this work and is not repeated.

When verified, original names and stock numbers for the outfits have been given. Otherwise a descriptive name is used. Note that where original wardrobe card illustrations were available, the outfit has not been redrawn for the feature page of this section.

With the patterns given in the first volume of this work, together with those in Volume 2, the doll seamstress will be able to create all of the original designs plus others from her own imagination. An example is creating the Starshine outfit by adapting the "Drenched Trench" coat pattern.

View 1
CRISSY SUNDRESS
Pattern Pieces R, V

This original tagged dress, found on a red-headed *Crissy*, is of pastel yellow, lavender, blue, and pink plaid gingham, and is teamed with yellow plastic *Crissy* shoes. Transparent yellow buttons are sewn down the front, which is open at about the knee, and two snaps fasten the open back.

Skirt - Cut two pieces of dress fabric 7in (18cm) x 8-1/2in (1cm). Sew together on long sides making a flat-felled seam. Gather along the 14in (36cm) edge to fit bodice.

Bodice - For straps, cut two pieces of dress fabric 3/4in (2cm) x 4in (10cm). Fold right sides together and stitch on long side; turn and finger press. Attach to bodice at indicators. Sew on bodice facing.

Top may be cut double for a nicer finish, in which case, sew darts in both pieces and install straps before sewing bodice pieces together.

View 2
CRISSY DOTTED SWISS A-LINE
Pattern Pieces DD, EE, FF, V

The dress is of lime green dotted Swiss with an eyelet-trimmed white cotton Bertha collar, finished with orange velvet ribbon belt, orange felt rose, and white lace-trimmed cotton panties.

View 3
CRISSY #8081-2 "FUNDERWEAR"
Pattern Pieces Z, AA, BB, CC, V

Fabric of this set of undies is a stretchy knit of apple green background printed with white apple blossoms with pink centers. Straps and bow trim are 1/8in (.31cm) pale pink satin ribbon. This pattern may also be used to create a swimsuit or sunsuit and cover-up.

View 4
VELVET PEASANT DRESS
Pattern Pieces S through Y

Bodice - Made of sheer white ribbed nylon with sewn-in vest of dark blue velvet, attached to cotton skirt of blue, red, white, and light blue print. A waistband of the skirt fabric is sewn into the waist seam. Tied at the center front neckline is a satin ribbon bow.

CRISSY #8038-8 "THE DRENCHED TRENCH"
Pattern Pieces E, F, L, M, N, O, P, Q, V

Cut from dark olive-green poplin, coat is unlined. Topstitching finishes all edges. Brass buttons give a double-breasted effect; brass buckle, ombre shaded scarf complete the ensemble. Coat is fastened with three snaps stitched under the three brass buttons closest to front edge of coat. Simple construction information is on pattern.

Scarf - Cut a piece of ombre-striped rayon satin 2in (5cm) x 10in (25cm). Machine bind all around with tight zig zag stitch.

Belt - Cut a piece of coat fabric 1-1/2in (4cm) x 11in (28cm). Turn in edges and topstitch on both sides. Buckle measures 5/8in (2cm) x 7/8in (2cm).

CRISSY #8087-9 "THE JEAN MACHINE"
Pattern Pieces D, G, H, J, K, V

Jeans are of heavy denim in natural color with unhemmed, fringed bottoms. They are printed all over with the word DUNGAREE in orange and brown. The long-sleeved red jersey top is attached to the jeans. The pull-over knit tank top is printed in a splashy brown, orange, and red design; a brown "leather" belt trimmed with two decorative 1/16in (.15cm) brass rivets completes the outfit.

| **VELVET #8124-0** **"LOVERLY"** Pattern Pieces A, B, C, V, W | Dark purple background cotton fabric printed with blue, white, and lavender flowers and green leaves. White, regular-sized ric rac adds pizzazz to the hem and sleeves and is stitched over the seam where the ruffle is sewn to the skirt. The dress is belted with a magenta pink velvet cummerbund tied with 1/16in (.15cm) white braid. Neckline and sleeves are fitted with narrow elastic. | **Skirt -** Use skirt pattern W, cutting hemline at the -V- mark. Cut a 2-1/2in (6cm) x 32in (81cm) ruffle from same fabric, gather to bottom of flared skirt. Dress is open down back, fastens with four evenly spaced snaps. **Other Outfits -** Use the pattern pieces given in this collection to create other outfits for the *Crissy* family taking your cue from the original wardrobe cards shown. |

Illustrations from the backs of three fashion outfit cards for *Crissy* and *Velvet* show the wide variety of styles available for the dolls.

Crissy and *Velvet* are trademarks of the Ideal Doll Corporation.

198

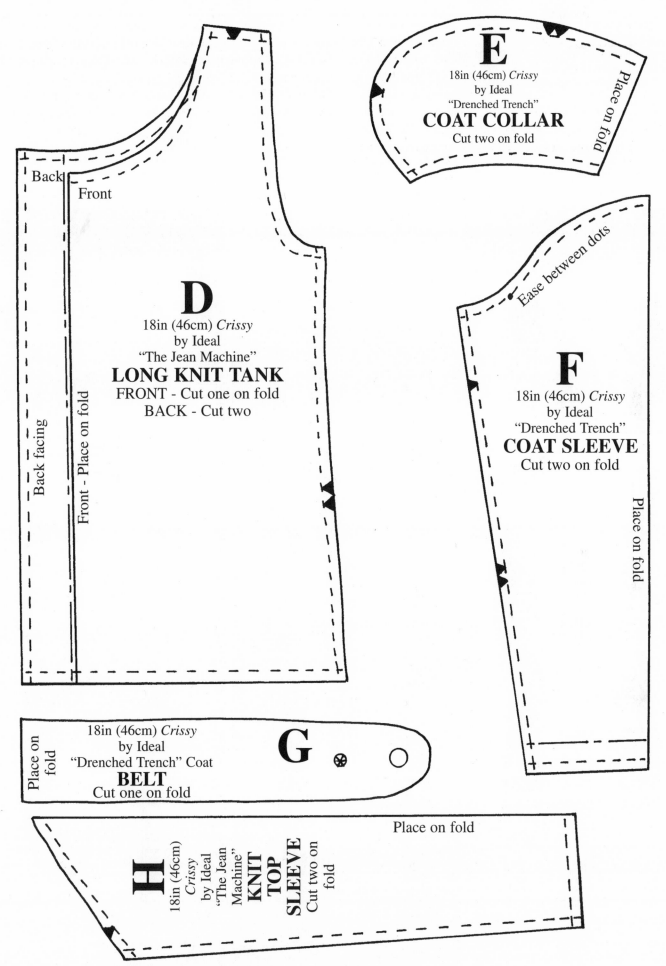

E
18in (46cm) *Crissy*
by Ideal
"Drenched Trench"
COAT COLLAR
Cut two on fold

Place on fold

Back

Front

D
18in (46cm) *Crissy*
by Ideal
"The Jean Machine"
LONG KNIT TANK
FRONT - Cut one on fold
BACK - Cut two

Back facing

Front - Place on fold

Ease between dots

F
18in (46cm) *Crissy*
by Ideal
"Drenched Trench"
COAT SLEEVE
Cut two on fold

Place on fold

Place on fold

18in (46cm) *Crissy*
by Ideal
"Drenched Trench" Coat
G
BELT
Cut one on fold

Place on fold

Place on fold

H
18in (46cm) *Crissy* by Ideal "The Jean Machine" **KNIT TOP SLEEVE** Cut two on fold

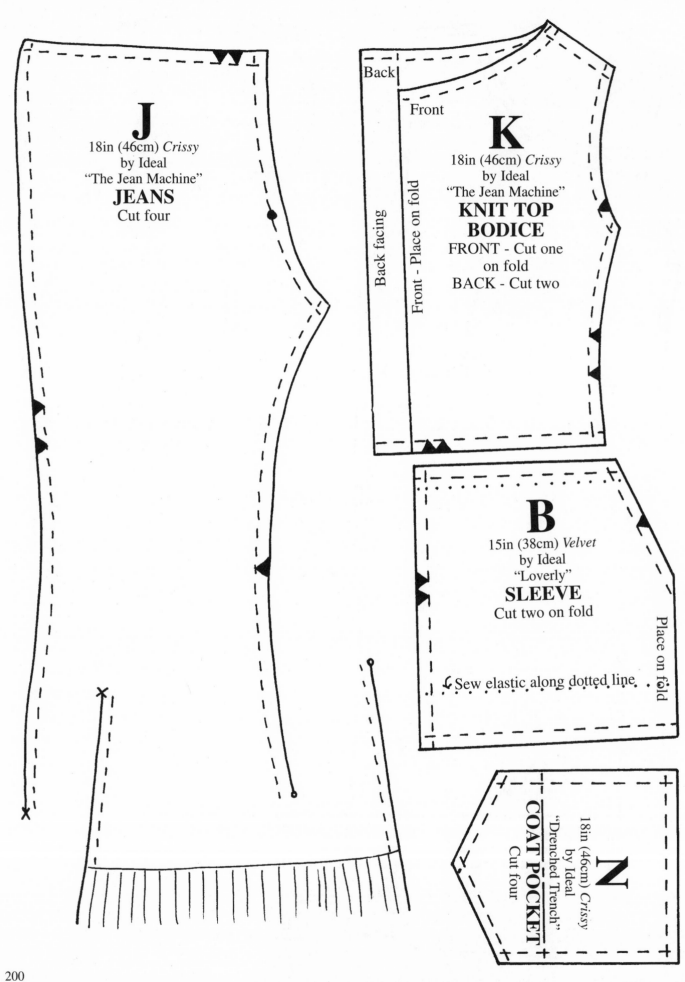

J
18in (46cm) *Crissy*
by Ideal
"The Jean Machine"
JEANS
Cut four

Back

Front

Back facing

Front - Place on fold

K
18in (46cm) *Crissy*
by Ideal
"The Jean Machine"
**KNIT TOP
BODICE**
FRONT - Cut one
on fold
BACK - Cut two

B
15in (38cm) *Velvet*
by Ideal
"Loverly"
SLEEVE
Cut two on fold

Place on fold

Sew elastic along dotted line

N
18in (46cm) *Crissy*
by Ideal
"Drenched Trench"
COAT POCKET
Cut four

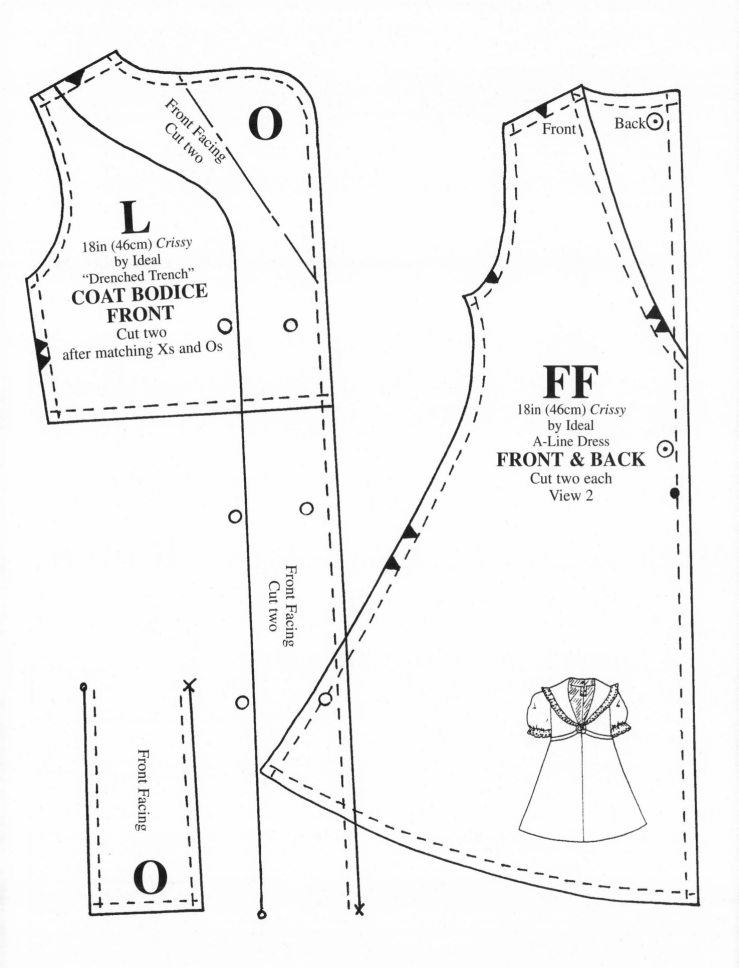

Front Facing
Cut two

O

L
18in (46cm) *Crissy*
by Ideal
"Drenched Trench"
**COAT BODICE
FRONT**
Cut two
after matching Xs and Os

Front　　　　**Back**

FF
18in (46cm) *Crissy*
by Ideal
A-Line Dress
FRONT & BACK
Cut two each
View 2

Front Facing
Cut two

Front Facing

O

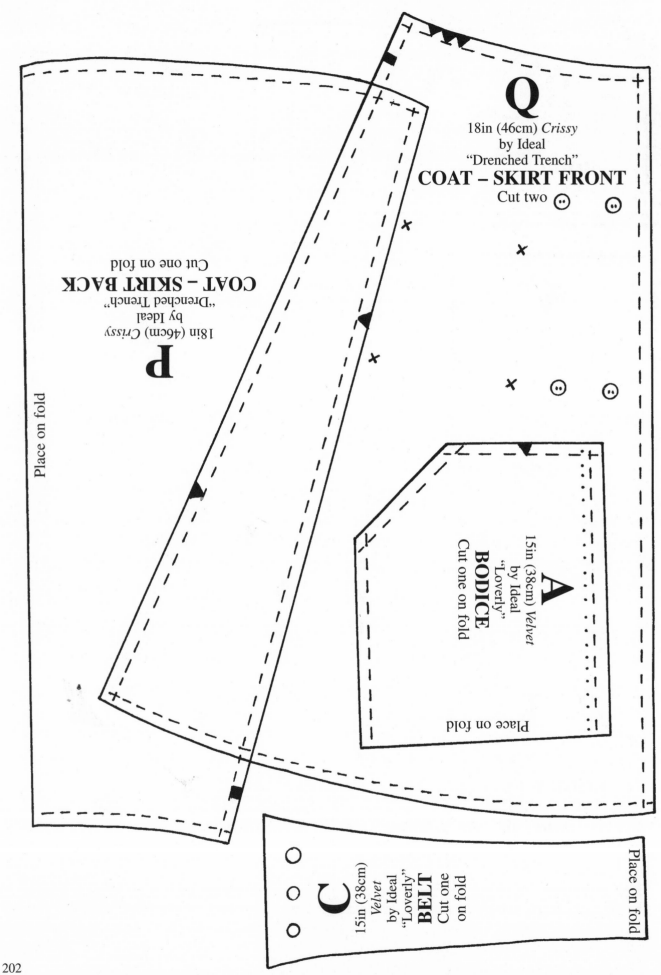

Q

18in (46cm) *Crissy*
by Ideal
"Drenched Trench"
COAT – SKIRT FRONT
Cut two

P

18in (46cm) *Crissy*
by Ideal
"Drenched Trench"
COAT – SKIRT BACK
Cut one on fold

Place on fold

A

15in (38cm) *Velvet*
by Ideal
"Loverly"
BODICE
Cut one on fold

Place on fold

C

15in (38cm)
Velvet
by Ideal
"Loverly"
BELT
Cut one
on fold

Place on fold

202

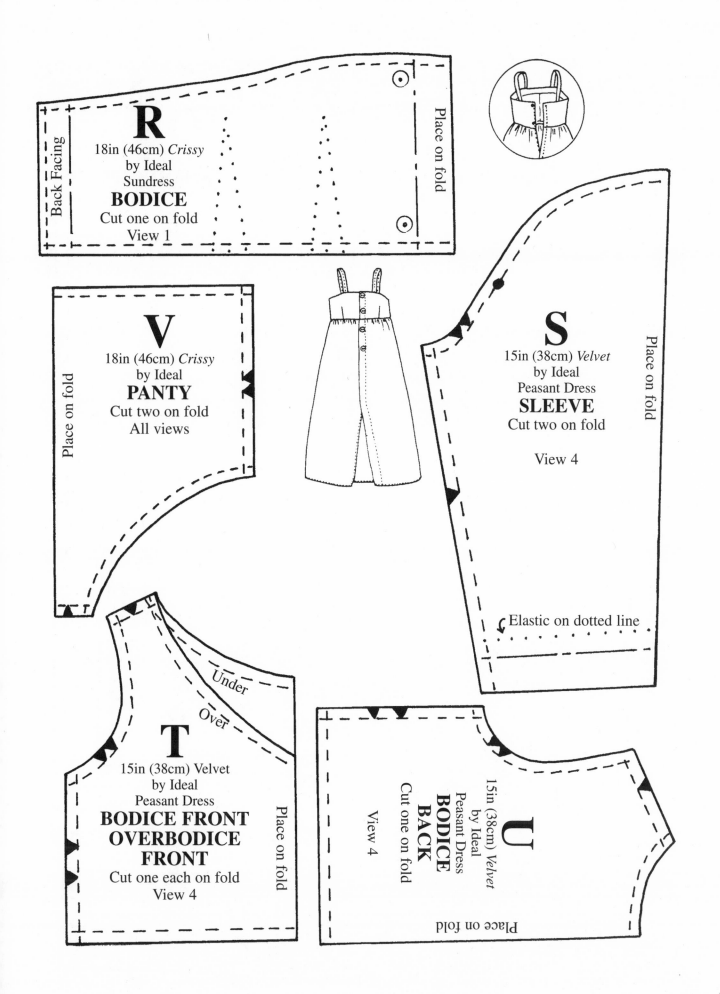

R

18in (46cm) *Crissy*
by Ideal
Sundress
BODICE
Cut one on fold
View 1

Back Facing

Place on fold

V

18in (46cm) *Crissy*
by Ideal
PANTY
Cut two on fold
All views

Place on fold

S

15in (38cm) *Velvet*
by Ideal
Peasant Dress
SLEEVE
Cut two on fold

View 4

Place on fold

Elastic on dotted line

T

15in (38cm) Velvet
by Ideal
Peasant Dress
**BODICE FRONT
OVERBODICE
FRONT**
Cut one each on fold
View 4

Under

Over

Place on fold

U

15in (38cm) *Velvet*
by Ideal
Peasant Dress
**BODICE
BACK**
Cut one on fold

View 4

Place on fold

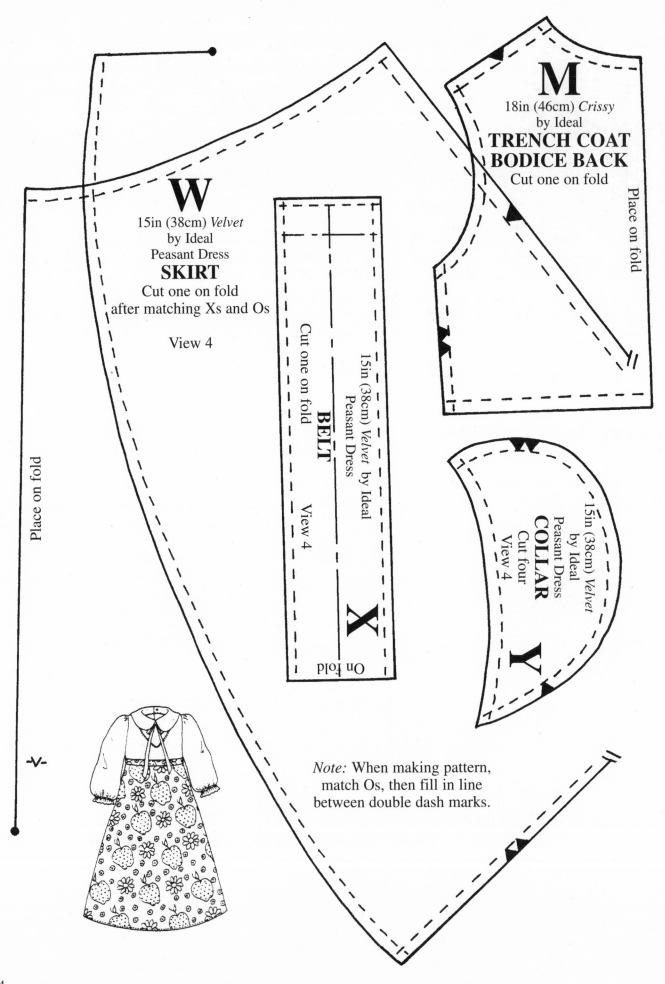

W

15in (38cm) *Velvet*
by Ideal
Peasant Dress
SKIRT
Cut one on fold
after matching Xs and Os

View 4

Place on fold

M

18in (46cm) *Crissy*
by Ideal
TRENCH COAT
BODICE BACK
Cut one on fold

Place on fold

15in (38cm) *Velvet* by Ideal
Peasant Dress
BELT
Cut one on fold
View 4

X

On fold

15in (38cm) *Velvet*
by Ideal
Peasant Dress
COLLAR
Cut four
View 4

Y

Note: When making pattern,
match Os, then fill in line
between double dash marks.

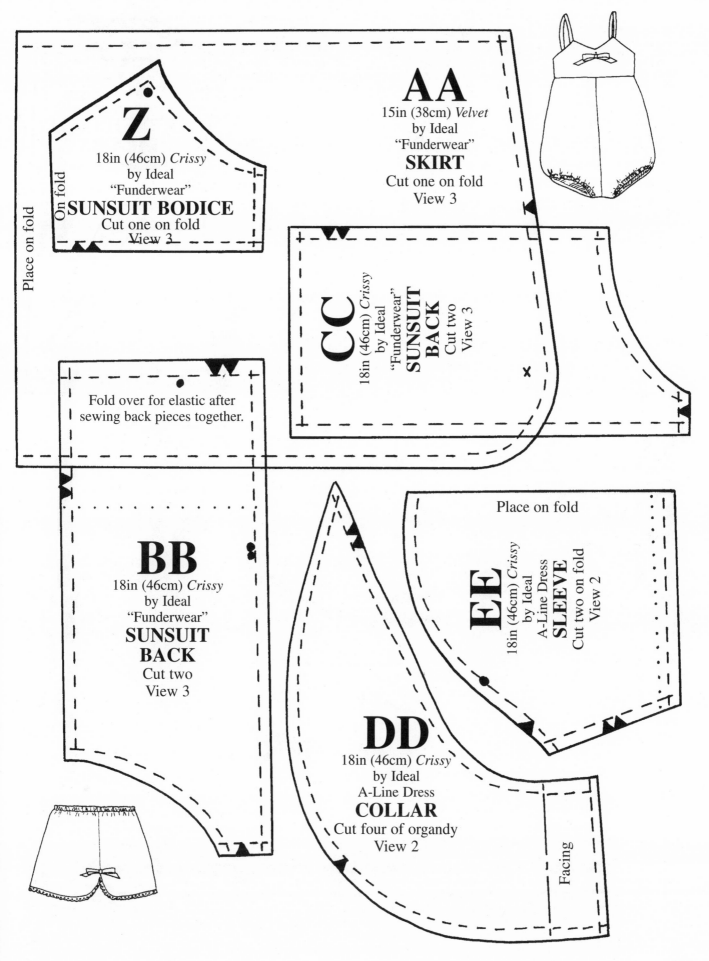

Z

On fold

18in (46cm) *Crissy*
by Ideal
"Funderwear"
SUNSUIT BODICE
Cut one on fold
View 3

Place on fold

AA

15in (38cm) *Velvet*
by Ideal
"Funderwear"
SKIRT
Cut one on fold
View 3

CC

18in (46cm) *Crissy*
by Ideal
"Funderwear"
SUNSUIT BACK
Cut two
View 3

Fold over for elastic after
sewing back pieces together.

BB

18in (46cm) *Crissy*
by Ideal
"Funderwear"
**SUNSUIT
BACK**
Cut two
View 3

Place on fold

EE

18in (46cm) *Crissy*
by Ideal
A-Line Dress
SLEEVE
Cut two on fold
View 2

DD

18in (46cm) *Crissy*
by Ideal
A-Line Dress
COLLAR
Cut four of organdy
View 2

Facing

205

View 1

View 2

View 2

View 3

View 4

View 5

View 6

12in (31cm)

Shirley Temple

by Ideal Doll Co.
1982

WARDROBE FOR A 12in (31cm) SHIRLEY TEMPLE
by Ideal - 1982

Note: For the 8in (20cm) dolls reduce these patterns to 75% of original size.

View 1
"STOWAWAY"
Pattern Pieces A through G

This costume consists of a peacock blue brocade jacket, completely lined with fine white cotton, fastened with black frog closures of very narrow black elastic. The pants are black brocade, anklets are white, slippers are black velvet. Construction is simple and classic.

View 2
"HEIDI"
Pattern Pieces G-1 through O, W

Bodice - Lower bodice is cut from green cotton with white yoke, embroidered with yellow flowers with red centers. Stems of flowers are narrow light green ricrac. Green satin ribbon covers the lower edge of yoke where it meets green bodice. Neckline is finished with 1/8in (.31cm) white eyelet. Cuff uses same eyelet plus 1/8in (.31cm) green satin ribbon over seam. A pearl and gold pin fastens at center front.

Skirt - Cut a piece of dark green fine cotton 5-1/2in (14cm) x 24in (61cm), including seam allowances. Turn up 1in (3cm) hem with machine stitching. Run gathering stitches along remaining long edge. Sew back seam together, leaving top 2in (5cm) open. Pull gathers to fit bodice.

Apron - Cut a piece of small-patterned white cotton eyelet yardgoods 5in (13cm) x 18in (46cm), including seam allowances. Cut a piece of 1/4in (.65cm) or 3/8in (.9cm) wide woven decorative tape. The original has black background with very narrow white edges, red flowers alternating with green leaves and white flowers. Sew tape to apron 1in (3cm) from bottom. Cut a piece of 1/2in (1cm) white eyelet edging 18in (46cm) long and sew to bottom hem of apron. Turn 1/8in (.31cm) hems on both short ends of apron. Gather remaining long side to fit waist of doll. Attach 18in (46cm) piece of white bias tape to top of apron as waistband and ties.

Bonnet - Cut two from pattern on fold. Seam together along ABC with 1/2in (1cm) white eyelet edging sewn into seam with only 1/4in (.65cm) to outside. Turn and seam C to D. Turn to right side, take tiny tuck on each side of back seam at dotted lines. Attach piece of small, round elastic at bottom center back seam as chin strap. Turn back "wings" along broken lines.

Klompen (Wooden Shoes) - Cut blocks of lightweight carving wood the size of a diagram on pattern page. Trace these views onto the wood and carve away excess areas as shown in illustration. Note: Both ends of the shoe are shown in the square. Do not carve both ends the same. Dotted lines show area to be carved out on inside for foot.

Suggestion: Cut a practice shoe from fine-textured Styrofoam or bar soap before embarking on woodcarving.

Petticoat - Cut one piece on fold from fine white cotton. Cut a piece of very fine nylon net 2in (5cm) x 24in (61cm); gather 1/4in (.65cm) from one edge of long side. Machine stitch to inside of petticoat along dotted line indicated on pattern. Attach 1/2in (1cm) lace along bottom edge.

Wig for this doll has pale blonde, soft, fluffy top and front with large looped braids hanging down on either side. The other five have classic Shirley-style wigs.

View 3
"LITTLEST REBEL"
Pattern Pieces P, Q, Q2, S, U, HH

Dress - Made of black cotton print with tiny nosegays of pink, lavender, and white with green leaves. Skirt, and half-slip are the same as Heidi's. Pantalettes are edged with insertion lace threaded with pink satin ribbon, and bottom is finished with narrow white eyelet.

Apron - Cut a 10in (25cm) piece of 3-3/4in (10cm) white eyelet ruffle and gather to waistband/tie belt made from white bias tape, allowing plenty of length for tying bow and streamers. Cut one dickey from pattern on fold, attach 4in (10cm) strip of eyelet edging on each side. This goes from front waistband, over the shoulder, then down and attaches to waistband in back on either side.

Black sox and black velvet shoes finish the ensemble.

View 4
"STAND UP AND CHEER"
Pattern Pieces V, W, X, X2, Y, Z

Probably the best-known Shirley Temple outfit is this sheer nylon dress with red polka dots and trim. There is red satin ribbon at the waist sewn into the back facing only at each side of back opening. Neck edge and bottom edge of skirt are finished with red cotton bias tape.

The white nylon underskirt is made from a piece measuring 3-1/2in (9cm) x 20in (51cm). A net ruffle is sewn to the inside of the piece before it is gathered and then it is sewn into the waist seam along with the skirt. The bodice is lined with the same plain white nylon. The skirt of the dress is a piece of polka dot nylon measuring 4in (10cm) x 24in (61cm). Sewn to the back of the panties are three rows of 1/2in (1cm) ruffles with very narrow red edging.

Fastened at the throat of this dress is a tiny "gold" brooch with a red paste stone set in its center.

This costume uses several design features from other costumes. The dress is of very fine, pale pink cotton with white dots, lace-trimmed hem, lace at neck and wrists. A tiny heart "locket" is sewn at the center front of neckline. The apron is of solid color pale pink very fine cotton, with lace trim and a snap fastener at the back. Pale pink sox complement the dress.

Petticoat - Same as Heidi, pattern piece S.

Pantaloons - Same as Littlest Rebel and Heidi, pattern piece U.

Dress - Skirt: Piece of dress fabric 5in (13cm) x 22in (56cm), including seam allowances, gathered to bodice. Leave open 2-1/2in (6cm) from waist down back seam. Add lace along bottom edge of skirt.

Apron - Cut a waistband 1in (3cm) x 7in (18cm) from pale pink cotton. Cut a 9in (23cm) circle from same fabric and cut in half. Run gathering stitches along straight cut edges of each half circle. Trim round edges of both half circles with narrow lace. Pull gathering threads to fit waist of doll and attach to waistband. Finish with two small bows of very narrow pink satin ribbon. (See detail.)

Another well-loved Shirley outfit is the sailor suit. This one has dark blue cotton uniform blouse trimmed with gold braid on sleeves, red anchors on shoulders; tie is 11in (28cm) length of 1/4in (.65cm) red satin ribbon; collar is white cotton trimmed with gold braid. Bell bottoms and hat are white cotton. Hat has stitched brim and fastens with gold elastic strap under chin. Shoes are black; socks are white nylon.

Not shown but also issued in the series were "Rebecca of Sunnybrook Farm", "Dimples", "Poor Little Rich Girl" (two outfits), "Suzannah of the Mounties", and "Wee Willie Winkie". These costumes may be constructed using assorted pattern pieces given here.

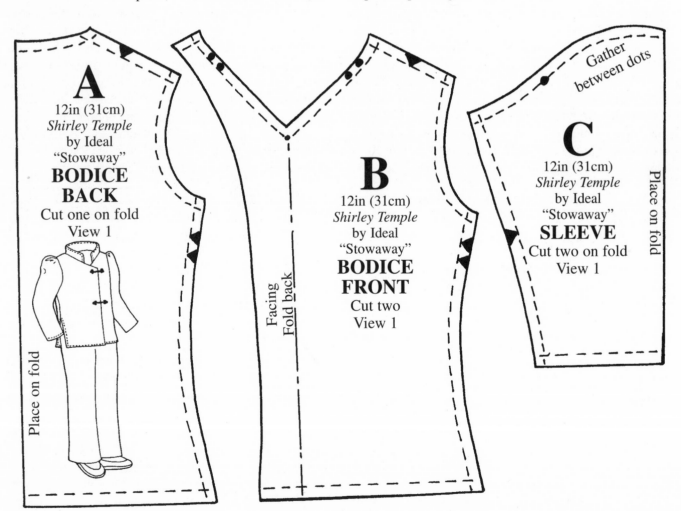

A

12in (31cm) *Shirley Temple* by Ideal "Stowaway" **BODICE BACK** Cut one on fold View 1

Place on fold

B

12in (31cm) *Shirley Temple* by Ideal "Stowaway" **BODICE FRONT** Cut two View 1

Facing Fold back

C

12in (31cm) *Shirley Temple* by Ideal "Stowaway" **SLEEVE** Cut two on fold View 1

Gather between dots

Place on fold

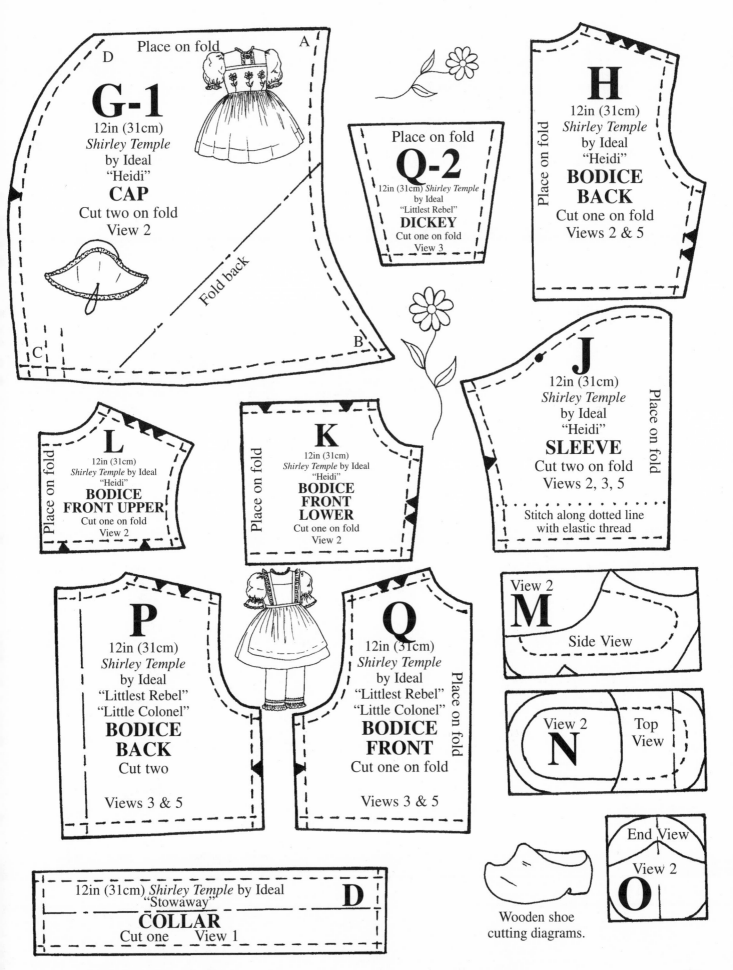

D
Place on fold
G-1
12in (31cm)
Shirley Temple
by Ideal
"Heidi"
CAP
Cut two on fold
View 2
Place on fold
A
Fold back
C
B

Place on fold
Q-2
12in (31cm) *Shirley Temple*
by Ideal
"Littlest Rebel"
DICKEY
Cut one on fold
View 3

H
12in (31cm)
Shirley Temple
by Ideal
"Heidi"
**BODICE
BACK**
Cut one on fold
Views 2 & 5
Place on fold

J
12in (31cm)
Shirley Temple
by Ideal
"Heidi"
SLEEVE
Cut two on fold
Views 2, 3, 5
Place on fold
Stitch along dotted line
with elastic thread

L
12in (31cm)
Shirley Temple by Ideal
"Heidi"
**BODICE
FRONT UPPER**
Cut one on fold
View 2
Place on fold

K
12in (31cm)
Shirley Temple by Ideal
"Heidi"
**BODICE
FRONT
LOWER**
Cut one on fold
View 2
Place on fold

M
View 2
Side View

P
12in (31cm)
Shirley Temple
by Ideal
"Littlest Rebel"
"Little Colonel"
**BODICE
BACK**
Cut two

Views 3 & 5

Q
12in (31cm)
Shirley Temple
by Ideal
"Littlest Rebel"
"Little Colonel"
**BODICE
FRONT**
Cut one on fold
Place on fold

Views 3 & 5

N
View 2
Top
View

O
End View
View 2

Wooden shoe
cutting diagrams.

D
12in (31cm) *Shirley Temple* by Ideal
"Stowaway"
COLLAR
Cut one   View 1

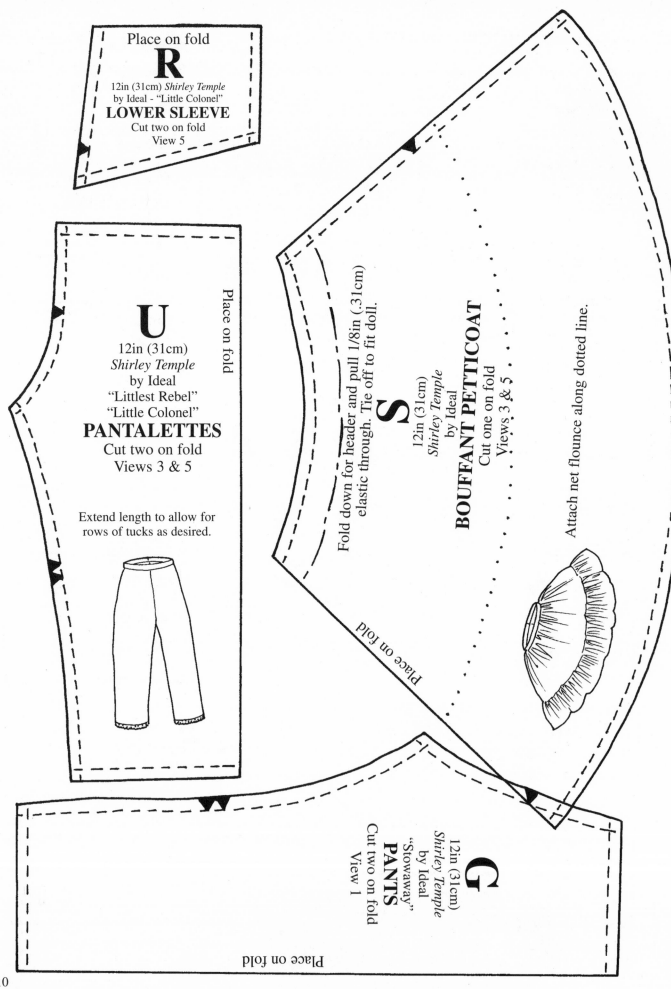

Place on fold

R

12in (31cm) *Shirley Temple*
by Ideal - "Little Colonel"
LOWER SLEEVE
Cut two on fold
View 5

U

12in (31cm)
Shirley Temple
by Ideal
"Littlest Rebel"
"Little Colonel"
PANTALETTES
Cut two on fold
Views 3 & 5

Extend length to allow for
rows of tucks as desired.

Place on fold

Fold down for header and pull 1/8in (.31cm)
elastic through. Tie off to fit doll.

S

12in (31cm)
Shirley Temple
by Ideal
BOUFFANT PETTICOAT
Cut one on fold
Views 3 & 5

Attach net flounce along dotted line.

Place on fold

G

12in (31cm)
Shirley Temple
by Ideal
"Stowaway"
PANTS
Cut two on fold
View 1

Place on fold

210

V

12in (31cm)
Shirley Temple
by Ideal
"Stand Up and Cheer"
**DRESS
BODICE**
Cut one   View 4

Place on fold

Back

Front

W

12in (31cm)
Shirley Temple
by Ideal
"Stand Up and Cheer"
PANTY
Cut two on fold
View 4

Place on fold

12in (31cm) *Shirley Temple*
by Ideal
SHOE SOLE **X2**
Cut four
View 4

Z

12in (31cm)
Shirley Temple by Ideal
"Stand Up and Cheer"
SLEEVE
Cut two on fold
View 4

Place on fold

On fold   12in (31cm) *Shirley Temple* by Ideal   **X**
SHOE
Cut two on fold
View 4

T

12in (31cm)
Shirley Temple by Ideal
"Little Colonel"
UPPER SLEEVE
Cut two on fold
View 5

Place on fold

Y

12in (31cm)
Shirley Temple
by Ideal
"Stand Up and Cheer"
PETTICOAT
Cut two on fold
View 4

Place on fold

Attach net
ruffle here

Attach 1/8in (.31cm) lace here

F

12in (31cm)
Shirley Temple
by Ideal
"Stowaway"
**SLIPPER
SOLE**
Cut two
View 1

E

SLIPPER
Cut two
View 1

12in (31cm)
Shirley Temple by Ideal
"Stowaway"

211

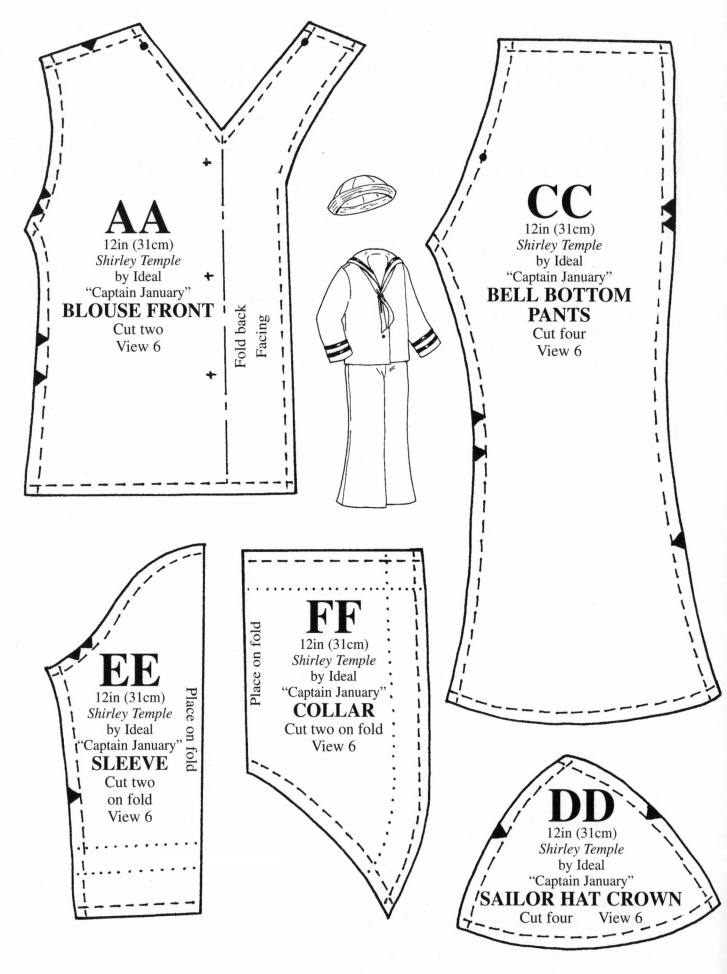

AA
12in (31cm)
Shirley Temple
by Ideal
"Captain January"
BLOUSE FRONT
Cut two
View 6

Fold back

Facing

CC
12in (31cm)
Shirley Temple
by Ideal
"Captain January"
**BELL BOTTOM
PANTS**
Cut four
View 6

EE
12in (31cm)
Shirley Temple
by Ideal
"Captain January"
SLEEVE
Cut two
on fold
View 6

Place on fold

FF
12in (31cm)
Shirley Temple
by Ideal
"Captain January"
COLLAR
Cut two on fold
View 6

Place on fold

DD
12in (31cm)
Shirley Temple
by Ideal
"Captain January"
SAILOR HAT CROWN
Cut four   View 6

GG

12in (31cm) Shirley Temple by Ideal
"Captain January"

HAT BRIM

Cut two on fold   View 6

Place on fold

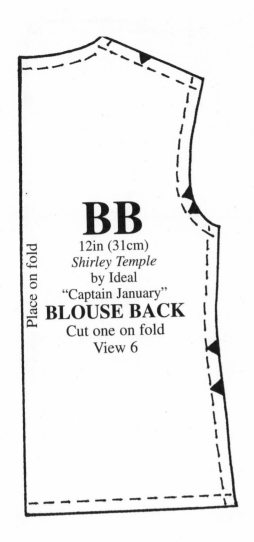

BB

12in (31cm)
Shirley Temple
by Ideal
"Captain January"

BLOUSE BACK

Cut one on fold
View 6

Place on fold

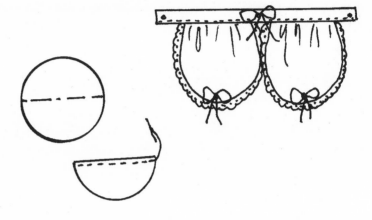

Detail - Little Colonel
Costume

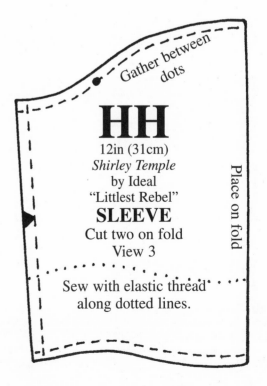

Gather between dots

HH

12in (31cm)
Shirley Temple
by Ideal
"Littlest Rebel"

SLEEVE

Cut two on fold
View 3

Place on fold

Sew with elastic thread along dotted lines.

1980s
Original On-The-Doll Outfits

Various Manufacturers

17in (43cm) Kimberly Cheerleader
by Tomy

18in (46cm) Punky Brewster
by Lewis Galoob

17in (43cm) Lady Luminous
Manufactured in Japan

View 1

View 1

View 2

View 3

As stated before, since on-the-doll clothes, those in which the doll was sold, are usually lost or worn out, it seems wise to try to preserve a record of these fashions for future generations of doll lovers. Such has been the goal of this work since the conception of the first volume.

An understanding of the fabrics of each period is essential for anyone wishing to construct an authentic costume. The ubiquitous denims along with gingham, chambray, corduroy, and other classic fabrics continued in popularity during the period.

Nylon, polyester, cotton, and blends of synthetic and natural fibers were common, although a trend toward 100% natural fibers strengthened. Wool and synthetic blends were used in suits and coats; rayon made a comeback during the decade, after a long period of neglect by those who preferred the newer synthetics. Inevitably, blends of rayon and other fibers came to market.

View 1
17in (43cm) *LADY LUMINOUS* SWIMSUIT & COVER-UP SKIRT
Pattern Pieces A, B, C
Manufactured in Japan

Lady Luminous seems almost an unknown among collectors in America; however, the doll rates high for quality construction of both doll and wardrobe. She is included here as an example of what a high-fashion doll can be; she is a hybrid of the old store window mannequins, in her stance and presentation, and the usual teen and fashion dolls of collecting fame. You will want to do your best sewing for her, using fine fabrics, linings, buttons, and threads.

Her body is realistically sculptured with firm, believable breasts and rounded buttocks, well-defined collar bones, well-proportioned ears, and long, slender hands with long, polished nails. She is not, however, completely natural in some proportions as we shall see, although her face seems more a portrait face than most other fashion dolls.

She is also presented as the subject of a lesson for doll seamstresses - a lesson in borrowing patterns and a lesson in proportion. *Miss Seventeen, Cherie, Lisa Littlechap, Super BARBIE®*, and *Lady Luminous* all have adult proportions; however, patterns may not be interchangeable simply by reducing or enlarging to the correct height size.

Dolls can be as different from one another in size and shape as humans are unlike each other. Two 17in (43cm) or two 21in (53cm) dolls, for example, may not have the same proportions, even though both are modeled as late teenagers or young adults. Treat each doll as an individual and you will seldom go wrong.

Lady Luminous is a product of the very late 1980s and the first years of the 1990s. Therefore, a suitable wardrobe for her may follow current fashion trends by reviving older ones. So many of the fashions of these years were a kind of *de ja vu* style which strongly reflected, even duplicated, the styles of then recent decades. For this reason she is a very good candidate for some experimentation in judicious pattern swapping.

Let us compare the 17in (43cm) *Lady Luminous* with the 18in (46cm) Miss Seventeen. In preparing this section, I had wanted to reduce the abundant patterns for the 18in (46cm) doll to fit the smaller one, and had struggled with my calculator for several minutes, always coming up with the same numbers. With a difference in height of only one inch, or approximately 6%, why was I unable to speedily fit *Miss Seventeen*'s patterns to the shorter *Lady Luminous*? It didn't make sense that the patterns for *Miss Seventeen* proved far too large for the Lady when I applied the 6% reduction principle.

The Lady stood on my drawing table as I worked, clad only in her swimsuit. From time to time, I glanced at her, trying to fathom the mistake in the math I was using. Suddenly I realized that the Lady has a rather small head for her height, as do many of the fashion figures drawn for advertising. It was then I became aware that her legs were disproportionately long for her height. She is 17in (43cm) tall and more than half of that height is in her legs, leaving a relatively short and slender body. I discovered that *Miss Seventeen* measures 5in (13cm) shoulder to waist while the Lady in question is a mere 3-1/4in (6cm) on the same line, something more than a 6% difference.

Lady Luminous was meant to represent a real fashion model. *Miss Seventeen*, on the other hand, was fashioned after the first *BARBIE®* with a prominent bust and legs somewhat more in proportion to her overall size, though still long and slender. The problems inherent in exchanging patterns between these two dolls became evident: It would be necessary to do some fitting and correcting before cutting fabric.

The *Miss Seventeen* swimsuit, reduced to 94-95% may prove just right for the Lady since the fabric of choice would be stretchy and forgiving and may even call for further reduction. For other outfits, it would be wise to use a tape measure and calculator and do some calculations to prevent headaches later in the fitting.

Having said all this, I sincerely hope not to have discouraged the reader from experimenting with pattern exchanges. Such a project can be a rewarding adventure in sewing and is to be encouraged.

There were at least three models of this doll, one with

a reddish-brown short, bobbed hairstyle, wearing the brown Lycra™ knit swimsuit with French high-cut leg openings, shown here.

Over the suit is a polished cotton cover-up skirt in a splashy, watercolor style of print in light shades of green, blue, yellow, and peach on a creamy white background. There are five smooth white buttons down the front of the skirt, all non-functioning. The waist is held with a tacking stitch and the length of the skirt falls open. The skirt is easily slipped over the hips with the use of elastic at the waist.

A second doll I have seen wore a beautifully tailored dressy gray suit with appropriate accessories. A third doll wore a fabulous dinner dress. Each doll had a different hairstyle and make-up and therefore a very different appearance. Even the complexions were different shades, keyed to the hair coloring.

Here now is your challenge with your favorite large fashion doll: Seek out patterns to adapt and create a unique wardrobe for your doll. Let your imagination and creativity loose. Perhaps you will want to venture into the 21st century, creating your own personal vision of the fashions of the future (see "Term Paper" later in this book for more challenges).

Swimsuit - The original is of a rich, warm brown, somewhat shiny stretch fabric with a neck strap fastened with a single hook and eye.

1. Turn down a very narrow hem on the top front edge a to a.

2. Sew back and front pieces right sides together on side seams and crotch.

3. Cut 1/2in (1cm) self bias and bind back and sides, leaving extra for neck strap. Try suit on doll and mark for length of strap and placement of fastener.

4. Hem leg openings.

Cover-up Skirt - Cut pattern piece C on paper on the fold. Lay out flat and mark one side for fold, then cut this doubled C pattern on fold of fabric. Waistline measurement should be 8in (20cm) and hemline should measure 22in (56cm).

1. Turn back 1/2in (1cm) on each end for front facings, press and baste.

2. Make a narrow hem along bottom of skirt.

3. Fold over 1/4in (.65cm) along top edge and baste. Measure doll's waist and cut a piece of 1/8in (.31cm) elastic, being sure to allow for hip width. Sew elastic along top (waistline), stretching as you sew.

4. Attach smooth white buttons (non-pearl) as shown on pattern, stitch waistline together.

View 2
18in (46cm)
PUNKY BREWSTER
JEANS OUTFIT
by Lewis Galoob Toys, Inc. 1984
Pattern Pieces D through H

Punky's pants and jacket are made of lightweight denim, topstitched with classic yellow-orange thread. Self-fabric belt loops, two on the front and one at center back, as well as the false pockets on the jacket, are stitched with the same thread. Cuffs are finished with a narrow jeans hem and turned up to the outside. There is a yellow belt with a Velcro™ fastener. Jacket is accented with topstitching and closes with a zipper in front.

The sleeveless top is of lightweight sweatshirt fabric in a shade of aqua. All openings are bound with matching aqua bias tape.

View 3
17in (43cm) *KIMBERLY*
CHEERLEADER **OUTFIT**
by Tomy Corporation, 1981
Pattern Pieces J through L

This outfit consists of a circular red cotton skirt lined with white cotton that shows about 1/16in (.15cm) below the lower edge of the red skirt. The top is white cotton knit with a personalized red megaphone painted on the front (fig. 1). Panties are white cotton knit; high anklets are nylon. Shoes are red and white soft vinyl sneakers, two red bows are tied in the long, blonde hair, and two pompons of red and white streamers complete the cheerleader effect.

Skirt - Cut a circle 4-3/4in (12cm) in diameter of red cotton for the skirt. Cut a circle 5in (13cm) in diameter of white cotton for the lining. Cut circles 1-1/2in (4cm) in diameter from centers of these two pieces for waist. Sew circles together along the outer edge, turn, and press so that lining forms an even, narrow trim along the outer edge of the skirt.

Cut a 1-1/2in (4cm) back opening, turn in narrow edges and blindstitch. Baste waistlines together and try skirt on doll. Make any adjustments required in waist opening.

Cut a 9in (23cm) x 1in (3cm) piece of red cotton for waistband. Fold and press in half lengthwise. Sew to skirt, fasten with one Velcro™ fastener.

Sweater - Before assembling the top, use fabric paint, following manufacturer's directions, to duplicate fig. 1 on the front bodice. When paint is completely dry, assemble shirt.

Cut bias of shirt material to finish sleeves and to make the narrow stand-up neck binding. Apply three evenly spaced Velcro™ fasteners on back of shirt.

Panties - These cotton panties are cut on the fold at the crotch with seams at the sides. Turn down the top edge and oversew very narrow elastic to fit the doll. Leg openings are turned under in a narrow handkerchief hem.

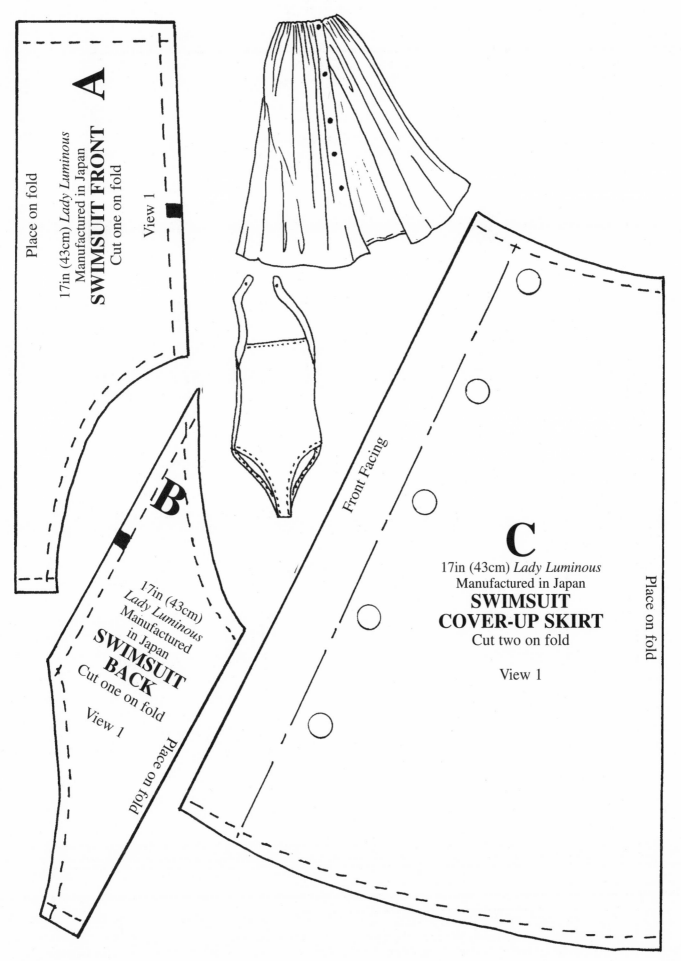

A

Place on fold

17in (43cm) *Lady Luminous*
Manufactured in Japan
SWIMSUIT FRONT
Cut one on fold

View 1

B

17in (43cm)
Lady Luminous
Manufactured
in Japan
**SWIMSUIT
BACK**
Cut one on fold

View 1

Place on fold

C

17in (43cm) *Lady Luminous*
Manufactured in Japan
**SWIMSUIT
COVER-UP SKIRT**
Cut two on fold

View 1

Front Facing

Place on fold

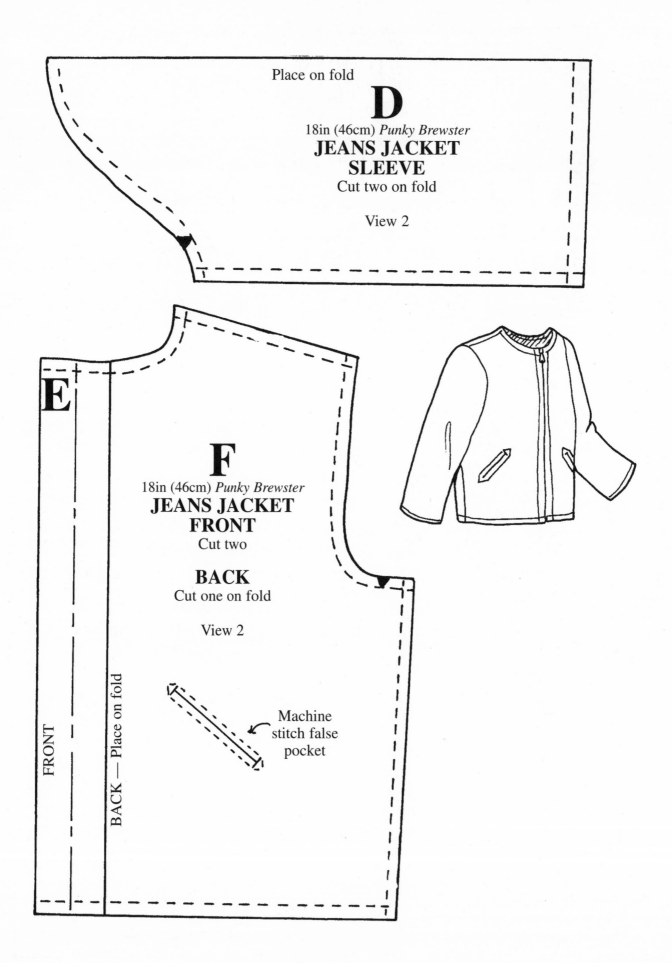

Place on fold

D

18in (46cm) *Punky Brewster*
JEANS JACKET
SLEEVE
Cut two on fold

View 2

E

F

18in (46cm) *Punky Brewster*
JEANS JACKET
FRONT
Cut two

BACK
Cut one on fold

View 2

FRONT

BACK — Place on fold

Machine
stitch false
pocket

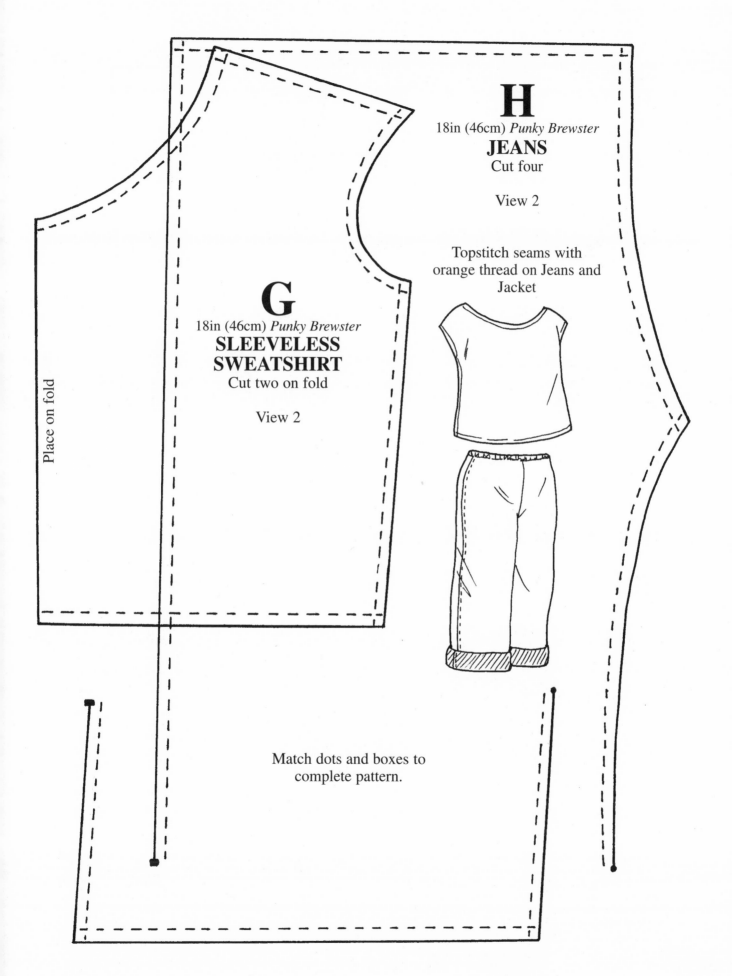

H

18in (46cm) *Punky Brewster*
JEANS
Cut four

View 2

Topstitch seams with
orange thread on Jeans and
Jacket

G

18in (46cm) *Punky Brewster*
**SLEEVELESS
SWEATSHIRT**
Cut two on fold

View 2

Place on fold

Match dots and boxes to
complete pattern.

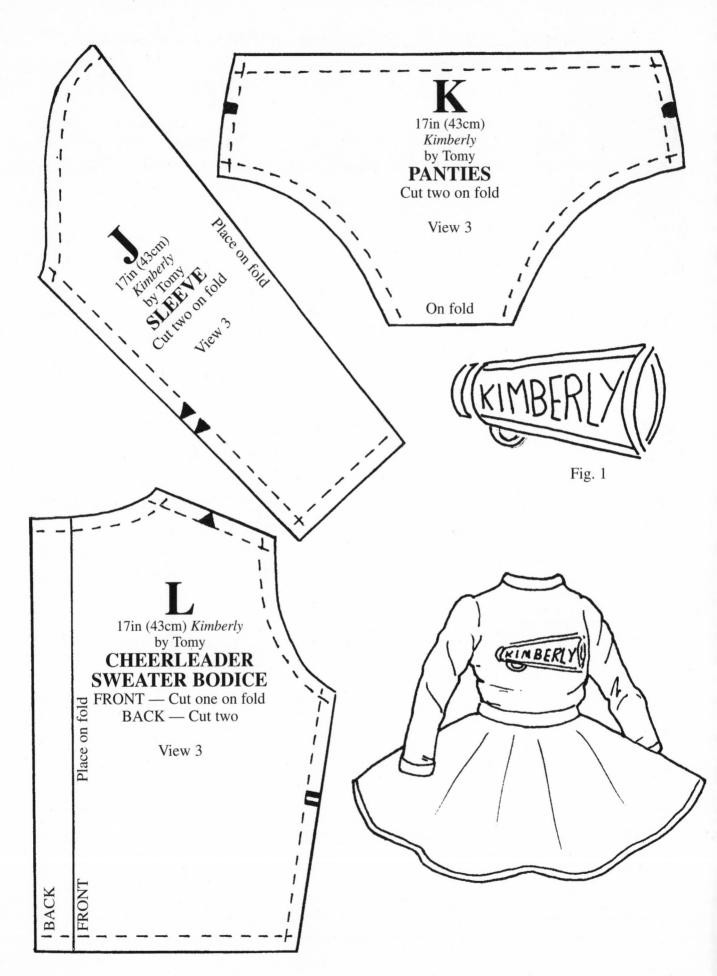

K

17in (43cm)
Kimberly
by Tomy
PANTIES
Cut two on fold

View 3

On fold

J

17in (43cm)
Kimberly
by Tomy
SLEEVE
Cut two on fold

View 3

Place on fold

KIMBERLY

Fig. 1

L

17in (43cm) *Kimberly*
by Tomy
**CHEERLEADER
SWEATER BODICE**
FRONT — Cut one on fold
BACK — Cut two

View 3

Place on fold

BACK

FRONT

View 1

View 2

View 3

View 4

View 5

View 6

View 7

View 8

View 9

View 10

Wardrobe
for 1980s 15-16in (38-41cm)
Slim Modern Child Dolls
such as Sasha, Boots Tyner Children,
and others

WARDROBE FOR 1980s 15-16in (38-41cm) SLIM MODERN CHILD DOLLS
Fits dolls such as Sasha, Boots Tyner, etc.

Most of these simple patterns are self-explanatory; however, a few notes have been included here when it seems they are needed. Variations and non-illustrated pieces are included at the last of this text.

View 1
SAILOR SUIT
Pattern Pieces A, B, C, D, E, H, J

Make this sailor suit of heavy white cotton, trim it with dark blue bias sewed flat (or use flat braid), and finish with red cotton tie. Or try dark blue lightweight wool with red trim and a dark blue or black tie for a winter look. The hat is of heavyweight white cotton, stitched in parallel lines all around the brim. This adds some rigidity to the brim.

View 2
BALLET TUTU & SLIPPERS
Pattern Pieces K, L, M

The tutu is of pink stretch knit with a skirt of very fine nylon net or sheer nylon marquisette. Shoes may be cut from heavy pink satin or lightweight kid leather. Add variety by using sparkle knit fabric for the suit.

View 3
BOAT SHIRT & TENNIS SHORTS
Pattern Pieces N, DD

The shirt and shorts are cut from a light blue knit with dark blue knit trim. For a girl doll, try two shades of pink or lavender.

For the turn-back collar of the shirt, slit the front neckline to heavy dot, bind with the darker trim, and turn down along dot-dash line. Shorts are similarly open to dot and trimmed as above.

View 4
NIGHTGOWN OR LONG DRESS
Pattern Pieces FF, GG, HH

Use this pattern for a nightgown of dainty flowered flannel, dimity, puckered cotton, or other lightweight cottons. Trim as desired.

Pattern also offers a variation of a short dress as well as a long dress which may be belted or allowed to hang loose. *Another possibility:* Make some adjustments and create a robe or housecoat from this pattern.

View 5
BASIC DRESS
Pattern Pieces S through X

Finish collar first, then sew shoulder seams of bodice and lining. Pin collar to right side of bodice, pin white lining, right side in, over collar so collar is on inside of the sandwich. Seam together around neck opening and down back of bodice. Clip, turn, press.

Slit center back of skirt to double dots on pattern. Cut a 2in (5cm) x 3-1/2in (9cm) piece of dress fabric and stitch to back opening. Slit facing, turn, press.

Run gathering threads along top of skirt. Pull threads to fit bodice and attach; topstitch over with raw edges of gathers turned upward.

Finish sleeves and cuffs; sew into armholes. Hem dress with machine stitching, or hemstitch by hand if preferred.

Note: When sewing for collectors' dolls always use the finest thread available and trim seams carefully to make seams less bulky. If sewing for a child's play doll, use regular thread and seam allowances for maximum strength.

Dress Variations

For a pleated dress, using basic dress pattern, cut skirt section wider by placing 1in (3cm) to 2in (5cm) from fold, pin, cut. Use this extra width for pleating or for fuller gathered skirt.

For a long dress, add 4in (10cm) to length of basic dress skirt.

For a smocked dress, using longest machine stitches, pull three rows of even gathers across top sections of skirt and tie off firmly, embroider over gathering threads, then attach to bodice. Repeat on sleeves.

View 6
JOGGING SUIT
Pattern Pieces O, P

Lay jacket out flat and sew mock raglan stitching from underarms to neckline. Sew contrasting knit bias tape along tops of sleeves as indicated by double lines. Insert 3in (8cm) to 3-1/2in (9cm) zipper in front of jacket, leaving tape on top and zipper in full view (zipper should match bias trim and is considered a decorative item in this application). Sew underarm seams. Bind neckline and cuffs with knit bias.

Turn up hem with machine stitching or make casing and insert cord for tie front if desired.

For pants, lay each out flat and stitch contrasting knit bias down outer leg (along fold), leaving 1-1/2in (4cm) loose at bottom for stirrups. Hem each leg. Sew seams C-D of each unit, then seam units together back and front at D-E. Turn down waist to form casing and insert narrow elastic. Attach stirrups inside legs at inseams.

View 7
SHIRT & JEANS
Pattern Pieces Y, Z, AA, BB, CC

Use denim and topstitching for a real "jeans" look, or cut from chambray, striped ticking, gingham or broadcloth for a different style. For ease of construction, add pockets and topstitching before sewing main pieces together.

The knit shirt uses scraps of knit tee shirt material, or may be cut from good parts of a worn shirt. Finish neck opening and sleeves with bias cut from same fabric, or bind with commercial bias tape. Add pocket before sewing main pieces together, but take care in placement of the pocket.

View 8
RAINCOAT & HAT
Pattern Pieces OO through UU

Make this rainy day outfit from heavy, stitchable plastic, oil cloth, or nylon. Line both pieces if desired.

View 9
SPORT SHORTS
Pattern Piece EE

These shorts may be teamed with various shirts and jackets in this collection. Make them of denim, gingham, broadcloth, chambray, etc. Trim as desired.

View 10
HOODED CAR COAT
Pattern Pieces HH, KK, LL, MM, NN

This coat is good made of corduroy, heavy double knit, or lightweight wool, lined or unlined. Sew pockets in place before sewing in lining. Try a tan corduroy with coordinated plain lining. Add a plaid scarf with fringed ends.

Not Pictured
PLEATED SKIRT

Cut a rectangle 4in (10cm) x 20in (51cm). Finish one long side with a narrow hem. Pleat other long side evenly to 10in (25m). Baste pleats in place and steam press. Sew back seam. Measure doll's waist and cut a piece of 1/8in (.31cm) flat elastic to that measurement plus 3/4in (2cm). Turn down top of skirt 1/8in (.31cm). Sew elastic to inside of skirt, pulling elastic to fit as you sew.

Not Pictured
SWEATER

Use blouse pattern without front opening. Check for proper length. Cut from loosely knit fabric or from heavy knee sock. Staystitch with machine around all pieces before assembly. Use collar pattern given.

Not Pictured
UNDERWEAR & ACCESSORIES
Pattern Pieces F, G, JJ, VV, WW, XX, YY

Cut underwear from good sections of tee-shirts. Makes nice, soft, non-bulky underthings. For girls' undies use only the narrowest and lightest cotton lace. Use the zig zag option on your machine for nice edge finishing or turn under a very narrow hem all around.

Use discarded stockings. Make shoes and slippers of heavy leather gloves.

Knit undershirt-pattern piece F
Knit underpants-pattern piece G
Knit stockings-pattern piece JJ
Underpants-pattern piece VV
Rib knit stockings-pattern piece XX
Ankle socks-pattern piece YY
Tie slippers-pattern pieces ZZ, Z2

ABOUT CLOSINGS & FASTENERS

You may wish to use the modern Velcro™ closing material for these clothes, especially when making clothes for a play doll. There is, however, no substitute for nicely worked buttonholes and attractive buttons. Small snap fasteners are also appropriate; however, standard hooks and eyes are a bit bulky.

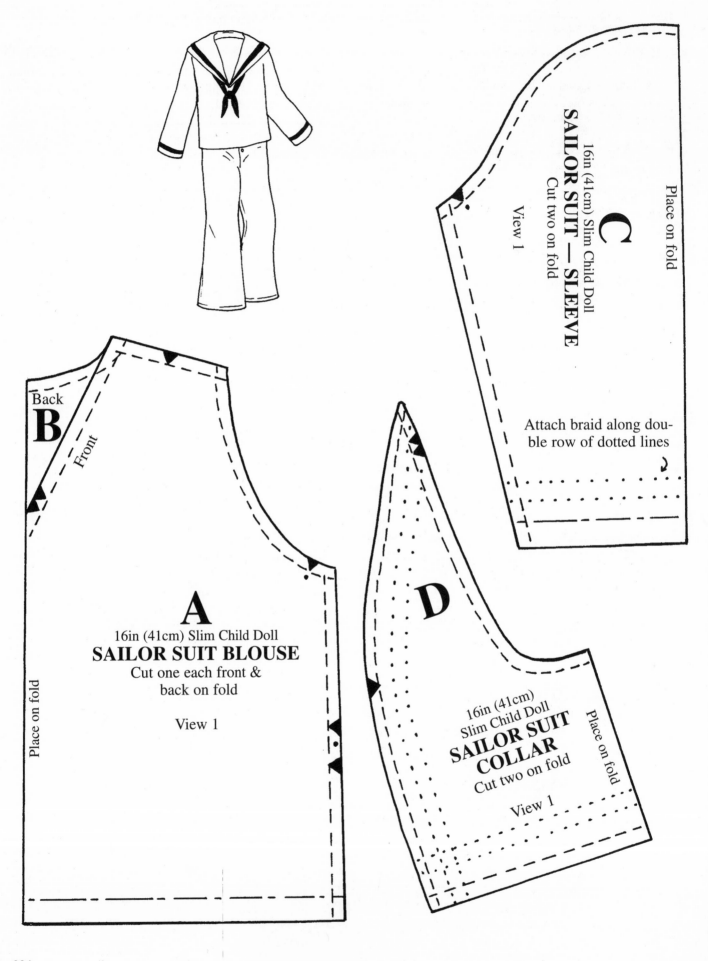

C

16in (41cm) Slim Child Doll
SAILOR SUIT—SLEEVE
Cut two on fold

View 1

Place on fold

Attach braid along double row of dotted lines

B

Back

Front

A
16in (41cm) Slim Child Doll
SAILOR SUIT BLOUSE
Cut one each front &
back on fold

View 1

Place on fold

D

16in (41cm)
Slim Child Doll
**SAILOR SUIT
COLLAR**
Cut two on fold

View 1

Place on fold

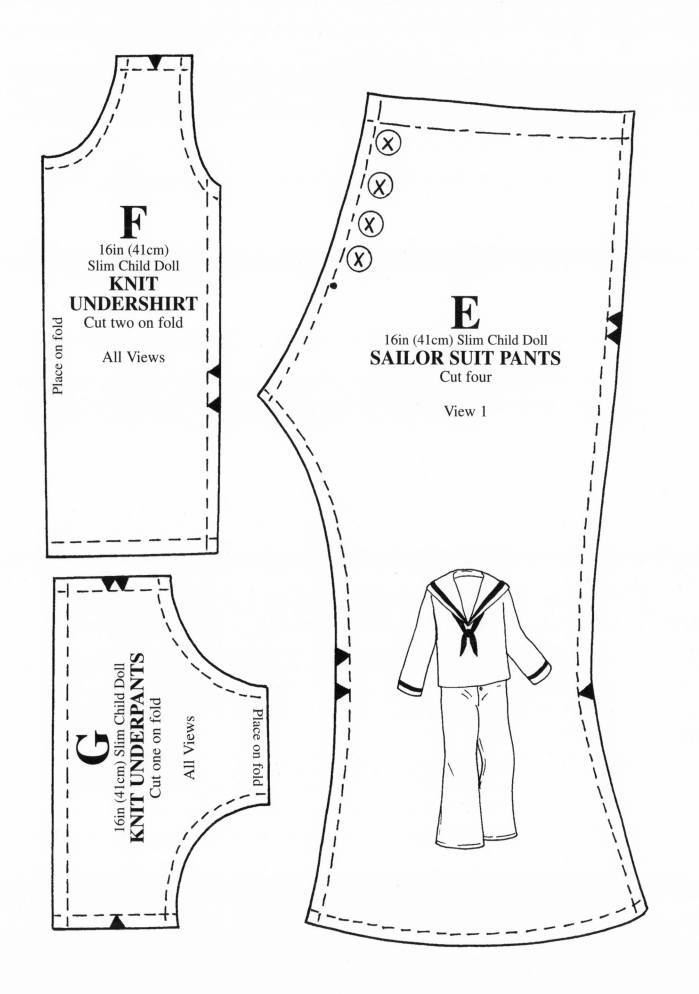

F
16in (41cm)
Slim Child Doll
KNIT UNDERSHIRT
Cut two on fold

All Views

Place on fold

E
16in (41cm) Slim Child Doll
SAILOR SUIT PANTS
Cut four

View 1

G
16in (41cm) Slim Child Doll
KNIT UNDERPANTS
Cut one on fold

All Views

Place on fold

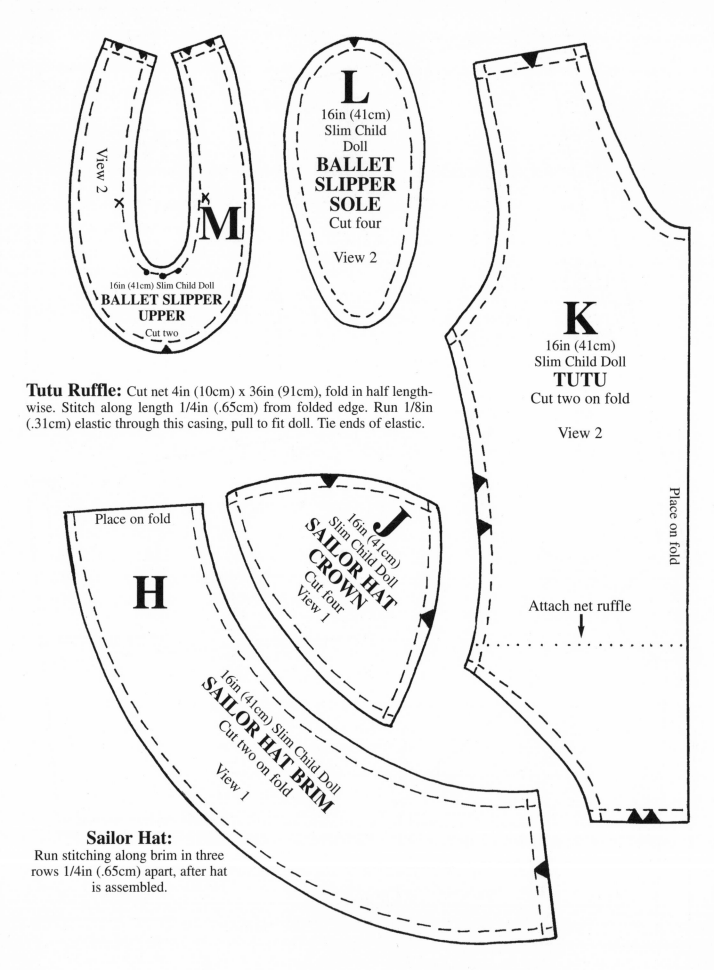

View 2

L
16in (41cm)
Slim Child
Doll
**BALLET
SLIPPER
SOLE**
Cut four

View 2

M

16in (41cm) Slim Child Doll
**BALLET SLIPPER
UPPER**
Cut two

K
16in (41cm)
Slim Child Doll
TUTU
Cut two on fold

View 2

Place on fold

Attach net ruffle

Tutu Ruffle: Cut net 4in (10cm) x 36in (91cm), fold in half length-wise. Stitch along length 1/4in (.65cm) from folded edge. Run 1/8in (.31cm) elastic through this casing, pull to fit doll. Tie ends of elastic.

Place on fold

H

J
16in (41cm)
Slim Child Doll
**SAILOR HAT
CROWN**
Cut four
View 1

16in (41cm) Slim Child Doll
SAILOR HAT BRIM
Cut two on fold
View 1

Sailor Hat:
Run stitching along brim in three
rows 1/4in (.65cm) apart, after hat
is assembled.

226

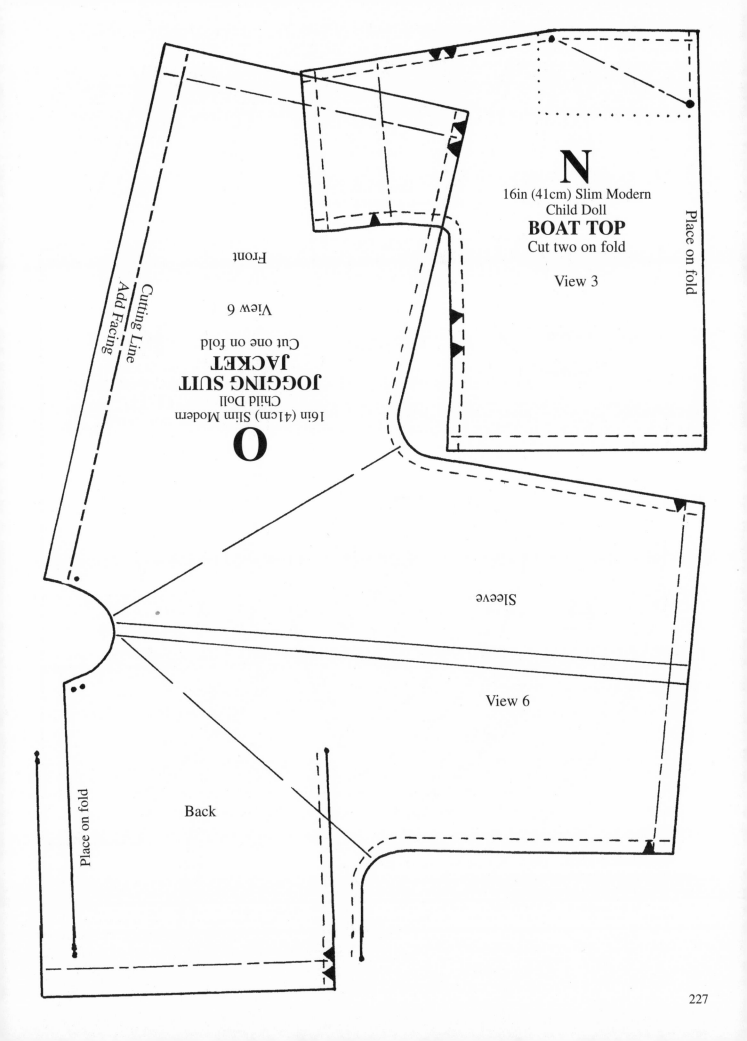

N

16in (41cm) Slim Modern
Child Doll
BOAT TOP
Cut two on fold

View 3

Place on fold

Cutting Line
Add Facing

Front

View 6

Cut one on fold
**JOGGING SUIT
JACKET**
16in (41cm) Slim Modern
Child Doll
O

Sleeve

View 6

Place on fold

Back

227

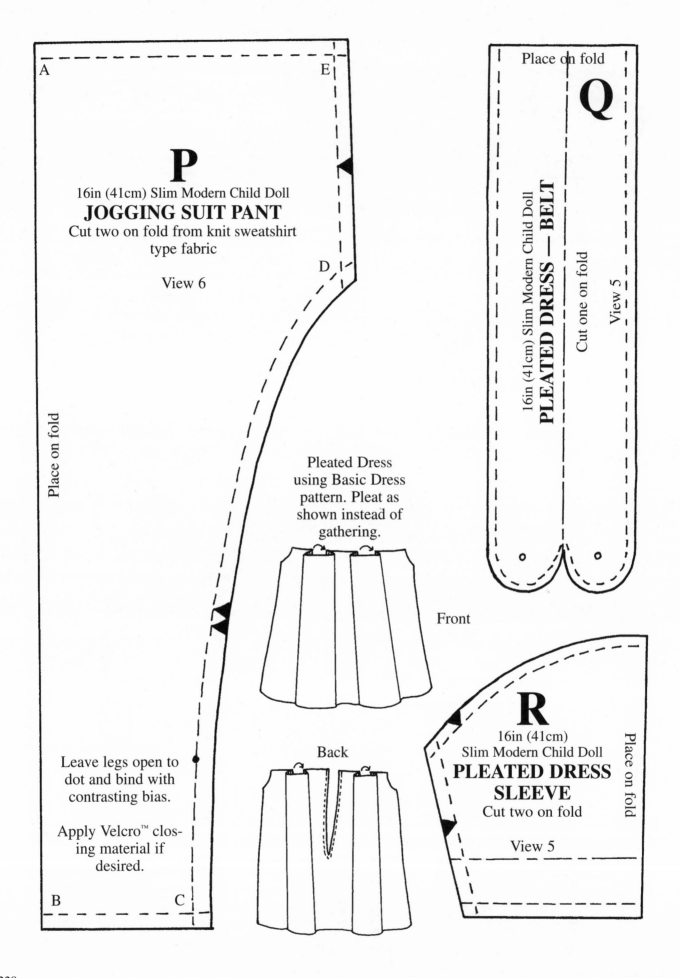

P

16in (41cm) Slim Modern Child Doll
JOGGING SUIT PANT
Cut two on fold from knit sweatshirt
type fabric

View 6

A

E

D

Place on fold

Leave legs open to
dot and bind with
contrasting bias.

Apply Velcro™ clos-
ing material if
desired.

B

C

Pleated Dress
using Basic Dress
pattern. Pleat as
shown instead of
gathering.

Front

Back

Q

Place on fold

16in (41cm) Slim Modern Child Doll
PLEATED DRESS — BELT
Cut one on fold

View 5

R

16in (41cm)
Slim Modern Child Doll
**PLEATED DRESS
SLEEVE**
Cut two on fold

Place on fold

View 5

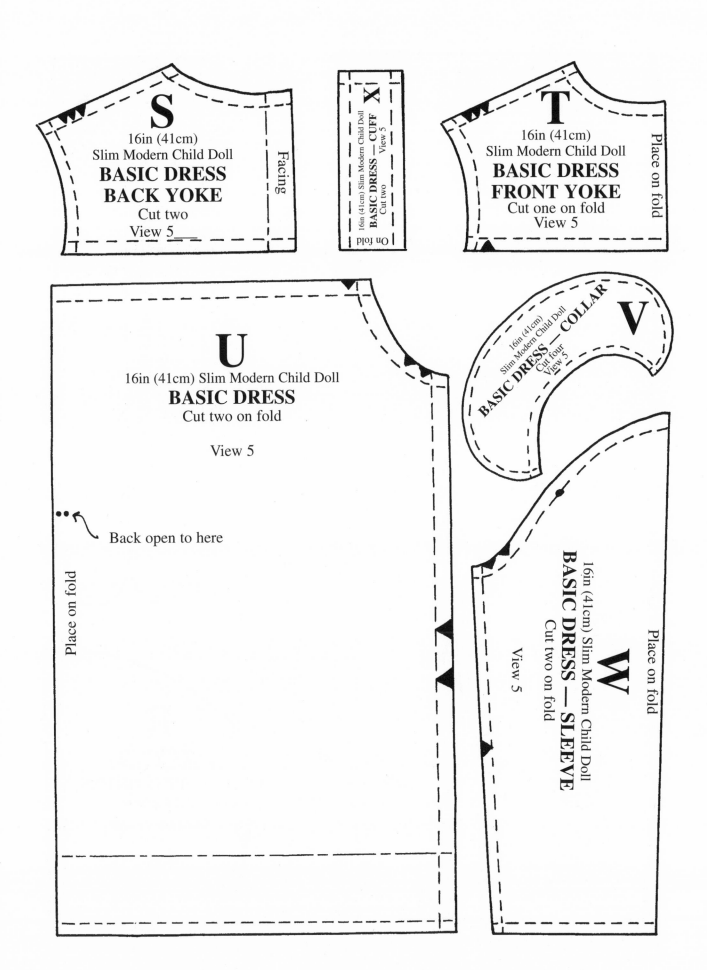

S

16in (41cm)
Slim Modern Child Doll
**BASIC DRESS
BACK YOKE**
Cut two
View 5

Facing

16in (41cm) Slim Modern Child Doll
BASIC DRESS — CUFF X
Cut two
View 5
On fold

T

16in (41cm)
Slim Modern Child Doll
**BASIC DRESS
FRONT YOKE**
Cut one on fold
View 5

Place on fold

U

16in (41cm) Slim Modern Child Doll
BASIC DRESS

Cut two on fold

View 5

Back open to here

Place on fold

16in (41cm)
Slim Modern Child Doll
BASIC DRESS — COLLAR
Cut four
View 5

V

16in (41cm) Slim Modern Child Doll
BASIC DRESS — SLEEVE
Cut two on fold

View 5

W

Place on fold

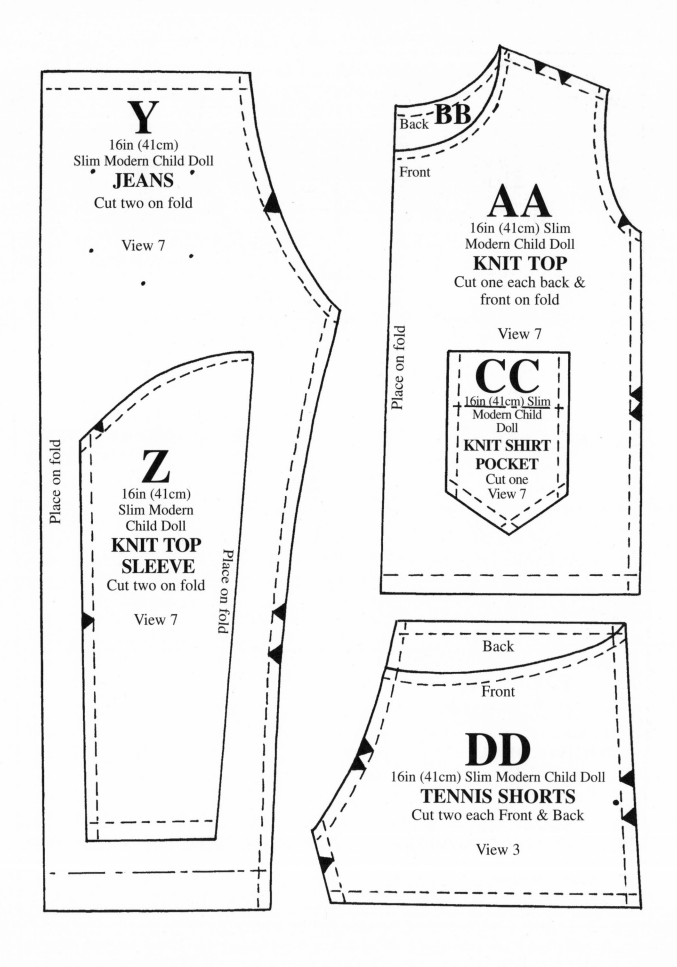

Y

16in (41cm)
Slim Modern Child Doll
JEANS
Cut two on fold

View 7

Place on fold

Z

16in (41cm)
Slim Modern
Child Doll
**KNIT TOP
SLEEVE**
Cut two on fold

View 7

Place on fold

Place on fold

Back **BB**

Front

AA

16in (41cm) Slim
Modern Child Doll
KNIT TOP
Cut one each back &
front on fold

View 7

Place on fold

CC

16in (41cm) Slim
Modern Child
Doll
**KNIT SHIRT
POCKET**
Cut one
View 7

Back

Front

DD

16in (41cm) Slim Modern Child Doll
TENNIS SHORTS
Cut two each Front & Back

View 3

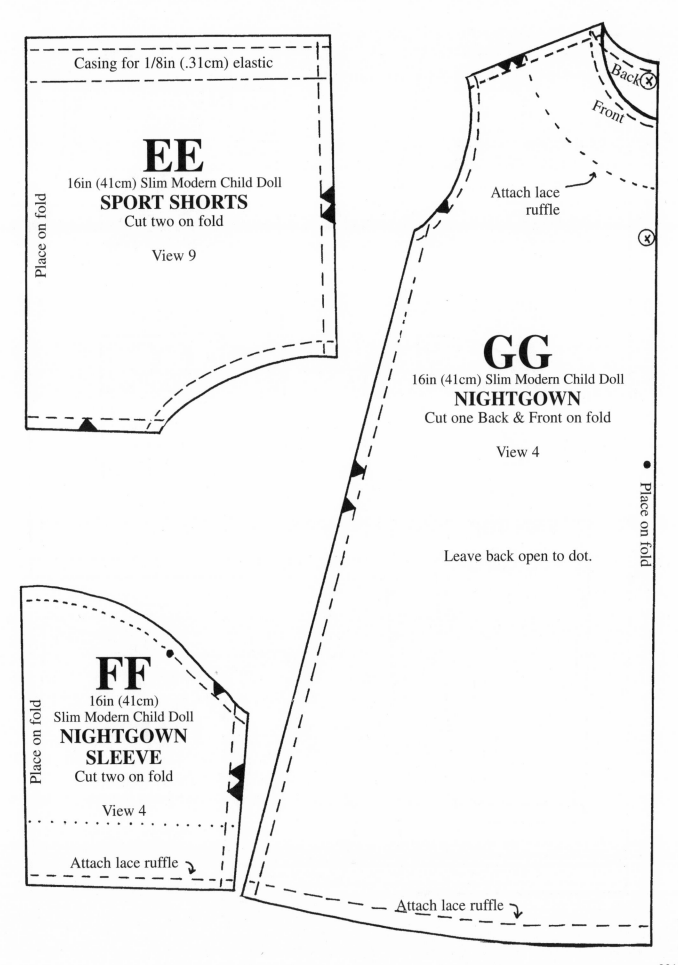

EE
16in (41cm) Slim Modern Child Doll
SPORT SHORTS
Cut two on fold

View 9

Casing for 1/8in (.31cm) elastic

Place on fold

GG
16in (41cm) Slim Modern Child Doll
NIGHTGOWN
Cut one Back & Front on fold

View 4

Leave back open to dot.

Attach lace ruffle

Back

Front

Place on fold

FF
16in (41cm)
Slim Modern Child Doll
**NIGHTGOWN
SLEEVE**
Cut two on fold

View 4

Place on fold

Attach lace ruffle

Attach lace ruffle

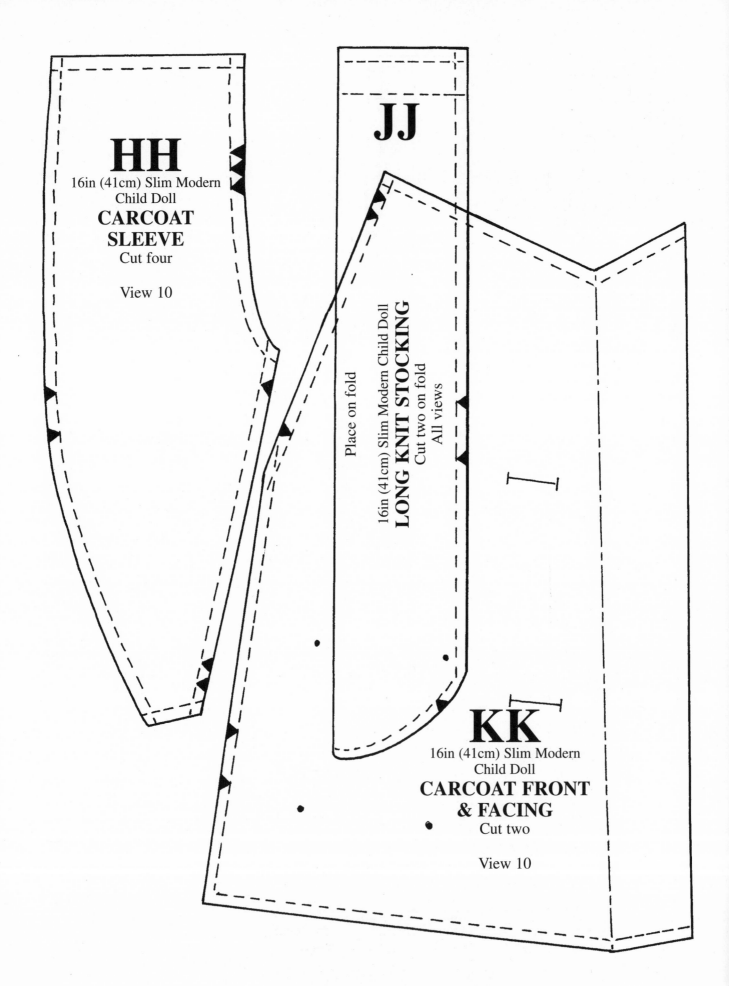

HH
16in (41cm) Slim Modern
Child Doll
**CARCOAT
SLEEVE**
Cut four

View 10

JJ

Place on fold

16in (41cm) Slim Modern Child Doll
LONG KNIT STOCKING
Cut two on fold
All views

KK
16in (41cm) Slim Modern
Child Doll
**CARCOAT FRONT
& FACING**
Cut two

View 10

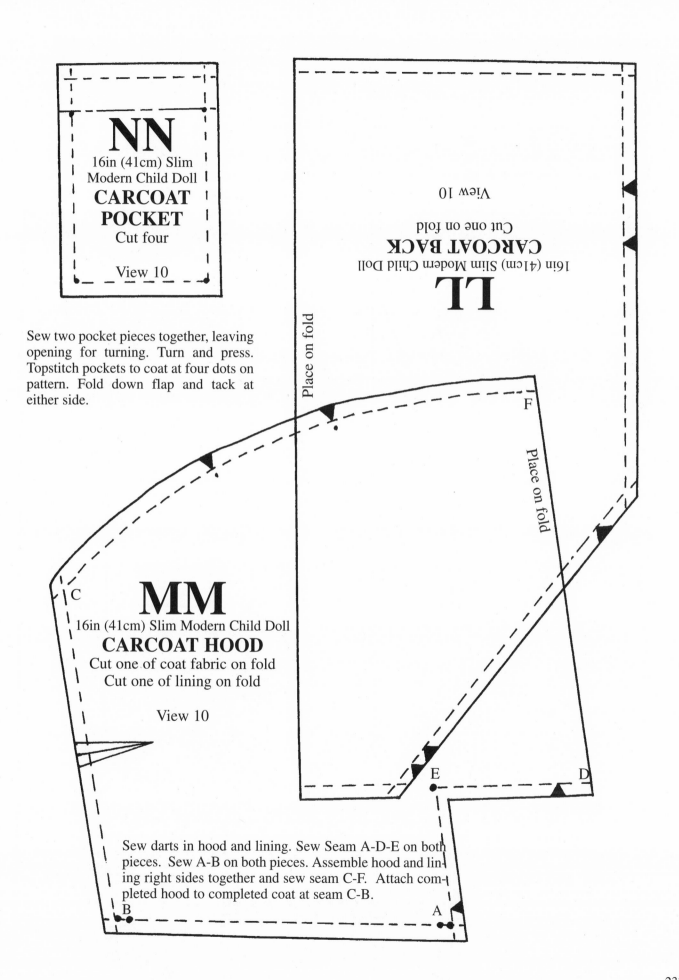

NN

16in (41cm) Slim
Modern Child Doll
**CARCOAT
POCKET**
Cut four

View 10

Sew two pocket pieces together, leaving opening for turning. Turn and press. Topstitch pockets to coat at four dots on pattern. Fold down flap and tack at either side.

CARCOAT BACK
16in (41cm) Slim Modern Child Doll
Cut one on fold
View 10

LL

Place on fold

Place on fold

F

MM

16in (41cm) Slim Modern Child Doll
CARCOAT HOOD
Cut one of coat fabric on fold
Cut one of lining on fold

View 10

C

E   D

Sew darts in hood and lining. Sew Seam A-D-E on both pieces. Sew A-B on both pieces. Assemble hood and lining right sides together and sew seam C-F. Attach completed hood to completed coat at seam C-B.

B   A

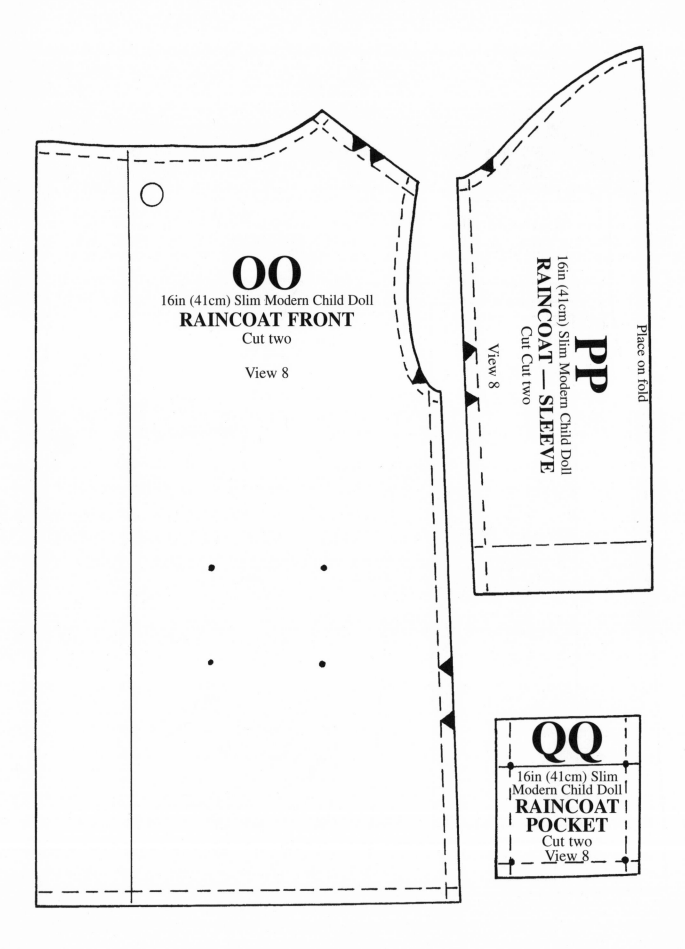

OO
16in (41cm) Slim Modern Child Doll
RAINCOAT FRONT
Cut two

View 8

PP
16in (41cm) Slim Modern Child Doll
RAINCOAT — SLEEVE
Cut two

View 8

Place on fold

QQ
16in (41cm) Slim
Modern Child Doll
**RAINCOAT
POCKET**
Cut two
View 8

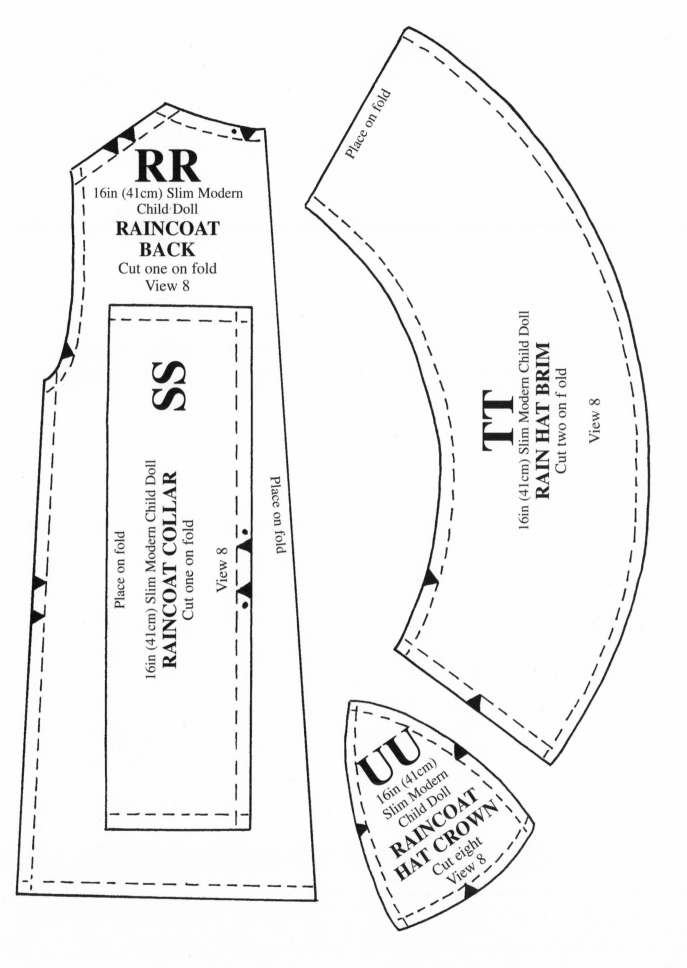

RR
16in (41cm) Slim Modern
Child Doll
**RAINCOAT
BACK**
Cut one on fold
View 8

SS
16in (41cm) Slim Modern Child Doll
RAINCOAT COLLAR
Cut one on fold
View 8

Place on fold

Place on fold

TT
16in (41cm) Slim Modern Child Doll
RAIN HAT BRIM
Cut two on f old
View 8

Place on fold

UU
16in (41cm)
Slim Modern
Child Doll
**RAINCOAT
HAT CROWN**
Cut eight
View 8

235

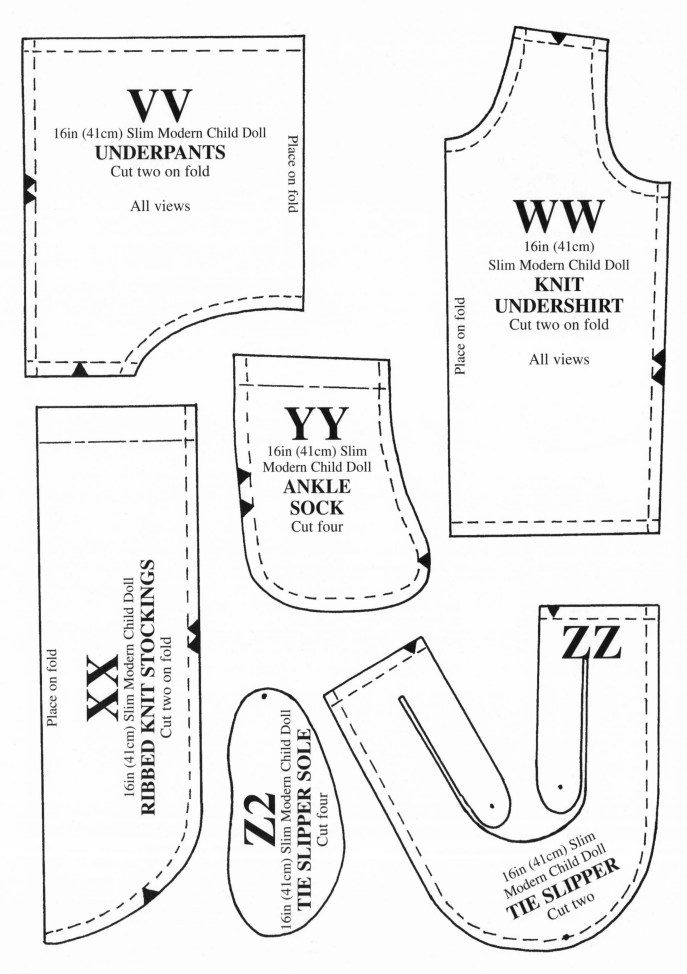

VV

16in (41cm) Slim Modern Child Doll
UNDERPANTS
Cut two on fold

All views

Place on fold

WW

16in (41cm)
Slim Modern Child Doll
**KNIT
UNDERSHIRT**
Cut two on fold

All views

Place on fold

YY

16in (41cm) Slim
Modern Child Doll
**ANKLE
SOCK**
Cut four

XX

16in (41cm) Slim Modern Child Doll
RIBBED KNIT STOCKINGS
Cut two on fold

Place on fold

Z2

16in (41cm) Slim Modern Child Doll
TIE SLIPPER SOLE
Cut four

ZZ

16in (41cm) Slim
Modern Child Doll
TIE SLIPPER
Cut two

Wardrobe
for
21in (53cm)

MODERN ARTIST DOLLS

For dolls such as:
Elena and Sabine by Jennifer Esteban
Tess by Elaine Campbell
Willow and Hilary by Dianna Effner
Kathy by Annette Himsteadt
and many others

View 1

View 2

View 2

View 3

View 4

WARDROBE FOR 21in (53cm) MODERN ARTIST DOLLS
Various Artists and Manufacturers

The long-legged, barefoot-child artist dolls which appeared in the late 1980s continued in popularity and in increasing numbers in the 1990s. These dolls, the creations of a fairly large number of international artists, are noted for their size (usually between 20in [51cm] and 30in [76cm]), their life-like features, and their beautiful, realistic hairstyles, as well as their bare feet. Some of these dolls are available in molds for the doll artisan and present a special adventure in doll dressmaking. They may be dressed in fantastically trimmed outfits or in simple, realistically styled play clothing. A bonus, in my opinion, is that the larger-sized clothing is much easier to make, fit, and trim than smaller sizes, although a considerably higher yardage is required, resulting in higher costs.

Fabrics for the dresses are often calico or dainty printed cottons in florals, checks, or stripes with organdy for aprons or trim. Underwear is of lawn or other very fine, soft cotton. Variations on this theme are, of course, at the whim of the doll dressmaker. There is no rule to say that corduroys, vel-vets, worsteds, or other fabrics may not be used. In fact, the artists who create these dolls sometimes select such fabrics as appropriate to particular designs.

Carefully chosen trimming often makes the outfit. On underwear use small embroidered flowers and leaves, either hand-embroidered or those purchased in a fabric shop by the yard. (Do not, however, use them by the yard on the underwear. They are meant to be used here merely as delicate touches.) Narrow ribbons, proportioned for the doll, add important touches as bows and streamers or in insertion lace.

Always use correctly proportioned braids, bindings, zippers, and buttons. Nothing is more detracting than a huge, out-of-proportion row of buttons down the front of an otherwise wonderfully constructed and finished outfit.

Dress the doll in her underwear and check measurements before beginning the outer clothing. Thus you are assured of good fit *over the underwear* when the dress is finished.

View 1
BLOUSE & SKIRT or DRESS
Pattern Pieces B, C, D or E

For attached bodice, cut bodice pattern as shown. To make a separate blouse, extend bottom edge of bodice pattern 1-1/2in (4cm) or to fit your doll. Finish with narrow rolled hem. Finish neckline with trim of choice.

Make skirt of dress following peasant skirt instructions. Attach to bodice or make an inset waistband following directions for inserting slip waistband.

For extra fullness on the ruffled, drop-shoulder blouse, add another inch on fold side when cutting. (Pin pattern 1in [3cm] from fold.) Assemble blouse and sleeves. Run double gathering threads along top edge but do not gather. Measure around doll's shoulders. Cut a piece of 2in (5cm) to 3in (8cm) wide pre-ruffled eyelet to shoulder measurement plus 1in (3cm) for seam. Sew end pieces of ruffle together, press seam flat. Gather top of bodice to fit ruffle and baste together. Machine stitch all around. Finish with bias tape.

For ruffle of same fabric as blouse, cut a piece two or three times the shoulder measurement, depending on fullness desired. Hem one long side; run double gathers along other long side. Stitch ends together and proceed as with pre-ruffled piece.

To finish sleeves: Make a casing 3in (8cm) from bottom edge of sleeves on inside and run narrow elastic through to fit over doll's hand. Finish bottom edge with narrow rolled hem or lace edge.

The basic blouse design may be varied, limited only by your imagination. Flip through this book and borrow from other patterns. Change the length of a sleeve or the shape of a collar, etc.

View 2
SLIP & PANTALETTES
Pattern Pieces A, B, C, F

Pantalettes - Make pantalettes first. For waistband length, measure doll's waist plus 2in (5cm) and cut 2-1/2in (6cm) wide. Cut from same fabric as slip.

Slip - This slip has a set-in waistband. Measure doll's waist over the pantalettes for waistband. Cut two pieces of slip fabric 1-1/2in (4cm) wide and the length of the waist measurement plus 1-1/2in (4cm). Place a mark or sewing pin on waistband 3/4in (2cm) from each end.

Sew the two panels of the slip skirt together. Open a slit down center back to dot shown on pattern. Run double gathering threads around top of skirt to within 1/2in (1cm) on either side of back slit. Bind slit with self bias. Gather skirt to fit waistband between marks; baste to waistband, wrong sides together, spreading gathers evenly (unfinished seam edges will be on right side of slip), machine stitch.

Sew bodice pieces together at shoulder and side seams; press seams open. Fold under and baste back facings as indicated on pattern. Run double gathering threads along waistline to 1/2in (1cm) from either side of back opening. Attach to waistband as above.

Press under all edges of remaining waistband piece, pin, then baste over sewed-in waistband, covering all raw edges. Turn in ends of waistband (trim off excess length if necessary), and blindstitch closed. Topstitch close to edge all around on machine using small stitches. Note: For best results, do not skip the basting step.

Make buttonholes and sew on buttons, or use snap fasteners.

Sew very narrow lace all around neckline and armholes. Use a wide pre-ruffled lace or eyelet along bottom edge and along dash line above hem ruffle. Add insertion lace threaded with matching ribbon, if desired. Eyelet trim may be used instead of lace for a "country" look.

Slip variation I - Cut slip skirt at dash line above hemline. Make self-ruffle of slip fabric measuring 50in (128cm) by 2in (5cm). Seam short sides together; press seam open. Finish one long edge with narrow lace. Run double gathering threads along remaining long edge. Pull gathers and sew to bottom of slip skirt. Or attach pre-gathered 2in (5cm) wide lace ruffle to bottom edge.

Slip variation II - For a blouse/slip combination, make slip with variation I and bodice using dotted line for neckline. Finish bodice with sleeves and large ruffled Bertha collar. Trim sleeves and edge of ruffled collar with same narrow lace as skirt of slip. Trim neck edge with self-fabric bias.

Finish outfit with flower-printed peasant skirt.

View 3 **GATHERED PEASANT SKIRT**	Measure doll's waist over underwear. Add 1-1/2in (4cm) to the waist measurement for waistband length and cut 2-1/2in (6cm) wide. Measure from doll's waist to desired skirt length. If

adding a ruffle, subtract the width of the ruffle. Cut a piece of skirt fabric the skirt length plus seam allowances and from 36in (91cm) to 60in (152cm) long, depending on fullness desired and size of doll. Stitch back seam of skirt to within 3in (8cm) of waistline and blindstitch seam allowance for back opening.

Cut ruffle from same fabric, of desired width by 60in (156cm) to 72in (182cm) long, depending on fullness of skirt. Sew short ends of ruffle together, press seam open. Finish one long edge of ruffle with hanky hem or with very narrow lace as desired.

Run double gathering threads along remaining long edge of ruffle; do not pull gathers. Pin ruffle at four equidistant points to bottom edge of skirt. Pull gathers evenly to fit, then seam to skirt.

Run double gathering threads along waistline of skirt. Pull gathers evenly to fit waistband and attach to waistband as above.

If desired, a sash may be added. Cut two pieces of skirt fabric, each measuring 4in (10cm) by 24in (61cm). Put a narrow hanky hem on long sides of sash. Fold over one end of each piece right sides together and stitch along side to point the sash. Fold over unpointed ends and attach to waistband. If desired, piece may be cut double, seamed right sides together, and turned.

View 4 **ELASTIC-TOP PEASANT BLOUSE** Pattern Pieces G, H	For elastic-top peasant blouse, follow construction detail sketches to run a casing along top edge of blouse (figs. 1-3). Insert elastic. Put

blouse on doll and pull elastic to fit. Tie off.

Sleeves may be extended to add push-up fullness, or may be finished as sleeves in View 1. Trim blouse with lace or ruffle if desired.

Not Shown **SHAWL**	Measure your doll beginning at one wrist, up the length of the arm, across the shoulders in back, and down the other arm

to the wrist. Use this measurement as the long side of a right-angle triangle of interesting fabric. Fringe the two short sides of the shawl and finish long side with a narrow rolled hem.

Shawl may be draped across one shoulder, thrown over both shoulders and tied loosely in front, or draped over her arms at the elbows and allowed to hang down in back. This shawl is great for a gypsy or country girl look.

TO MAKE A GYPSY GIRL COSTUME

Using the patterns and instructions in this section, make a peasant blouse, a ruffled peasant skirt, and a ruffled petticoat. Add a bolero from another pattern set in this book. Use plain, plaid, or flowered prints in combinations that work together. Red, green, white and gold make a striking costume.

Make a head scarf of a silk triangle by measuring from one of your doll's wrists, up the arm, across the shoulder, down the opposite arm to wrist. This is the long side measurement of a right-angle triangle. Trim scarf points with fake golden coins and golden bells. Tie around her head gypsy-style.

From the same silk, make a sash for her waist measuring 4in (10cm) to 6in (15cm) wide, depending on the size of your doll. Measure the doll's waist and add 4-6in (10-15cm) for the knot plus enough length so that both ends of the sash hang about three-quarters the length of her skirt.

Add a golden shower-of-coins belt, necklace, and ankle bracelets, gold hoop earrings and arm bracelets, give her a tambourine or a crystal ball, and you'll have a gorgeous gypsy girl. (Her adornments denote the extent of her wealth and prestige in her community.)

TIPS FOR THE COUNTRY GIRL LOOK

While the country girl look is every bit as charming as the gypsy girl look, country girl is somewhat more demure. Rose or daisy prints and eyelet add charm. Starchy white cottons suggest line-dried clothes under blue skies and ironing days in a country kitchen.

To customize a plain white apron, appliqué it with flowers and leaves cut from the dress fabric. Or embroider forget-me-nots in an attractive design across the apron. Trim the sleeves of the dress with white cotton cuffs edged in narrow eyelet. Repeat the eyelet around the neckline. Finish bottom edges of apron and skirt with wider matching eyelet. Ruffle the same wide eyelet over the shoulders of the apron.

Use a checked gingham for the dress and incorporate some gingham into the trim for the apron as bias trim, pockets, or insets. Again, embroidered forget-me-nots on gingham are a traditional and lovely decoration.

These are only a few of the styles in which the modern artist dolls may be dressed. They also look wonderful in antique styles; never feel inhibited about crossing over into the previous century for ideas. In particular, the styles of the late 1890s, as well as the early twentieth century, may be adapted with great effect. Use plenty of white dimity, lawn, and organdy, insertion lace and ribbon, keeping all in good proportion. (See Sewing for *Twentieth Century Dolls, Volume I* for several antique patterns that may be adapted for the modern dolls.)

Above all, avoid synthetic fabrics when sewing for these dolls. Their design seems to demand the use of natural fibers.

See Sarah's wardrobe for additional ideas for the artist dolls.

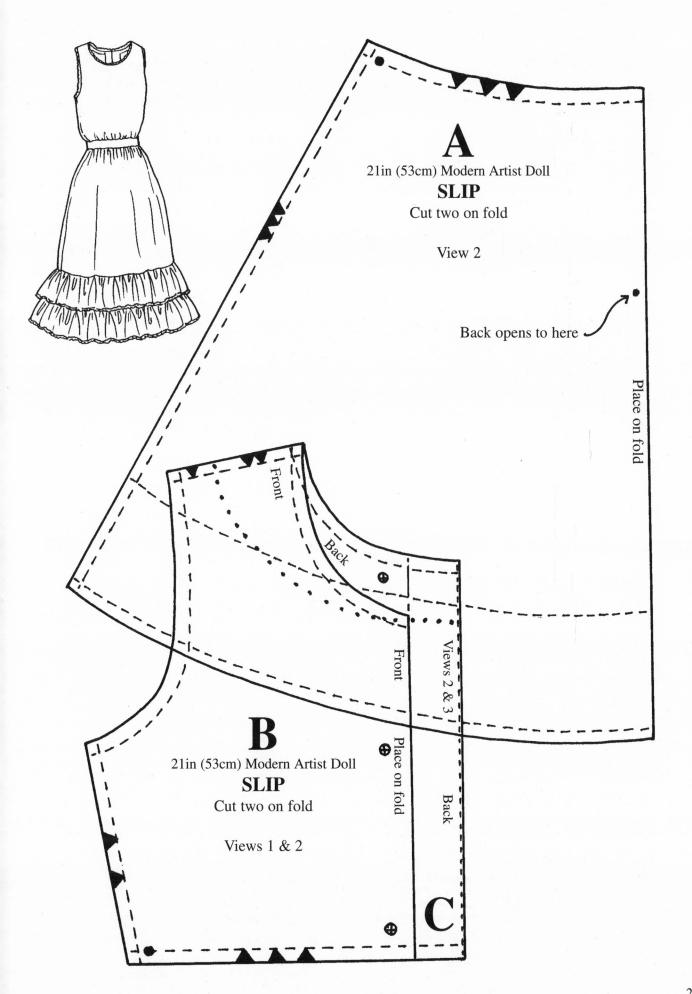

A

21in (53cm) Modern Artist Doll
SLIP
Cut two on fold

View 2

Back opens to here

Place on fold

Front

Back

Front

Views 2 & 3

B

21in (53cm) Modern Artist Doll
SLIP
Cut two on fold

Views 1 & 2

Place on fold

Back

C

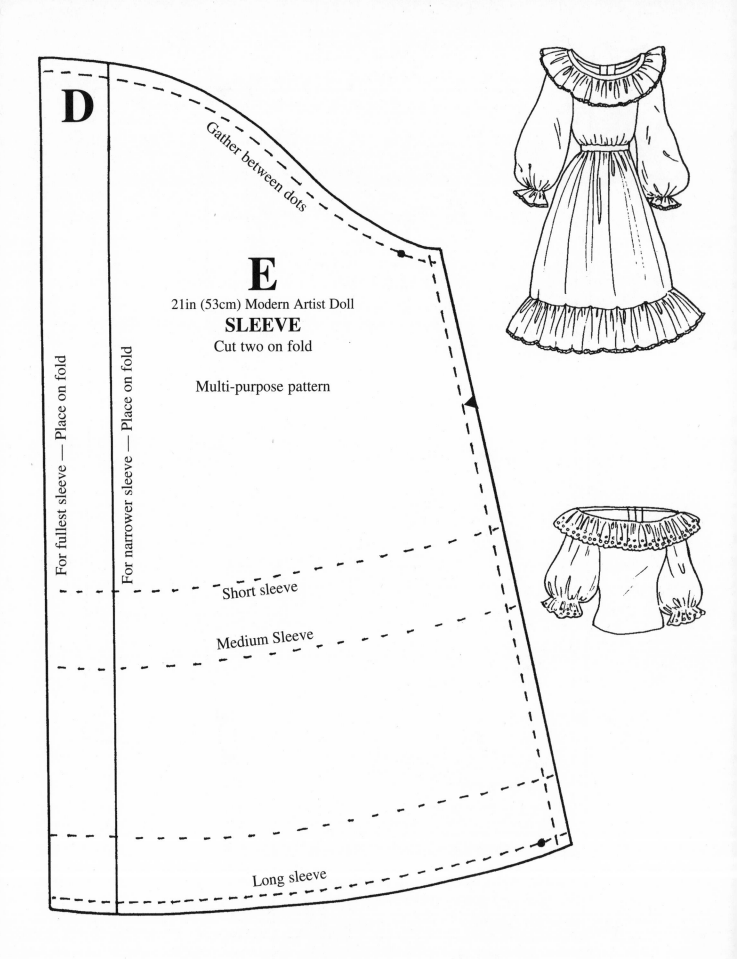

D

Gather between dots

E

21in (53cm) Modern Artist Doll
SLEEVE
Cut two on fold

Multi-purpose pattern

For fullest sleeve — Place on fold

For narrower sleeve — Place on fold

Short sleeve

Medium Sleeve

Long sleeve

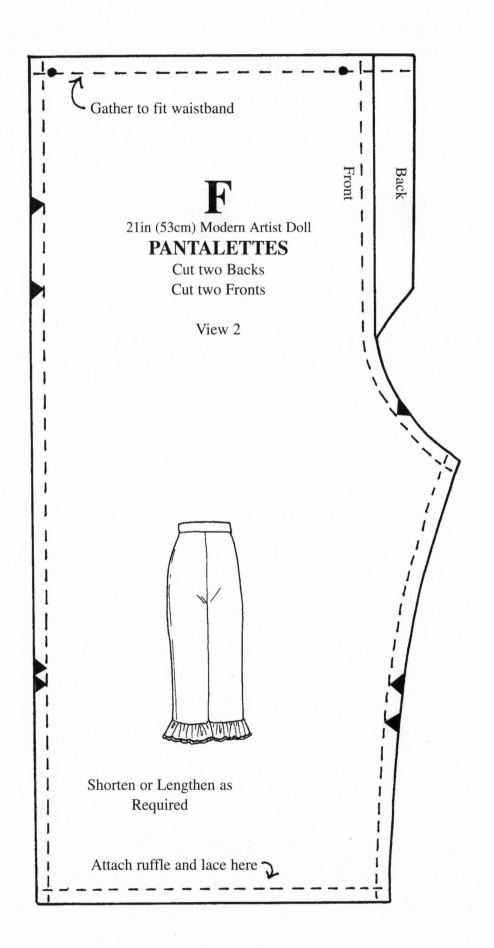

Gather to fit waistband

Front

Back

F

21in (53cm) Modern Artist Doll
PANTALETTES
Cut two Backs
Cut two Fronts

View 2

Shorten or Lengthen as
Required

Attach ruffle and lace here

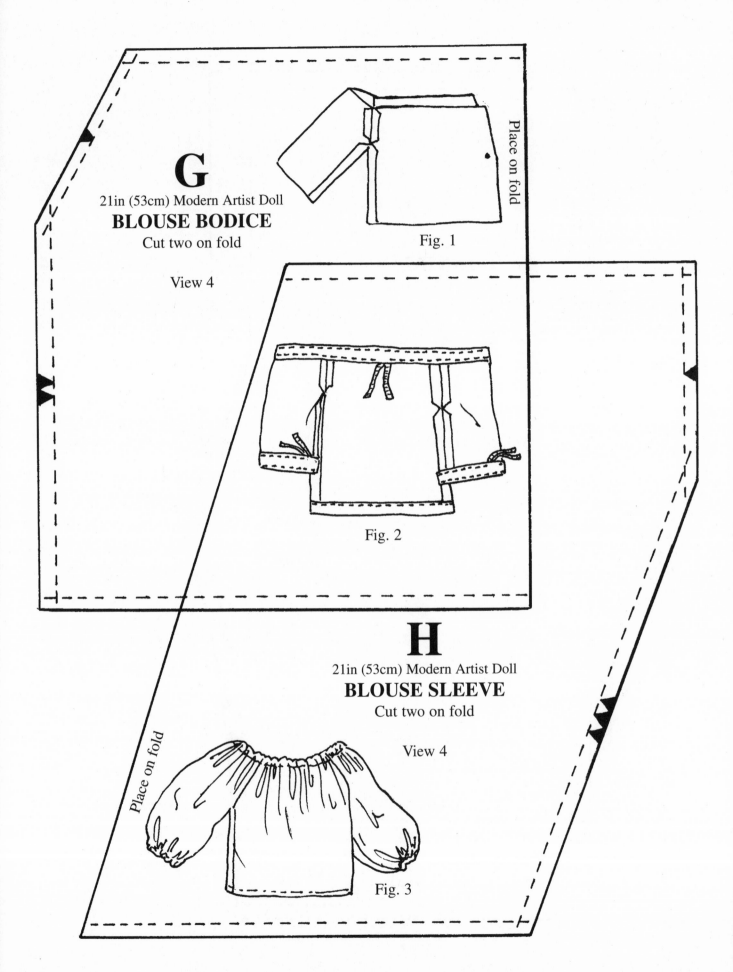

G

21in (53cm) Modern Artist Doll

BLOUSE BODICE

Cut two on fold

View 4

Place on fold

Fig. 1

Fig. 2

H

21in (53cm) Modern Artist Doll

BLOUSE SLEEVE

Cut two on fold

View 4

Place on fold

Fig. 3

Romantic Fashions for
22in (56cm)

Sarah & Daniel
and
Other 1980s and 1990s
Artist Dolls

(Sarah by Nicholas Bramble)

View 1

View 8

View 6

View 7

View 2

View 3

View 5

View 4

Dolls by modern artists provide particular challenges to the doll costumer. Selecting a style of clothing that will be a counterpoint to the character of the doll, enhance its features, and give the best presentation, will contribute to the believability, the representation of humanity of the doll.

Years ago I interviewed the late Nicholas Bramble and he told me the story of his *Sarah*. The doll was a portrait of a child he saw in Porto Bello Road during one of his jaunts into the flea market stalls that proliferate there.

When he saw the child, he immediately thought what a wonderful doll he could make after her. Eventually, he was able to gain the permission of the child's guardian, her grandmother. Originally he planned a limited edition of 100 dolls, but found he did not enjoy long productions of the same work. The repetition did not suit his artistic temperament and he ended the edition at 30 dolls. Nevertheless, my *Sarah* is marked on neck and box 29/100.

I digress, however. The point is that understanding the doll, *Sarah*, becomes a mandate to dressing her appropriately. She is a little girl - not a lady. We will not choose for her satin and fur. Rather we will dress her in gingham, calico, muslin, dimity, lawn or percale in styles appropriate to her perceived lifestyle and age.

The original dress is of cream dimity printed with sprays of flowers and leaves in a warm medium brown that picks up the color of *Sarah*'s eyes and contrasts beautifully with her auburn mohair wig. Tied about her waist is a wide peach-pink satin sash which echoes her lip, cheek, and eyelid coloring. She wears a necklace of tiny pearls which shows off her long neck to perfection. Her look is pensive. As you can see in the cover picture, she has just put down her book and stares off into space as though considering what she has just read. A very serious young lady is *Sarah*; I cannot picture her dressed extravagantly. It would seem a trespass of her very nature.

View 1 shows *Sarah*'s original dress, and the underthings, View 2, are also her originals. The remainder of this pattern section has been developed by designing directly to the doll "from scratch" as the saying goes.

Recognizing that many dollmakers are producing boy dolls and may need patterns for them, I have developed several styles for 22in (56cm) boy dolls and the name *Daniel* arbitrarily has been chosen for this generic young fellow.

Many of the patterns for *Sarah* will also fit well into a plan for *Daniel*, as you will see. Again, here is an opportunity to borrow and adapt patterns for your needs. Possibilities are nearly endless.

View 1
SARAH ORIGINAL LONG-SLEEVED DRESS
Pattern Pieces A through E

Bodice - Sew shoulder seams, press, and lay out flat. Turn under and press 1/2in (1cm) facing on either side of back opening. Install neck ruffle as described below.

Before constructing sleeves, decide whether to sew the sleeve into the bodice before or after the bodice side seam is sewn. Admittedly, joining completed sleeves and bodice gives the neatest finish. However, laying the entire unit out flat and installing the sleeves before the side seaming is done is much easier. Neither method is exclusively and absolutely correct. It is your decision.

Ruffles about the neck and sleeves are doubled lengthwise, then gathered to fit. This gives a nice finish with no hems to make.

For the neck ruffle, cut on the bias a piece of dress fabric measuring 24in (61cm) x 3in (8cm) and fold wrong sides together lengthwise, turn ends inside 1/2in (1cm), and press, or seam as desired. Run double gathering threads and pull to fit neckline. Pin to neckline, then pin 3/4in (2cm) self-bias, right sides together to the neckline over the ruffle and baste through all layers. Stitch the seam, turn bias to wrong side and blindstitch. Finish ends with a few hidden stitches. Bias edge should show 1/4in (.65cm) around neckline.

For sleeve ruffles, cut on the bias two pieces of dress fabric measuring 12in (31cm) x 2-1/2in (6cm). If setting completed sleeves, sew short ends of ruffle together, fold in half and press. Gather to fit sleeve. Sew bias as above, pull bias to inside to cover seam.

To set sleeves, ease fullness into sleeve opening without making gathers.

Note the extra patterns for alternate bodices. Dotted lines on pattern piece A indicate suggestions for applying lace or other trim for a different look.

Skirt - Cut on the straight a piece of dress fabric measuring 42in (106cm) x 18-1/2in (47cm). Use fig. 1 to mark skirt for tucks on one long side. Sew two short ends together with a 1/2in (1cm) seam, within 3in (8cm) of waist edge on side opposite tuck marks. Press back seam flat. Note that if the fabric you choose for this dress is too heavy, the skirt will be much too bouffant. If the fabric is soft and fine, the very full skirt will hang beautifully.

Begin at lower edge, following marks and referring to diagram, fig. 1, make hem and tucks. Be sure to baste and press as you go; this is much easier than taking out incorrect stitching later. Each tuck will overlap the preceding one just as the lowest tuck overlaps the hem seam, thus hiding each seam. Finished length of skirt is 11in (28cm).

Run double gathering threads along waistline of skirt, pull gathers to fit bodice, and seam together.

Sash - The original sash is a piece of peachy-pink silk measuring 48in (122cm) x 6-1/2in (17cm), with a side-point. (See fig. 1, 1950s 14in (36cm)-18in (46cm) *Hard Plastic Dolls* p. 95.) Fold fabric lengthwise and sew together, leaving a turning opening. Trim seams, turn, press. Close opening. Tie in large bow at back.

Refer to View 4, alternate dress bodices, for variations on this theme. Also, note dotted lines on bodice pattern A. Use these lines to add trims such as lace, embroidered or woven trims, or hand-embroidered motifs for a different look.

Slip - For slip skirt, cut a piece of fine white cotton measuring 33in (84cm) x 11in (28cm), which allows 1/4in (.65cm) each for waist seam and hem. Run double gathering threads on one long side to within 1in (3cm) of each end, but do not pull. Sew short sides together to within 3in (8cm) of gathered side for back seam and facing. Turn under and press 1/4in (.65cm) on one long side. Baste 3/4in (2cm) lace to underside, covering turned back edge. Using wide zig-zag stitch, sew all layers together, or straight-stitch together along fold and edge of turned-back edge, allowing edge of lace to cover raw edge of slip fabric.

Sew shoulder seams of bodice, lay out flat. Fold over both back pieces 1/2in (1cm) for facing. Turn edges 1/8in (.31cm) to right side along neckline and armholes and cover with matching lace, finishing as for hem. Sew side seams, finishing ends.

Pull gathering threads of skirt to fit bodice and seam. Sew three snap fasteners on bodice back.

Pantalettes - Cut these from same fine cotton as slip and trim in same manner. Turn down a 3/4in (2cm) casing at waist. Finish bottoms of legs with 3/4in (2cm) lace same as slip. Pattern may be adapted for panties, shorts, slacks, or jeans.

These two sleeve patterns, plus sleeve C, suggest a wide variety of possibilities for creating additional styles for either doll. Note that while sleeve C is eased into the armhole and sleeve is not cuffed or gathered, sleeves H and J are gathered at shoulder and cuff. Both are quite full. Here are some ideas; your imagination will provide more:

1. Extend sleeve C as needed and finish with a shirt cuff, finishing with decorative buttons to simulate cufflinks or make true cufflinks by linking two buttons and working buttonholes in French cuffs.

2. Turn up lower edge 1/4in (.65cm) and run elastic for a push-up sleeve.

3. Measure up from lower edge and sew in elastic for a different ruffled sleeve or run elastic through a casing.

4. Use either N or O to make a sleeve for a "gambler's shirt for a boy doll or a peasant blouse for a girl doll.

5. Use the medium width full sleeve N as a coat sleeve.

These patterns are truly versatile. Below are enough possibilities for an entire wardrobe:

1. The two widths of sleeves suggest opportunities for different looks in many applications.

2. Sleeves may hang loosely, be sewn to cuffs or gathered with elastic in a casing, or they may be caught up and tacked to make an irregular or "scrunched" look.

3. Neckline may be gathered with elastic in a casing, gathered and bound with self-bias, or gathered to a self-ruffle or wide lace.

4. Neckline may be sized to fit the shoulders or for an off-shoulder look.

5. Waist may be left loose and straight for a separate top, gathered to a skirt to make a dress, gathered to an inset belt as a top or as a dress bodice, or may be shaped with the dart shown on pattern.

Couple the gambler's shirt with this black vest; put a watch in the vest pocket with a chain across the chest. Cut the vest from black felt, satin, worsted, or heavy cotton. It may be lined with solid black satin, or with a multi-colored satin in a very small print.

Make pockets from 2in (5cm) squares or add a point. For a perfect point, draw a 2in (5cm) square, find the center of bottom line, make a mark 1/4in (.65cm) below the bottom line center and draw lines to each lower corner from that point.

To make a criss-cross belt for the back, cut two pieces of vest fabric or satin measuring 2in (5cm) x 5in (13cm).

Fold each in half lengthwise, point one end of each. Sew raw ends into side seams at dots on pattern. Pull together in back through a pair of rings or a buckle. Adjust to fit doll.

Make a vest of bright colors in velvet or satin for the girl doll's gypsy costume; sew on coins and bangles.

For a country girl or boy, choose appropriate fabrics: Denim, pinwhale corduroy, chambray, gingham, checks, or even unbleached muslin. Each of these fabrics suggests entirely different images and will give unique results.

View 6
SARAH VEST JACKET DRESS
Pattern Pieces C, H, J, L, M

Dress - With white cotton, construct slip bodice and slip skirt, but do not pull gather threads or attach skirt to bodice. Make dress skirt of desired fabric, but do not pull gathers. Pin skirts together with slip inside and pull gathers to fit bodice. Pin bodice with right side to right side of dress skirt. Baste all three pieces together, then sew as one. Trim inside seam if necessary or cover seam with single bias tape.

Vest Jacket - Vest and sleeves may be made of same fabric as skirt or of a solid or patterned fabric which contrasts with skirt. Sleeves of this vest may be of a white fabric to simulate a blouse worn under the vest. Style of cuffs is designer's (your) choice.

View 7
22in (56cm) *DANIEL* SHIRT, STRING TIE, TROUSERS, CUMMBERBUND
Pattern Pieces P, Q, R, S, K, Choice of Sleeve

Shirt - Use quality fabric and some real shirt tailoring techniques on this shirt. Look at a man's shirt and note the details which make it look good, such as topstitching on the collar and down the front. Cuffs and seams are also topstitched. For shirt pockets, follow instructions for pockets, View 5 above.

Make your own cuff pattern: Measure your doll's wrist, allow for seams and the overlap where the cuff buttons. As for width, decide just how dramatic looking you want the cuffs to be and cut accordingly. Use good pearl buttons small enough to be in proportion to the garment. Or make a French cuff and use small decorative buttons for cufflinks.

String Tie - Black silk, rayon, cotton, or velvet are good choices for this tie. Measure around the doll's neck, letting the tape measure hang down to simulate the length you want, allowing for the bow. It always amazes me how much ribbon or tie it takes to make a bow, so don't measure short on this. As to width, again the size of the doll must be considered, but generally the tie will be very slim, as suggested by its name. Turning a piece as narrow as this one can be a chore, but it is not impossible. Finish with simple squared ends.

Trousers - Lightweight wools, blends, heavy silk or cotton, all may be employed in constructing these pants or slacks. For dress slacks, using a white sewing pencil, mark the front crease and press. Sew along this crease as near to the edge as possible for a "permanently pressed" crease. If your vision sees turned-up cuffs on the pants, be sure to allow extra length, at least two inches for the 22in (56cm) doll, but more for larger dolls.

Extend pattern piece K to length required for your doll, cut a paper pattern and check size on your doll. Extra width may be added by moving the straight line to the left the required distance divided by four. Thus if your doll needs four more inches, you will only need to move the line 1in (3cm) to the left. Of course, if there's that much difference in girth, you need to check the crotch seam line also. It may prove easier to enlarge the whole thing proportionately on a copy machine.

Width of pant leg is another consideration. Some styles require a fuller cut than others. Jeans, for example, have varied greatly in width from one period to another. Make the adjustments required to meet your needs.

Cummerbund - Cut a piece of fabric to doll's waist measurement over clothes, plus 2in (5cm). Double the finished width measurement you want and add 1/2in (1cm) for seams. With right sides together, sew down one long side and across short end. Clip seam and turn. Try on your doll, determine the amount to turn in at the open end, and blindstitch closed. Make small pleats in each end to make the cummerbund "squash" nicely across front. Sew two or three snap fasteners to close.

Eyeshade - Trace the gambler's eyeshade in the *Whimsies* section and adjust to fit your gambler.

View 8
THREE HATS
Pattern Pieces V through CC

Either the billed cap or the feathered beret is suitable for boy or girl dolls. Vary the fabric and trim to create everything from a billed corduroy cap to a voile hat to match a dress. For a romantic effect, make a rose-trimmed hat to match the doll's dress or work one of straw or hatter's horsehair. (See first volume for instructions.) Any of the hats may be lined for stiffness or made floppy with a soft fabric.

The patterns given are designed for versatility. Choices of contour, length, width, and style are indicated on the pattern pieces. The "button" indicated on pieces V and W are finishing touches which may be used on berets or caps. Cut out the circle or oval from matching or contrasting fabric, run a gathering thread around the outer edge, pull as tightly as possible and knot off securely. Smooth out the resulting unit and space gathers evenly. Pin then baste to cover the point at which hat pieces are sewn together at the crown. Either blindstitch button to cap or topstitch on machine. Or turn cap to inside and stitch at center so button is loose around the outside edge. If the cap or hat is lined, the button may be secured from the outside by lifting the outer edge and tacking it to the crown at the seam lines.

A worthwhile suggestion: Familiarize yourself with the possibilities of these patterns. Make up the various styles in muslin or sheeting. See how the brim fits to the crown using the alternate cutting lines (AA). Determine the angle of the bill if it is made wide (BB) or narrow (CC). Investigate the differences in appearance when using the rounded line of crown Y as opposed to the straighter line of crown X. Compare both X and Y when elongated (Z).

Keep such samples on hand for future reference and make note of which pattern pieces were incorporated into each sample. If you sew often, this will be an aid. If you sew occasionally, the information will be invaluable.

Further Suggestions for
GIRL DOLLS
Pattern Pieces F, G, N, O, T, U

These pattern pieces are extra tools for changing patterns to create new styles. Do not hesitate to try something different by exchanging one of these pieces for an existing pattern piece in a garment set. Just be vigilante for any adjustments that may be required.

If you're trying for a complete wardrobe, make a shawl for your doll or devise an apron, falling back on patterns found elsewhere in this volume. Find a pattern for a large "Bertha" collar for a new look in a blouse or dress. Design a cloth coat with a "fur" collar; patterns are to be found herein. Or how about a sailor dress, a raincoat, pajamas, flannel nightgown? There is no end to what can be done with pattern swapping and adapting, and you can do it.

Further Suggestions for
BOY DOLLS

Patterns for boys are often difficult to find. Here are some possibilities for using the copy machine to develop a collection of patterns for your modern boys. All of these were found in browsing through the first volume of this work:

1. The Schoenhut collection, based on original outfits, pp. 67-76, contains several likely patterns.
2. *Dr. John Littlechap*'s wardrobe includes sports, dress, and professional outfits suitable for borrowing (pp. 207-211).
3. Sailor outfits abound in both volumes; check to see which one fits your doll best.

4. *Shirley Temple*'s pajamas on p. 147, View 1, would make nice overalls with a few changes, such as a square bib and straight straps and buckles.
5. There are several romper suits in the first volume.
6. On p. 205 is a shirt and crawlers set which has possibilities.
7. The original *Buddy Lee* patterns, pp. 80-88 (courtesy of H. D. Lee Company) may be lengthened, widened, or otherwise altered. Or they may fit your doll perfectly as is.
8. *Jerri Lee*'s outfits on pp. 178-181 are perfect basic patterns for developing new patterns for your doll.

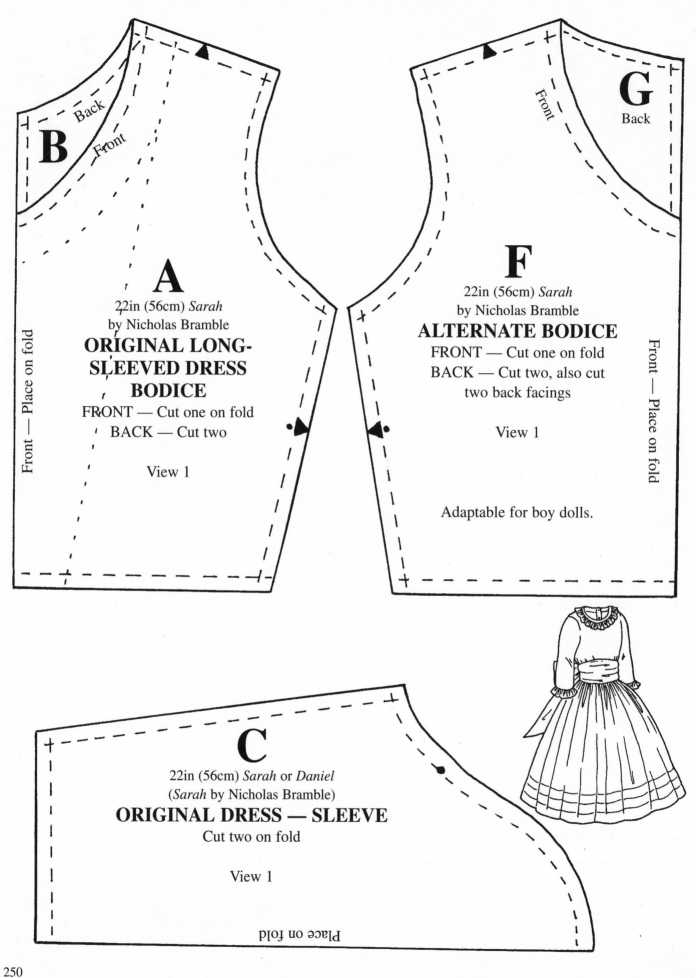

B

Back

Front

A

22in (56cm) *Sarah*
by Nicholas Bramble
ORIGINAL LONG-SLEEVED DRESS BODICE
FRONT — Cut one on fold
BACK — Cut two

View 1

Front — Place on fold

G

Back

Front

F

22in (56cm) *Sarah*
by Nicholas Bramble
ALTERNATE BODICE
FRONT — Cut one on fold
BACK — Cut two, also cut
two back facings

View 1

Adaptable for boy dolls.

Front — Place on fold

C

22in (56cm) *Sarah* or *Daniel*
(*Sarah* by Nicholas Bramble)
ORIGINAL DRESS — SLEEVE
Cut two on fold

View 1

Place on fold

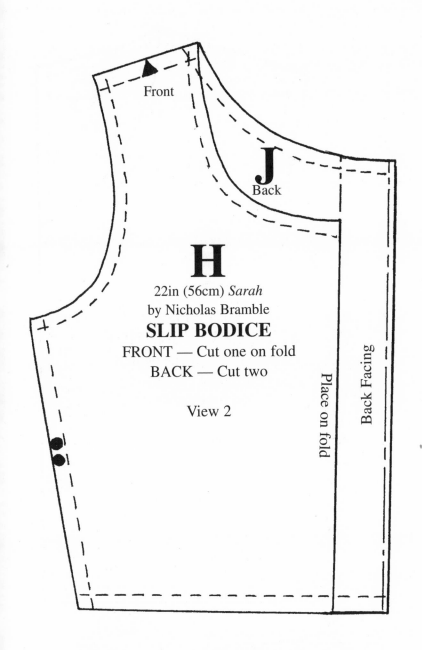

H

22in (56cm) *Sarah*
by Nicholas Bramble
SLIP BODICE
FRONT — Cut one on fold
BACK — Cut two

View 2

Front

J

Back

Place on fold

Back Facing

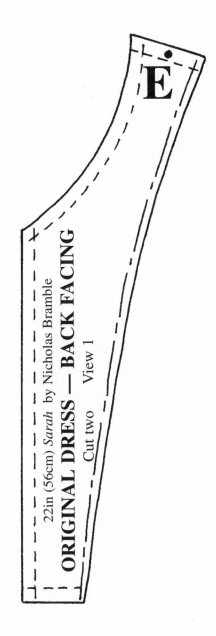

E

22in (56cm) *Sarah* by Nicholas Bramble

ORIGINAL DRESS — BACK FACING

Cut two   View 1

D

22in (56cm) *Sarah*

DRESS BACK FACING

Cut one on fold   View 1

On Fold

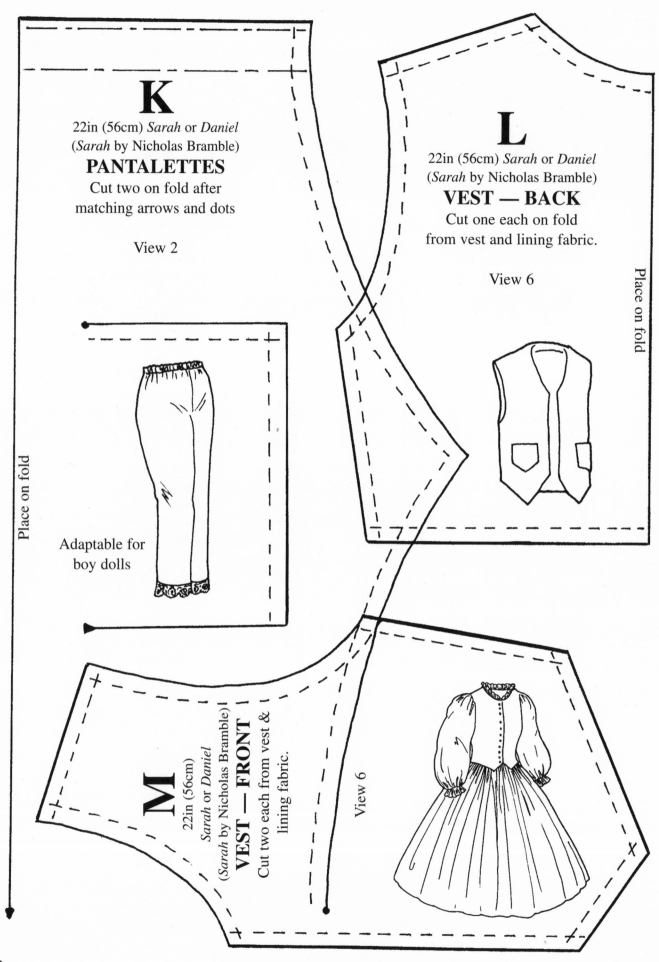

K

22in (56cm) *Sarah* or *Daniel*
(*Sarah* by Nicholas Bramble)
PANTALETTES
Cut two on fold after
matching arrows and dots

View 2

Adaptable for
boy dolls

L

22in (56cm) *Sarah* or *Daniel*
(*Sarah* by Nicholas Bramble)
VEST — BACK
Cut one each on fold
from vest and lining fabric.

View 6

Place on fold

Place on fold

M

22in (56cm)
Sarah or *Daniel*
(*Sarah* by Nicholas Bramble)
VEST — FRONT
Cut two each from vest &
lining fabric.

View 6

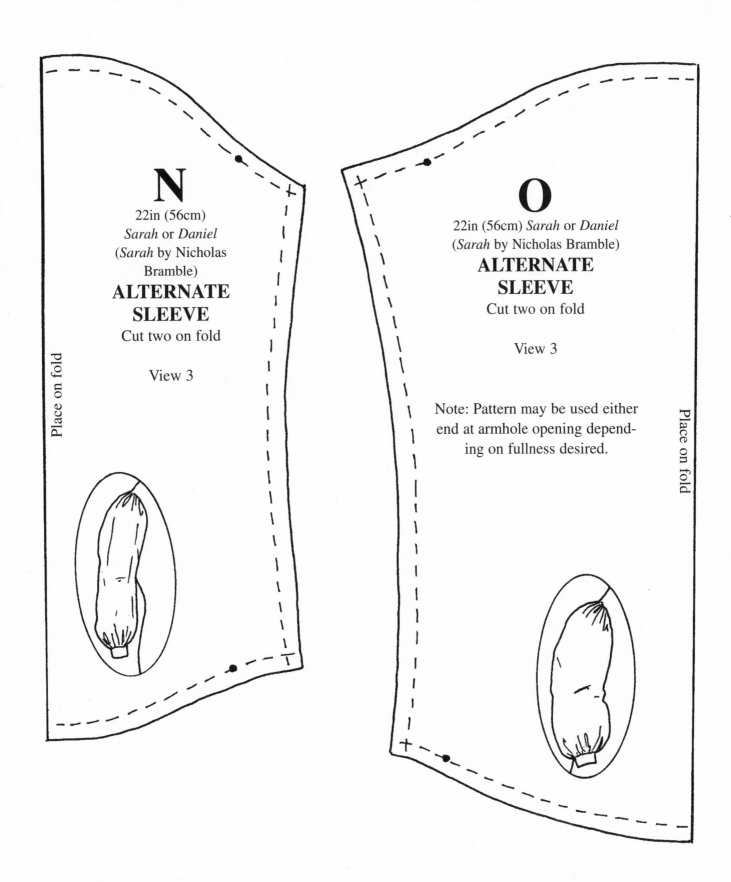

N

22in (56cm)
Sarah or *Daniel*
(*Sarah* by Nicholas
Bramble)
**ALTERNATE
SLEEVE**
Cut two on fold

View 3

Place on fold

O

22in (56cm) *Sarah* or *Daniel*
(*Sarah* by Nicholas Bramble)
**ALTERNATE
SLEEVE**
Cut two on fold

View 3

Note: Pattern may be used either
end at armhole opening depending on fullness desired.

Place on fold

Make a paper pattern of the diagram shown as Fig. 1. Measure carefully amd mark off the spaces, labeling each fold and stitching line. Fold the paper to check your measurements. Each tuck should cover the preceding stitch line.

Transfer the marks to fabric with a sewing pencil, press lower two folds and stitch.

Continue up the skirt, folding, pressing, and seaming, one tuck at a time.

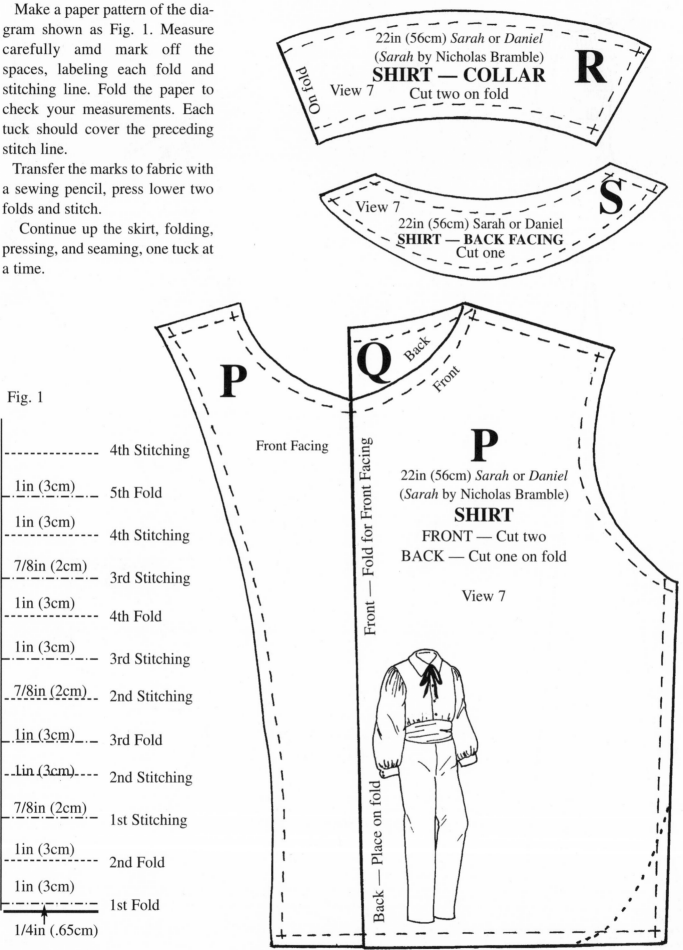

On fold

22in (56cm) *Sarah* or *Daniel*
(*Sarah* by Nicholas Bramble)
SHIRT — COLLAR **R**
View 7
Cut two on fold

View 7
22in (56cm) Sarah or Daniel
SHIRT — BACK FACING **S**
Cut one

Fig. 1

4th Stitching
1in (3cm) — 5th Fold
1in (3cm) — 4th Stitching
7/8in (2cm) — 3rd Stitching
1in (3cm) — 4th Fold
1in (3cm) — 3rd Stitching
7/8in (2cm) — 2nd Stitching
1in (3cm) — 3rd Fold
1in (3cm) — 2nd Stitching
7/8in (2cm) — 1st Stitching
1in (3cm) — 2nd Fold
1in (3cm) — 1st Fold
1/4in (.65cm)

P

Q Back
Front

Front Facing

Front — Fold for Front Facing

Back — Place on fold

P
22in (56cm) *Sarah* or *Daniel*
(*Sarah* by Nicholas Bramble)
SHIRT
FRONT — Cut two
BACK — Cut one on fold

View 7

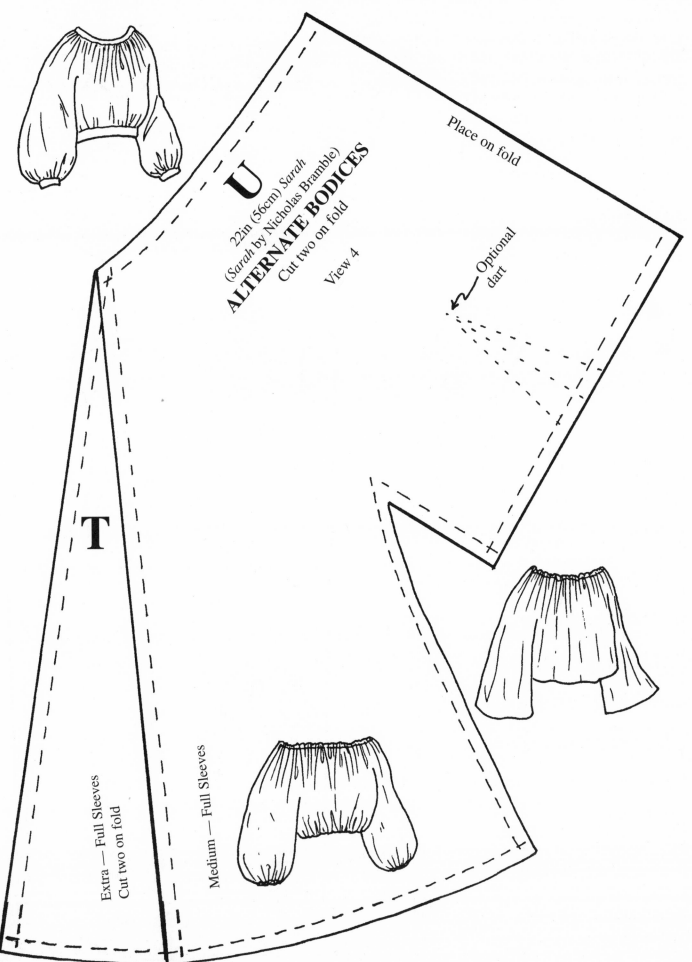

U

22in (56cm) *Sarah*
(*Sarah by Nicholas Bramble*)
ALTERNATE BODICES
Cut two on fold

View 4

Place on fold

Optional
dart

T

Extra — Full Sleeves
Cut two on fold

Medium — Full Sleeves

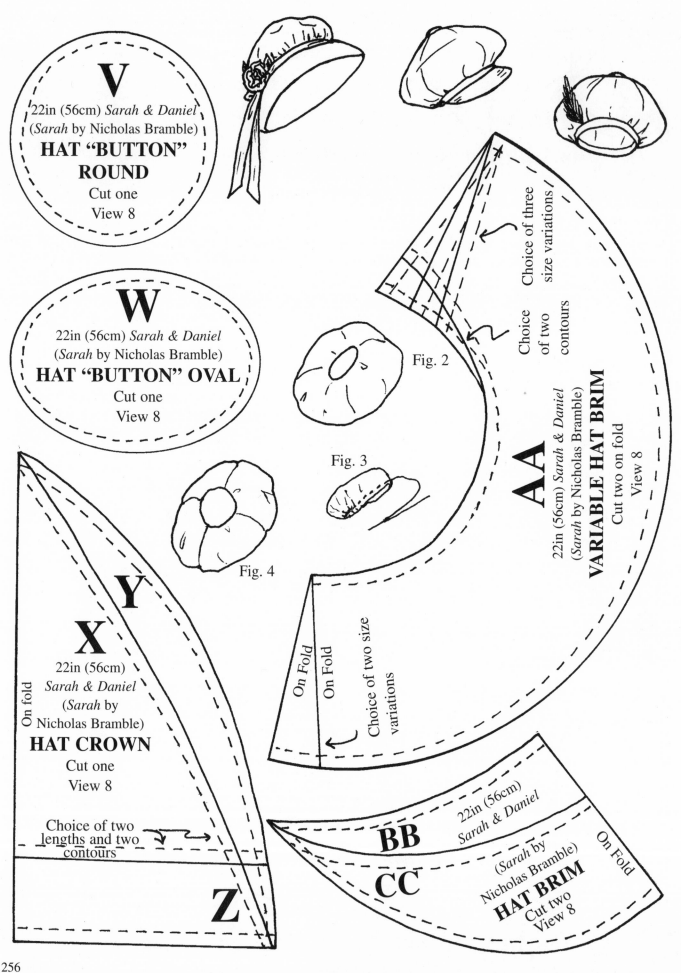

V

22in (56cm) *Sarah & Daniel*
(*Sarah* by Nicholas Bramble)
HAT "BUTTON" ROUND
Cut one
View 8

W

22in (56cm) *Sarah & Daniel*
(*Sarah* by Nicholas Bramble)
HAT "BUTTON" OVAL
Cut one
View 8

Fig. 2

Fig. 3

Fig. 4

AA

22in (56cm) *Sarah & Daniel*
(*Sarah* by Nicholas Bramble)
VARIABLE HAT BRIM
Cut two on fold
View 8

Choice of three size variations

Choice of two contours

On Fold

On Fold

Choice of two size variations

X

Y

22in (56cm)
Sarah & Daniel
(*Sarah* by
Nicholas Bramble)
HAT CROWN
Cut one
View 8

On fold

Choice of two lengths and two contours

Z

BB

CC

22in (56cm)
Sarah & Daniel
(*Sarah* by
Nicholas Bramble)
HAT BRIM
Cut two
View 8

On Fold

Term Paper
Creating A 1990s
Cutting Edge Wardrobe
for
17-18in (43-46cm) Slim Modern Dolls
Meet
The Terrific Triangle, The Super Square, and
The Remarkable Rectangle
Original JGA Concepts

View 1

View 2

View 4

View 3

View 5a

View 5b

View 6a

View 6b

View 7a
View 7b

View 8

The unstructured look came into its own in the 1980s and 1990s with the introduction of an assortment of knit blends and 100% cotton knits. Soft, stretchable, and washable, these quality fabrics became abundantly available. Savvy designers took advantage of the opportunity to create constructions that were both versatile and wearable, possibly in answer to the needs of working women who were trying to do and have it all. With budgets and time stretched to the limit, women wanted something simple yet stylish that provided options for creating more than one outfit per garment. And they wanted reasonable prices, comfort, and washability.

Working with the basic knit units, designers were able to produce fashions featuring fluid drapery and flowing lines suitable for office wear, shopping, or an evening out. Television's home shopping programs featured many of these designer collections, with print and plain pieces that combined to create elaborate wardrobes from relatively few garments.

Basic to this approach to fashion were coordinating pieces that reversed, turned upside down, or changed places with other units. Skirts became blouses; jackets turned around to button in the back; short-short skirts draped the shoulders over dresses or rolled into belts or twisted about the head as turbans.

Extending the versatility of these pieces was the combination of print and plain fabrics often used in the same garment. Sleeves might be printed or of a different, though coordinating color. Fronts and backs of garments might not match in color or print design. Key to these styles was the careful selection of coordinating fabrics.

Other styles played off plain garments against printed ones featuring the same color, such as a jacket in a large, flowered print with a plain skirt that picked up one of the colors in the print. And finally, plain or printed fabrics of the same color or pattern were paired for a more conservative look. The possibilities with these unitized fashions seemed endless.

This collection reflects those attitudes and may be a boon to doll seamstresses wishing to dress one or a bevy of the dolls of the period.

View 1
THE TERRIFIC TRIANGLE

For the 17-18in (43-46cm) doll, the triangle measures 20in (51cm) x 14in (36cm). Make as many of these as you wish for your dolls, using all the various fabrics selected for your "designer collection." (You are the designer.)

Lay fabric out flat and fold carefully, making sure no creases exist on the under side. Pin the material together along the fold and outer edges. With ruler and white sewing pencil or chalk, mark 10in (25cm) on the fold, then 10in (25cm) out from one end of the first mark, maintaining a 90° angle.

Connect the ends of these two lines with another line which should measure 14in (36cm). Cut carefully along the outer two lines, but not on the fold. Remove pins and open out and there is your triangle. Make a handkerchief hem all around this piece.

The triangle may be used as a turban, shawl, belt, hip wrap, babushka, halter-top, or a variety of other fashions, including a very modern bathing suit.

View 2
THE SUPER SQUARE

A 12in (31cm) square of knit fabric, hemmed all around, in print or plain, or one of each, will be a welcome addition to your doll's wardrobe. As with the triangle, the square may be utilized in a variety of ways. Wrap the square for a sarong skirt, hang it over the doll's shoulder and fasten with a pin made from a decorative button. Scrunch and pin it into a hat, using colorful big-headed straight pins as hat pins. Twist it around for a sun top with the short-short skirt. Throw it over that daring swimsuit you just made from the triangle.

View 3
THE REMARKABLE RECTANGLE

Suggestions here are for three different lengths of skirts made from rectangles. Other units may be constructed from these same rectangles, the mysteries of which I will leave for the reader to discover. Use your imagination; the rectangle is indeed remarkable.

Each of these three skirts is constructed in the same way. Fold and sew the side seam, turn up a narrow hem, turn down the top 1/8in (.31cm) and stretch while sewing in 1/8in (.31cm) wide elastic which equals your doll's waist measurement plus 1/2in (1cm) for seam. (*Note:* This step may be done prior to sewing the side seam; however, if neatness counts, sew the elastic after sewing the side seam.)

Short-short skirt - Cut a rectangle measuring 8in (20cm)W x 4in (10cm)L. Note that the second measurement refers to the length of the skirt.

Medium-length skirt - Cut a rectangle measuring 8in (20cm)W x 6-1/2in (17cm)L.

Long skirt - Cut a rectangle measuring 8in (20cm)W x 10in (25cm)L. Note that these measurements may be adjusted for fuller or narrower skirts, or if your doll measures smaller or larger than 17-18in (43-46cm) in height, or if the doll happens to be more or less slender than the doll for which I have created these patterns.

View 4
THE ASTONISHING A-LINE

Here again versatility is the word. A-line dresses, skirts, and coats seem always in style. Make at least one of these just for the exercise because here also is a lesson in pattern drafting.

First, using a T-square, draw a rectangle measuring 7in (18cm) x 12in (31cm). Cut out the rectangle pattern, being careful to follow the lines. Fold exactly in half short side to short side. Open out flat and draw a light line along the fold.

Measure from the light center line 2in (5cm) to either side and make a light pencil mark on the top line of the square. Using your ruler, draw lines from these two dots to the lower corners of the rectangle. These are the sides of the skirt.

Now measure down 1/4in (.65cm) from the top edge at the center, making a light mark. Beginning at one upper corner of the skirt, with the edge toward you, draw a swooping curved line from one corner, down to the 1/4in (.65cm) mark, and back to the opposite corner. Don't worry if your first attempt does not work out; keep trying.

Next, on the opposite long side, measure 1/4in (.65cm) from each corner and set a light mark on each short side. Turn the paper so that the edge is away from you. Sketch a swooping curved line from the one dot down to the center line on the edge and then to the other side dot.

Bear in mind that in both cases above, what I have called a "swooping curve" is a very gradual change of direction, which should give the skirt just the right "hang," a slightly curved line.

The length of this skirt may also be varied as was that of the straight skirt in View 3, above, and it is finished in much the same way. For the A-line, however, cut two pieces and sew side seams.

Variations on this A-line theme are many. For example, cut a shorter A-line and sew together at the waist with the longer skirt for a peplum effect (see illustration). The peplum may be applied to dresses as well, which you will create by combining units and pattern pieces from this collection.

The width of this skirt may be varied to create a "swing skirt," as shown in the illustration, omitting the peplum. Or sew side seams within 1in (3cm) of the top, bind with bias tape all around the top, and add bias tape straps for an A-line sun dress.

Views 5a, b
THE ELASTIC DRESS, THE A-LINE REVISITED TWO VERSIONS

Using your A-line pattern, cut two pieces and sew one side seam. Lay out flat and insert 1/8in (.31cm) elastic across the two pieces, using your doll as a guide to the length of elastic required. (Refer to Views 5a, 5b, and fig. a) Note that view 5b shows the effect of inverting the dress shown in view 5a.

For the second version (not shown) run the elastic at the top and waist, leaving the bottom free, thus creating a completely different dress.

Views 6a, b
THE JACKET cum SWEATSHIRT
Pattern Pieces A, B,C

Jacket - This jacket will present better if the front and neckline are faced, giving a more professional finish to the garment. Use the pattern to make facing patterns. Try using a multi-color tweedy knit for one of your projects. Select multi-colored buttons that pick up the colors of the knit for a couture touch. Perhaps a braid trim using these same colors may be found. Use this braid to trim all edges to add snap. If you are a devoted doll seamstress, the result will be worth the extra trouble.

Sweatshirt - Following dotted lines on pattern piece B, cut two on the fold. Use sleeve pattern C. Ready-made knit cuff material may be added to bottom edge, sleeves, and neckline, or they may be neatly turned under and hemmed. This garment may be worn with a belt or sash, or allowed to hang free.

Sash - Cut a piece of contrasting plain or print knit measuring 4in (10cm) x 24in (61cm) and make a narrow hem all around. If desired, cut two of these pieces, sew right sides together, leaving an opening for turning. Turn, close the opening, and topstitch all around in matching or contrasting thread or use thread that picks up a color from the print. Fringe may be added to the ends for a different look.

This sash may be worn as a neck scarf or stole, wrapped around the head for a turban, wound around upper body for a halter top, or draped about the hips over a skirt or dress.

Views 7a, b
PEPLUM JACKET OR BLOUSE
Pattern Pieces D, E, F

Jacket - Using all three pattern pieces, construct the front-opening jacket with the six buttons. The garment may be lined so that it is reversible; facings may be cut using the patterns as guides, or all edges may be bound with self-bias.

Blouse - Using a lightweight fabric, blouse is constructed same as the jacket above. For a pull-over blouse, use only the back pattern piece and the sleeves (D, E). Bind the neck edge with bias or facing, or add a ruffle or decorative trim, as desired. Note that you may have to cut out the neckline to accommodate your doll's head, depending on its size.

Bonus Dress - Try extending the front and side lines of this pattern to a length required for your doll, either street length or ball gown length. Add or subtract details. The results may prove quite extraordinary.

View 8
THE UBIQUITOUS SHOULDER PAD
Pattern Piece G

The shoulder pad cannot be ignored in a discussion of the fashions of this period. "Football shoulders" were in evidence everywhere off the field of play during these years. For those with naturally broad shoulders the trend became a nightmare. Removing the pads was not a solution. Since the garments were cut to accommodate the extra width, removing the pads merely created a droopy shoulder line. Fortunately, over-large shoulder pads come and go and as fate would have it, these went.

Complete each garment before constructing the shoulder pads. As you stuff the pads, place them in the garment from time to time and try them on the doll. You will be able to judge when the thickness is just right for your doll and for the garment.

And now, congratulations. Your term paper is complete and you've graduated. You are now a genuine Doll Fashion Designer!

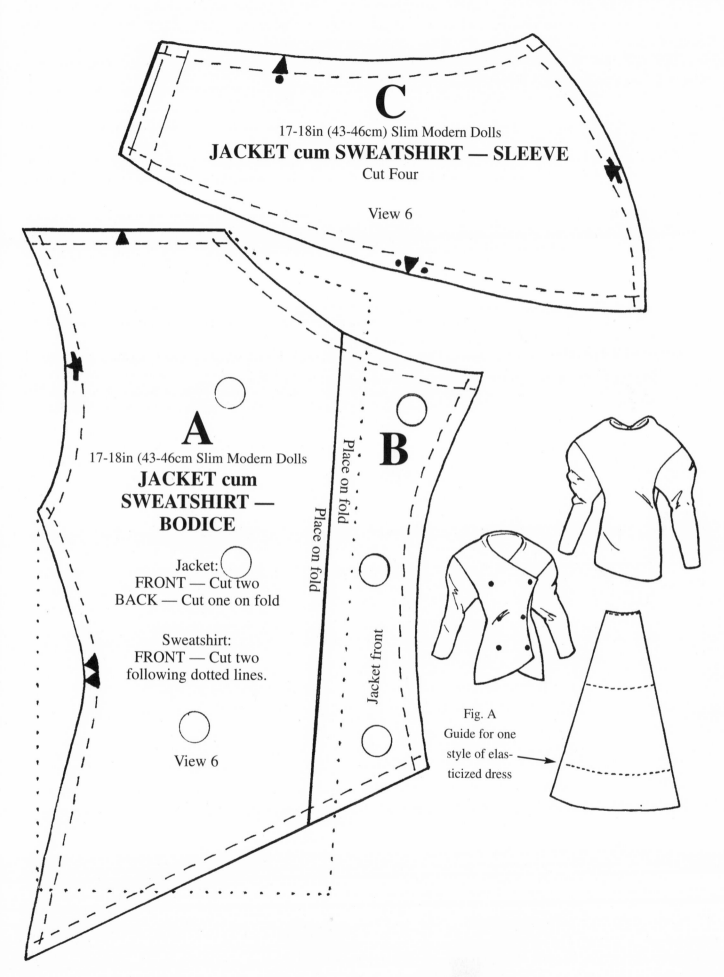

C

17-18in (43-46cm) Slim Modern Dolls

JACKET cum SWEATSHIRT — SLEEVE

Cut Four

View 6

A

17-18in (43-46cm Slim Modern Dolls

JACKET cum SWEATSHIRT — BODICE

Jacket:
FRONT — Cut two
BACK — Cut one on fold

Sweatshirt:
FRONT — Cut two
following dotted lines.

View 6

B

Place on fold

Place on fold

Jacket front

Fig. A
Guide for one
style of elas-
ticized dress

261

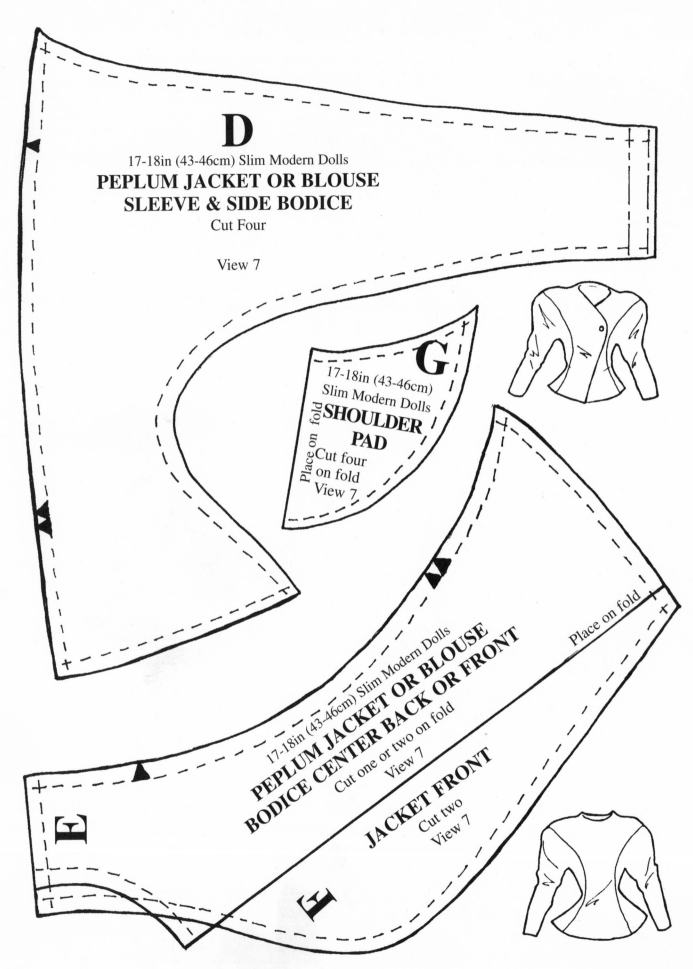

D

17-18in (43-46cm) Slim Modern Dolls
**PEPLUM JACKET OR BLOUSE
SLEEVE & SIDE BODICE**
Cut Four

View 7

G

17-18in (43-46cm)
Slim Modern Dolls
**SHOULDER
PAD**
Place on fold
Cut four
on fold
View 7

E

17-18in (43-46cm) Slim Modern Dolls
**PEPLUM JACKET OR BLOUSE
BODICE CENTER BACK OR FRONT**
Cut one or two on fold
View 7

Place on fold

JACKET FRONT
Cut two
View 7

E

BIBLIOGRAPHY

Anderton, Johana Gast.   *Collectors Encyclopedia of Cloth Dolls, The*,
Des Moines, Iowa: Wallace-Homestead
Book Co., 1986.

Johana's Dolls,
A Reprint of Her Columns and Articles,
North Kansas City, Missouri:
Athena Publishing Company, 1975.

More Twentieth Century Dolls,
From Bisque to Vinyl, Vols. I and *II,*
Revised Edition, Wallace-Homestead
Book Company, 1979.

Sewing for Twentieth Century Dolls,
Wallace-Homestead Book Company, 1972
Revised Edition, 1979,
Hobby House Press, Inc., Cumberland, Maryland:
1996.

Twentieth Century Dolls,
From Bisque to Vinyl, Revised Edition,
Des Moines, Iowa: Wallace-Homestead
Book Co., 1976.

"Doll Clothing," Dolls — A Complete Bibliography, ed. Nancy Anne Lutz,
Newport Beach, California: The Doll Works, 1981.

About The
AUTHOR

Johana Gast Anderton began writing and drawing at an early age. As a first-grader, she sent poems and drawings to the children's page of the *Kansas City Journal Post*. Johana's first efforts for collectors was a pioneer work on what is commonly known today as "Depression Glass." Before going out of print, *The Glass Rainbow, the Story of Depression Glass* went through eight printings and is now considered a collector's item in itself. The author is well-known in the doll and paper doll worlds for her *Twentieth Century Dolls* series of reference books, hundreds of magazine and newspaper articles, and dozens of black-and-white and full-color paper doll sets published in collector magazines and as convention souvenirs.

She is a founding member of the Original Paper Doll Artists Guild (OPDAG), a member of the executive board of the Modern Doll Convention (MDC), a member-at-large of the United Federation of Doll Clubs (UFDC), and a charter member of the Sun, Sand, and Sea Paper Doll Collectors Club of Florida. She has created souvenir paper dolls for MDC since 1984, with the exception of 1986 and acted as MDC Souvenir Book editor for several years. Her specially commissioned full-color paper dolls have been given as souvenirs for UFDC regional conferences across the country. She is also a doll designer; her pattern book, *Sewing the Last Christmas Doll*, first in a series, is now in its fifth printing. Also in the works is a series of dolls she hopes to have produced by a mold company. In her spare time she works on a book of fairy tales for children and two novels she hopes to publish "some day".

Her activities have included teaching oil painting, instructing YWCA craft classes, personal appearances on television, radio, and at antiques and doll shows and conventions throughout the country. Her experience in planning and directing conventions has made her, she says, much more appreciative of such functions. She also teaches occasional workshops and does some lecturing, an activity that is necessarily limited by her full schedule.

In 1972 she founded her own publishing company, Athena, and produced books on a variety of subjects in the collectibles field written by well-known authors. Of interest to doll collectors are *The American Doll Artist, Vol. II* by Helen Bullard; *Dressing Dolls in Nineteenth Century Fashions* by Albina Bailery; *Much Ado About Dolls* by R. Lane Herron, and the *Collectors Art Series* paper dolls and coloring books. The Athena books were sold to American Broadcasting Company in 1976 and were subsequently published by Wallace-Homestead Book Company and Chilton Books.

After living in Florida for thirteen years, Johana and husband, Harold (Andy) returned to the Kansas City area in 1995. There she has a spacious studio in which to work and her first major project has been completion of this second volume of authentic doll clothes patterns for Hobby House Press. She looks forward to completing several more doll books and paper doll designs in the coming years.

Other books by the Author:
The Glass Rainbow, The Story of Depression Glass
Sewing The Last Christmas Doll, Story, Paper Doll, and Patterns
For further titles see Bibliography.
Edited: *Favorite Recipes from OPDAG; a Collection of Recipes and Paper Dolls*
Coming Next Year: *Sewing for 20th Century Dolls, Volume 3*